T0382723

The Age of Entrepreneurs]

This landmark research volume provides the first detailed history of entrepreneurship in Britain from the nineteenth century to the present. Using a remarkable new database of more than nine million entrepreneurs, it gives new understanding to the development of Britain as the world's 'first industrial nation'.

Based on the first long-term whole-population analysis of British small business, it uses novel methods to identify from the 10-yearly population census the two to four million people per year who operated businesses in the period 1851–1911. Using big data analytics, it reveals how British businesses evolved over time, supplementing the census-derived data on individuals with other sources on companies and business histories. By comparing to modern data, it reveals how the late-Victorian period was a 'golden age' for smaller and medium-sized businesses, driven by family firms, the accelerating participation of women and the increasing use of incorporation as a significant vehicle for development.

A unique resource and citation for future research on entrepreneurship, of crucial significance to economic development policies for small businesses around the world, and above all the key entry point for researchers to the database which is deposited at the UK Data Archive, this major publication will change our understanding of the scale and economic significance of small businesses in the nineteenth century.

Robert J. Bennett is Professor Emeritus and Research Director in Geography at the University of Cambridge, UK. His research covers SME policy, economic development and the history of entrepreneurship, chambers of commerce, and business associations. His recent publications include *Entrepreneurship, Small Business and Public Policy* (Routledge, 2014) and papers in multiple journals, including *Business History*.

Harry Smith is a Research Associate at the Cambridge Group for the History of Population and Social Structure, UK. He is a historian with interests in eighteenth- and nineteenth-century social and economic history, entrepreneurship and the history of class and towns (especially Birmingham). He has published articles in various journals, including *Business History* and *Midland History*.

Carry van Lieshout is a Research Associate at the Cambridge Group for the History of Population and Social Structure, UK. She is a historical geographer with interests in gender, entrepreneurship and natural resources. She has published articles in various journals, including *The London Journal* and *Geopolitics*.

Piero Montebruno is a Research Associate at the Cambridge Group for the History of Population and Social Structure, UK. He holds a PhD in economic geography and is a trained medical doctor with interests in entrepreneurship, surrogacy and slums and heavy-tailed distributions. He has published articles in various journals, including *Business History*.

Gill Newton is a Research Associate at the Cambridge Group for the History of Population and Social Structure, UK. She is a data scientist whose interests include large-scale datasets and demographic behaviour, mortality and the occupational structure of nineteenth-century Britain. She has published widely in population history and its methodologies.

Routledge International Studies in Business History

Series editors: Jeffrey Fear and Christina Lubinski

For more information about this series, please visit: www.routledge.com/
Routledge-International-Studies-in-Business-History/book-series/SE0471

The Age of Entrepreneurship

Business Proprietors, Self-Employment
and Corporations Since 1851

**Robert J. Bennett, Harry Smith,
Carry van Lieshout, Piero Montebruno
and Gill Newton**

LONDON AND NEW YORK

First published 2020
by Routledge
2 Park Square, Milton Park, Abingdon, Oxon OX14 4RN

and by Routledge
605 Third Avenue, New York, NY 10017

First issued in paperback 2021

Routledge is an imprint of the Taylor & Francis Group, an informa business

British Library Cataloguing-in-Publication Data
A catalogue record for this book is available from the British Library

Library of Congress Cataloging-in-Publication Data
A catalog record for this book has been requested

ISBN 13: 978-0-367-78559-8 (pbk)
ISBN 13: 978-1-138-06443-0 (hbk)

Typeset in Bembo
by Apex CoVantage, LLC

Contents

Foreword

This book has sought a very ambitious goal: to identify as far as possible and to analyse the whole population of business proprietors in Britain over 1851–1911 and to link the individual data for this period to aggregate data running up to the present. That this goal has been largely achieved is due to the skills and commitment of the team that has worked on this, and the main funding that has supported it from the Economic and Social Research Council (ESRC), additional funding from the Cambridge Isaac Newton Trust and support for piloting for 1881 from the Leverhulme Trust. This has been fundamental to achieving the production of this book, and also the data deposit of the main 1851–1911 database at the UK Data Archive known as the 'British Business Census of Entrepreneurs' (BBCE). The book is mostly restricted to analysis of England and Wales. While Scotland's data unfortunately was not ready for analysis in this book, it has since been added to this database deposit. Fundamental to all this has been the availability of the electronic version of the census data for 1851–1911 in the Integrated Census Microdata (I-CeM) at UKDA SN7481 which has made the identification of entrepreneurs within the censuses feasible. We especially acknowledge our debt to these organisations and the individuals behind them.

This book has been a team effort; however, it is important to specify how responsibilities for authorship were deployed. Bob Bennett led on Chapters 1–4, 5.4 and 6; Harry Smith led on Chapters 7, 5.3 and 9–11; Carry van Lieshout led on Chapters 8 and 5.2 and provided input into 7.3, 7.4 and 7.7; Piero Montebruno was responsible for all econometric estimation, the main inputs to Chapter 6, led on Chapter 2.4, and developed the models for reconstruction and agricultural entrepreneurship allocation described in Chapter 4 used throughout the analysis. Carry van Lieshout had main responsibility for the 1851–81 database throughout, including assimilating the 1871 data from S&N, as well developing the directors' database. Harry Smith had main responsibility for the 1891–1911 database, developed the occupational and urban classifications, and guided the key decisions on reconstruction choices. Gill Newton developed the original format of the extraction algorithm to identify employers in the 1881 census funded by the Leverhulme Trust and, supported by ESRC, helped manage the database and edit some chapters. This was a multidisciplinary effort, with Harry Smith the main historian, Carry van Lieshout the main historical geographer and Piero Montebruno the econometrician and economic geographer. Dragana Radicic, who was employed by the ESRC funding for its first year as the econometrician, was responsible for the early stages of portfolio analysis (reported in Radicic et al., 2017), some data coding of entrepreneurs and the factor analysis classifications for 1891 (see WP 7, WP 8 and WP 10). Max Satchell was employed from ESRC funding to provide guidance and inputs on GIS sources and was responsible for manipulating the various GIS source data cited below to provide the transport coding used in Chapter 6 and elsewhere. Joe Day was employed by the Isaac Newton Trust funding to help manipulate the S&N data for 1871 into a compatible format with I-CeM, especially the spatial coding, and was also crucial in providing the RSD GIS boundary files cited below. Sophy Arulanantham was supported by ESRC funding to help with administration. The figures were drawn by Phil Stickler at the Cambridge University Geography Department Cartographic Unit, with the exception of Figure 5.6 which was drawn by Piero Montebruno.

The book also owes a great debt to many other advisors and supporters. We would particularly like to thank Leigh Shaw-Taylor and Alice Reid who were co-investigators at Cambridge funded by ESRC who have been generous with advice and other supports that have made the research possible. Amanda Wilkinson (Essex) was also a co-investigator but unfortunately had to withdraw. Support and advice from others was particularly valuable in the early stages of interpreting I-CeM data. The team working on Alice Reid's *Atlas of Victorian Fertility Decline* project (ESRC grant ES/L015463/1) was very helpful to various stages of this work: especially Alice herself, Eilidh Garrett, Hanna Jaadla and Joe Day; they and Xuesheng You were also part of an I-CeM working group that met 25 times in the early stages of the project and was critical to database preparation. In addition Kevin Schürer has provided crucial additional help with I-CeM data cleaning, upgrading and advice. The overall environment of the Cambridge Group for History of Population and Social Structure (Campop) also made major contributions.

The ESRC support included five formal partners who advised at various critical points: Leslie Hannah (previously Tokyo University, then LSE), James Foreman-Peck (Cardiff), Stephan Heblich (Bristol), Olmo Silva (LSE) and Alex Trew (St Andrews). Les Hannah has been particularly generous with advice from the design stage of the project through to some of the detailed interpretations of business numbers and corporate activity, especially in Chapter 5. We are also very grateful to a range of other advisors who have helped us to surmount critical hurdles: Mike Anderson (Edinburgh), Mark Casson (Reading), Eddy Higgs (Essex), Matthew Woollard (UKDA) and, at Cambridge, Richard Smith, Tony Wrigley and Martin Daunton. Les Hannah, Janette Rutterford (Open University) and Naomi Lamoreaux (Yale) advised on coding directors and their companies.

We have also benefited from the help of research assistants. Checks and filling out I-CeM truncated lines in 1861 using National Archive sources was undertaken by Mark Latham, Gavin Robinson, Tiffany Shumaker and Rebecca Tyler.

Gavin Robinson also helped match 1851 I–CeM truncated lines to census transcriptions from S&N Genealogy Supplies (TheGenealogist.co.uk). In Scotland similar work with truncated lines was done by Tobias Lunde, Annette Mackenzie and Amber Stevenson. Coding directors and their companies was assisted by Walter Jansson. Most additional data keying and parsing was undertaken by AEL Data and 1881 by Thymus.

Acknowledgements

The ESRC provided the main funding that supported this research under project grant ES/M010953: *Drivers of Entrepreneurship and Small Businesses*. In addition, piloting of the research for 1881 draws from Leverhulme Trust grant RG66385: *The Long-Term Evolution of Small and Medium-Sized Enterprises (SMEs)*. Additional support for the coding of the 1871 census data was supported by the ESRC project with additional support from the Isaac Newton Trust research grant 17.07(d): *Business Employers in 1871*.

The main database for the censuses for 1851–1911 derives from K. Schürer, E. Higgs, A.M. Reid and E.M. Garrett, *Integrated Census Microdata, 1851–1911, version V. 2 (I-CeM.2)*, (2016) [data collection]. UK Data Service, SN-7481, http://dx.doi.org/10.5255/UKDA-SN-7481-1; enhanced version, see: E. Higgs, C. Jones, K. Schürer and A. Wilkinson, *Integrated Census Microdata (I-CeM) Guide*, 2nd ed. (Colchester: Department of History, University of Essex, 2015). The I-CeM data for 1851–61 and 1891–1911 were transcribed by FindMyPast (FMP) using the original manuscript censuses at TNA. For 1881 the database coding was derived from K. Schürer and M. Woollard (2000), *1881 Census for England and Wales, the Channel Islands and the Isle of Man (Enhanced Version)* UKDA, SN-4177, transcribed by Genealogical Society of Utah and Federation of Family History Societies. This 1881 source has been used as well as I-CeM for 1881.

In addition, we are especially grateful to S&N for preparing the data to infill truncated lines in I-CeM in 1851 and for providing the entire dataset used for 1871; we especially thank Mark Bayley at S&N for his help and advice for this data extraction using algorithms written by Gill Newton and Carry van Lieshout.

GIS acknowledgements

The geographical boundary files for mapping parishes derive from A.E.M. Satchell, P.M.K. Kitson, G.H. Newton, L. Shaw-Taylor and E.A. Wrigley (2016), *1851 England and Wales Census Parishes, Townships and Places*.

Continuous parish boundaries were created using the methodology developed by Wrigley (2011) by A.E.M. Satchell, G. Newton, K. Schürer, C. Roughey,

M. Anderson and L. Shaw-Taylor (2018), *Continuous Parish Units of England, Wales and Scotland 1851–1891*; and A.E.M. Satchell, G. Newton, K. Schürer, C. Roughey, M. Anderson, L. Shaw-Taylor (2018), *Continuous Parish Units of England, Wales and Scotland 1851–1911*.

This Satchell et al. (2016) dataset is an enhanced version of N. Burton, J. Westwood and P. Carter (2004) *GIS of the Ancient Parishes of England and Wales, 1500–1850*, Colchester, Essex: UK Data Archive (May 2004), SN-4828, which is a GIS version of R.J.P. Kain and R.R. Oliver (2001), *Historic Parishes of England and Wales: An Electronic Map of Boundaries Before 1850 with a Gazetteer and Metadata*, Colchester, Essex: UK Data Archive, SN-4348.

The boundary files for RSDs were created by J.D. Day (2016), *Registration Sub-District Boundaries for England and Wales 1851–1911*. This dataset was created by the *Atlas of Victorian Fertility Decline* project (PI: A.M. Reid) funded by ESRC grant ES/L015463/1. The RSD files were created using the Satchell et al. (2016) boundary files source and its sources, as listed above.

The distances to population centres used in Chapter 6 were prepared by Max Satchell from parish centroids in the I-CeM GIS (Satchell et al., 2016, above) and town centroids from L. Shaw-Taylor, A.E.M. Satchell, E. Potter and D. Bogart (2017), *Candidate Towns of England and Wales, c. 1563–1911 GIS shapefile*. Description of the dataset can be found in M. Satchell, *Candidate Towns of England and Wales, c. 1563–1911 GIS Shapefile*.

Documentation of all GIS files at the Cambridge Group for History of Population and Social Structure (Campop) can be found at: www.geog.cam.ac.uk/research/projects/occupations/datasets/documentation.html.

Law-Robson urban population files are from R.J. Bennett (2012), *Urban Population Database, 1801–1911*. (Law–Robson–Langton database), SN-7154, http://doi.org/10.5255/UKDA-SN-7154-1; University of Salford, Department of Geography; University of Manchester, Department of Geography; University of Oxford, School of Geography and the Environment [original data producers].

Part 1

New methods to interpret historical trends

1 Entrepreneurship over time

1.1 Introduction

This book provides the first large-scale, long-term and whole-population assessment of the history of entrepreneurship in Britain in detail from the nineteenth century to 1911, and in lesser detail up to the present. It develops and uses a remarkable new database of more than nine million persons identified as employers and self-employed over the period 1851–1911 that allows whole-population analysis of 'all' entrepreneurs, and then links them to modern trends. In lesser detail we also examine proprietors of limited companies. This gives a capacity for a new understanding of the development of British entrepreneurship as the world's 'first industrial nation' through 'big data'. As British economic history is often used to interpret international development and policies for small businesses, the book also provides new material for comparative analysis.

The analysis uses the England and Wales population census on business proprietors and own-account self-employed as its main source. This provides a surrogate 'British Business Census of Entrepreneurs 1851–1911' (referred to throughout as the BBCE database). The database itself is a major resource for economists and business historians that has been deposited at the UK Data Archive, for which this book provides an entry point; supplementary material is provided in working papers (referred to as WPs, listed in the references). While Scotland's data unfortunately was not ready for inclusion and analysis in this volume, it has since been added to this database.

We term the 1851–1911 period the 'age of entrepreneurship'. This is for two main reasons. First, it was associated with a general rise in the number of businesses of all sizes. Despite the setbacks of the agricultural depression in 1873–96, and the trade depression in the 1880s to early 1890s, this was a period of rapid population and economic growth. To a significant extent population growth was a key driver of demand, acting like a rising tide that raised all ships so that most businesses had potential to prosper. But, second, the end of the period of our detailed study marked a turning point. By 1911 many industries were consolidating; the limited company was becoming a compelling form of industrial organisation; transport developments allowed the economy to become more integrated regionally and nationally so that large firms could expand into almost all local areas through brand development, branches and attempts to exert monopoly control; individual sole traders and small businesses were experiencing more intense competition; market entry was becoming more difficult as capital requirements in many sectors increased; and the expansion of large firms, public bodies and civil administration, often offering higher and more stable wages, increasingly attracted many of the most able and reduced the attractions of entrepreneurship with its inevitable uncertainties and risks. Moreover, if there had been any doubt about future evolution, this was buried by the cataclysm of World War I. The loss of many of the young adult population, the needs of the war effort, the interrelated development of large-scale government and business management techniques (such as Taylorism and Fordism) and the turn of government policy mainly to support industrial consolidation all pointed towards subsequent developments where small-scale proprietors faced greater challenges, unless they were in niche or technologically protected markets or prepared to take decreasing returns. Over the long term, the peak of entrepreneurship over 1901–11 was not to be approached again until the late 1990s.

The book fills two major intellectual and data gaps at the most basic level. First, for *entrepreneurs* it provides the first historical large-scale data and analysis of the characteristics of entrepreneurs at the scale of the whole population and how they compared with non-entrepreneurs and how they changed during rapid industrialisation. Second, for *businesses* the book allows assessment of evolution developed by sector, firm size (measured by employee numbers), corporate and non-corporate forms and geographic location. This provides new assessments of entrepreneurship rates and their evolution, the location of entrepreneurial 'hot spots', changes of business concentration by firm size, variation between sectors and the speed of changes. It also allows understanding of how entrepreneurial decision makers were influenced by their personal characteristics such as age, gender, family and household structure and how individual characteristics interacted with business sectors, geographical environments and changing transport access. Our results challenge tropes of late-Victorian entrepreneurial decline and the limited extent of female entrepreneurship.

The present chapter introduces the definitions and data used and the main themes of entrepreneurship analysis over time. The other chapters comprising Part 1 review previous understandings and theories of entrepreneurship that inform the long-term analyses (Chapter 2) and summarise how the data used in this analysis were constructed and enriched (Chapter 3). Part 2 of the book gives an overview of the main trends in business numbers by type and the sector changes that the new data reveal (Chapter 4). Chapter 5 develops new insights into the evolution by business size and different institutional forms (as self-employed, employers, partnerships and corporations).

Part 3 of the book then presents different dimensions of micro-entrepreneurial change that led to different aggregate outcomes. Chapter 6 introduces a statistical method for understanding the influences on entrepreneurial choice of different personal characteristics, such as age, gender, family and household structure. These are assessed along with the effects of different sector market opportunities, geographical location and the role of changing locational opportunity in a period of rapidly developing transport infrastructure. This leads to some important new insights into questions that have previously been difficult to examine for this period, such as 'What makes an entrepreneur' and 'What contributes to opportunities for entrepreneurship and growth'. The following chapters then engage in more detail with specific dimensions: demography and the family firm (Chapter 7), gender (Chapter 8), geographical locations (Chapter 9), migration (Chapter 10) and diversification through development of portfolios of business activity (Chapter 11).

1.2   Defining the entrepreneur and entrepreneurship

The information now available in the BBCE allows 'entrepreneur' to be defined in this book as *the proprietor who is responsible for the business at a given point of time.* Their businesses are also defined broadly to include all those run by individual sole proprietors, both those who employed others and the self-employed 'working on own account' who employed only themselves; those run by individuals working in partnership or joint enterprises as 'firms'; and those run by directors of incorporated entities. The book focuses on all individuals who ran all businesses, covering the full size range from the smallest to the largest. The definition is as broad-ranging as possible so that it can be applied to understanding the whole population, can be integrated with modern definitions and is supported by data collected now and in the past.

More precisely we define 'entrepreneurship', enlarged in Chapter 2, as *the process of decision making to draw together resources to produce an economic output of goods or services*; and we define 'entrepreneurs' as *those **responsible** for undertaking business activity who responded to business opportunities by trying to meet or anticipate demand and organise supply. They assembled factor inputs, achieving a return for their skills by successfully doing so, and bearing the risk if they failed.*

This book focuses on *entrepreneurship in business development.* However, it is accepted that entrepreneurship can be applied to many, perhaps any, field: ranging from business to government administration, social organisations, charities or the arts. It can also be applied at the level of chief executive, senior and middle managers and by artisans and basic workers. All types of activity at all levels are amenable to the application of the wide concept of 'entrepreneurial action' that pursues opportunities to improve current processes. Indeed modern business schools and other centres attempt to train people to be more entrepreneurial in all fields of endeavour (Shane and Venkataraman, 2000). But the focus here is on business development and the business proprietor: those who are actually in business to trade goods and services, have a level of meaningful discretion over price setting, make the key strategic decisions and take on the responsibility for the risks involved.

This definition, even with its restriction to business proprietors, is much broader than many modern studies of business entrepreneurship which use different approaches in different contexts and disciplines. For example Hébert and

Link (2009: 100–1) recognise that even among economists there are competing views on the role of the entrepreneur. They define entrepreneurs as performing at least 12 different, though overlapping, roles as economic agents: the person who assumes risk, who supplies financial capital, innovator, decision maker, industrial leader, manager or superintendent, organiser and coordinator, business owner, employer of factors of production, contractor, arbitrageur and allocator of resources. But this does not exhaust the possibilities. Mayer et al. (2018: 534) argue that there has been a failure to define entrepreneurship sufficiently precisely; Kitching and Rouse (2017: 568–9) conclude that context and research question are all-important: it is impossible to create a synthesis.

Much modern economic literature defines business entrepreneurs purely as those who *innovate*. Other literature focuses on those who assemble and coordinate factors of production chiefly through their organisation of the labour of others as *employers*. Yet others restrict attention to non-farmers. However, many modern studies widen the definitions to include entrepreneurship as an *attitude of mind* and psychological traits. Within these, there is an important field focusing on the development of entrepreneurial thinking among those who might consider business initiatives but have not yet started (*nascent entrepreneurs*). These are all valuable approaches, but for our purposes they are less relevant to whole-population study, and mostly inapplicable to what can be assessed for the historical period from the data available; furthermore, the distinction between innovative entrepreneurs and simple 'owners' has proved difficult to implement on any scale in modern research (Aldrich and Waldinger, 1990: 112–13). It is particularly problematic to exclude *farm businesses* since, for our period, they were about half of all business numbers and the interaction between farming and other enterprises affected all sectors. Indeed, we show they are an important element of nineteenth-century business development.

Given our aim of whole-population analysis, and given the historical data available, we limit the focus to *those currently operating a business at a specific point in time*. This does not, of course, restrict future analysis of our database to extract from it innovators, those who might be nascent entrepreneurs or who have specific traits, if sufficient information can be assembled to identify such sub-sets. The advantage of the whole-population database that has been assembled is that sub-sets can be extracted, but also when they are used it is possible to determine how special they are, and how they differ from, or are representative of, wider groups. This was impossible before the large-scale data now made available.

A key comparison we use is between entrepreneurs and workers. Workers are those who are not (currently) operating as the proprietors of any business and receive their income as wages or salaries. Entrepreneurs are those who receive their income as the residual of the profits of their enterprise after deducting all costs; they support themselves by their own direct endeavour, receiving no wage or salary but the residual of profits. This is the usual definition of entrepreneurial income (though sometimes confusingly referred to as an 'entrepreneurial wage'). This is the broadest definitional distinction used in the modern literature, which is also supported by historic data. The income distinction focuses on the different ways in which income is obtained: wages provide higher certainty but less control, because they rely on others to run the business; entrepreneurial income generally offers lower certainty but gives greater independence and potential for control of business decisions. We develop this distinction further in Chapter 2 where we confront alternative theories of business entrepreneurship and their historical applicability to whole-population analysis. This is then developed further in Chapter 6 where estimates are developed of alterative constrained discrete choices of entrepreneurial status between different forms of business organisation: as a waged employee, as an own-account sole proprietor, as an employer of others or as a director. We also give attention, as far as our data allow, to choices between partnership and sole proprietorship. In addition, within the discrete choice framework, we also investigate situations where entrepreneurship is applied to more than one business at the same time through portfolio diversification.

1.3   Re-positioning historical studies of entrepreneurship

The challenges of definitions of the 'entrepreneur' and scale of available data have been well recognised in the literature. A useful debate has emerged in business history on the need to develop larger-scale analyses and to move beyond case studies and small samples: Wardley (2001: 129) calls for greater 'development of generally accessible machine-readable datasets'. However, development of such databases has chiefly focused on corporate and large businesses, with the most significant research mainly based on the 100 largest firms (Hannah, 1983, 2014; Jeremy, 1998); nothing of scale for Britain has emerged on non-corporate and smaller businesses. Many studies in the 'new economic history' tradition following Landes (1969) have sought to construct larger databases to examine characteristics of entrepreneurs over time (Gatrell, 1977; Godley, 2001; Kay, 2009; Nicholas, 1999a). A recent example is Mokyr (2010: 197), who takes a broad view of the definition of entrepreneurs. In practice these use definitions of the 'great employers' or the 'economic elite' of significant business leaders who were also politically well connected. Mokyr's analysis of 1,249 British entrepreneurs is on a larger scale than many previous studies, and combines the information from Rubinstein (1977, 2006), Çrouzet (1985) and Honeyman (1983) and the *Dictionary of Business Biography*. But even this is a tiny sample of the whole population of entrepreneurs that existed over the period of analysis, and it is biased towards the successful and others large enough to gain attention, those with at least basic archival records and those whose health allowed them to live longer.

Nye (1991) and Mokyr (2010) have drawn attention to the important truncation effects in such studies. Any comparisons with the successful are constrained because we do not generally know who was surviving but struggling, who had failed, who were would-be entrepreneurs who had tried but gave up early and reverted to waged employment or became unemployed or those who never initiated action. Nye argues that if all the struggling, failed and would-be entrepreneurs were fully included the probability of success would be better understood, entrepreneurship rates would be lower and the rate of return to entrepreneurship would probably be negative. In other words, looking at the whole population, rather than at selected samples of the successful, radically changes the inferences that can be drawn about entrepreneurship. Ideally, we need better data on firm creation, longevity of firms, turnover rates, the extent of failures and their actual losses, as well as the opportunity costs of other activities in which they engaged. Such data are impossible to assemble in full for historical series, although the big data used in this book go some way in this direction. However, the alternative of focusing on samples of the successful or the 'innovators' has obvious selection bias and represents an unknown proportion of the total entrepreneurial population. Inferring from such samples to entrepreneurship rates, macro-economic effects and their role in economic growth can be entirely misleading.

Selection bias is a particular challenge to modern and historical accounts of the *entrepreneur as innovator*. Innovators usually can only be recognised by their success and prominence, or if they fail they are tracked only when they were previously successful or prominent; almost all the rest remain unknown and unstudied. For example, Baumol (2010) explicitly restricts his definition of entrepreneur to innovators. Casson (1982, 2010), a leading commentator on entrepreneurs in economic history, defines them as innovators who make the critical judgement decisions by entering or creating new markets in order *to extract rents and obtain above-average returns*. His review of nineteenth-century entrepreneurship (Casson and Godley, 2010: 225) takes the argument further, stating that defining entrepreneurs as we do, as the self-employed, 'is too narrow to be of much use in analyzing the Victorian economy' and is 'misleading, as entrepreneurship reduced self-employment rather than increased it, and those that were self-employed were not particularly notable for their entrepreneurship . . . there is much more to being an entrepreneur than being self-employed'. Their alternative is to define entrepreneurship as a scarce ability reflected in the scope to make above-average profits. Whaples (2013: 72) also argues that equating entrepreneurship with self-employment, as we do,

> can be unhelpful in at least two important ways. First, self-employed workers in many fields – landscapers, plumbers, truck drivers, accountants, day-care operators, and hair stylists, for example, – rarely make economic meaningful innovations. More importantly, the most economically important entrepreneurs aren't self-employed, but rather build and manage corporations with thousands of employees.

Casson and Whaples thus rule out defining the *full population* of self-employed as entrepreneurs (the definition we employ). Similarly the full population of small firms is dismissed as entrepreneurs since many are 'life-style businesses' not interested in growth; what Storey (1994) calls 'trundlers'.

These positions have to be challenged. There is nothing wrong with defining special cases of entrepreneurship as 'innovators', 'rent seekers', 'the highly successful', 'gazelles', 'high-growth orientated' or the 'economic elite'. For case studies and samples drawn under transparent and specific selection criteria these special cases provide valuable means to address specific research questions matching the selection criteria. And our counterpart of including all self-employed should not be seen as an exaggeration of the economic contribution of deliverymen, window cleaners or laundresses. We argue for breadth and balance: that selective definitions are too narrow to fully understand the significance of the differences and complementarities of entrepreneurship within the whole population. As summarised by Nye (1991: 134), defining entrepreneurship as Schumpeterian or only concerned with innovation is 'misperceiving the role of entrepreneurship'. Instead we should view the entrepreneur as learning 'through repeated failure . . . only now and then do one of these . . . entrepreneurs happen to luck out, . . . just as the odd player may win the lottery'. In comparison '"ordinary" successes are fully discounted in the marketplace'. This is a very helpful recognition of the distinction between the routine of entrepreneurial practice ('ordinary' survival in the market is itself challenging) and the few that obtain 'super-normal' returns, which they themselves could not expect *a priori*. Hence the focus on the exceptional limits the explanatory power of any conclusions regarding the nature of entrepreneurship. Without knowing the rest of the entrepreneurial population we do not know how the successful differ. Our alternative is to treat innovation as a separate issue, with innovators a sub-group within entrepreneurs as a whole.

Moving beyond selective samples to analyse the whole population has a range of advantages:

1   It removes selection bias of sampling only the successful, the prominent or the innovators.
2   Taking the whole population allows innovators, or other selections, to be positioned against the whole population to assess their specificness, and how far they really differ.
3   Using the population of the self-employed recognises that even these are relatively rare. From our estimates we now know that total self-employed were only 12 percent of the economically active in 1911; employers of others were only 4 percent. Radical innovators and transformers were only at most 0.01 percent. To put a microscope over these ignores the majority entrepreneurial activity which is an already small category.
4   Whole-population analysis gives understanding of the whole distribution. It is valuable to know about the less, as well as the more, successful. Definitionally, a focus on above-average profits must exclude most other businesses that are average or below-average but are nevertheless run by operating entrepreneurs. We can move beyond value judgements that distinguish one person's business from another by their *relative* success; for example:

    •   The interaction of entrepreneurship with opportunity, which is seen as the key distinction in modern entrepreneurship definitions (Shane and Venkataraman, 2000): those operating flat out and implementing many changes and innovations to achieve a good level of profit for their type of business but only able to achieve at best an average profit level because of constraints of market opportunities in their sector or location. The pejorative dismissal of these 'trundlers' fails to recognise that maintaining any business is challenging, and levels of below-average profits may require innovation just to survive.

- The importance of satisfying behaviour; that is, equating entrepreneurs with those who seek high profit as a goal ignores others who make important economic contributions but are content to achieve lower income if that suits their lifestyle.

- At the basic level, for some (often many) to make enough profit to survive is to have succeeded. Beyond satisficers many may only be able to achieve a basic income from the choice options available; that is, so-called necessity or survival entrepreneurs.

- Many of those who achieve above-average profits may have done nothing different from the rest of the distribution beneath them: they may just be lucky; they do not have any special characteristics. Indeed, a significant conclusion from most case studies of entrepreneurs, as Nye argues using the examples of Thomas Edison and Henry Ford, is that luck plays a big role for highly successful entrepreneurs. Focusing on the successful, therefore, often does no more than investigating chance. As Mayer et al. (2018: 534) conclude: such entrepreneurship has not been correctly measured.

5   Whole-population analysis is also less prescriptive about competition. It is implicit in entrepreneurship that the markets involved are contestable, but it is essential for definitions based on sustaining above-average profits to be rent exploiting that markets are partly non-contestable. Indeed, many definitions of entrepreneurship, discussed further in Chapter 2, have entrepreneurs as exploiting disequilibrium. To maintain the benefits of a disequilibrium requires non-contestability through a level of monopoly control. A rent-seeking entrepreneur is restrictive of the entrepreneurship of others. In contrast to this view, modern endogenous growth theory (as noted in Chapter 2) recognises the benefits of externalities from innovations that spill over beyond the initial inventor or innovator, recognising the gap between private and social returns. Generally, narrow rent-seekers inhibit long-term growth, and such control is usually possible only with actual or de facto grants of monopoly by the state (e.g. patent protection or relaxed regulation of anti-trust and monopolies). This in part explains the interaction between 'great men' and their political involvement: they needed to lobby to maintain their advantages. It is highly contentious that monopolies achieved in this way constitute business entrepreneurship at all, though it may constitute political entrepreneurship, a point well recognised in the types of entrepreneurship that Baumol (1990) distinguishes as 'productive, unproductive, and destructive'.

6   Selective definitions also separate entrepreneurs from the conditions within which they operate. We are particularly concerned in this book with the support from families, extended networks of relationships and specific geographical contexts. It is important to know how entrepreneurs compare with others on these dimensions. These are relationships we can begin to interrogate with whole population data but which are largely invisible within more selective approaches.

7   Perhaps most important is that selective definitions of entrepreneurship do not integrate with the economic definition of entrepreneurial income for the whole economy. They thus isolate analysis of entrepreneurship from analysis of national income and national economic growth because they cannot join up individuals to aggregates nor join historical and modern data. To be able to make inferences about the distribution of income between business profits and labour, or between one part of the business population and another, requires the total entrepreneurial population to be known. This is the information that Feinstein (1972) constructed for incomes as part of his estimates of historical national accounts for the UK and Kuznets et al. (1941) did for the US. With whole-population data we can now add to Feinstein's assessment and extend his estimates of self-employment income back to the 1850s. Following new estimates in Chapters 4 and 5, the changes in business numbers can be used to infer how profits were distributed across the population. This is only possible by calculating the total number of all entrepreneurs, of whatever kind, and not restricting attention to innovators.

On Casson's observation that entrepreneurship reduced self-employment in the Victorian period, we demonstrate that this is incorrect for most sectors. Moreover it reinforces the trope of late-Victorian decline. In contrast, the results now available in this book for the whole population show that entrepreneur numbers increased over the period from 1851 up to 1901. Entrepreneurship rates did decline in many sectors, against a rapid rise in the population, and compared to the total economically active. But this was a result generated more by the rapid expansion of the labour market for waged employment. The actual number of businesses stayed similar over the period, with increases in many sectors. Moreover the expansion in business numbers was strong for both individual own-account traders and for those who were employers of others. Expansion was even more rapid for incorporated businesses, once their popularity began to take off in the 1890s. As others have concluded, the trope of Victorian decline was a misinterpretation.

1.4   Drivers of entrepreneurship

We are covering a long period of development and change. Across this period many economic and social structures changed radically. To understand the rest of our analysis it is important to have a preliminary view of these changes since they acted as both drivers and outcomes of different forms of entrepreneurial development. There are many such drivers. We focus on seven main aspects.

Government policy and free trade

An important feature for modern readers to note is that there was little explicit government policy to support small business or self-employment in the eighteenth and nineteenth centuries beyond the use of bounties to encourage certain industries, with varying degrees of success, quite unlike modern government priorities (Hoppit, 2011). Indeed, historically governments had mainly explicitly intervened in the world of business to hold back small-scale business activities and 'interlopers' in trade by granting monopolies, such as to chartered companies or groups of adventurers (such as the East India Company), and through acquiescence in private Acts of Parliament that sought to establish statutory companies (of which the most important were canals, and then railways). A critical change in government policy occurred in the early nineteenth century to step even further away from interventions in trade and open up scope for open access to the economy as a whole by all comers – domestic and international. Liberal Tory governments of the 1820s revised the Navigation Acts and introduced new administrators to the Board of Trade, who were mostly leading advocates of further reform. From the 1840s a series of campaigns opened the British economy to 'free trade' at the start of the period of our intensive analysis, by repeal of the Corn Laws in 1846 and reform of the Navigation Laws in 1849. The age of entrepreneurship we primarily examine is, therefore, a period from the 1850s which was underpinned by a policy milieu and institutional orientation of Britain towards open trade. This was to remain essentially unchanged until World War I. For the main period we examine, these changes thrust Britain into the forefront of benefiting from low-cost imports, but made it vulnerable to competition from low-cost producers and subsidised goods and commodities from elsewhere, and cyclical sensitivity increased.

This background gives the context to the ease of market entry and relative ease of achieving business profits evident for the own-account traders and small firms that dominate much of our analysis: as Payne (1984: 42–4) noted, small businesses proliferated. Even for Lancashire textiles, large and long-established firms were under continual pressure from small firms and start-ups (Gatrell, 1977). This means that after 1851 changes in the general patterns of firm size growth were fairly modest. Certainly there were major new and expanding large firms. But small firms and own-account sole operators were dominant and increased in numbers up to 1901. As Marshall (1919: 92–3) argued, the mid-nineteenth century had 'an unprecedented combination of advantages [that] enabled businessmen to make money even when they were not throwing themselves with energy' into their business. The political and institutional climate encouraged this, and the opening to free trade helped to reduce many input costs and stimulate a feeling that opportunities were assessable to entrepreneurs.

But the effects of free trade began to profoundly change in the 1870s and 1880s. Initially agriculture prospered after the abolition of the Corn Laws; this was referred to by Prothero (1912) as the 'Golden Age of British Agriculture', covering the 10 years following 1853. However, from the early 1870s the price of grain in Europe fell dramatically following bulk imports from America as railways opened up the prairies and steam shipping radically cut freight rates. The development of tin canning from the late 1860s and the use of compressed air refrigeration from 1879 opened the way for cheap imports of meat and animal products from the Americas and Australasia, with the British and European prices of many farm products declining until about 1900 (Lawton and Pooley, 1992; Koning, 1994; Collins, 2000). The subsequent period from 1873, generally referred to as the 'Great Depression' in agriculture, lasted until about 1896. Depression of trade more generally affected industry from the mid-1880s into the 1890s with a *Royal Commission on the Depression of Trade and Industry* report in 1886. There were also challenges to the free-trade commitment from colonial import barriers by Australia and Canada introduced from the 1860s, and from the US McKinley Tariff of 1890, German tariff increases in 1902 and German stimulus to cartels across central European countries (Brown, 1943; Howe, 1997). However, no meaningful British policy changes were made to protect agriculture or other industries from external trade competition until World War I. Even after the war the commitment to free trade remained strong across the political spectrum until after the 'tariff election' of 1931, after which tariff control became the norm until the 1980s. The period we mainly examine opened British businesses to global price competition and increased cyclical sensitivity. Many businesses thrived, but many smaller businesses and own-account proprietors from the mid-1880s were faced with declining profits, with increasing numbers only able attain 'survival' incomes. This had a profound impact on bringing the 'age of entrepreneurship' to a close.

In addition, although the British state was laissez-faire with regard to international trade, it was increasingly interventionist in the labour market. Worries about factory work inspired a raft of legislation aimed at improving working conditions and regulating the labour market to limit hours and age of workers. The first Factory Act was passed in 1802, followed by further acts at frequent intervals throughout the nineteenth century. Such legislation mainly applied to women and children. Until the 1860s most restrictions affected mines and the textile trade, but this was progressively extended to cover most sectors by 1911. Regulations primarily covered workshops and factories, although enforcement was variable (Fraser, 2009; Fang, 1930). Other changes in legislation affected labour-market incentives through poor law reform and trade union legislation, whilst compulsory school provision accelerated improvements in the general level of literacy, numeracy and skills (Curthoys, 2004; Sanderson, 1995; Wallis, 2014). The effects of such policies on entrepreneurship are debated – some may have inhibited economic activity and others enabled it – but like all regulation they raised entry barriers and required more knowledge and skills which together with other changes favoured larger and more managerial enterprise structures. However, at the same time the application of regulations primarily to workshops and factories, the development of trade unions mainly within large firms and the incentives to work from poor law reform encouraged own-account development which was free of restrictions on hours and use of family labour.

Transport and communications

The period we examine in most depth, 1851–1911, saw many innovations in industrial, service and organisational processes which we address through their sector development in Chapters 4–11. But innovations in transport and communications transformed the context of entrepreneurship. The fundamental characteristic of entrepreneurship is responsiveness to opportunities. Transport and communications innovations introduced some radically new opportunities directly, as well as also profoundly reducing the costs of passenger travel and freight and accelerating the speed of transmission of goods and information.

Roads, canals and other navigable waterways were well-developed networks long before the 1850s. Canal improvements occurred after 1850 to speed up transit though locks and widen sections, but these had mainly local impacts. Roads also improved steadily after the 1820s with the introduction of horse-drawn rollers, from the 1870s with steam rollers and from the 1880s with the introduction of asphalt, mainly in cities. Additionally, from 1835 a succession of Highways Acts improved road upkeep across the whole network, after 1873 transferring responsibility for major roads from turnpike trusts to local government, removing toll barriers. But *road networks* did not change radically over the period from 1851 until motor vehicles became more common after about 1910, although electric trams revolutionised urban transport at a local level.

The more radical change was the development of railways. The first steam railways were built in the 1820s, but access to lines was fragmentary and piece-meal until after a period of rapid expansion following the railway 'mania' of the 1840s, so that only by 1850 was the basic trunk system complete enough to provide a network that connected almost all the large towns and cities (Mitchell, 1964; Turnock, 1998). This allowed rail to link markets nationally but primarily regionally. The major carriers shifted from road to rail for packages and parcel delivery over long distances during the late 1840s for the main carriers such as Pickfords and Chaplin & Horne (Turnbull, 1979: 126–33). Hence the start of our analysis in 1851 is the first point where England and Wales can be regarded as having an almost complete trunk rail network, with the following period the main time that could produce significant impacts from increased regional marketing opportunities that affected entrepreneurship and growth in business size. Also, as Simmons (1986: 312) stated, the mania period 'produced a system that was much unbalanced' with main emphasis on passenger transport. Over 1854–76 railways spread to almost all areas, fuelled by the main rail companies trying to prevent others getting their business through feeders (Jenks, 1944), and began to make more significant adaptations for commercial freight and agricultural produce. The developments after 1851 were thus a critical period where railways began to have more significant impact on reducing costs of assembling factor inputs and distribution of products, which opened entrepreneurs to opportunities for expanded market access.

Railway developments also aided a revolution in communications: radical changes to the volume and speed of message transmission through the postal service were now possible, covering all locations at a uniform rate irrespective of distance. The Post Office was a rapid adopter of rail, usually soon after lines opened. This became critical to introducing, across almost the whole country, rapid ordering and delivery between producers, wholesalers and customers and, after 1838 reforms, the rapid transmission of small payments through Post Office 'money orders' (Daunton, 1985). The impact on entrepreneurial market opportunities was increased still further after the 1883 Parcels Act introduced postal distribution of larger packages. The postal system also stimulated local carriers who transported goods between origins or destinations and rail access points (Sherrington, 1934; Robinson, 1986; Barker and Gerhold, 1995). The effects were revolutionary: letters delivered per year increased from 347 million in 1850 to 2.3 billion letters by 1900; postal transmission of small payments (of up to £5, increased to £10 in 1860) rose for small numbers in the 1840s to over 11 billion transfers per year by 1913, totaling £47 million (Daunton, 1985: 48, 72, 80–92). In addition a rapidly growing market for magazines and short novels was created through extensive development of station bookstalls supported by High Street newsagents and stationers. Postal distribution of printed papers by rail to these outlets rose from 159 million in 1875 to 732 million in 1913. Similar dramatic changes affected overseas mail and communications. Mostly heavily subsidised by various government contract systems and cartels, ocean-going mail communications allowed more rapid export and import trade development and more rapid decision making on investment and other decisions. This was supplemented from the 1850s when transmission speeds radically improved through the use of international cable communications. In addition the domestic telegraph cable system, nationalised in 1868, and telephones, nationalised 1912, became sub-divisions of the Post Office and created 'instant' business communications that supplemented the mail.

Population change

Over the period mainly considered in this book, the population of England and Wales rose from 17.9 million in 1851 to 36.1 million in 1911. Most of this growth was concentrated in towns, with considerable migration from rural to urban locations. This population growth alone was enough to promote entrepreneurship by increasing both demand for goods and services and the supply of entrepreneurs and workers (Gilbert and Southall, 2000). It was a key feeder to Payne's observation that profits were easy. The main population-led demands were most directly felt in the building and construction sectors, retail and services, leisure activities (which were focused in urban areas and resorts) and for the supply new consumer goods. The supply effects of greater waged labour fuelled the expansion of larger businesses and increased the attractions of waged labour compared with operating one's own business. The effects were the more significant because from the mid-1850s the real income of workers increased steadily until the 1880s, before growing again in the 1900s (Feinstein, 1972).

However, given the close relationship between starting a business and aspects of the life cycle (Davidoff, 2012; Aldrich and Cliff, 2003), changes in nuptiality, fertility and mortality also had important effects on entrepreneurship. By the end of this period, people were living longer, marrying later and having fewer children. Life expectancy at birth rose from 41.1 years in the 1850s to 50.9 years in the 1900s (Woods, 2000: 365), with nearly all of this improvement concentrated on children and younger adults, hence directly enhancing the size of the current and future workforce. Changes were slow (Schürer et al., 2018), with most of the change concentrated in the 1890s and early 1900s, but the tide had begun to turn. Life expectancy improvements continued more into older age groups, people were marrying later and having fewer children, and this may have contributed to a slowdown in entrepreneurial opportunity. Marriage age rose: the singulate mean age at marriage (SMAM) for women in England and Wales rose from 25.8 in 1851 to 26.3 in 1911 (Teitelbaum, 1984). Additionally, there were changes in the proportion of the population that never married; for both men and women the proportion never married fell between 1851 and 1881, before returning to 1851 levels in 1891 and continuing to rise thereafter (Garrett et al., 2001: 214–16), with more people living alone (Schürer et al., 2018). From 1891 women were marrying later or not at all, and men were more likely to have never married. These changes interacted with separate changes in marital fertility to drive overall fertility rates downwards so that the crude birth rate of 33.4 per thousand in the 1850s began to fall in the 1870s, reaching 24.3 per thousand in 1911 (Mitchell and Deane, 1962: 29–30). As a result the age pyramid slowly started to change, older people increased as a proportion of the population and younger people decreased from the 1890s onwards; this accelerated significantly after 1914. Hence the economically active population in this period was growing, but also beginning to age (Baines and Woods, 2004: 47–9).

There was also considerable geographical variation in the demography of Victorian and Edwardian England and Wales (Garrett et al., 2001), especially the sex ratio and the proportion of never married women, which in turn affected business proprietorship. Areas with high sex ratios (where there were more men than women) tended to have lower rates of never married women and thus lower levels of female labour force participation, and consequently lower rates of female entrepreneurship. This was most stark in the nineteenth century in mining areas (Shaw-Taylor, 2007). We examine these effects more fully in Chapter 9. The relationship between demography and economic activity interacted with economic and social status (Szreter, 1996; Barnes and Guinnane, 2012). It has been suggested that employers had lower fertility than workers or own-account sole proprietors (Szreter, 1996: 348–51). But as shown in Chapter 7 and 8 this relationship was complex and varied between sectors and family life stages. For example, as entrepreneurs tended to be older than workers, the increase in life expectancy increased the pool of potential entrepreneurs, but as many people started businesses when they married, the rise in age at marriage reduced the pool.

An additional aspect of demography is the interaction with cyclic and trend effects; this was first noted in Lösch's (1937) *Population Cycles as a Cause of Business Cycles*, but it is also embedded in Kuznets' (1926, 1940, 1974) assessment of causes of growth and fluctuations. Lösch noted that population change acts as a stimulus to economic changes: the reverse of Malthus' thinking. Increasing population size, which dominated the period up to World War I, offered the benefits of a long upswing: demand for goods and services rose, increasing labour was available and markets extended purely because there were more people. This also stimulated migration, locally, regionally and internationally, as we discuss in Chapter 10. As Payne suggested, profit opportunities were easy and small firms were stimulated. This could combine with expanded technical opportunities, as Schumpeter (1927, 1939) suggested, when entrepreneurs were more likely to invest or implement innovations, but population growth alone was enough to increase entrepreneurship. Lösch argued that entrepreneurship followed population changes, either to co-vary with it in periods of stable demographic trends or to lag population changes when there were disruptions such as population loss during major wars, other crises or epidemics. In our main period of analysis Britain did not experience major disruptions to population growth, but small disruptions occurred during the South African War in 1901–02; and the age of entrepreneurship was brought to an end by World War I and the pandemic flu epidemic of 1918. These combined major population losses with changes in state policy to favour protection and support for large businesses at the expense of small firms and own-account entrepreneurs.

Urban population growth

The main impact of population growth was in cities: rapid urbanization transformed the nature of entrepreneurial markets. Britain was already a more highly urbanised society than other developed countries by 1851, and its urban population continued to grow rapidly: as of 1851, 54 percent of the population of England and Wales was in towns, and by 1911 this had increased to 79 percent (Lawton and Pooley, 1992: 91). City size and city growth were strong correlates of economic growth throughout the eighteenth and nineteenth centuries in Britain (Hudson, 1989; Jackson, 1988a; Langton, 2000). Larger agglomerations had increasing scope to combine externalities, export multipliers of locally and regionally connected places and import substitution and reprocessing multipliers to further expand their markets (Jacobs, 1984). Crafts (2005) and Crafts and Mulatu (2005) found market potential of city foci *within* regions of Britain critical in explaining economic growth and competitiveness up to World War II, whilst *between* regions agglomeration had little benefit until nationally linked transport (mainly roads) was more widely available after World War II. Hence between-region differentiation, 'industrial districts' and diversity were key characteristics of nineteenth-century entrepreneurship.

Urban growth concentrated population at high densities that reduced business risk, increased externalities and increased competition. Demand was readily available in agglomerated urban areas, and among larger business owners a shared urban and civic culture facilitated trust between proprietors, encouraged supportive institutions such as banks, agents and other intermediaries, and aided organisations like chambers of commerce and business clubs, which helped press for greater national political involvement and influence for business needs (Gunn, 2000; Morris, 1990; Clark, 2000; Bennett, 2011; Hoppit, 2018). In addition urbanisation increased the 'contextual variety' and breadth of entrepreneurship opportunities (Boschma, 2009; Jacobs, 1969). For smaller entrepreneurs urban life could bring other advantages, most obviously in the external economies noted by Alfred Marshall which provided a locally tuned labour market and skills, infrastructure and ready markets for suppliers and sales. This was further enhanced through the historic development of industrial districts with concentrated firms in particular industries in certain locations. In such locations costs of labour management, transport, information sharing and capital were usually lower given the networks and shared culture which developed between businesses and families (Marshall, 1961; Wilson and Popp, 2003; Popp and Wilson, 2007; Reeder and Rodger, 2000). Although such advantages could become hindrances over time, as was the case in the Lancashire cotton industry in the early twentieth century (Wilson and Singleton, 2003), this was not occurring on any scale before World War I. As well as generic benefits for all businesses, an important aspect was increased opportunities for female labour force participation and the chances of women becoming business proprietors (Smith et al., 2018).

It was also at the urban level that most infrastructure was developed. The period from the 1850s saw major infrastructure expansion such as new/improved roads, omnibuses and trams, sewers and, increasingly, gas, water and later electricity. All these development offered business opportunities and were often initiated by private business, frequently as limited companies. However, as time progressed municipal government became increasingly involved in infrastructure concerns, as well as welfare services and education provision. This could be encouraged by the strong representation of business proprietors on councils, but developments were not without tensions that could set manufacturers against retailers, merchants and professionals, which led to increasingly vigorous debates about the appropriate extent of municipal enterprise and the effect of industry on local environments (Hamlin, 1988; Hennock, 1973; Prest, 1990).

Incorporation, managerial control and capital markets

Up to the mid-nineteenth century, British businesses had two main avenues for finance. They could fund their business through investment from family members or familial contacts, as many small companies and family firms continued to do, or they could borrow from banks or finance houses (Ashworth, 1962: 88). While the banking system expanded through the nineteenth century, it was criticised for mainly providing short-term loans, and finance houses were mainly accessible only to large businesses. With the increase in scale of fixed capital requirements in several nineteenth-century sectors such as iron and steel, many projects were beyond the means of business owners or had long lags between setup and profitability that made short-term banks loans in appropriate. Limited companies could also raise capital through shares, but this was limited before the 1844 Joint Stock Companies Act. Even then wider share ownership and raising of capital was restricted until the introduction of general limited liability in 1856 and its extension in 1862. Limited liability protected individual directors and shareholders if a company became insolvent, holding them liable only to the extent of the nominal value of their shares. However, incorporation was generally stimulated more by the increasing needs for capital, rather than limiting risk (Hannah, 1983), and from the 1860s increasing numbers of companies sought capital through the stock market, especially for iron and mining, as well as cotton and shipping. As a result listings on the London and provincial stock exchanges became increasingly important compared to private capital raising (Cottrell, 1980).

Although there had been some resistance to incorporation, by the 1880s confidence in limited companies and wider share financing was high among borrowers and lenders, which meant that companies were able to draw their capital from a multitude of small streams. The addition of fixed-income securities, such as preference shares and debentures, which offered a guaranteed return, made shareholding less risky, more accessible and more applicable to a wider population (Rutterford et al., 2011). Between the 1870s and 1910s the number of commercial and industrial companies listed on the stock exchange expanded dramatically. While domestic industrial and commercial companies only accounted for 1 percent of all value quoted on the London Stock Exchange in 1870, by the 1913 they accounted for almost 10 percent (Cottrell, 2004). However, the attractions of incorporation developed much more quickly in some sectors than others: it was most important for large companies in sectors such as iron and steel, mining, utilities, textiles, and foreign investments. This meant that corporate entrepreneurship was often highly sectorally focused, whereas non-corporate entrepreneurship continued to cover all sectors, as evident in the analysis in Chapter 6.

Incorporation not only changed the nature of finance, it also encouraged changes to internal management and hierarchy. Schloss (1899) argued that managers and foremen emerged first as a means to control large enterprises in limited companies, though the practice was also more widespread. He stated it was becoming significant in the 1890s. But Taylorism, the systematic organisation of management mainly through line management, multiple foremen and hierarchical remuneration systems, became dominant only after World War I (Taylor, 1911; Littler, 1982: 48–63; Gospel, 1992, 2008). The depression of industry in the 1880s has been credited as being important in beginning the crucial shift towards hierarchical control. Landes (1969: 231) and Littler (1982: 72–8) considered that the 1880s began to shift the balance of bargaining permanently away from the craft master towards the employer as a result of the pressure of declining prices on profits, increasing competition from the US and Germany, and the decrease of working hours as a result of factory legislation. We certainly discern a shift towards larger firms in the non-corporate sector becoming important from the 1880s, which was coincident with the accelerating rise of corporate numbers (see Figures 5.10 and 5.11). There was indeed the beginning of a systemic shift underway, but, as concluded by Hannah (1983), the main impact of these changes followed World War I.

Overseas investment and opportunities for entrepreneurs elsewhere

The effects of incorporation and wider shareholdings widened entrepreneurial opportunities, but may also have narrowed them by increasing competition for private financing and career aspirations. A major theme in the historiography of nineteenth-century British entrepreneurship has been that overseas investment competed with home-based businesses. Some argue that British banks favoured investment in foreign securities rather than British manufacturing, meaning that smaller companies and start-ups in new and innovative sectors found it more difficult to raise money on the stock exchange, and the competition for funds from rewarding international investments may have squeezed the UK market away from domestic investment as a whole (Kennedy, 1991; Cain and Hopkins, 2002), though this remains contentious (Cottrell, 1980; Edelstein, 1982; Daunton, 1991). A significant proportion of British capital in this period was held abroad, with estimates ranging from one-quarter to two-fifths (Pollard, 1984: 491). This could have diverted attention from long-term domestic funding opportunities compared to countries like Germany (Kennedy, 1991). However, how far this systematically harmed British industry is controversial. It is also important to remember that a significant amount of British overseas financial activity was in firms concerned with the movement of commodities, which was essential to much British industry. Also many UK multinationals also traded substantially domestically, and foreign firms also invested in the UK (Buckley, 1989). The situation was therefore complex, with any bias towards overseas investment damaging some firms and rewarding others, while the international nature of much of British large-scale manufacturing meant that international finance was vital to certain areas of the British economy.

The historiography of nineteenth-century British entrepreneurship has also argued that the pattern of British capitalism was set by aristocrats who successfully married pre-capitalist status with successful agrarian capitalism to create a form of economic activity which became the ideal in Britain. Occupations which allowed for the maintenance of an aristocratic lifestyle while also being economically efficient thus came to dominate British life; hence, it is argued, why commerce and particularly finance in the City of London prospered, and industry supposedly failed or declined, in the second half of the nineteenth century. 'Gentlemanly capitalism' looked down on full-time employment, production and economic interaction with those deemed socially inferior; thus, inevitably, British manufacturers failed to innovate compared to industrial entrepreneurs elsewhere (Wiener, 1981; Rubinstein, 1993, 2006; Cain and Hopkins, 1986, 1987, 2002). These arguments also remain contentious (Daunton, 1991).

The biases of 'gentlemanly capitalism' and overseas investment have generally been argued to be at the expense of large-scale manufacturing. But, as already noted, concentrating on big business means ignoring the majority of entrepreneurs in this period for whom local banks and loans raised through familial and friendship networks remained more important (Capie and Collins, 1996; Collins and Baker, 2003; Cottrell, 2004; Davidoff, 2012). Furthermore the focus on the financing of industry ignores the increasingly important service sector, which provided employment for about 30 percent of the population of England and Wales in 1856, rising to about 45 percent in 1913 (Lee, 1984; Broadberry, 2014). We can redress the previous imbalance of attention by focusing on the entrepreneur, and in Chapter 6 we investigate how corporate and overseas directors differed from non-corporate entrepreneurs and the most numerous – own-account proprietors. Turning our attention to smaller businesses and including the service sector suggests that the detrimental effect of overseas investment on British entrepreneurship has been exaggerated. This confirms the arguments by Daunton (2007: 131–65) that, first, smaller business were always likely to be less reliant on the City of London for finances, and second, British investment overseas by spreading risk helped create financial stability and encouraged the growth of consumerism which in turn stimulated entrepreneurship in the service sector as goods not only have to be made, but they also have to be distributed, advertised and sold. The result was the overall growth of the non-corporate domestic sector as well as the overseas sector (which was mainly corporate).

The organisation of work

The growth of large firms and the increasingly common presence of incorporated enterprises radically affected the organisation of work over the period we analyse, affecting entrepreneurship along four main dimensions (Gospel, 1992; 2008: 421–4). This is a core aspect of our later analysis in Chapters 4 and 5, and also affects how we interpret the data that can be interrogated. First, technological drivers shifted the balance of power away from small artisans and craftsmen towards large and more capital-intensive machinery in factories and large-scale business organisations. For our period this varied sectorally depending on skill levels and the extent of technological changes occurring. Second, there were crucial changes in labour markets that made waged labour more attractive: relatively high and stable wages, increasing regulation that improved working conditions and reduced working hours, increased holiday allowances, greater influence of trade unions and a shift in cultural norms towards improved working conditions and managerial responsibility in the face of declining prices and increasing foreign competition. Third, there were changing social norms that accorded higher status to salaried professional and managerial roles than to small traders. This also affected attitudes towards the role of women in the workplace and entrepreneurship, the starting age of employment, and the value of compulsory education, professional examinations and training. These went hand in hand with a large expansion in the number of salaried jobs, notably in clerical, administrative and teaching roles (Crossick, 1977). Fourth, changes in business organisation and technology enabled increased size of firms, and the sectors in which large sizes were most common (textiles, mining, railways and manufacturing) expanded, which increased the role of hierarchy within the workplace towards foreman and managers, and away from personal control, family firms, own-account trading and owner management.

These trends are important for the distinction between those who had a significant degree of control over contracting, price setting and their working conditions, which we take as entrepreneurs, and those who had to accept working conditions and prices set by others, who we take as waged workers. This distinction has sometimes been assumed to be defined by occupational titles such as 'master craftsmen'. Master craftsmen were traditionally entrepreneurial, possessed their own tools, often assembled their own raw materials, operated from their own premises, trained apprentices and managed one or more journeymen to whom they paid wages and perhaps gave board and keep (Woodward, 1995). This included 'family craftsmen' who had family as assistants, apprentices and co-partners (Fang, 1930: 8). These continued after 1851 as an important part of the own-account self-employed, as well as among small employers. Many were still able to set prices, even if this could be constrained by limitations on pricing autonomy caused by general economic conditions and increasing dependence on one or a limited number of wholesalers who could operate list prices or otherwise restrict profits. But only at the extreme, where the 'truck system', sweating and other strong controls operated, did own account effectively operate at waged rates; usually own account had more autonomy than the de facto waged.

Hence among the trends we examine between own account, employers and companies, the own account may be the most ambiguous. Littler (1982) argued that indirect craft control and gang systems continued on a large scale up to World War I in many industries, such as iron foundries, mining, shipyards, the building industry, glass production and potteries, and through kinship networks in textiles, such as through cotton minder-piecer systems (see also Schloss, 1899: 197–202; Bendix, 1974; Samuel, 1977; Lazonick, 1990). However, we do not find that pattern affecting entrepreneur groups. Although the census used the term 'master' in its instructions, generally respondents and enumerators used the term 'employer', with 'master', 'mistress' or similar terms limited to, and generally synonymous with, autonomous employers or own account (see Chapter 3). Hence, although over the course of the nineteenth century the decline in status and use of the concept of the traditional master was certainly a major driver of change, it was used in the census mainly for own-account operators, and does not appear to have been commonly self-declared by census respondents for internal contracts, team or gang work. Although Landes (1969: 231) and Littler (1982: 72–8) date the start of the shift from craft masters to managerial control to the 1880s, the term 'master' was already largely obsolete in its traditional usage by 1851.

1.5   Data sources

The data and GIS resources used in this book are fully listed in the Foreword. They are mainly derived from the digitised census records transcribed for 1851–1911 made available by the Integrated Census Microdata (I–CeM) project (Schürer et al., 2016; Higgs et al., 2015). In addition other sources of census transcription are used to infill substantial gaps and truncations in I–CeM, to generate enriched data on directors and companies, to extend the coverage up to the present, and to support wider analysis of transport, local environments etc. The full, cleaned and enriched database for 1851–1911 constitutes the surrogate 'British Business Census of Entrepreneurs' (BBCE) deposited at the UK Data Archive.

The population censuses collected the information of employers and those operating as self-employed on 'own account', including the employee size of their businesses, 1851–81, but little of this information was published at the time, and what was published has been little used by historians. The first attempts to analyse aggregate entrepreneurship levels and rates in Britain before 1911 by Bowley (1919, 1937), Feinstein (1972) and Clark (1957) used published census tables as a key resource. Indeed Clark noted that 'the only valid source of information in this field is from census returns'. Where other sources of statistics to measure entrepreneurship have been developed in different countries, including Britain, he concluded that 'it is doubtful whether any of these yet can be regarded as equally reliable with the census itself' (Clark, 1957, 495–6). He confirmed the approach taken in this book: that for large-scale assessment of entrepreneurship before 1911 there is no alternative to starting with the census, although other sources can be used to supplement and validate it. The population census was also recognised as a possible source for business study by Clapham (1926, 1932, 1938), but with only the limited published records for the 1851 census, and no access to the full data in the original census response, he, like all other scholars, was unable to make progress. Moreover it was subject to the selective coding, errors and omissions by the GRO (see WPs 4 and 13).

Research that was held back by the previous absence of digitised original census records is now possible. Using the new database constructed here we can move on from the previous lacunae. However, the records created in I–CeM are not straightforward to use to identify entrepreneurs and required extensive efforts of data extraction, supplementation and enrichment from additional data to construct the BBCE. This book uses this database, provides an introduction to the data and hence offers the key entry point for developing further research. However, the book focuses on interpretation. Fuller information on the database is given in Chapter 3, is available in detailed data guides with the database documentation at UKDA, and in the web-based working papers listed in the references.

1.6　Conclusion

This chapter has introduced the definitions of entrepreneurship, the data used in this research and the main themes of analysis over time. The remaining chapters of Part 1 of the book review previous understanding and theories of entrepreneurship that inform the long-term analyses (Chapter 2). Chapter 3 extends the discussion of how the data used in the analysis were constructed and enriched. These discussions form the basis for the following parts of the book. Part 2 overviews the main trends in business numbers by type and sector changes, the evolution of business size and different institutional forms (as self-employed, employers, partnerships and corporations). Part 3 presents different dimensions of micro-entrepreneurial change, first through a statistical overview of the main patterns of influence on entrepreneurial choice from different personal characteristics, household structure, sectoral market opportunities, alternative forms of business organisation, geographical location, and the role of changing locational opportunity in a period of rapidly developing transport infrastructure. This is followed by detailed assessment of different dimensions of gender, the family and family firm, geographical location and transport development, migration, and portfolio diversification of business activity.

2 Entrepreneurship in theory and historical practice

2.1 Introduction

This chapter introduces the main lines of previous theoretical debate on historical development of entrepreneurs and identifies the points of departure of this book. The chapter examines the main theories of entrepreneurship and self-employment, and their relation to endogenous growth. Entrepreneurship is a central process for economic development. Its core is a decision maker who draws together resources to produce an economic output for sale of goods or services. Chapter 1 defined entrepreneurs as the proprietors who are responsible for the business at a given point of time: those who successfully develop activity by assembling factor inputs to produce new outputs and who try to anticipate demand and organise its supply. This is a broad definition that is focused on whole-population analysis. The rest of the chapter enlarges and deepens this idea of entrepreneurship.

The theory of entrepreneurship is often claimed to be underdeveloped. Baumol (2010: 2) states that 'entrepreneurs usually lurk in the background – largely concealed, but present under certain circumstances . . . [and] are almost entirely excluded from standard theoretical models of the firm'. Baumol is particularly critical of the focus of economic theory on static comparisons, and begins to develop approaches based on inter-temporal change. Casson (1982, 2003: 9) asserts that 'there is no economic theory of the entrepreneur'. Barreto (1989) argues that the role of the entrepreneur simply disappeared from economics because it could not be made consistent within the microeconomic theory of the firm. Mayer et al. (2018) argue that there is no adequate economics-based definition. These views from the field of economics contrast with those of the fields of management, business studies and small firm research which have a large theoretical literature. Although the literature is usually not as formalised and focused on production and pricing decisions, as sought by economists, this literature provides valuable insights. From historical studies we can also use theoretical discussion from a range of important contemporary historical commentators. The modern literature's focus on the traits and characteristics of the type of person most likely to be an entrepreneur is, however, difficult to use for historical analysis because personality characteristics are rarely recorded in historical records.

Because this book is a study of long-term historical change it is important to view theories through the lenses of the writers who have tried to understand entrepreneurship at points of time contemporary with the historical processes examined. Often these theories are presented within texts as an evolution of ideas which have been improved over time to reach the level of modern understanding (see e.g. Kirzner, 1979: 37–52; Parker, 2018, 2004: 39–43; Baumol, 2010: 11–34; Casson, 2010: 6–8; Peneder, 2001: 3–24), and many often conclude that the defining characteristic of the entrepreneur is innovation (e.g. Hébert and Link, 2009; Casson, 2010; Whaples, 2013). However valuable this modern understanding is, in many ways it misses a crucial point: that earlier writers developed their understanding in the context of the economic conditions of the time they observed. Their observations offer valuable contemporary insights into the different processes they encountered that they believed were 'entrepreneurship'. Of course their understanding may have been imperfect, but they did not take an exclusive view of entrepreneurs as innovators. Their observations are the more valuable since many were themselves entrepreneurs, on any definition, who understood business from the inside: Cantillon was a prosperous merchant in the Anglo-Irish trade and financial intermediary who successfully anticipated the collapse of the 1720 'Mississippi Bubble'; Say founded a successful textile manufacturing business; Schumpeter was a venture capital entrepreneur and banker, as well as an academic. Even Marshall, although primarily concerned with theoretical principles, undertook many visits to UK business premises and knew business well at the practical level, as reflected in his texts, and Knight, primarily known for his entrepreneurship theory, worked close to practice.

It is also useful for historical understanding to conceptualise any one period as *not* defined by a single confluence of entrepreneurial categories; rather each period had dominant entrepreneurial forms for many of the largest and most prosperous businesses, but at the same time had a multi-layered development of other businesses following other entrepreneurial forms at other scales or in other sectors. Our account therefore tries to move away from a single view towards a more nuanced account that is capable of embracing what was going on across different parts of the whole business population. We are not focused on just a few pathbreakers or 'gazelles', nor innovative 'disrupters' who made transformative leaps of business practice, nor the activities of dominant sectors. We try to embrace conceptual development from the eighteenth-century 'merchant entrepreneur', which was a dominant entrepreneurial form preceding but continuing into our detailed analysis of the nineteenth century, through widened entrepreneurial developments for self-employment and the factory system in the nineteenth century, and its challenge by growing business incorporation at the end of the nineteenth and through the twentieth centuries and into the modern economy. We emphasise the need to maintain a perspective of multi-layered responses: at any one time different entrepreneurial processes co-existed and 'dominant forms' often characterised only parts of some sectors.

In this chapter we first outline (Section 2.2) the modern approaches most relevant to our historical analysis. Section 2.3 then demonstrates how historical theorists can be used to enlarge on interpretations of their contemporary world. In Section 2.4 we expand the discussion to use modern endogenous growth theory as a bridge to the geographical and other analyses in the following chapters.

2.2   Modern theoretical framework

Various definitions of 'entrepreneur' have been provided, often with different approaches used in different contexts and disciplines; indeed Mayer et al. (2018), Kitching and Rouse (2017) and Baker and Welter (2015) conclude that it is impossible to create a synthesis of the term that is applicable to all situations: definition of context and research questions are all-important. Our concern here is to adopt a practical definition that is as wide-ranging as possible and that can be applied to understanding the whole population of entrepreneurs, is as non-selective as possible, can be integrated with modern definitions and is supported by the data collected in the past. The broadest definition used in modern literature, and supported by historic data, is that entrepreneurs are individuals who are/were self-employed. It is for this reason, as we argue in Chapter 1, that we take the whole of the self-employed as business proprietors.

The self-employed are individuals who support themselves by their own direct endeavour and receive no wage or salary. In an economist's definition, they receive income or remuneration as *the residual of the profits of their enterprise after deducting all costs: entrepreneurial income.* Marshall (1961) refers to this as 'entrepreneurial withdrawals': the amount in money or goods used by entrepreneurs as living expenses, wealth accumulation and other costs not associated with the expenses of carrying on the business. The deductions from entrepreneurial income include payments to creditors, wages and the costs of other factor inputs. Economists will normally try to go further and separate the remuneration of capital, enterprise and risk-taking. But in most historical analyses and for micro-enterprises it is not usually possible to fully separate these different contributions. However, we have to be aware of three different elements: rewards to capital investors, to enterprise producers, and to entrepreneurs for the scale of risks they bear.

The definition of entrepreneurs as the receivers of entrepreneurial income is simplistic, but it is simple to make operational and covers the full range of different enterprises. While self-employment is the simplest form of entrepreneurship (Blanchflower, 2000: 473), it is inclusive of all categories of business by size and legal structure. Clark (1957: 506) noted that it measures 'those who actively control their own business, either on their own or in partnership'. The three main categories, and the ones that are available from both the historical and modern records, are individual own-account proprietors who employ no one but themselves (whether individually or in partnership), employers of others in both large and small firms and (with suitable caveats about different forms of governance, tax and legal definitions) those who are directors of incorporated enterprises. These categories accord with most previous economic analysis that has defined entrepreneurs as the recipients of entrepreneurial income: the total of business proprietors, own-account self-employed and limited companies. This is the measure used by Feinstein (1972) in his historical national accounts, extended in time coverage by Mitchell (1988) and relied upon by most historians. It is the same as the Kuznets et al. (1941) study of the US.

Our broad definition follows Parker (2004: 43–5), who provides a systematisation of the full range of self-employment choices, and Peneder (2001: 2–24), who shows how entrepreneurship theory relates to all forms of business activity. The starting point is profit earned by entrepreneurial activity, defined as the remuneration obtained from sales of a given volume of goods and services, after taking account of all input costs. This allows profits to be compared with the wages of workers in comparable situations, but derived in an entirely different way. The comparison can be extended to incorporated businesses, though incentives can vary since directors can receive income as dividends paid from profits, capital gains or wages that may be linked to profits. For non-corporate businesses the difference between profits and wages provides the incentive to take waged employment or to undertake entrepreneurial activity, intermediated by personal factors and opportunities. At the individual level these incentives underpin the fundamentals of all economic choice models of entrepreneurship, and at the aggregate level of a whole economy differences between wages and profits imply a disequilibrium that would incentivise switching from the lower to the higher source of income (until demand for, and supply of, the different forms of employment come into equilibrium). The incentives anticipate as well as respond to current profit opportunities, taking account of the actions of others on the potential for future profits (Mises, 1949). Indeed, Mises saw markets themselves as an entrepreneurial process by transmitting through prices (or profits and wages) aggregate information on supply and demand conditions and competitive conditions (Cantillon's 'rivalness'), to reveal opportunities for individual entrepreneurs: what Kirzner (1997: 73) summed up as 'the everyday business world, in which each entrepreneur seeks to outdo his rivals . . . by offering consumers a better deal'. This does not require 'novelty' or 'innovation' per se, but rather responsiveness to opportunity at either the micro (each deal) or macro scale (business strategy). Indeed this was the core of Nye's (1991: 134–5) critique of selective definitions such as innovation:

> that truly rational businessmen consider not just short-run profit maximising opportunities for investment but take into account the difference between long-and short-run benefits, properly discounting future returns. . . . In a competitive market, the heroic investor, no matter how unique, will simply find his rents bid up to the point where his skills and willingness to take risks earn no supernormal returns.

The definition of entrepreneurs as the receivers of entrepreneurial income has been a starting point for developing a wide range of theoretical contributions and analyses in economics, management and other disciplines. It can be made more complex by assessing how different factors influence choices: for example the effect of compensating differentials of different working conditions, demographics, individual preferences, cultural and psychological differences, degrees of risk aversion, product market conditions, different competitive environments and ease of market entry or other barriers. In the simplest cases, the economic theory of the choice of being waged or entrepreneur can be used to estimate the probability of choices (as we seek in Chapter 6), and can be extended to estimate equilibrium numbers of firms supporting (at given firm sizes) and different numbers of entrepreneurs (which is not attempted here).

The idealised economic model is a valuable starting point for historical investigations. But for our analysis at the scale of the whole population it is difficult to apply directly, given the data constraints on the information available. Most importantly, we do not have historical data on wages and profit levels in the detail required for the whole economy. Moreover, as Parker (2004: 266–7) notes, modern literature is still developing with regards to specifying the models. In the management and business studies literature this is indicated by the wide range of different studies undertaken that are usually partial analyses of specific factors or situations (for recent reviews see Hébert and Link, 2009; Baker and Welter, 2015, Mayer et al., 2018; Parker, 2018).

'Choice' framework

In this book we follow the established approaches of choice analysis. We identify the different types of entrepreneur in each period, we compare them with non-entrepreneurs under controlled definitions and we estimate the influence of different factors and opportunities on the choices that individuals made, within the constraints of the data now available (Chapter 6). This assesses choices as separate options through logit and multinomial alternatives. This, and the fact that we are dealing with the whole population, not a sample, reduces, albeit not entirely, the need to control for selection bias. This contrasts with those studies that have to start by selecting and defining what they are sampling; for example, all studies of innovation. Our approach also avoids the need for data on wages or risk. As Kuznets et al. (1941: 406) noted, where there is no information available, recourse has to be made 'to bold assumptions'; in our case we have to assume that choice reflected various unobservable variables, of which wages were one key element. Similarly, although following Knight, Say and Cantillon in using the concept of risk to define aspects of entrepreneurship, this is chiefly to clarify where decisions lie. In practice risk is a complex concept, not easily measurable at the level of detail required in historical data, and in some ways misleading because in the whole business population we analyse many established proprietors were not significant risk takers. For example, they had sufficient scale that insured their risk in new ventures or, if incorporated, their risks were not personal, but rather passed to capital providers and shareholders. And, as noted earlier, it is not usually possible in micro-enterprises to separate the remuneration of capital, enterprise and risk-taking, since these are consolidated under a single business head.

The choice framework is shorthand for the amalgam of real choices, constrained choices and the availability of opportunities from which to choose. In reality individuals do not have an open choice. Many can only obtain waged employment. For others self-employment without employees may be an attractive choice, allowing for independence, but it can also be the only option because there is no waged employment available: 'necessity' and 'survival' entrepreneurism.

The range of choices and opportunities available to existing or potential entrepreneurs is also constrained and mediated by factors that influence individuals; other influences on their households, family and social context; and the externalities and opportunities of their wider geographical milieu. Over time these circumstances and influences change, leading to opportunities to shift status either way between the options of entrepreneurship and waged employment, to expand entrepreneurial earnings or to diversify activities as a portfolio of initiatives (perhaps even mixing waged and entrepreneurial activity). Our analysis seeks to investigate these different situations.

At the *individual level* choice and opportunity are mediated by:

- Individual skills: education, experience and aptitude.
- Gender: which often constrained female independence and access to finance until the Married Women's Property Act of 1882.
- Marital status: provided joint resources of a household unit that often advantaged the married over single people.
- Age: in some contexts young entrepreneurs thrive, but entrepreneurs often have a higher age profile than workers as a result of using their experiences, receipt of inheritance or use of accumulated savings, wider networks, or greater preference for independence.
- Ethnicity: positive or negative influences on members of ethnic minorities or other immigrants.

At the *level of households*, family or social context (the group level) choice and opportunities are mediated by:

- Position of the individual within the household: whether they were the head, spouse, child or other type of household member or not part of a household at all but operating as single individuals in their own house or lodgings. This influenced the extent to which part-time, part-waged, unwaged or other internal labour or social supports might be available and how far it was controlled through patriarchy or matriarchy.
- Economic activity of other individuals resident in the household: mixing waged and entrepreneurial work can be a strategy to manage the higher risks associated with business proprietorship.
- Household assets: land, premises or tenancy, tools, equipment and wealth, and the extent to which these could be pooled.
- Social status: wider social status associated with the household's social position, occupation, inheritance, and the social networks these opened or closed.

- Household and family size: an indication of the amount of income required to sustain all individuals and the number of potential contributors to raise this income.

The *externalities of location* include a range of constraints and opportunities:

- Specifics of a location: its size and diversity of opportunity, openings or barriers to access and market entry, its economic character as urban, rural, industrialised, craft-based, and the existing firm-size distribution and its sectoral structure. These all condition what Marshall (1961: 270–4) identified as the *externalities of a place*:
  - Knowledge spillovers between different businesses in the locality; namely, the ability to become quickly aware of new opportunities
  - Availability of specialised inputs, services and supporting industries.
  - Pooled labour market benefits from specialised and adaptable skills.
- Accessibility of location: centrality or peripherality within the economy as a whole, distance to nearest local market centres and their size and characteristics, accessibility to wider locational opportunities regionally and nationally and openness to export opportunities abroad.
- Specific transport access and its quality: presence or absence of useable roads, waterways, railways, port infrastructure and nodal points.

These characteristics (individual, group and locational) were critically important to historical entrepreneurship and remain so today.

The analysis of choice and opportunity is developed in the following chapters through different levels of investigation for the whole entrepreneurial population 1851–1911, and in most depth for the period 1851–81, where more detailed census information is available on most employers for the size of their workforce. We can also investigate choices to operate as an incorporated business. We engage with incorporated businesses through their directors using data enrichment and linkage to information derived from the census, but there are limitations both to the information available on directors and its capacity for linkage. The literature on the corporate form provides some important indicators of the incentives for different types of self-employment within a choice framework. For Chandler (1962, 1977, 1990) the choice of incorporation was driven by the advantages of hierarchical authority and management capacity that gave internal economies of scale and scope, whilst for Alchian and Demsetz (1972) there were information, tacit knowledge and capacity benefits to joint team production. Williamson (1985) broke these down into various transaction cost advantages of the corporate form. A larger enterprise also has greater capacity to control knowledge within itself, thus offering advantages of bringing new products or innovations to market and limiting market entry by others (Geroski, 1995). This can extend to whole R&D departments for a large enterprise that small firms and sole proprietors could never match. Jensen and Meckling

(1976) focus specifically on entrepreneur/manager choices and principal–agent relations of those inside and outside the firm. This has stimulated an important literature comparing different legal forms of incorporated businesses focusing on shareholder and corporate financial controls (La Porta et al., 1998, 1999, 2008). However, Jensen and Meckling (1976: 311) note that what matters most are the actual relationships between the individuals concerned, and these apply as much to the proprietor-employer choice as to choice of incorporation: the monitoring costs of principal (owner-manager or entrepreneur), bonding costs of agents (co-entrepreneurs and employees) and residual transaction costs (and losses).

For many small enterprises, and most of those considered here, the main issue of choice is whether to extend sole proprietorship from working on one's own to a business employing others; incorporation represents a further step beyond. Sole proprietors with no employees are a base case of zero agency costs (Jensen and Meckling, 1976; Ang et al., 2000). The crucial step of taking on employees indicates decisions to engage in business expansion, but also to take on higher management and other transaction costs, as well as bonding costs and the risks and challenges of managing agency effects. Incorporation offers some advantages in terms of increased capital resources and spread of risk, but introduces further transaction costs and agency effects. A non-corporate employer as a firm, or a corporation, has developed decision making beyond individual entrepreneurism; as Penrose (1959: 31) observed these firms are autonomous units, with decisions framed in the light not just of personal incentives, but from the perspective of the resources and impacts for the enterprise as a whole. A firm as a whole can be viewed as entrepreneurial (or not). It will succeed or fail from the strength of it competences and dynamic capabilities to pursue competitive market opportunities. However, here we focus on individuals as proprietors. As noted by Barreto (1989) this allows escape from the straightjacket that the theory of the firm imposes on entrepreneurship.

As with the choice between entrepreneurship and waged employment, embedded in decisions about business organisation are choices related to interactions between individuals' characteristics, their household, family, social milieu and local externalities and opportunities. Many entrepreneurs attempt to avoid the transaction and agency costs of becoming employers by utilising inputs from their spouse or family. These are informal, sometimes 'unwaged', and lead to important issues of social hierarchy that are especially important in our period given Victorian and Edwardian gender relations and the role of patriarchy and matriarchy. If employers, they may avoid the transaction and agency costs of becoming incorporated, especially the loss of direct control this usually implies, but even when incorporated they might retain control by keeping their company 'private' with shares held by trusted networks of family or friends. These are important dimensions for analysis of firm size in Chapter 5 and family firms in Chapter 7.

These theoretical considerations and their previous historical development by Cantillon, Say, Marshall, Knight and others suggests that we can develop historical analyses based on how people responded through choices that balanced uncertainty against their personal characteristics, ability, opportunity, information available to them and other factors. Although we cannot observe all these characteristics in our historical data, we can use the choice framework to interpret those data we do have. Those individuals favouring higher certainty generally preferred waged employment that relied on others to face the challenges of running a business. As Knight (1921: 282–3) argued the supply of entrepreneurs depends on the extent of people's abilities across four dimensions: their willingness to undertake the role of entrepreneur, which he states as most fundamentally depending on their degree of risk aversion; their power to give satisfactory guarantees (e.g. to creditors), which in turn depends on their experience, assets and extent of other backing (such as family supports) deriving from the extent of their opportunity through personal, locational context; the degree of coincidence of these three factors; and the extent to which there is a broader social, geographical and institutional context that encourages effective judgement of opportunities across the population – in our case primarily the institutional context of Victorian and Edwardian England and Wales.

The choice framework for sector opportunities

The choice framework provides the basis for our analysis. This will be influenced by the local and national markets and contextual factors, as well as by the specific trading sectors concerned. Marshall and Kirzner were among the first to focus on the importance of sectors as the locus of competitiveness of an entrepreneur's environment. Kirzner argued that alertness to opportunities was a distinguishing characteristic of entrepreneurs, and that sectors were one of the main contexts in which opportunities were opened (or closed). This is supported in 1850s historical data by Crossick (1978: 47) who argued that an effect of seeing successful firms locally helped to create the 'perception of the opportunity for skilled artisans to leave dependence on employment and to work on their own account . . . a view of the openness of economic opportunity'. For small artisan sectors Crossick recognised that the distinction was 'often a flimsy one', less a perception of social opportunity than work opportunity: 'to cease being an employee following the instructions of an employer'. Crossick found little earnings differential between own-account workers and the same craftspeople in employment. But for a few that employed others he found that there was considerable scope to develop earnings and status.

We cannot in our historical data directly investigate competition effects on behaviour, but we can investigate what Marshall (1961: 270–4) termed industrial districts, and what Kirzner (1973: 89–101; also see Ekelund and Hébert, 1983 Peneder, 2001) termed different 'situational contexts' using sector as a lens through which to classify different competitive environments. Sectors shape choice and are a core element in our analysis. Sector characteristics that are particularly important to the scale and form of entrepreneurship are:

- Entry costs
- Barriers to access and sunk costs

- Scalability; that is, the minimum enterprise size and how far growth involves small steps or large increments in inputs (particularly labour and capital requirements)
- Skill levels needed and specialisation, and the scope for their subdivision
- Tangibility or intangibility of assets (extent of R&D and other technological assets, human capital and skills)
- Degree of innovation and novelty of product or service
- Overall scale and market opportunities of the sector
- Interactions with other sectors through extent for knowledge and other spillovers, and skilled labour pooling

Some sectors have much lower entry barriers than others favouring easier start-up and individual self-employment, particularly where market entry is possible without premises and with little or no equipment. Many small and ephemeral trades had such characteristics: errand boys, delivery agents (such as newspaper sellers), porters or window cleaners, who needed little to operate other than their labour. With such easy market entry, own account predominated but was subject to intense competition and received no more than marginal income. This was often an entry route into work, especially for the young. At the next level were artisans who needed only a few tools: sweeps and many building trades, such as plasterers and bricklayers.

Small-scale market entry was also favoured where home could function as business premises. Householders could operate lodgings, others took in laundry or other work or opened their front room as a small shop or beer seller. For farmers the opportunities could be greater as their premises were usually larger and there was land for expansion, so that lodgings, innkeeping, the carrier trades and more significant retail development was possible when opportunities were available (as for example with the opening of new transport infrastructure or new demand from local industries such as mine development). Some sectors were more easily scalable through adding more personnel, which is the case with most service industries, especially where this could be done through using family members. This favoured own-account proprietors that could scale up in small increments and divide roles between individual partners.

If the main way to scale up is by increasing personnel, small firms and individual self-employed can often compete effectively, as in care industries, retailing and other services. In the nineteenth century it also characterised industries where large-scale factory manufacture was less able to compete with the individual, such as high-skilled artisan manufactures (jewellery, instruments, watch and clock making), sectors where small manufactures could compete on quality or some types of product specialisms (shoes, clothing, many food manufactures), or where the industrial conditions favoured small and localised operators such as washing and laundry (even after large-scale steam laundries began to take over), local retail, merchanting and trading, as well as many building and construction trades (painters, plasterers, bricklayers). Many of these sectors have been regarded as 'traditional' industries compared to those where factories and corporations had most strongly developed, or in modern times where electronic trading is possible, but many of these nineteenth-century small trades remain an important part of modern small business and self-employed activity.

An additional aspect favouring self-employment is level of specialised skills and their aggregability. Fields especially favourable are those where knowledge can be aggregated into 'experts' or skilled personnel and cannot be easily subdivided. This characterised many professions, such as specialist engineers, architects, doctors and lawyers, midwives, and musicians and some other performers. These groups frequently operated (and many still operate) as individual self-employed, even where a major part of the industry where they worked operated through waged labour; for example, engineers as consultants to major mining companies, ship builders or chemical industries; doctors and surgeons as employees of hospitals and poor-law infirmaries; architects and design engineers in the building industry and major contractors for construction projects. Throughout the nineteenth century these specialists were frequently self-employed individuals, acting for many clients, sometimes combining waged and self-employed activity. But by the 1890s many professionals were beginning to develop as major businesses, usually operating as partnerships employing waged clerks and assistants.

Sector effects are also important when considering evolution of the whole economy. Modern comparisons of entrepreneurship rates distinguish between countries or regions with high or low agricultural sector concentrations. Generally high self-employment rates occur in farming. Hence locations with high proportions of farming have high entrepreneurship rates, even when the rest of the economy is less developed. This occurs in developing countries as well as in some advanced economies where the agricultural sector remains large. Similarly in nineteenth-century Britain the proportion of businesses in the agricultural sector was very large which led to high entrepreneurship rates in remote farming areas such as Wales. The change in entrepreneurship rates with economic development is a key trend taken up by Clark (1957) and Kuznets (1966), and is also a major distinction taken up by Blanchflower (2000) and Parker (2004) comparing self-employment in modern economies. Hence it is critical to understanding changes in entrepreneurship that interaction between farming and other sectors is assessed. Whilst many modern studies exclude farm businesses because they have 'very different characteristics' (Parker, 2004: 11), for our period they were a significant proportion of all business numbers, many were the initiators of change in their local economies through diversification and the developments in farming shed employees who migrated to cities and industry. In an economy in transition, as Britain was in the nineteenth century, the interaction between farming and other enterprises was crucial.

Innovation

As noted in Chapter 1.3, the definition of entrepreneurship is often restricted in much modern research to those who were innovators, and whose innovations were radical and Schumpeterian. Similarly, in one of the most theoretically based contributions from economic history, Casson (1982; 2010: 3) defines entrepreneurship as 'good judgement [that] leads to timely innovation and profitable arbitrage'. Even Kirzner (1979: 108–18), who diverges from Schumpeter (1942), nevertheless sees entrepreneurs as those who exploit disequilibrium opportunities, although these can be continuous improvers capable of exploiting any minor opportunities for additional profit-making. Although widening the concept to define an entrepreneur as someone who specialises in exercising judgement, the historical cases of Casson (2010: 19–23) and Casson and Godley (2010) define entrepreneurs as 'project managers' who identify innovative market opportunities offering significant short-term economic 'rents'. Indeed, many authors start with innovation without considering alternative definitions of entrepreneurship (e.g. Jovanovic and Rousseau, 2007).

Given our focus in this book on whole-population analysis of entrepreneurs we treat innovation as a separate issue from that of entrepreneurship, where innovators are a sub-group within entrepreneurs as a whole. But for future analysis our identification of the whole business population offers opportunities for a range of subsequent selective studies, for which a focus on sub-samples of innovators is readily possible. This also avoids the selection bias of innovation studies, for which most definitions are essentially arbitrary. Acs and Audretsch (1990), for example, include novel products, processes and services. Similarly the Community Innovation Survey (EU, 2001) emphasises firms' own view of whether they have innovated; this often introduces upward bias by including almost anything as innovation. Even Baumol (1990; 2010: 18) accepts that most innovation is developed by processes of incremental improvement and that Schumpeterian change is often the result of accumulation or acceleration of incrementalism. This echoes Marshall (1961: 597) who differentiated between 'active' entrepreneurs opening new methods and passive entrepreneurs who 'follow beaten tracks'. Modern empirical approaches usually adopt wide definitions of innovation. Whole-population analysis overcomes this arbitrariness and allows subsequent research to sample innovators as a sub-group within the entrepreneur population.

2.3   The historical basis of entrepreneurship

Modern theories of entrepreneurship are useful, but we must also understand historical entrepreneurship in the context of the times and within the understanding that contemporaries held of what entrepreneurship involved for the decision makers. Their concept was wide, viewing the entrepreneur not just as a transformative innovator but embracing all types of proprietors, all sectors and all sizes of business. The earliest writers, Cantillon and Say, are of critical importance, as they established a theoretical framework that introduced the core concept of incentives to choices; this embraced all sectors and levels of activity from the greatest to the humblest business; it distinguished the returns on capital from returns to superintendence, administration and judgement; and it recognised that sector and skill differences, opportunity and ease of market entry are key influences on incentives through offering different risks, returns and opportunities. This has been the basis for the modern theoretical extensions that seek to understand individual choice: Cantillon and Say thus provide the natural link to historical understanding of entrepreneurship and how we should now interpret it.

Richard Cantillon and the eighteenth-century entrepreneur

Cantillon's *Essay on Commerce*, written around 1734 and published in French in 1755, is credited with introducing the term 'entrepreneur'. There were earlier uses of the term in French from the Middle Ages in the form of 'entre-prendre', someone who does something as a contractor, and Jacques Savary's (1723) *Dictionary* defined it as a project undertaker, manufacturer and master builder.[1] 'Adventurer' and 'projector' were also widely used in earlier literature before Cantillon (Hoselitz, 1951; Gough, 1969), but it was Cantillon who first developed the *concept* of entrepreneur into a theoretical approach relevant to modern interpretations. As Brewer (1992: 10) argues, Cantillon's *Essay* was the first systematic treatment of economic principles in an abstract way that modern economists would recognise. Indeed Spengler (1954: 281, 424) argues that Cantillon has a 'good claim to having been the principal forerunner of both the classical and neo-classical schools' of economics; 'the first writer to describe at so great length the supposedly self-adjusting . . . character of the economic system'.

It is usually argued that the French term entrepreneur was translated as Cantillon's English term 'undertaker', which in the eighteenth century generally suggested a contractor. But we cannot be sure whether Cantillon conceived the concept in French or in English, and it is believed that he wrote in both languages. The original 1734 English version of the *Essay* was destroyed by fire, and may never have been completed, and the French version was not published until after Cantillon's death; there may also have been several text versions.[2] The English translation of Cantillon's 1755 edition provided by Higgs is the version of Cantillon's text most widely known, which we follow.[3]

Here it is most useful to analyse what Cantillon meant by the term entrepreneur in English. His first use of the term in French is 'petits entrepreneurs and marchands'. This is rendered in English as 'undertakers and merchants' (p. 12), and 'merchants and factors' (p. 14). From this and later uses it is clear that Cantillon was coining a concept for the world he knew, that collectively meant merchanting, factoring, contracting, assembling and risk-taking. It was not a concept about innovation, nor about attitude of mind per se, though later he commented on differences between cultures in extent of entrepreneurship. Most importantly he saw entrepreneurship in the activities of both large-scale merchants and manufacturers of the day and in the small traders and farmers.

Cantillon's main contribution of significance for interpretation here is that he provided the first grasp of the concept of entrepreneurial income as the residual after costs of inputs, organisation and capital, and that he conceived this as covering all forms of business activity and all forms of self-employment. He also made a huge conceptual leap by focusing on an individual's actual activity and the choice incentives they faced, rather than their social status (a leap that the designers of the nineteenth-century census unfortunately did not make). These contributions opened opportunities for understanding not available to Adam Smith, who failed to distinguish entrepreneurship explicitly, or to distinguish profits as investment returns on capital from the profits from superintendancy. For Cantillon 'The farmer is an undertaker who promises to pay the landowner, for his farm or land . . . without assurance of the profit he will derive from this enterprise' (p. 62), who 'conducts the enterprise on his farm at an uncertainty' (p. 63). Similarly, the

> merchant or undertaker . . . buys the country produce from those who bring it or order it to be brought on their account. They pay a certain price following that of the place where they purchase it, to resell wholesale of retail at an uncertain price. Such undertakers are the wholesalers in wool and corn, bakers, butchers, manufacturers and/merchants of all kinds.
>
> (pp. 65–6)

Their risk is uncertainty about sales:

> The undertakers can never know how great will be the demand in their city, nor how long their customers will buy of them since their rivals will try all sorts of means to attract customers to them. All this causes so much uncertainty among these undertakers that every day one sees some of them become bankrupt.
>
> (p. 66)

Again: 'The manufacturer cannot foretell the profit he will make selling his cloths and stuffs to the merchant tailor' (p. 66). Similarly: 'the draper is an undertaker who buys cloths and stuffs from the manufacturer at a certain price to sell them again at an uncertain price, because he cannot foresee the extent of demand' (p. 67), and 'shopkeepers and retailers of every kind are undertakers who buy at a certain price and sell in their shops or the markets at an uncertain price' (p. 67). Cantillon then lists all other types of entrepreneurs, who similarly 'live at uncertainty': from pastry cooks and innkeepers to 'the undertakers of their own labour who need no capital to establish themselves . . . like needlewomen, chimney sweeps, water carriers' and 'master craftsmen like shoemakers, tailors, carpenters,/wigmakers, etc. who employ journeymen', as well as 'undertakers of their own labour in art and science, like painters, physicians, lawyers, etc.' (pp. 69–70). He also included beggars and thieves as entrepreneurial, anticipating some modern authors.

Cantillon's conception is thus close to the modern use of entrepreneur we adopt: the recipient of income from profit, and covering all types of business endeavour by business proprietors, large and small, and not a narrow range of innovators. Cantillon also included, as we do, all those trading as self-employed individuals: they were as much entrepreneurs 'in their own labour' as the great merchants. He was also responsible for establishing the entrepreneur as distinct in having to manage risk: 'If there are too many . . . some who are the/least patronised must become bankrupt; if they be too few it will be a profitable undertaking which will encourage [others] to open shops . . . and so it is that the undertakers of all kinds adjust themselves to risks' (pp. 68–9). As a result, Cantillon argued that (apart from large aristocratic landowners), the important distinction is between the entrepreneurs who accept risk in their trades, and wage labour that passes the risk to others: 'all the inhabitants of a state . . . can be *divided into two classes, undertakers and hired people*; and that all undertakers are as it were on unfixed wages and the others on wages fixed so long as they receive them' (p. 71, emphasis added). He also argued that intermediary managers or bailiffs were de facto entrepreneurs: 'overseers become undertakers, will be the masters of those who work under them' (p. 79). This foresees the need to understand larger businesses and limited companies through both their directors and managers. His approach also provides a contemporary argument for our use of bailiffs as surrogates for large farm proprietors.

Of course, it is right to criticise Cantillon that he was more useful in understanding the taxonomy of different incomes, choices and sources of risk than providing a fully developed theory, or that he did not fully grasp the significance of uncertainty.[4] Nevertheless, his insights provide invaluable contemporary observation in an abstracted way that confirms the value of choice theory and the importance of sector-based opportunities as a means to interpret historical entrepreneurship.

Jean Baptiste Say and the early nineteenth-century entrepreneur

One of the first commentators to expand the definition of entrepreneurship and to recognise more detailed interactions with the wider labour market was the textile manufacturer Jean Baptiste Say. His initial 1801 study was augmented a number of times and is best known through its first English translation of the French fourth edition which is its fullest development (Say, 1827).[5] Observing the world he knew as a manufacturer and merchant, Say viewed the entrepreneur as the 'master-agent or adventurer' who had both the capacity for 'superintendancy' and applied it. The profits gained by an entrepreneur came from the assembly and application of skills and knowledge. Say explicitly distinguished this from Adam Smith's capitalist, commenting that Smith did not grasp the nature of entrepreneurship as distinct from wider capitalism (II: 102–3, and n. 1). Say drew directly from English business experience, having completed his education in England and being initially employed by London sugar merchants, before developing his own business in France.

In many ways Say's definition was a natural extension of Cantillon. But he set the theoretical base more widely. This led to a number of important distinctions that carry through into modern theories. First, that the main difference from wage workers was the return entrepreneurs gained from the application of knowledge: 'the art of superintendence and administration'. This requires 'judgement, perseverance, and knowledge of the world as well as of business', which relies on ability to estimate demand, means to produce, employ necessary personnel, buy the right amount of raw materials and find markets. This ability is a mix of skills and talents. Second, Say went further in recognising that the availability of this mix has limited supply, and lack of success in application (business failures) further limits supply (II: 103–4), what Kirzner (1979: 146–9) termed ability of 'alertness' to perceiving opportunities and making effective implementation. Hence Say argued that entrepreneurship is relatively rare. Third, Say recognised why sector differences arise. Different industries require different levels of personal capacity, skills and knowledge which lead to different levels of entrepreneurial profit or return. Fourth, that capacity applies across all levels of entrepreneurship, with levels differentiated between routine and more specialist skills, the level of demand and supply for those skills and ease of market entry. This underpins options for an individual's choices between wages or entrepreneurial returns. Hence, like Cantillon, Say recognised the distinction between returns to entrepreneurship and returns to capital, but went further in identifying different levels of return for level of skill and noting that unskilled waged labour is the base case for comparison.

As an example Say (II: 105–6) compared the *farmer*, who may succeed with routines and relatively limited exploitation of knowledge usually of only 'two or three kinds of cultivation', with large-scale *commerce* which has long-return periods on investment requiring significant planning and assembling of investment and other inputs and which needs greater skills, especially of anticipating markets and demand, and knowledge of prices, transport, risks and the customs and laws of locations where goods are sent (especially important for exports) and sound judgement of agents and other intermediaries to act for them in different and often distant markets. Say did not argue that farmers were not entrepreneurs, but that they were paid less as the skills were more common, and commerce was paid more because the skills were greater and the knowledge required much greater. But commerce also varied. Retail dealers 'for the most part pursue routines quite as mechanically as the generality of farmers', so that their returns will be lower than more complex commerce.

Say considerably extended Cantillon's brief comparison of entrepreneurial skills with *waged labour*. This is valuable as an early nineteenth-century commentary on the distinctiveness of entrepreneurship which applies widely to the big data we investigate. Waged employment as a basic labourer had no entry costs and required low or no skills; it was open to 'any man who is healthy' so that wages would be low and usually only sufficient to support a family to maintain the supply of more labourers (II: 107–10). Similarly Say argued that female work will be poorly paid 'because a large proportion of them are supported by other resources than their own industry [i.e. husband's wages], and can, therefore, supply the work they are capable of at a cheaper rate than even the bare satisfaction of their wants', for example, as rural spinners (II: 112). In this Say captured the modern concept of survival or necessity entrepreneurs; what he calls returns at a level of 'necessary subsistence' (II: 115).

The key comparison Say made was between the demand and supply for different levels of skill, with those who had little or no skills as unskilled waged labour used as a base category of subsistence returns. This recognised that entrepreneurs who are skilled as assemblers of resources (including employing labour) have choices that are entirely different from those available to unskilled labourers. Say (II: 119–20) made a particularly valuable comment using the example of 'masters', the traditional term for skilled artisans that we use in some extractions of census data that adopted this terminology. For masters there are 'few . . . who could [not] exist for several months, or even years, without employing a single labourer; and few labourers that can remain out of work for many weeks without being reduced to severe distress'. Although aware of demographic issues identified by contemporaries such as Malthus, Say highlighted a key difference as the relative supply and demand for each type of skill. Of significant value here is his contemporary identification of 'master' as a category of small-scale entrepreneur who had a significant level of control and choice compared to waged labour.

A further distinction identified by Say, which has been highlighted in most modern commentary on his work because it interrelates with innovation, is that entrepreneurs had a key role as implementers of *applying* scientific knowledge and invention (although not themselves creators of scientific knowledge). He noted that science and knowledge is 'transmissible in a few pages and circulated in greater abundance . . . there is never a necessity to recur to [use or consult] those from who it originally emanated' (II: 100); it can 'circulate with ease and rapidity from one nation to another' and cannot normally be protected for any length of time, and indeed scientists are usually in the forefront of disseminating their ideas (I: 53). Say recognised that these 'spillovers' mean that the return to scientists is low and this can be used as a justification for government support (also see Baumol, 2010: 12). This underpins some of the later discussion by Schumpeter and modern theories of innovation. Hence Say concludes that the 'wealth of Britain is less owing to advances in scientific acquirement . . . than to the wonderful practice of skill of her adventurers in the useful application of knowledge' (I: 53).

These distinctions led Say to define entrepreneurs as 'possessed of the means of reducing the knowledge into practice; who should have first made himself master of all that was known of that particular branch of industry, and afterwards have accumulated, or procured, the requisite capital, collected artificers and labourers, and assigned each his respective occupation' (I: 51). Successful industry therefore had three prerequisites: the availability of knowledge, the application of knowledge and the organised application of labour and other inputs. These activities are usually performed by different people who receive different returns in relation to their supply and demand (I: 46). But the key contribution of entrepreneurship is assembly: the combination of ideas with its application, relevant knowledge and skill. For this reason Hébert and Link (2009: 20) refer to Say's entrepreneur as 'the guardian of equilibrium': spotting opportunities for arbitrage which, once exploited, bring the economy back into equilibrium and remove scope for super-normal profits unless monopolies can be maintained.

This has become a central feature of the modern more limited definition of opportunities used by Kirzner and Casson.

John Stuart Mill, Alfred Marshall, factories and large-scale entrepreneurial development

Even at the time when Cantillon and Say were writing there were large businesses, but from the early nineteenth century on many more firms grew in size. Significant eighteenth-century leaders of factory development such as Josiah Wedgwood, Richard Arkwright, Robert Peel, Matthew Boulton and James Watt were certainly viewed as entrepreneurs in the modern senses of the word (see e.g. Fitton and Wadsworth, 1958; Chapman, 1967; Berg, 1993). But over the nineteenth century the factory became a larger and more frequent phenomenon, employing increasingly larger proportions of the population, and becoming almost synonymous with capitalism. Indeed the term 'entrepreneur' was not much used by Victorian contemporaries: more common were 'industrialist', 'capitalist', 'merchant', 'manufacturer' and sometimes 'master'.

By the time of John Stuart Mill's (1867) *Principles of Political Economy*, capitalists were identified as one of three productive classes who provided capital and contributed 'no other labour than that of direction and superintendence'. Indeed, Mill noted the unfamiliarity of the term 'entrepreneur' in English. Unlike Adam Smith, he followed Say, and is primarily responsible for re-introducing into English writing from the 1840s the term 'entrepreneur' and the distinction between the separate profits of those who lent capital and industry (or superintendence).[6] For Mill, their 'entrepreneurial wage' was their extra return for management, echoing Say. Mill also saw this as having potential as a monopoly rent, requiring 'great assiduity, and often, no ordinary skill'. This provided the direct point of entry for Marshall (1961: 432) and modern understanding.[7]

Towards the end of the nineteenth century, Alfred Marshall was able to draw some of these understandings together in order to better formalise the position of entrepreneurship. Although primarily associated with being the foundation of neoclassical economics, and giving a primary place to the role of economies of scale in encouraging large-scale production, Marshall also provided valuable insights into contemporary smaller and medium-sized businesses as a result of undertaking a wide range of visits to British business premises in the late nineteenth and early twentieth centuries. The business world he knew was at the practical level, not just as a theoretician. His experience covered a period of British history that he argued was characterised by free competition and a diversity of large and small firms co-existing in most industries. Generally, he observed that no single firm was sufficiently dominant to influence market prices. Rather, firms competed to reduce variation in prices, profits and hence returns on capital to a minimum, with a tendency towards an industry rate and similar returns across industries. This occurred because higher returns attracted capital from those businesses with lower returns, forcing improvements in efficiency or changes in factor costs or loss of trade and business closure. These adjustments occurred across all businesses within a sector, and between sectors (Marshall, 1961: 297–8, 315–8, 606–15). This was a view of the economy we would now term 'neoclassical economics', but it was based on observations of actual industries at the time.

Marshall called entrepreneurship 'business power': the supply of managerial expertise. He put this into a general equilibrium setting by arguing that there was a general rate of profit for each trade reflecting each sector's market conditions. In his earliest major work (joint with his wife: Marshall and Marshall, 1879: 114–34) different types of entrepreneurs were treated as similar agents operating under the same price and other signals, whether they were individual masters, owner-managers or the managers of large enterprises. They each responded to the same managerial challenge: 'much of the work of business is so difficult, and requires . . . such a rare combination of natural qualities, that the earnings of management got by it may be very high' (Ibid.: 115). This resulted in different entrepreneurial profits in different sectors, depending on the level of specialisation and rarity of the entrepreneurial skills required. Although the field for market entry and success for the individual master and small business was narrowing, especially in manufacturing, where economies of scale and the application of standardisation and factory production normally gave considerable advantages, small firms continued to grow. 'Though the small producer is constantly threatened with extinction . . . yet he survives' because of a superior ability to deliver specialised products and cater for the general increase in demand for new inputs from large-scale producers so that 'the number of small businesses is constantly growing' (Marshall, 1919: 247–8). In his *Principles* he rationalised this as the advantages of the strong managerial oversight available to the small proprietor: the master's eye is everywhere reducing the scope for information asymmetry and gaps in understanding, principle–agent problems, divisions and delays in responsibility, as well as reducing needs for checks, coordination and messaging. This was especially beneficial in high-value trades (Marshall, 1961: 284).

Marshall (1919: 235–49) recognised emerging challenges to small firms. First, the rise of the limited company provided a permanence to organisations that small businesses dependent on a single owner or family were unlikely to achieve because of succession problems – whereas a company could in theory carry on forever. Second, mergers and oligopolies between companies increasingly allowed greater internal economies of scale and market control so that they could buy up or squeeze out small ones unless, as Marshall argued, smaller ones had sufficient countervailing advantages from local external economies or sector markets operated to favour individualised high-skilled products, or that larger firms were unable to efficiently manage internal bureaucracies.

The economies of scale and other advantages of the factory system have been discussed more widely in numerous studies. For example Ashton (1961: 25) summarised the 'factory system' as primarily 'a particular means of organisation', for which success indicated entrepreneurship: its owners and managers having 'to anticipate demand, to modify, and even sometimes create it . . . due to extraordinary adaptability and to rapid and incessant improvements' (Ibid.: 91).

For many nineteenth-century commentators it was a magnificent creation, and Wright (1882, 1883) eulogised it as an instrument of 'civilisation' in increasing output and wealth and freeing arduous labour through mechanisation. Ure (1835: 13) defined the factory system as the combined operation of many orders of workpeople tending machines in a single set of premises continuously impelled by a central power, with highly developed division of labour. Ure (1835: 42–3) is important in recognising at an early date that factory proprietors had to depend on managers, thus allowing the development of agency behaviour; but he still saw the proprietor as the key decision maker. Similarly, in the major debate in the 1830s on working conditions, Royle (1833: 5) contended that 'the man of property, the Capitalist, who devotes all his time, who applies all his energies to increase his wealth, by building mills and factories, and so employing the poor', was the key figure where decisions lay. Indeed Ashton (1961: 417) sums up the general position as the 'absolute and uncontrolled power' of the employer.

Although factories were not without criticism by contemporaries and subsequent historians, especially for their effects on working conditions and for their importance to elite social and political thought (Webb and Webb, 1920; Joyce, 1980; Gray, 1996; Stedman Jones, 2013), many Victorian writers eulogised large-scale capitalists and factory proprietors. The most widely cited, Samuel Smiles, in a series of biographical books on *Character* (1871), *Thrift* (1875) and *Duty* (1880), and especially his first book on *Self-Help* (1859: 2), argued that anyone through hard work, determination and temperance could 'elevate and improve themselves by their own free and independent action'. These books were extraordinarily widely read and very influential: *Self Help* was one of the small number of books working-class people and anyone literate encountered, alongside the Bible and Dickens. They would have been known to most of the entrepreneurs in our census data, and may have motivated some. They disseminated a view that anyone following their strictures could potentially become a successful Victorian industrialist. The contemporary discourse was supported by numerous personal accounts and other commentary arguing the scope to move from small beginnings to great wealth. Such an autobiography was Robert Owen's (1857: 25–6), the major industrialist and idealistic social reformer, who wrote that from a small foundation in a rented workshop with three mule machines he was able to progress to 'those palace-like buildings which were afterwards erected by the firm, – of the princely fortunes . . . made by them . . . [which] from small beginnings produce very different results to any anticipated by us when we commence'. Other commentaries are assembled by Ward (1970: 77–140). They shaped much historiography of the period (Taylor, 1997; Smith, 2015).

Whilst many contemporary commentators saw large-scale businesses and the factory as synonymous with entrepreneurship, for small traders there were no such plaudits. As Payne (1988: 22) notes, small businesses were the 'regiments of the anonymous' and many middle-class Victorians increasingly viewed 'trade' (meaning both small businesses and self-employment) as lower status

Table 2.1 Nineteenth-century industrial systems, modified after Fang (1930: 8)

System	Own-account traditional master craftsman	Merchant	Factory
Capital			
• Nature	Circulating and fixed	Primarily circulating	Circulating and fixed
• Extent	Small	Medium	Large
Mode of production			
• Workplace	Shop, home	Home, shop	Factory
• Technique	Handicraft	Handicraft	Machine
Method of sale			
• Market	Local, national	National, international	National and international
• Sale	Consumer Merchant	Consumer Merchant	Wholesaler

and distasteful, preferring salaried administrative and clerical posts. This shift in preferences was to accelerate up to and after World War I. However, most of the period we investigate saw different systems overlapping with each other. Fang (1930), following Day (1927), characterised these into three 'industrial systems' which he considered to co-exist in the 1840s and continue throughout the nineteenth century: the 'craftsman system', 'merchant employer', and 'factory', as shown in Table 2.1. This summarises the shifting balances between the master craftsman as an own-account proprietor operating their own premises, often from home; the merchant and contractor mainly 'putting out' or operating through investment in international project opportunities; and the factory. As we noted in Chapter 1, we expect all these systems to co-exist in our analysis.

Frank Knight, choice and diverse entrepreneurship

Knight's significant contribution to the theory of entrepreneurship was the development of a wider understanding of choice, albeit noting that choice was often constrained by opportunity. Knight is also a valuable link between periods. Writing at the end of our period of intensive study, mainly in 1915–16, he was close to the business choices available at the time we identify as a peak of entrepreneurial activity immediately prior to the change point of World War I. Indeed, although explicitly aiming at a theoretical contribution, his book is full of references to contemporary business practice and characteristics. Like Marshall, whose work he knew and admired, he sought to found his theory on reality (Knight, 1921: 15), but took it forward to the point of departure for much modern scholarship that has developed choice theory further.[8]

Following Cantillon, entrepreneurs were viewed by Knight (1921: 243–4) as taking on risk by trying to anticipate demand and organising supply. We adopt this approach; they are assemblers of factor inputs, achieving a return for their skills in successfully doing this. Knight viewed the size of organisations as deriving from advantage of assembling as great a number as possible of organisational tasks across different areas of risk. This gave advantage to larger size by trading off higher- against lower-risk activities, in the same way as an insurer. This could be across different customer markets (as we assess for aggregate sectors in Chapters 4 and 5), different products, services or activities (as we assess for portfolios in Chapter 11) or different fields of factor supply. A larger organisation should be better able to ride out failures of different strategies and markets, and over time the short- and medium-term fluctuations of economic conditions. For Knight an entrepreneur was thus an 'assembler' or 'aggregator' of risk.

Writing in 1915–16 Knight followed Marshall and most contemporaries who saw the attributes of entrepreneurship increasingly favouring large corporations. Partnerships could achieve the same results, but were generally more limited by their ability to unify interests between partners and among external agents (such as creditors) (Knight, 1921: 253; see also Hansmann and Kraakman, 2000: 406). A formal corporation gained not so much from its limitation of liability, but from its 'permanence', ability to aggregate risks and to market to consumers through the scale of its brand and advertising.

Knight discussed at length the important qualities of being an entrepreneur, which we address in Chapter 6, opening the way for investigating the characteristics of the individual. His key conclusion was that success depended on measured judgement between 'rashness or timidity' (p. 283), which in turn derived from experience and extent of previous efforts or trial and error (pp. 281–4). This reflected the two specific entrepreneurial inputs of exercising control (management) and combining resources (to reduce uncertainty). He argued that the extent of differential profit can be judged from the size of a firm's employment, a measure we adopt in the absence of other data on scale. If entrepreneurs employed only themselves, they were merely substituting remuneration for wages or 'contractual income' from putting out. If employing others, then the extent and costs of their workforce was a measure of their contractual costs, after which was their entrepreneurial profit which should be well above that of the waged labour to be worthwhile. Hence he concluded that individual self-employment mainly operated as an alternative to the wage economy, whilst employers had the potential to reap higher or entrepreneurial extra returns. Without employing others there was little or no scope for this 'excess' income. Hence, with regards to the analysis in this book, the distinction between employers and own-account self-employed was a starting point for identifying the extent of different types of entrepreneurship in the economy. A successful entrepreneur was able to make competitors and non-entrepreneurs pay more for the inputs they required as long as they could maintain this advantage. In modern terms this is the 'rent' that an entrepreneur can achieve over general factor costs (Casson, 1982) or the opportunities of a hitherto unexploited project (Casson, 2010: 42; following Kirzner, 1979), what Kirzner refers to as opportunities for arbitrage and Schumpeter saw as the opportunities to exploit the benefits of new initiatives for as long as possible.

However, few employers have the opportunities to extract 'excess' income. First, they often merely achieve an income that is similar to the general market as if they had been waged, although they may improve their lifestyle or 'social status' by substituting working for someone else by working for themselves. Second, some of the most successful entrepreneurs employ no one else. Hence employer versus own-account status may not distinguish between those with higher potential incomes. In modern times this second group is characteristic of many early stage technology entrepreneurs. Historically it was typical of many financial intermediaries that were involved in establishing large-scale business operations but were themselves only small employers or employed no one else (as for many of the project-type entrepreneurs summarised by Casson and Godley, 2010). Many of the second group can be identified by their role as company directors. The company employed the staff, and the director obtained a large return by taking a substantial share of the 'dividend' of the company, capital gains or a 'wage'.

Schumpeter, Keynes, Mises and entrepreneurship dynamics

Immediately following these earlier writers were Schumpeter, Keynes and Mises, who reflected the developments of late Victorian changes in their experiences up to the 1940s. Joseph Schumpeter's (1927, 1939) most significant impact on modern entrepreneurship study has been his thesis that relatively slow changes in the rate of innovation are disrupted by short periods of accelerated technical change where 'disruptive technologies' rapidly impact many industries; now usually referred to as 'creative destruction' through 'disruptive' or 'Schumpeterian innovation'. Disruption comes from new goods, new methods, new markets, new sources of supply or new forms of business organisation (such as changes in market control) (Schumpeter, 1934: 66). Disruptive periods represent the time for golden entrepreneurial opportunities.

However, because we focus on the whole entrepreneurial population and include innovators as only one type of entrepreneur, albeit an important one, our main concern is what Schumpeter's ideas indicate for the rest of the entrepreneurial population. For this his preoccupation with the interaction of individuals with dynamics of the economy is most valuable, but this has been less emphasised in the literature (Peneder, 2001; Campagnolo and Vivel, 2012).

Our interpretation of Schumpeter's theory is aided by improved understanding of his personal entrepreneurial experiences which has recently become possible following the path-breaking archival study of his papers by Peneder and Resch (2015). Schumpeter began his career as an academic in Graz in Austria with his *Theory of Economic Development*, the book where he first fully recognised entrepreneurship, originally published in 1912 and translated into English in 1934. However, after World War I he shifted into entrepreneurial projects: first from 1919 acting as an advisor, investor and joint figurehead of a venture capital group of closed-ended funds for factory development in new technologies (such as glass and electricity), and second in 1921 converting a Vienna family bank into a joint stock investment bank. Both ventures succeeded for a time, but in 1924 both collapsed leaving huge debts. The period covered Austrian hyper-inflation 1921–22, a radical devaluation of the currency in 1922, a bull market in shares that burst in 1923, followed by a severe credit squeeze and collapse of many banks in 1924–29, including Schumpeter's. His business model in many ways followed one classic entrepreneurship approach: venture-financed projects. But, hounded by creditors, his entrepreneurial failures drove him away from Austria. After his appointment at Harvard in 1932 he re-engaged with venture finance in Massachusetts, where he bridged the emerging divide between the economics faculty and business school.

His subsequent successful intellectual contributions thus must be seen in the context of continuing personal involvement in projects of venture finance in innovative industries. Peneder and Resch (2015: 1342) identify three critical aspects that informed his views: understanding the entrepreneur as the under-taker of projects who made something happen; understanding profit more widely than income, such as capital gains and the launching of joint stocks through initial public offerings; and the match of successful innovation opportunities to the good fortune of an individual's decisions within specific points in the economic cycle (a timing which Schumpeter himself largely failed to achieve). Subsequently, some of this was included by Keynes' *General Theory* in his conceptualisation of 'animal spirits'. Keynes famous discussion of 'animal spirits' was partly concerned with what he termed 'enterprise': 'the activity of forecasting the prospective yield of assets over their whole life'. This follows Mises' (1949) emphasis on anticipation which was also key to Schumpeter. As summarised by Keynes, the 'spirits' of foresight and optimism play a vital part in determining the actions of business owners: 'individual initiative will only be adequate when reasonable calculation is supplemented and supported by animal spirits, so that the thought of ultimate loss which often overtakes pioneers . . . is put aside as a healthy man puts aside the expectation of death'. As a consequence, optimistic anticipation, psychological factors and calcula-tion must all be considered in trying to understand how entrepreneurs act, and how this affects the economy as a whole (McKibbin, 2013: 78–106; Keynes, 2015, 213–17). Mises (1949: 113) introduced into the concept of anticipation not only the ability to weigh opportunities and economic events, but also the anticipation of the action of others to the same opportunities, and thus weighing the whole competitive process through market responses. Peneder (2001: 11–24) sees this as the fundamental basis of modern understanding of entrepreneurship.

Hence the key insight that Schumpeter and subsequent thinkers offer for our analysis of historical entrepreneurship is the linkage of the dynamic opportuni-ties within the economic cycle with the reaction of individuals. The golden periods of Schumpeterian disruptive innovation opportunities are reflected in increases in entrepreneurship rates as many others follow entrepreneurial and technological pioneers to gain the benefits of the high returns and rents that are possible in the early and middle stages of innovating in an upswing. However, as the technology matures and becomes widely adopted the market opportunities for entrepreneurs become saturated, increases in returns first begin to slow and entrepreneurship rates stabilise, and then fall, resulting in consolidation to maintain returns through scale economies, which in turn lead to more uniform products opening the way for future disruptive change. Kuznets (1940: 261–8), approaching these cycles from a different perspective, reinforces the view that the best entrepreneurship opportunities arise in an upswing, and contract in a downswing.

There remain many disagreements over the causes of these changes, with Mises (1949: 11–12, 255) correctly criticising Schumpeter for confusing entrepreneurial action and changed conditions (economic and technological). But the conceptual advantage is to give insight into how entrepreneurs can gain from the good fortune of cyclical opportunities as well as through effort and good judgement of risk. This insight also integrates understanding of the behaviour of individuals with the aggregate of the whole economy: increasing or decreasing the incentives to 'animal spirits' (Francois and Lloyd-Ellis, 2003: 530). The macro effect is to stimulate the overall numbers of innovators and entrepreneurs who share, or anticipate a shared positive view of the prospects of the economy and invest in an upturn, and share a negative view and risk aversion in a downturn. This is pro-cyclical. Over the long term this will produce declines in entrepreneurship in historical data for depressions, suggested by Kuznets (1940: 261) to be 1814–27, 1870–96, 1925–39, and increases in boom periods, such as 1843–57, 1898–1911, with slowdowns in downturns, and accelerations during upturns.

The value of Schumpeter's ideas relating to the cycle have been given renewed attention in the light of the severe global downturn after the 2008 financial crisis and in recessions of the 1970s and 1980s. However, as Parker (2011: xi–xii) points out, Kuznets' (1940) and Mises' (1949) critiques demonstrate how Schumpeter did not fully develop his ideas for the business cycle, though his work certainly stimulated others to look at the potential processes involved. Kuznets argued that Schumpeter's link between short-term changes and unequal entrepreneurial activity was not demonstrated, nor was the link of these inequalities to bunching that might lead to business cycles. Hence cyclical effects on entrepreneurship remain controversial.

Location factors in entrepreneurship: von Thünen, Weber and Lösch

Entrepreneurship does not take place in an empty space; it is intimately bound up with the specifics of location. Location offers local facilities, infrastructure externalities and varied access to other places. It is also an important aspect of residential and life cycle preferences. This has been built into modern theories of spatial economics and economic geography developing from Thünen, Weber and Lösch.

Location was recognised by Cantillon, Say and other early writers as offering market constraints and opportunities, with the contrast of rural and town locations often noted as we reviewed above. However, the first significant attempts at a more specifically locational perspective on entrepreneurs were made by Johann Heinrich von Thünen (1826/1966) for farmers, and Alfred Weber for industry (1909/1929).[9] Although entrepreneurship as such was less considered than the effect of transport on costs on production and hence on profits, both writers provided important contemporary theoretical insight into locational effects for our period of detailed analysis.

Thünen was concerned with the time and effort of travel undertaken by farmers and their workers: travelling to fields to cultivate them; transporting fertilisers and other inputs, especially night soil; and travelling to markets to distribute assembled products. This was a theoretical perspective at the level of the farm unit. It is particularly valuable for our analysis in establishing an understanding of the effects of distance on farm production and marketing in a period when transport was dependent on walking or carriage by horse and cart, but was being heavily affected by rail. This constrained local farming operations to a de facto limit from a market or key access point to rail. This defined the normal catchments of the farms using market towns to about 5 miles for a heavy cart, 15–20 miles for a light cart, with exceptions of up to 30 or 40 miles for infrequent exchanges with more remote locations (Everitt, 1976: 179–84; Barker and Gerhold, 1995: 15–20). This pattern began to be disputed by canals from the 1760s, and more radically modified by the development of railways from the 1820s but especially after the 1850s. Electric trams became important after the 1880s, and motor transport began to dominate urban taxis, omnibuses and some lorries in the 1900s, but motor vehicles became generally significant and important for farming only after about 1910.

Weber focused on the effects of transport costs on the assembly of raw materials and other factor inputs for a factory, and the subsequent effect of transport costs on the distribution of finished goods. His conclusion was that a factory would be located at the point where costs were lowest. Each possible location would have its own individual potential production costs depending on local price differences and the quantity of inputs required. Weber's contribution was to recognise that if all these other costs were held equal, then locational effects on an entrepreneur would be reduced to finding *the point of minimum transport cost*: the location with the lowest possible combination of freight costs for raw material assembly and shipment costs for the finished product. His approach allows different locations to be compared and the effects of different influences on transport costs to be assessed, such as the effect of transport networks and assembly points (stations or ports), the role of political or physical boundaries or differences in terrain.

Development of these locational theories to embrace the specifics of entrepreneurial decisions by August Lösch (1952) in the *Economics of Location* sought to combine Thünen and Weber, and expand them to a general equilibrium framework. This assumed substitution between factor inputs and locational costs occurred at each stage so as to maximise marginal entrepreneurial income against marginal costs. He considered business *location in the general sense* to be the choice which achieved that maximisation. This holds for settlements and wider economic landscapes (regions, countries). The result would be adjustments of individual business decisions to achieve the profit maximisation, with location costs being one major input into this calculus. This combined with *location in the narrow sense* of a site, which will be occupied by 'those prepared to pay most for it'. Lösch (1952: 246–8) considered that entrepreneurs could (in theory) rank all possible locations and then evaluate alternatives in terms of their revenues, transport costs and site prices. A choice could then be made that maximised profits and minimised locational and other costs, but also factored in the competitors for different sites and hence relative site costs that an entrepreneur was prepared to pay depending on how many other businesses sought the same site and their preparedness to pay for it. This moved on from Weber by combining profit maximisation with transport cost minimisation, the trade-off between the two and the level of competition between locations. Hence 'in any given locality everything is produced for which neighbouring competition leaves room' (Ibid.: 249). However, Lösch recognised that actual locations will differ from those that might be optimal (Ibid.: 329–30): first, because removal itself is costly and there are often other personal reason for inertia; second, because actual locations have depended on economic history so that the worst located may have failed, or will be the least capable of undertaking a move, whilst the most profitable will be those already in the best locations; but, third, once a firm is located, suppliers and markets to some extent adjust to it, as do potential competitors and competitor sites (what Lösch called 'the accident of an early start'; a form of monopsony, which also relates to path dependency), so that existing locations will continue despite disadvantages – until some disruption occurs (often a Schumpeterian technological change). This also recognised that local monopoly (giving control over prices) and monopsony (giving control over suppliers) was strongly influence by transport costs and degree of accessibility.

Lösch, living in a later period when motor transport and wider travel were common, made much of the distinction of locational decisions between entrepreneurs and workers which also applies before 1911. Although recognising that the locations of workers and businesses were interdependent, he argued that workers were relatively untied and entrepreneurs were more tied to locations. In addition to the specifics of sub-optimality noted above, this was because of four fundamental differences between workers and entrepreneurs which influenced choice: first, workers could more easily transfer between sectors, whereas entrepreneurs were generally more constrained; second, profits were more sensitive to location than wages; third, an entrepreneur's factory or premises was not easily moved, and re-location would not be considered unless there were large differences in costs or profits to be obtained; and fourth, 'it is easier for an adequate number of potential workers than for potential entrepreneurs to make the sacrifice that would permit the establishment of a factory in the locality . . . either voluntarily or of necessity' (Lösch, 1952: 244–5).

Lösch was also keen to use his theoretical insights to aid practical decision making, and dedicated a large part of his *Economics of Location* to assessing current locational patterns and the costs of different locations using mainly the census of manufacturers and other more local business surveys in the US. He devoted extensive discussion to decisions on optimal market areas over which a trader should operate, demonstrating that many businesses sought to distribute too widely and had poor control over pricing of distribution. An entrepreneur's profit could be increased by reducing market area and total sales, but this varied by size of firm and type of industry. Generally he concluded that smaller areas should predominate for retail businesses like groceries, medium-sized market areas for wholesalers and larger areas for manufacturers, especially where they were more specialised. The differences were explained by the contrasts of freight costs between sectors, but also by the level of fixed costs in different sectors, the value of their goods, degree of specialisation, frequency of purchase and perishability and the income or market potential of each settlement (Lösch, 1952: 396–410). Assembly at nodal points of transmission such as a station or port was key:

> Every railway station . . . is a collecting point in miniature. Each is surrounded by its small supply area . . . . A larger supply area surrounds (the larger nodal stations), and the price at each stopping palace is equal to that at the superior nodal point less the freight [cost)] . . . finally are the few great ports that export.
>
> (Lösch, 1952: 188–9)

2.4   Aggregations: endogenous growth, externalities and industrial districts

We engage with aggregations of entrepreneurial activity at two levels in this book: for the whole economy to assess numbers and rates of entrepreneurship over time and at a local level to assess concentrations in different locations. Entrepreneurial activity of individuals, when aggregated over all businesses, is a strong influence on an economy as a whole. This has been recognised since the outset of historical theorising. The success of a country was held to depend on the success of its entrepreneurs by Cantillon and Say, and is embedded in Marshall. Kirzner (1985: 71–2) referred to 'the development of a nation's economy over time as a process made up, to a major extent, of the interaction of innumerable individual acts of mutual [entrepreneurial] discovery'. However, the link between the individual level and the aggregate in more modern economic theory has been problematic. Traditionally economic theory left entrepreneurship out of consideration, relying on external technological changes to explain national or local-level economic growth, and the micro-economic theory of the firm to explain the individual level. Barreto's (1989: 157) key conclusion was that entrepreneurs were excluded because they did not allow the consistent self-contained theoretical model to operate unhindered: 'The entrepreneur is shorthand for uncertainty, imperfect information, and the unknown'.

Modern economic growth theory has tried to re-introduce or endogenise entrepreneurship. Most attention has focused on how entrepreneurship explains how growth escapes from diminishing returns (Romer, 1986; Barro and Sala-i-Martin, 1995). Entrepreneurship is one endogenous factor that can overcome diminishing returns by introducing new products and services; others are human capital investment (e.g. through improved education) and institutional and policy improvements. Innovation and R&D is also endogenous, and is sometimes included with entrepreneurship as a whole or treated separately. It is argued that these factors increase returns through spillovers from externalities. Individual entrepreneurship achieves returns for initiators, but also creates spillovers to others by transmission through supply chains and wider factor markets and knowledge spillovers which cannot be entirely controlled by inventors which allow take up and adaptation by third parties (as recognised by Say). These entrepreneurial spillovers can be either Kirznerian (from arbitrage or new opportunity) and Schumpeterian (technological or innovation based): both increase overall economic growth (see e.g. Romer, 1990; Segerstrom et al., 1990; Aghion and Howitt, 1992; Acs et al., 2009; Baumol, 1990, 2010). Krugman (1991) shows how these spillovers lead to agglomeration in different locations, giving Marshall's 'industrial districts' a base in modern trade theory. However, as noted by Peneder (2001: 140–52), while trade theory can include agglomeration effects it ignores Marshall's other concern of localisation – sector specialisation – which is key to nineteenth-century analysis. Peneder attempts to extend the model by using different labour pools offering different profit and entrepreneurial opportunities for each sector.

Endogenous factors linked to agglomeration inevitably focus attention on urban locations. In our analysis beginning in 1851 most of the population was urban, and cities were already the centres of well-defined clusters, trading networks and 'industrial districts'. These clusters continued to expand in scale and importance into the twentieth century (de Vries, 1984; Crafts, 1985, 1997), and we find them dominant throughout our analysis (Chapter 9). They were especially important for manufacturing and large-scale financial and commercial centres. They offered increasing returns to scale since their wider externalities generally increased with the size of place and the firms within it: the larger they were, the easier matching of business needs and available workforces, and the greater the collective sharing of infrastructure and communication investments (Duranton and Puga, 2004; Piori and Sabel, 1984; Scott and Storper, 1987; Hirst and Zeitlin, 1991). Cities and industrial districts overlapped, both providing the micro-level opportunities that underpinned endogenous growth. Moreover, this tended to be self-reinforcing. An individual business, region or country that was successful at one stage of development tended to stay ahead, whilst those that were behind tended to stay behind. This path dependence was important at both the macro level of a whole economy, in local districts and at the micro level (North, 1990, 2005; Mokyr, 1990, 2009). Entrepreneurs tended to remain entrepreneurs, entrepreneurial families tend to encourage the next generation, strongly entrepreneurial locations tended to remain strong. Such 'hysteresis' effects (Congregado et al., 2009) led to long-term persistence of spatial clusters.

Whilst we are not concerned in this book with formal economic models, modern theory is indicative of the situations that our analysis has to tackle: identifying the different sectoral and locational contexts for entrepreneurial development and assessing their effect on choice (as examined in Chapters 4–6 and 9). This is particularly important for whole-population analysis where different firm sizes and sectors are important. As Marshall noted, small businesses and own-account proprietors depend on externalities and institutional structures, whereas large firms have more capacity to 'make their own environment' or influence government to improve policies. Small firms have to draw much more heavily from the externalities of what is generally available.

2.5   Implications for analysis

This chapter has focused on how theories of entrepreneurship can be developed for whole-population analysis based on combining modern theories of choice with historical insights from Cantillon, Say, Marshall, Knight, Mises, Schumpeter, Kirzner and others, up to the insights from modern endogenous growth theory. The definition of entrepreneur used is broad-based: those who successfully developed activity by assembling factor inputs to produce new outputs and who tried to anticipate demand and organise its supply. We have also emphasised the need to assess layers of development, with multiple types of entrepreneurship going on at the same time, and variations between firm size, sector and the types of person involved. Our approach is not limited to considering innovation; this reflects the nature of our data, our evaluation of the existing theories and the relevance of more expansive conceptions of entrepreneurship to nineteenth-century Britain.

This is the starting point for the rest of the book. Chapter 3 shows how the historic records of the census and other sources can be extracted to identify entrepreneurs as defined from this theoretical approach. This is applied over time: in depth for 1851–1911, and in lesser detail for 1921–2011. These data are then used in Chapter 4 to provide an overview of entrepreneurship development for employers and own-account individuals compared to workers, and in Chapter 5 by firm size, and in lesser detail for corporations. The choice model which is the key element of theories of entrepreneurship is estimated for whole-population analysis in Chapter 6. The following chapters then investigate the different dimensions of the family firm (Chapter 7), gender (Chapter 8), geography (Chapter 9), migration (Chapter 10) and diversification through business portfolios (Chapter 11).

Notes

1 See Redlich, 1949, and Hoselitz, 1951: 194ff, who summarise earlier uses of the term, and Savary, 1723.
2 The origin of the 1755 text is confusing. Cantillon's original text was lost but much circulated in other publications. A major part was published in Postlethwayt's *Universal Dictionary of Trade and Commerce* of 1749. Higgs (1931: 383) states that most of this *Dictionary* followed

Cantillon's *Essay*, including all comments on entrepreneurs. A more detailed analysis by Jevons (1881) and Johnson (1937) shows how the different entries by Postlethwayt used Cantillon; see also Murphy (1986). However, a recent study by van den Berg (2012) demonstrates that there must have been multiple and differing versions of the text so that neither the 1755 French version nor Postlethwayt's extraction can be considered definitive.

3 Higgs, ed., 1931; here page numbers are quoted from the Cantillon 1755 edition, with '/' to indicate page breaks, as reproduced in Higgs' parallel texts; see also Brewer, 1992: 22–7, 50–4; Hébert and Link, 2009: 7–12.

4 However, he clearly did not 'fail to proceed beyond the stage of taxonomy in the theory of the entrepreneur' as stated by Williams, 1978: 16; on uncertainty see Hébert and Link, 2009: 13.

5 The quotations that follow are from the 1827 edition which has two volumes. This edition does not differ substantially in the main argument from the first and intervening editions, but gives more detail and examples. It is a curiosity that in the French original text Say mentions 96 times in the first edition of 1803 and 138 times in the sixth edition of 1841 the word 'entrepreneur', while in the first English translation from the 1827 fourth edition by R. Prinsep the word appears only once and in a footnote. Instead 'adventurer' is used because 'The term *entrepreneur* is difficult to render in English . . . For want of a better word, it will be rendered into English by the term *adventurer*'. Thus, in the first translation the word 'entrepreneur' is invisible. Hoselitz, 1960, reviews Say's personal background in textile production.

6 Compare Mill, 1867, 137–9, 400–416 and Smith, 1904: i, 50–51, 55, 89–100.

7 See Williams, 1978: 47. Hébert and Link, 2009: 13, 24–35, 49–54 discuss the specific British conceptual developments leading up to Marshall.

8 He also advanced the range of previous American conceptual developments into 'a meaningful synthesis': Hébert and Link, 2009: 64.

9 Both von Thünen and Weber depended on other writers: see reviews of the early literature by Lösch (1952) 5, 18–23, 184–191, 261, 330, and Isard (1956) 27–53.

3 New insights from historical big data

3.1 Introduction

Key parts of this book analyse the entire population of entrepreneurs 1851–1911. It seeks to fill previous major gaps in knowledge of business numbers and size distribution in nineteenth-century Britain. As Jeremy (1998: 31) stated, historical data on small business populations is so scarce that economy–wide understanding of business dynamics has been impossible. Mokyr (2010: 197) notes a fundamental lack of information about the scale of entrepreneurship over time. Hannah (2007: 415) refers to nineteenth-century data on business numbers as a 'statistical dark age'. The effect is particularly severe for understanding small firms and the overall firm-size distribution. As Crossick and Haupt (1995: 40) note, 'the vitality of small enterprise was not sufficiently important to shape the gathering of statistics', and Payne (1988: 22) observed that small businesses were the 'regiments of the anonymous'.

This chapter shows how the data gap can be filled using the electronic version of the census (I–CeM), supplemented from other sources. The chapter describes how I–CeM presents many challenges because the businesspeople have to be identified and extracted from the rest of the population through carefully targeted searches and gaps and deficiencies in I–CeM overcome by supplemental data. Moreover, because the census was not designed as a business census its coverage is imperfect. To fulfil the aim of obtaining as complete a business coverage as possible as a surrogate 'British Business Census of Entrepreneurs', this book also uses other sources to fill census gaps. The main gap infilled is for corporations (limited companies). Section 3.2 of the chapter introduces how the census can be used to identify business proprietors. Section 3.3 discusses how the census data are aligned over time. Section 3.4 outlines how the census data have been enriched to include company directors. Section 3.5 summarises the definitions of aggregate business sectors used in subsequent analyses.

As noted in Chapters 1 and 2 we define business proprietors and entrepreneurs as widely as possible, with information and coding added to the database so that different groups and categories can be selected by users as required to answer different research questions. The core of available information is the statement or imputation of employer status given in the census, usually obtained from information on occupational activity. From this and other resources, the base objective is to identify *business proprietors*: those who were at the date of the census (or equivalent date where other data have to be used) *currently* the responsible individuals bearing the risks of running private business enterprises, however small, and even if they did this alone with no other individuals involved (as self-employed individuals).

The business proprietors active at any point in time fall into five categories:

1   Sole proprietor with no employees (own account)
2   Sole proprietor with employees
3   Partnership with no employees
4   Partnership with employees
5   Company directors

These categories coincide with the same categories used in most modern formal definitions, although technical detail may vary: for modern UK population censuses (ICSER, 1951; OPCS, 1977) and similar surveys such as the Labour Force Survey (LFS), the General Household Survey (GHS), and the Family Expenditure Survey (FES), although company directors were imperfectly included in censuses and other surveys until very recent years. As another comparator, categories 2 and 4 are equivalent to modern tax regulations for employers with responsibility to deduct tax at source (PAYE), whilst categories 1, 3 and 5 and the proprietors in categories 2 and 4 fall under self-assessment for income tax, or (if they are venture capitalists) are remunerated through income from dividends or capital gains and taxed on those sources through self-assessment or corporate taxation. Of course, these categories may not be entirely distinct, and a given person may be simultaneously in two or more categories.

3.2   The census as a source for understanding entrepreneurship

The population census is the main source used. It allows most business proprietors to be identified where they are non-corporate; that is, they are not limited companies. However, because the population census was not a business census, its imperfections of coverage have to be understood and corrected or infilled. To achieve the aim of generating a final database which is consistent, accurate and as complete as possible, it is important to fully understand how the data were derived. The census records now available for analysis reflect seven stages of database assembly: (i) design of the census forms and instructions given to householders; (ii) actual responses by householders to the instructions; (iii) local administration that gathered the responses, recorded them and exercised quality controls; (iv) subsequent preservation of records, including any losses, and muddling of entries; (v) modern transcription of what has survived; (vi) modern coding of entries; and, finally, (vii) tailored coding and manipulation of the entries for our analysis, including any data editing, cleaning and further coding.

The census was designed by the General Register Office (GRO), who responded to advice and pressures from others such as the Royal Statistical Society and Local Government Board, but generally followed their own line (Higgs, 1988, 2004: 61–2; Porter, 1986). The GRO also had to tailor administration to the skills available from local collectors of information and central processing clerks. The census was a survey undertaken by local administrators (enumerators) working under registrars for larger areas. Census returns were normally filled in by the head of household, returned to the enumerator on the census night or the next day. These household returns were then entered by the enumerator into census enumerator books (CEBs), and the books for the whole district then sent via the registrar to the GRO in London. At the GRO they were then processed by census clerks to produce published tables. Researchers now have available only the CEBs, except for 1911, when the GRO dispensed with them and used the original household returns, which are what is now available. The data processing by the GRO and any cleaning or recoding of responses is no longer available to us, but it is built into the published tables. From the digitised records now available, we must begin with the CEBs for 1851–1901 and the householder returns for 1911. The National Archives (TNA) has then overseen a process of scanning the original records and transcription from the scans (or from previous versions on microfilms). TNA has used commercial partners for transcription: mainly Ancestry, FindMyPast (FMP), and S&N: The Genealogist. For 1881 the transcriptions were first undertaken by the Genealogical Society of Utah (GSU), and then incorporated into Ancestry and FMP. FMP and Ancestry have also sourced some of their transcriptions from earlier work by local family history societies. However, S&N re-transcribed all years, including 1881.

Potential deficiencies at each stage have to be managed. The 1841 census was the first to be administered directly to households, and 1851 was the first occasion where all householders gave full occupational information. As a relatively new instrument the census design and wording of some questions was imperfect by modern standards, which constrains analysis. Similarly, the local enumerators, though generally efficient, were variable in quality so that both wider and narrower variances were introduced into the CEB records of householder responses than the actuality. Equally important, although the census achieved a near total coverage of the population, non-responses to some questions were a major feature, rising in some cases to one-fifth of the adult population: this particularly affects the information on employment status as employer, own account or worker in later censuses. Hence, whilst there was a legal requirement to respond to the census, not all questions were answered, or answered correctly. However, tests of census responses against other information in a range of cases studies have demonstrated that inaccuracies were relatively small. For example, where age can be verified from other sources, estimates show 70–96 percent accuracy to 1–2 years. Age accuracy was lower for unskilled, partly skilled and professions, and for the 10–29 and 50–59 age groups (Thomson, 1996; Perkyns, 1996). Various tests undertaken by Schürer and Woollard (2000, 2002) and Woollard (1997a, 1999) suggest that whilst there are certainly inaccuracies at the household level and in small localities, across the country these errors are small and there is generally 'a high level of internal consistency' (Woollard, 1997b: 57). ICSER (1951), OPCS (1977) and Bellamy (1953: 307–8) observed that accuracy, which was more problematic in earlier censuses, steadily improved.

Once gathered by the GRO the paper records were preserved in their offices or other government departments, and eventually transferred to TNA (Higgs, 2005). The tortuous history of preservation and transfer to TNA muddled some of the records and resulted in the loss of others. About 2 percent of the England and Wales population was lost in 1851, and 3.7 percent in 1861, with minor losses for later years. The digital scanning of the CEBs for 1851–1901 and of the householder responses for 1911 also resulted in missing some entries, muddling some entries between locations and introducing some duplicate records. The transcription from these images was carried out by several contractors with varying accuracy at both the general level (1851 is recognised as being relatively inaccurate, and 1881 very accurate), and at the level of batches of records by particular transcribers for locations in a given year. Most problematic, the description of employers, where it included employees, is usually a long string of information, which was sometimes systematically truncated or ignored by transcribers. For 1851 and 1861 transcription omissions are a substantial part of the total entrepreneur records which have to be infilled. Transcriptions by FMP were then input used by the Essex University team for the I–CeM database, which is the starting point for modern research. I–CeM, as well as including any errors or omissions from enumerator and GRO processes, preservation and transcription, introduced other features that have to be managed. The most important of these relate to how data were coded, and their accuracy, for employer status, occupations, location, relationships within the household and birthplace.

Our analysis uses census information for two periods in different levels of depth. Our main analysis is at detailed individual level for all people included in the censuses 1851–1911. This is big data covering 161 million people from the original individual records. A second part of our analysis is undertaken in lesser depth in order to connect the historic information to modern censuses. This uses the later census information drawn from published tables for 1921–2011, and additional special tabulations for 2011. These two periods of coverage are complementary, but offer scope for different depths of analysis. They are discussed in turn below.

The censuses 1851–1911

The historic censuses for which we can access individual records give information on entrepreneurs in two different ways. In the first period, 1851–81, a question was asked as part of the occupation information on whether individuals were employers or masters, and, if so, the number of employees, and acres if a farmer. In 1881 census instructions to householders were:[1]

> In TRADES, MANUFACTURES or other Business, the Masters must, in all cases, be so designated. – *Example: 'Carpenter – Master, employing 6 men and 2 boys;'* inserting always the number of persons in the trade in their employ at the time of the Census. In the case of Firms, the number of persons employed should be returned by *one partner* only.

The farmer's instructions were:

> FARMERS to state the number of acres occupied, and the number of men, women, and boys, employed on the farm at the time of the Census. – *Example: 'Farmer of 317 Acres, employing 8 Labourers and 3 Boys.'* Sons or daughters employed at home or on the farm should be returned – *"Farmer's Son"*, *"Farmer's Daughter"*. Men employed on the farm and sleeping in the Farmer's house must be described in the schedule as *Farm Servants*.

These instructions differed in minor detail but were similar for the whole period 1851–81 (except for how some women's activities were recorded). They provide invaluable information that we use for those who were employers and farmers, and on many partners. However, for 1891 and subsequently the instruction to give information on employee numbers and farm acres was dropped. The 1851–81 population censuses are thus the only ones ever undertaken that attempted to give full workforce-size information.

From 1891 a question was introduced to the census which has been continued in different forms up to the present. As well as their occupation this instructed people also to record their *employment status*: whether they were an employer, own account or worker. In 1901 the specific wording was contained in instructions over the column for 'Profession or Occupation' under which were three sub-columns:[2]

> 'Write opposite the name of each person engaged in any trade or industry, either
>
> (1) *"Employer"* (that is, employing persons other than domestic servants)
> (2) *"Worker"* (that is, a worker for an employer); or
> (3) *"Own account"* (that is, neither Employer nor working for Employer, but working on own account).'

The information was collected in the same way in 1911 and in similar ways up to 2011. But in 1891 the first use of this question adopted a different format where the respondent had to tick one of three columns after the occupation column, which were headed: (1) 'Employer', (2) 'Employed' and (3) 'neither Employer nor Employed' which was defined in notes as 'when the person neither employs other workmen in his trade or industry, nor works for a master, but works on his own account'.[3]

The details of the specific differences in questions over 1851–1911 and their implications are discussed in WPs 2, 3 and 4. A critically important issue arises from the change in questions between 1881 and 1891. For the whole period most employers were explicitly designated, though the information was collected in different ways. However, only from 1891 were employer, own-account proprietors and workers explicitly identified. This leads to a major discontinuity in the data available, as summarised in Table 3.1. The result is that, whilst we can extract employers for 1851–81, these are somewhat incomplete so that missing employers have to be identified; whilst own account and workers have to be identified and separated from each other. This involves a lengthy process of data editing which we refer to as 'reconstruction'. It is described more fully in Chapter 4 and at length in WP 9. The results of this reconstruction are believed to be good estimates of the actual business population, although the accuracy varies between business sectors.

For 1891–1911 a different range of data problems arise. All these censuses had a significant number of non-respondents to the employment status question. These were 16, 18 and 20 percent of people, respectively, in 1891, 1901 and 1911 (once the non-economically active are removed: scholars, retired, those living off own means etc.). Moreover, the non-responses were systematically more likely to occur among women, relatives who were not household heads, and in some sectors (especially the professions, and those operating businesses in their homes, such as lodging-house keepers, laundresses, or milliners): see WP 4. This source of non-response bias is compounded for 1891 by deficiencies in the design of the census question which leads to a misallocation bias between employers and own-account proprietors which systematically overestimates the former. An

Table 3.1 How entrepreneurs are identified in each census year, 1851–1911

	1851–81	1891–1911
Individual entrepreneurs	*Employers* identified in all years, though coverage varies before 1891 and has to be infilled.	
	Firm size: employee nos. and farm acres given.	
	Own account reconstructed.	*Own account* identified explicitly.
	Partnership and partners identified for some businesses.	
	Company directors: some identified in census; others enriched from directories and linked to census records.	
	Most *portfolio businesses* identified.	
Non-entrepreneurs	*Workers and unoccupied* have to be separated.	*Workers* identified explicitly.

Source: BBCE database.

extensive correction and re-weighting of the data has to be undertaken before the information can be used for reliable analysis (Bennett et al., 2019a; WP 11). This is discussed fully in Chapter 4. For users of the database deposit it is important to be aware of the variation in coverage of the different entrepreneur categories in each year and to use appropriate strategies that are provided in the database documentation *User Guide.*

Table 3.1 also summarises the other categories of entrepreneur for the period. Some *partnership* businesses were identified in the census, but this is partial. As business proprietors all partners are treated as separate individuals in this book. However, additional codes identify partner status in the database, following Bennett (2016). For partners co-resident within the same household, additional information is used to code those within family business structures. Similarly, most corporate businesses will have multiple *directors* which have to be dealt with through special coding. Unfortunately, the recording of directorships in the census is partial, and data enrichment is necessary (see Section 3.4).

Portfolio businesses, where an individual ran two or more identifiably separate businesses at the same time, are another special case, for which the census gives a very good record. About 8–10 percent of identified business people had portfolios (Chapter 11). For these it is essential to remove spurious portfolios where other activities recorded in the census are purely titles of rank (e.g. alderman), or reflect employee status (e.g. a grocery proprietor who was also a post master employed by the Post Office).[4] We are focused solely on business portfolios. As described in Chapter 11, employee activities and more general by-employment can be included by other researchers if desired.

Workers are not the main subject of this book or database. But, as noted in Chapter 2, they are an important baseline comparator category of those who were *not* business proprietors or entrepreneurs at the time of the census record. They can be investigated to assess how far their personal or other characteristics differ from those who were entrepreneurs. In any case it is critically important to be able to distinguish workers in order to identify entrepreneurs. Hence the database contains codes to classify workers as well as the self-employed, at various levels of certainty as to their status. Definitions are of course complex, and individuals often moved category across their lifecycle.

Extracting and identifying entrepreneurs 1851–1911

For the later censuses 1891–1911 employers and own-account entrepreneurs can be identified using the question on employment status, which is coded into I-CeM. Although there are biases in the responses to this question that have to be corrected, as discussed above and in Chapter 4, they provide a direct entry point for identifying the entrepreneurs which are the main focus of this book.

However, in the earlier censuses 1851–1881 the responses to the instructions outlined above, where employers were asked to give their employee numbers or for some own-account proprietors to identify them as masters, have not been coded in the I-CeM database. The information is available only as embedded within the original occupational strings. This is a complex alphanumeric list of information expressed in no uniform wording or order. Examples in 1881 were John J. Crosbie of Chipping Barnet, who was a 'gold pen & writing ink manufacturer employing 30 men & 6 boys', and James Smith of Derby, a 'clothing contractor employing 210 females & 26 males'. Extracting and coding these employers is a lengthy and multi-stage process. First, the entire population of 17–26 million records for each census year has to be searched to identify potential candidates as employers who have such strings. Second, the numbers of their employees in each category (and for farmers their acreage) has to be identified and parsed into a consistent data structure. Lastly, the output and especially all anomalous cases must be checked, processed manually and cleaned where necessary, and false positives discarded. The method used was piloted in a first extraction for 1881 (Bennett and Newton, 2015). This method was refined for 1851, 1861 and 1871, and extended to infill any 1881 individuals previously missed.

The method used two algorithms. The first searched the occupational text strings of all individuals to find those that match regular expressions that identify employers. These include: sequences of text that include digits or written number words, terms connoting employees and the presence of 'employs' or 'employing' and its abbreviations and synonyms. The second algorithm split (parsed) into separate variables the relevant parts of the full occupational strings of those identified by the first algorithm as employers into sector, number and category of employees, and acreage where appropriate. This identifies as potential employers around 15 percent of all unique census occupational strings, but as many of these were unique to one individual, such strings account for less than 1 percent of the population (including children) as a whole. Each character, word or phrase in each string was compared to 'dictionaries' of expected patterns, to determine which part of the string to place in each of the new employer variables. These dictionaries were 'seeded' initially with the most common patterns and then extended iteratively to encompass the most numerous exceptions, until a relatively small residual of strings that could not be processed remained. By this means 80 percent of the extracted strings were parsed. For farmers the additional information available from the instruction asking 'farmers to state the number of acres occupied' was easier to identify and over 90 percent of acreages were parsed by algorithm. The residual of up to 30,000 strings per census year left after applying algorithms was then processed by hand using research assistants and checked by the authors. In addition, all long strings that were not picked up by the algorithm were inspected, and if relevant, were added and parsed by hand. Other checks were then performed on all the largest employers.

The terminology for employees varied widely: including 'hands', 'labourers', 'persons', 'assistants', 'journeymen/women', 'apprentices', 'servants', 'clerks', etc., as well as men, women, boys, girls, sons, daughters, males, females, people and employees. The final database assigns employees into the following categories:

- Men, including descriptors that were obviously men, such as tradesmen
- Women, including descriptors easily identifiable as women, such as shopwoman

- Boys, including lads
- Girls, including young ladies
- Labourers, with indoor and outdoor labourers added up
- Apprentices
- Journeymen/women
- Male, when gender is stated but no indication of age, such as 'son' or contractions such as '20 men and boys'
- Female, when gender is stated but with no indication of age, such as 'daughter' or contractions such as '14 women and girls'
- Children, including young persons and contractions such as 'boys and girls'
- Other, including non-gendered titles and occupations such as servants, clerks, assistants, baker, hands or where contractions include both males and females and/or unknowns, such as '65 men, women, and boys' or '9 men and apprentices'

Where descriptions fitted more than one category they were assigned in the order listed above; this only applied to a small number of fewer than 100 female labourers in 1851.

The employers identified in this way required significant additional cleaning and supplementation. The occupation strings for 1871 are not provided in I-CeM and were acquired for employers and masters from a separate source (S&N); these were mostly complete (see WP 12). However, 1871 occupational data for workers and many own-account categories were not available so that analysis with the 1871 data is restricted to employers. For 1851 and 1881 the I-CeM occupational string field was truncated at 99 or 100 characters, and for 1861 at 49 or 50 characters (see WP 3). The occupational information often exceeded these limits, and long strings were likely to be employers with employees as these required more characters. All these potentially truncated strings were checked manually against the original CEBs and infilled if there was important information beyond the truncation point. For 1861 this involved checking about 35,000 people identified as probable employers with missing information. Those over 99 or 100 characters in 1851 and 1881 were very small in number and easily infilled. Additionally, I-CeM for 1851 has incomplete transcriptions. This is geographically specific, reflecting the batch inputting of data. The gaps affect most or all of 14 counties (including the crucial counties of Lancashire, Cheshire and London), and all or part of 210 Registration Sub-Districts (RSD) in 87 Registration District areas. The total missing records number about 55,000 employers. These were infilled by additional data obtained from S&N (see WP 3). Various other features of the data also had to be cleaned (Bennett and Newton, 2015), one of the most important of which was split occupational descriptors. This occurs particularly for wives, who are misattributed information from their husbands in the line of above in the CEB. These strings must be linked and attributed to the correct person and erroneous entrepreneur removed.

In addition to employers, algorithmic extraction was also applied to identify own-account proprietors. The primary search terms were 'master' and 'mistress', following the census instructions. Other search terms identified asset owners, partners, directors and other special cases of proprietors. However, whilst the identification and parsing of employers was highly successful, and generally correlated with the small number of tables of employers published by the GRO (see WP 13), the identification of own account was very restricted. Subsequent reconstruction, discussed in Chapter 4 for 1851–81, indicates that only about 5 percent of own account were identified by searching 'master'/'mistress'.

Entrepreneurs in the censuses 1921–2011

The later censuses are used here to join up the historic and modern data. The data from the censuses 1921–2001 are derived solely from published tabulations, but for 2011 special tabulations were commissioned as well as using published tables.

The connection between the early censuses 1851–1911 and later are fairly straightforward because the question on employment status introduced over 1891–1911 was carried forward up to the present. The 1921 census used a question format almost identical to that in 1901–11: this asked the householder to write opposite each person *'Employer'*, *'Own Account'*, or *'Worker'*. From 1931 the terminology was changed to the modern definition of self-employment with or without employing others: 'employs others for purposes of his or her own business' or 'neither works for an employer nor employs others for business purposes'.

The later censuses from the 1921 question explicitly included *all sectors* of employers, whereas previously the question could be read as only applying to 'trades and manufactures'. In addition all employees were required to state the nature of their employers' business and the name of the employer (and whether a person, firm, company or public body). This allowed more accurate industry tabulations since the census 'compilers used local directories' of the main employers to allocate employees to the appropriate category of industry.[5] Although this was mainly used as a check only for larger firms, and no employer information was reported in tabulations, the publications from 1921 should give more accurate industry coverage. The basic method of asking the question was maintained subsequently up to 2011, but with no 1941 census because of World War II.

Over this period being an employer and working on own account were consistently defined, so that with some caveats over detail, the self-employment counts 1921–2011 should be comparable. The main difficulties are: (i) there are differences in how published tabulations included employers, managers and own account in some years; in particular managers and foremen were included with employers in tabulations in 1931, and partially in 1951; (ii) part-timers were included in the occupation questions from 1931, but their treatment in tabulations varied; and (iii) there was an inconsistency for those working for an employer in their own houses as 'out-workers', who were classified as own account in 1951 and 1961, resulting in some own-account proprietors 'in seemingly unlikely occupations';[6] however, this is similar to earlier censuses and accords with modern freelance and outworking; consequently, outworking is a consistent ambiguity from 1851 to the present day. However, these differences in inclusions and definitions can be adjusted to create consistent time series.

3.3   Aligning the census data over time

Consistent definitions and alignments are required to make comparisons over the whole period 1851–1911, and extensions up to 2011.

Occupations

For all proprietors the occupational description identified their occupation in the business; that is, the type of task undertaken. This was not an industry or sector description but is the main census information we now have in order to align over time. Although it has deficiencies in mapping to industries, it was generally a well-administered part of the census, providing a valuable way of categorising different entrepreneur characteristics. Its main limitation is where householders gave limited, very generalised or imperfect information. Additionally, there were differences between the occupational classifications used over time, some of which are difficult to align. In general these have been overcome for 1851–1911 by using the occupational dictionaries provided by I-CeM, which provide correspondences between each census year. We normally use the I-CeM occode, which was based on the 1911 census occupational coding, which covers 797 categories (Higgs et al., 2015), and sometimes the 1881 coding (Woollard, 1997a). But for most the analysis these are too detailed and potentially misleading for tracking across different censuses, given the administrative changes that occurred. Hence for much of the analysis, and for comparison with later censuses, more aggregate alignments are made (see Section 3.5). For most cases alignment over time, and attribution to sectors, is possible only if the information is used at a fairly broad level, and not for minor sectors or very narrow trades. This is the same method used for estimating different contributions to GNP by Feinstein (1972: 226–7) for the UK, and Kuznets et al. (1941: 113) for similar information in the US, who both judged the results, with similar constraints, to be adequate.

Sectors

Whilst occupations defined the nature of the work done, industry defined the type of business it was done for, and sector defined the broad industry markets relevant to entrepreneurs. Thus, for a blacksmith occupation, shipbuilding might be industry and narrow sector, and manufacturing the broad sector. However, because the distinction between industry and occupation was not well understood in early censuses any mapping to business sector is imperfect. The absence of census information on industry was criticised by Booth (1886) and was partially remedied from 1911. For this reason, we develop aggregated sectors used for most of the analysis. We use two levels of aggregation for 1851–1911, as discussed more fully in Section 3.5: one for 51 sectors and another for 17 sectors, referred to, respectively, as EA51 and EA17.

Sector coverage

The early censuses had an important deficiency that the instruction to give employer information, or to respond to the employment status question, could be misread to apply only to those working in 'trade or industry'. Respondents could have followed other census instructions instead. This is mainly an issue for four categories: the legal profession; medical profession; professors, teachers, writers, authors and scientific men; and persons engaged in commerce (merchants, brokers, agents, clerks, commercial travellers). It may also have had a more minor and variable effect for miners, engineers and construction trades. Although checks on this show that generally good coverage was achieved, the large non-response categories for 1891–1911 to employment status indicate that many professions, and proprietors operating from home, did not respond. In 1901, for example, 49 percent of barristers, solicitors and bankers and 43 percent of physicians did not give their employment status. This feature is aligned in reconstructions (Chapter 4).

Full and part time

The early censuses did not require respondents to state whether their occupation was full or part time but to state their 'rank, profession or occupation'. The only explicit terminology to exclude part time related to women, where there was an 1851 instruction that 'the occupations of women who are *regularly* employed from home, or at home, in any but domestic duties, to be distinctly recorded'.[7] A similar instruction was included up to 1881, but was dropped in 1891–1901, and in 1911 read: 'the occupations of women engaged in any business or profession, including women *regularly* engaged in assisting relatives in trade and business, must be fully stated'. The 1911 instruction also added that 'if more than one occupation is followed, state that by which living is *mainly* earned'.[8] This makes clear that 'regular' and 'main' occupations were implicitly the focus of the census enquiry, but the lack of explicit differentiation between full and part time will mean that some part-time occupations were included. The timing of the census in late March or early April and the absence of any question relating to the description of seasonal work was aimed by the GRO at excluding most seasonal employment, and this reduced the amount of part-time activity recorded. Nevertheless the census probably overestimates the number of full-time entrepreneurs active in each census year, but this is likely to remain a constant proportion of a workforce that similarly recorded some part-time activity.[9] The absence of general instructions about part-time activity, and the focus of any explicit instructions solely on women means that, despite the well-known problems of recording female occupations, the entrepreneurial activities of women may be more accurately recorded than often supposed (Roberts, 1988; Anderson, 1999; Higgs and Wilkinson, 2016). The retired were also treated in a problematic way (Woollard, 2002). The occupation question did not require current activity, but used occupation as a status that included former or retired occupations.

Subsequent census treatment varied: in 1921–31 part-timers were included in many tables; in 1951 they can be separated, but were not in all published tables; in 1961 they were included with full-time activity and cannot be separated; from 1971 part-timers were separately questioned, though tabulations varied on what was published. A 30-hour distinction between full and part time was introduced in 1951 and has continued to the present, though it was not explicitly used in 1961 and 1971 which referred to 'normal' hours as de facto full time. These changed definitions result in potential overestimates of full time in 1851–1931 (probably small), and in 1961–71 (probably large). Retired was introduced in the 1861 questions and maintained up to the present.

For entrepreneurs the distinctions may be less important in practice. Many successful entrepreneurs could earn considerable income whilst being only active part time, without other occupations; for example, by using their family or managers to operate the business, by combining with other employment, or they were retired but continued to participate. This could also apply to directors of companies who might earn several multiples of the income of waged earners, even if they spent only a few hours a week on the task. For females, part-time own-account lodgings, refreshments or home manufacturing businesses were often significant in income, even though it was mostly 'necessity' entrepreneurship (Davidoff, 1995). Kuznets et al. (1941: 113, 120–1) comments that 'partial employment has little meaning' for entrepreneurs, though he believed that the share of activity omitted from the US census for this reason was very small (but could cover a large number of people). In order to overcome some of these difficulties, Feinstein (1972: 227) and Chapman and Knight (1953: Table 18) used Ministry of Labour and National Insurance estimates after 1938 instead of the census to measure the total workforce. However, the census definitions are usually the base of official statistics.

Portfolios and by-employment

Portfolios are an important aspect of entrepreneurship, assessed in Chapter 11, and for directors in Chapter 6. Many entrepreneurs identifiable in the census return multiple business activities. In addition to business portfolios there were many others who had occupations additional to another activity. There is little early comment on this in the UK, but in the US Kuznets et al. (1941: 423) estimated ancillary activities in the 1930s to amount to about 2 percent of national income, but most were wage earners (contributing less than 0.4 percent of national income). If the main activity was domestic (managing the household) this should have been omitted from census returns. But if it was part of a portfolio of occupations it should be listed by census respondents. The 1851–1901 censuses asked respondents to list their occupations in order of importance, though in 1911 individuals were asked only to state 'that by which living is mainly earned'. As far as possible we identify these portfolios, but include only those that were part of business portfolios, and exclude by-employments from entrepreneurship. For directors, portfolios are identified through multiple directorships and any involvement in other businesses.

Female occupations

The wording and administration of the census had a number of deficiencies for how far female economic activity was assessed. Fortunately, most do not affect the original records; however published tables omit many wives' employments or ignore in-household female contributions to a business. For analysis using the CEBs the main problem is how wives' activities were recorded. For most years there was an explicit instruction to record wives' activity, as quoted above in relation to issues of part time activity. However, in 1891 a wife was to be treated the same as an employee whether or not she was a business partner: 'married women assisting their husbands in their trade or industry are to be returned as 'employed''. Similarly, relatives of farmers who were working on the farm were instructed to be recorded as 'farmer's son' or 'farmer's daughter', and the examples included in the 1851 to 1881 censuses listed a 'farmer's wife'. Respondents answering in a similar manner resulted in systematic under-recording for females on farms, and probably affected many female workers in domestic businesses such as shops. Conversely, in other cases some enumerators applied the occupation of the head to wives and other members of the household (often as 'ditto') which may have over-recorded female contributions (Higgs, 1987: 68). Inspection of the original CEBs makes it clear that the most common pattern in many areas was enumerators systematically leaving the occupations of many married women blank or just recording 'wife', which may or may not have been correct. This particularly affects home manufacturers and traders, farm and field workers and especially domestic servants (Higgs, 1987: 63–8; Higgs, 1995). Some enumerators returned up to 50 percent of women as blank. In addition, where female occupations were recorded, it is often unclear whether they were household supports to the family or were directly employed in the market-facing part of the family's trade or externally. This has some effect on our subsequent analysis (see Chapters 5, 7 and 8). From 1911 new enumerator instructions removed most of these difficulties, and the census became a more reliable count of women's occupations and other under-recorded groups (Hatton and Bailey, 2001).

A major problem for analysis is inconsistency of the numbers of married women enumerated with their husband's occupation; for example, as 'carpenter's wife' (I-CeM code 789). This was common (chiefly in farming, manufactures and construction), with more than 100,000 women recorded in this way for 1851–81, where they may have followed the 'farmer's wife' example, and in 1911. However, for 1891 and 1901 only a few thousand were recorded.

A method has to be chosen to treat this category consistently. If included, there is a severe disruption to trends. If excluded, some information is lost. As a description, this is an ambiguous category which includes women who were genuinely active in a family business, as well as those not necessarily economically active where the title indicated social or marital status. This varied by enumerator, so that it is impossible to correctly assign which of these women were economically active or not (You, 2014: 216). Hence in most subsequent analysis they are *excluded* to remove disruption of trends. This is imperfect but is the normal approach of researchers seeking consistent estimates of trends. However, as Feinstein (1972: 224) concluded, even after exclusions and compensations, 'it is not possible to obtain a completely uniform treatment . . . [which] must be accepted as an unavoidable limitation of the Census-based estimates'. Exclusion leads to some genuinely economically active women being removed, meaning we estimate the *lower boundary* of the married women's labour force participation and entrepreneurship rates.

'Own means'

This terminology was of longstanding, but was only introduced into census-explicit instructions in 1891: 'persons following no profession, trade, or calling but deriving their income from land, houses, dividends, or other private means' to return themselves as 'living on own means'. In 1901 and 1911 the explicit instruction was headed 'living on own means'. With nothing explicit about own means in earlier censuses, this had the effect of significantly increasing the numbers recorded from 1891. This affects active entrepreneurs who earned income from directorships and some estate and landed proprietors (see below), but this number is small. The main effect was on widows. There were 510,000 widows in I-CeM code 778 (own means) in 1891, and similar numbers in 1901–11, compared to 180,000 in 1881. This meant that over 1891–1911 some widows, who for earlier censuses responded in a way which may have included them within the economically active, in 1891–1911 became instead 'own means'. It is not entirely clear how they were recorded before 1891, but many were likely to be returned with their husband's former occupation because of the status associated with this, following instructions to married women discussed above. We exclude these from the economically active as part of general data cleaning since they were living on income such as annuities and were not active business proprietors. When combined with our exclusion of women giving their husband's occupation as discussed above, this should make census comparisons consistent (see Chapters 7 and 8).

Managers etc.

Another inconsistency is how managers and foremen were treated. These were relatively rare categories in the early nineteenth century, except for farm bailiffs. However, they became much more important by the late century as large employers became more numerous. For 1851–81 a decision can be made to include them or not as an entrepreneurial category. In general, we exclude managers and foremen, unless the information they give is unique: for example, if bailiffs give the number of employees in the business or the size of farm acres they are treated as 'surrogate' entrepreneurs for the purpose of including all businesses. For 1891–1911 they are included if they self-report as an employer or own account, but the numbers are small. For the 1931 census inclusion of managers in published tables among business proprietors, and in 1951 partial inclusion, requires adjustments. They are also included among directors where they are clearly a 'managing director'.

Partners

A business will have multiple proprietors if it is a partnership. In 1861–81 the workforce of firms was only meant to be reported by the senior partner. In 1851 and 1891–1911 there was no instruction regarding partners. Where they are identifiable, partners returned themselves as a mixture of employers and own account. From 1921 they were classified as self-employed (own account) in tabulations if they had no employees, and as employers if they had employees. However, the explicit instructions for respondents to identify themselves as partners was still inadequate, with tabulations relying largely on clerks using employer name descriptions as a guide. Because the census identification of partners is imperfect we choose not to analyse partnership in this book, but do use it as a means to identify entrepreneurs and hence proprietor numbers.

Employer inclusions

While our definition is, as noted previously, broad, there are some types of entrepreneur whose inclusion requires specific consideration.

1   *Financial entrepreneurs*: Those whose contribution brought together financial assets that others used to develop businesses (such as brokers, bankers, investment agents) are often excluded from explicit recognition in the census. They are included in our analysis where they gave employees, reported themselves as employers or own-account proprietors or where they were recognisable as company directors, but often this form of entrepreneurship was 'hidden' within an individual's general occupational descriptor. Many would be excluded anyway as they were not the prime business decision makers: most brokers, bankers, investment agents, asset managers and insurance fund managers were not the final decision takers within the businesses covered by the investments.

2   *Land and asset owners*: Asset owners who deployed their assets to develop businesses are an important class of proprietor; for example, mine/quarry owners, ship owners, barge owners, machine owners, and others with

physical or land-based assets as their main business basis. The census allows many of these to be identified and included as definite business proprietors. However, they could be resident (and hence enumerated by the census) in locations far from their businesses.

We exclude from analysis owners where the census records them solely as landowners and house proprietors. This is the same approach as Booth (1886) and Feinstein (1972). They are sometimes ambiguous as to possible business status. Many land owners, even very large ones, were not proprietors of businesses but occupied the space for personal use (Spring, 1971). While they were likely to employ individuals to maintain the household (domestic servants), such employment relations were usually of a different character to the employer–worker relationship in private businesses, though their role as employers of estate workers qualifies them as business proprietors where these workers unambiguously indicate contribution to the estate as a 'business'. House proprietors may or may not be actually letting their property. The census classification and terminology is unhelpful in both cases because of a lack of sufficient recorded information that allows business proprietors in these groups to be identified; however, it is clear that most recorded in this way were not in business and many were recorded as 'own means'.

3   *'Masters', outworkers and teams.* Outworking is difficult to analyse using the census; few people reported themselves as 'outworkers' or synonyms, and their employment status can be ambiguous. We include outworkers who reported themselves as own account or employers, but the majority of outworkers either returned themselves as workers or did not explicitly report their status as outworkers. In 1901 and 1911 some analysis can be undertaken using the 'at home' variable, where the census asked individuals to report whether or not they worked at home; however, this question has confused coding and high non-response.

We consider internal contract systems, putting out and sweating as not sufficiently autonomous to be included as entrepreneurs (see Chapter 1). However, we are reliant on self-reporting to maintain this distinction. For example, if a cotton spinner employed in a factory was also employing cotton piecers under them, they would be included if they reported themselves as an employer but excluded if they either gave no employee numbers (in 1851–81) or reported themselves as a worker (1891–1911). This relies on self-reporting: as detailed in Chapter 2, we treat entrepreneurship as it was understood by individuals themselves. Similarly, masters are included where they were likely to be independent proprietors, but excluded where they were likely to be employed. This distinction is mainly maintained by reference to their occupational strings; thus, barge masters were usually workers in this period and were mostly excluded, but master craftsmen were usually autonomous employers or own account and so were included. This is imperfect. For example, the distinction by Fang (1930) between own-account 'family craftsmen' and 'master craftsmen' outside the family in small firms does *not* seem to appear in the census (see Chapter 7). Hence, although Littler (1982) argued that much indirect craft control continued up to 1914, we find that despite the use of 'master' in the instructions in the census, generally respondents and enumerators used the term 'employer', with 'master', 'mistress' or similar terms limited to, and generally synonymous with, autonomous employers or own account. Only 28,628 individuals used 'master' or 'mistress' in any way to describe their occupation in 1851 and had employees; this reduced to 22,701 in 1881, and 11,780 in 1891. The use of 'master' or 'mistress' to indicate own account, not employing others, was larger: 44,887 in 1851, 31,756 in 1881 but only 4,192 in 1891.[10] This low level of use (less than 4 percent of entrepreneurs in 1851, and declining) occurred even though respondents were led to use the term by the phrasing of the census question.

Hence, although outworkers and worker-contractors are a problematic category in our analysis, generally they do not appear to have been recorded in the census. But the self-identification as entrepreneurs allows some outworking business proprietors to be identified. Thus, while recipients of putting out, outworking and the sweated trades were not price setters and are regarded as workers in this book, some putting-out groups that could set wages or prices locally for others they employed can be identified. They remained prominent in a few locations and sectors, showing up in census self-identification mainly in the glove making, hosiery, apparel and straw plait industries, especially for women in the East Midlands and counties immediately north of London (see Chapters 7, 8 and 9). This is consistent with our broad definition of entrepreneurship, as stated in Chapter 2, based on using nineteenth-century understandings of entrepreneurial activity to inform our analysis.

Location

The census is a return of those resident at a place at the time of the census. For most business proprietors this is exactly what is required; that is, businesses domiciled in Britain. However, there may be some misallocations between locations within England and Wales because the location of the residence used in the census was not the location of the business. This occurred frequently at the local level within urban areas, where a business may be located in a central area or industrial district but the proprietor lived in a suburban or rural location or even a different town. This type of mismatch will lead to only small geographical misallocations unless the analysis by location is made at a very small scale. Generally, census RSDs are used in this volume since these are mostly large enough to ensure that entrepreneurs' residences are in the same unit as their business, although this is less true in cities and London. Also, proprietors could be residents who had businesses in other regions around the country; particularly for London, Manchester, Liverpool, Leeds, Birmingham, Glasgow and Edinburgh. Some census respondents make this geographical difference clear by stating their business location, but this was rare. There is little that can be done about this. The effect will be small, but it may include some of the larger businesses. Our references to geography assess this potential effect on analysis and mapping.

Additionally, three types of foreign business proprietors are allowed for, all of which are also more likely to occur in large cities. First, English- or Welsh-owned business proprietors but operating abroad; these are generally excluded from census information and rarely gave employee numbers if they were large employers so that any distortion is insignificant. Second, there are foreign-based proprietors who were recorded in the census because they were visiting England or Wales at the time. These are almost always recorded as visitors in a private house, or boarders if in hotels. Unfortunately, a foreign visitor cannot usually be distinguished from a visitor from another part of the UK. Their foreign birth may be indicative, but a foreign-born visitor may equally be a UK resident away from home on census night; indeed, this occurs for some well-known entrepreneurs in the census. The effect of foreign visitors on calculations of total business numbers will to some extent be netted out by those from the UK who were aboard on census night; but the balance may differ between sectors. This can be controlled through their recorded status as boarders and visitors. Third, there are English- and Welsh-based directors of foreign-based companies, which have been identified as far as possible using data enrichment.

Boundary changes

Each individual in the I-CeM is coded to parish of residence. Above the parishes were RSDs, Registration District (RDs), Counties and then Divisions (a regional level; 11 for England and Wales). Unfortunately, many of the boundaries of these units changed over time, especially in the 1890s as administrative changes responded to increasing urbanisation. This makes some comparisons difficult. We use the original boundaries for each year in many cases, especially for RSDs. But where precise comparisons are essential over time we also use 'continuous parishes'. These are based on Wrigley's (2011) method, as implemented by Satchell et al. as listed in the data acknowledgements. It amalgamates parishes to their smallest possible later common boundaries parishes where boundaries have changed. This reduces the total number of parishes but allows consistent geographical comparison over time. There are two formats of the continuous parishes available: for 1851–91 and for 1851–1911. Because the later series involves many more large-scale aggregations the main continuous parishes used in this volume are for 1851–81. The RSDs are not continuous so that mapped units differ by census year, though the differences are usually small.

Urban areas

We use a set of urban definitions derived from Law (1967) and Robson (1973). This is based on aggregating the parishes that constituted the largest towns of

10,000 population and over in each census year. This allows larger urban places to be distinguished from rural areas, as well as classifying other areas that have a mixture of rural areas and small towns (of 2,500–9,999 population) which we term 'transitional' (see WP 6). The rural distinction was set at RSD population densities below 0.3 persons per acre.

3.4   Corporations and company directors

The census extractions and reconstruction yield a database of mainly non-corporate businesses which it is believed to be nearly complete. However, this provides very little information on limited companies and their directors. For these, different sources have to be used.

First it is necessary to decide where the entrepreneurial responsibility in an incorporated business rests. This issue has led to a wide literature that takes various positions about the different roles of shareholders, other investors and lenders, directors, and managers as the main decisions makers (Chandler, 1990; Hannah, 2007; Cheffins, 2008; Foreman-Peck and Hannah, 2012; Campbell and Turner, 2011; Acheson et al., 2015). We want to focus on equivalent definitions for corporate as for non-corporate businesses. For non-corporates we identify business proprietors as those who were currently the responsible individuals bearing the risks of running the enterprise. Whilst shareholders, lenders and managers all bear risks, legally it is the directors who are the main decisions makers and who bear the direct responsibility for strategic business decisions. Directors are particularly relevant in the period 1851–1911 where most domestic corporations were relatively small, and many were held as de facto private companies where the main shareholders and directors were the same people. However, there were an increasing number of large and complex businesses where director control was delegated to managers. These were major employers, and included important businesses, such as the railway companies, major shipbuilders, steelworks, chemical production, tobacco production and breweries (Hannah, 1983). But these were still numerically a small proportion of the corporate sector. Hence the focus on directors is a justifiable way to identify the overwhelming majority of corporate decision makers using big data with a uniform definition; more sophisticated approaches could be developed with detailed information on individual companies.

The information used to identify directors is taken from the census itself, where many individuals self-identified as director, and from the *Directory of Directors*. This was first published in 1879 and then appeared annually. Because the *Directory* appeared early each year with a late addendum, it was essentially a record of the directors for the previous year. Hence, for alignment with the census undertaken in March-April, the following year is taken as the best comparison, omitting the addendum; that is, 1882 used for 1881. The number of directors identified from each source is shown in Table 3.2.

The *Directory* information was keyed and then coded by director type and company type (WP 14). Company type was coded to industry sector as far as

Table 3.2 Directors identified for each census year in England and Wales and their record-linkage to the census

Census year	1881	1891	1901	1911
N. of directors in *Directory* database	7,243	10,473	15,415	18,010
N. linked with census	2,704	3,348	5,107	7,041
% linked	37	32	33	39
N. of directors identified in census not linked in *Directory*	218	698	2,268	6,990
Total director sample linked to census	2,922	4,046	7,375	14,031

Source: BBCE database.

possible consistent with the sector codes used for non-corporates (see below); however, utilities were extracted from manufactures and coded separately to give an additional sector for director analysis, not used in other parts of this book. Coding to location of the main business activity aimed to identify those whose business was mainly based in England and Wales; some were multinational, and some remain unknown. Information on the names of companies, addresses in the *Directory of Directors* and additional information in the *Stock Exchange Year Book (Official Intelligence)* and Whitaker's *Red Book of Commerce* were used for this coding (WP 14).

As far as possible directors were searched in the census and the records linked. Linkages were usually most successful where a full address was available for the director. However, addresses for directors were often unsatisfactory, giving only a business address, which would not usually link easily with the census, or giving an address for a whole town (e.g. just 'Nottingham'). The search strategy for data matching was an algorithmic match on location, initial and variations of surname in order to cast a wide net and then manually narrowed based on address and exact first name and surname. Directors were ranked on a declining scale of match confidence: the top-ranking matches provided either an exact match on first name, surname, and census street address or first initial, surname, and 'director' in the census occupation. The second-tier matches were as above, but with two people of the same name living at the same address. Third- and fourth-tier matches did not match the exact street address, usually as it was not available in the directory, but were still positively identifiable by exact name and location (city if urban, county if not), matching census occupation to a director's title or occupation (MP, J.P., colonel, etc.), an unusual name, or a matching middle name. Third-tier matches were identified within this sample based on at least three criteria; fourth on fewer, but were still deemed accurate matches. The majority of matches were either tier 1 or 3. Directors who were included in the *Directory* under their title, such as Lord Grosvenor, were matched manually as the census recorded them under their given names. Finally, a reverse match was made of all people identified in their census occupation as a director to the remainder of the *Directory*.

As shown in Table 3.2, overall data matching allowed 18,203 directors to be linked with their census entries (35.5 percent linkage rate, reasonably uniform across years). A further 10,171 directors were identified in the census who were not in the *Directory* (although these can rarely be linked with company information). Whilst later publications use all directors, this book uses only those with census identifiers (the bottom row in Table 3.2); these are included in the BBCE data deposit; hence we refer to the data as mainly non–corporate.

3.5   Aggregation of occupations

Our analysis is undertaken at various levels of aggregation. In many cases we are concerned with individual business sectors or occupations. I–CeM's occode provides 797 categories for such close analysis. But it is often useful to aggregate these to see the wider picture. Aggregation is also more robust because it is less likely to be distorted by misunderstandings from census respondents or confused in I–CeM coding.

As noted earlier the census gathered information on occupations, which defined the nature of the work done, but for business analysis we are often more interested in the industry sectors, namely the type of business such work was done for, including the distinction between working on own account, employing others and working for others. A major aim of aggregations was to attempt to group occupations into similar sectors of like groups of related activities, and like groups of organisational structure (employers, own account or workers). Two aggregations are used throughout the following chapters. These aggregations cover the entire economically active population and are defined at two levels: EA17 for 17 groups of occodes and EA51 for 51 groups of occodes (Tables 3.3 and 3.4). These are based loosely on the approach to census coding developed by Booth (1886) and Armstrong (1972), discussed and defined more fully in WP 5. Because the last four sectors of EA17, and the last seven of EA51 are non–entrepreneurs, we often used the reduced set of EA13 and EA44 sectors in subsequent chapters. In addition, numerous incorporated utilities led us to code this as a separate category for the analysis of directors as EA18. The aggregation to sectors is aided by the fact that many of the census categories 1851–1911, although referred to as occupations, were more accurately industries. Indeed the 1921 census, which instituted a more thorough industrial coding, noted that 'the classifications used in 1911 and earlier were only in part occupational, . . . in a large proportion of cases the distinction was industrial rather than occupational'.[11] However, we have tried to re-code to an industrial attribution.

It is recognised that all aggregations gain and lose information and that, for the period covered, the census occupational descriptors only imperfectly map to industries. Occupations also make very imperfect distinctions between 'makers' and 'dealers'. EA17 and EA51 keep makers and dealers together where they cannot be easily separated over the entire 1851–1911 period; this has significant benefits for the alignment of reconstructed numbers. But it is accepted that

Table 3.3 Aggregate industrial sector groups: entrepreneurship classification of economically active for EA17 sector classification

Aggregate EA17	Summary title
1	Farming, other agriculture and fishing (including farming labourers and family workers)
2	Mining and quarrying
3	Construction
4	Manufacturing (including utilities)
5	Makers and dealers
6	Retail and ironmongers
7	Transport
8	Professional and business services
9	Personal services
10	Agricultural produce, drink and tobacco manufacturing
11	Food retailing
12	Lodging and refreshment
13	Finance and commerce
14*	*Public administration, military, clergy*
15*	*Domestic and service staff*
16*	*Undefined general labourers*
17*	*Persons of property with no stated occupation*
[18]	[Utilities] – used only for analysis of directors

Source: BBCE database.

* Note that groups 14–17 contain only workers (if there were entrepreneurial services or other staff in the related I-CeM categories, they were corrected to the other categories).

Table 3.4 Detailed industrial sector groups: entrepreneurship classification of economically active for EA51 sector classification

Aggregate EA51	Summary of census occupation descriptors
1	Farming, fishing, market gardeners, horse breeding and keeping
2	Coal mining
3	Other mining and quarrying, brickmaking, gravel, salt works
4	Construction operatives (masons, bricklayers, thatcher, plumbers etc.)
5	Machinery manufacturing
6	Tool and weapons manufacturing
7	Iron and steel manufacturing, bolts and nails
8	Blacksmiths
9	Other metal manufacturing (copper, tin, brass, whitesmiths, etc.)
10	Ship, road and rail vehicle manufacturing
11	Earthenware and glass manufacturing

Aggregate EA51	Summary of census occupation descriptors
12	Gas, coke, water and chemical manufacturing
13	Leather, fur, hair and bone manufacturing
14	Wood manufacturing (sawyers, coopers, cane workers)
15	Furnishing manufacturing (cabinet makers, French polishers, undertakers)
16	Printing and paper manufacturing (paper, cardboard, printers, bookbinders)
17	Waterproof goods manufacturing (floor and oil cloth, rubber etc.)
18	Woollen manufacturing (woollen goods, carpets, blanket, flannel)
19	Cotton and silk manufacturing (including ribbon, weaving, dyeing, bleaching etc.)
20	Other textile manufacturing (flax, hemp, rope, jute, lace, tape, thread)
21	Clothing manufacturing (tailors, milliners, hosiery, hats, gloves, umbrellas, buttons, leather)
22	Shoe, boot, clog manufacturing
23	Agric. produce manufacturing (millers, refiners, bakers, confectioners)
24	Drink and tobacco manufacturing (maltsters, brewers, distillers, tobacco and pipes)
25	Watch and instrument manufacturing
26	General manufacturing (manufacturers, mechanic, artisan, machinist)
27	Ocean, inland and dock transport
28	Road and rail transport
29	Coal dealing
30	Timber, hay, corn and agricultural produce dealing
31	Clothing and dress dealing (drapers, hosiers, haberdashers)
32	Food sales (butchers, fishmongers, cheese mongers, milk sellers, grocers)
33	Lodging and drink sales (wine and spirits, hotels, inns, coffee houses)
34	Communications (publishing, newsagents, stationers and telecoms)
35	Household and personal goods dealer (earthenware, glass, jewellers)
36	Ironmongers
37	Other retail (general shopkeeper, huckster, hawker)
38	Chemists, druggists
39	Merchants, banks, insurers and brokers
40	Other commerce (accountants, salesmen, travellers, officers of cos.)
41	Construction management (builders and contractors)
42	Professions (barristers, solicitors, scientific pursuits)
43	Professions (doctors, dentists, artists, performers, education)
44	Personal services (washing and bathing, hairdressing, chimney sweeps)
45*	*Public administration, clergy*
46*	*Military*
47*	*Domestic service*
48*	*Undefined general and factory labourers*
49*	*Factory hand (textile, undefined)*
50*	*Commercial clerks*
51*	*Persons of property with no stated occupation*

Source: BBCE database.

* Note the last seven groups contain only workers.

this is not fully satisfactory; it is however, the best that can be done without significant assumptions about making or dealing that cannot be validated at the individual level from the structure of the original census responses.

3.5   Conclusion

This chapter has described the nature of the data available in the census relating to entrepreneurship, how we have extracted that data, the assumptions made with regards to certain special groups and how the data have been enriched. Throughout the development of the BBCE database we have relied primarily on the employment status information provided by individuals. For 1891–1911 such self-reporting provides information on most entrepreneurs. For 1851–81 self-reporting identifies many employers and a smaller number of own-account masters. These are then supplemented through a reconstruction process which is based on the self-reporting by each individual and adjusted to take account of the data available in 1891–1911. Although imperfect, we have been guided throughout by the responses made by the respondent business proprietors themselves. Different challenges arise with regards to alignment with the later censuses and other data. However, overall, as complete coverage as possible of the whole population of entrepreneurs has been achieved, and hence a surrogate business census has been constructed.

The remainder of this book uses these data to answer a series of questions about the characteristics and behaviours of these entrepreneurs. In doing so it rests on the assumptions outlined in this chapter; however, it is also possible to control for and check most assumptions in the analysis that follows. These data represent the largest and most complete database available for the study of historical entrepreneurship, and what follows illustrates both the new insights obtained regarding the history of business in England and Wales and the possibilities created by the use of big data.

Notes

1 'General Instruction', Census of England and Wales, *Householder's Schedule*, 1881; Parliamentary Papers 1883, No. 43, vol. LXXX, Appendix C.
2 'General Instruction', Census of England and Wales, *Householder's Schedule*, 1901.
3 'General Instruction', Census of England and Wales, *Householder's Schedule*, 1891.
4 The Post Office was a major state employer, with a workforce increasing from 25,192 in 1860 to 46,956 in 1880, 113,541 in 1890, 167,075 in 1900, and 212,310 in 1910. Local postmasters and sub-postmasters were 11 percent of these numbers (Daunton, 1985: 194–5).
5 *Census General Report*, 1921: 86.
6 *Census General Report*, 1951: 127.
7 'General Instruction', Census of England and Wales, Householder's Schedule, 1851; emphasis added.
8 'General Instruction', Census of England and Wales, Householder's Schedule, 1911; emphasis added.

9 Except for women 1901–11, where dropping the explicit instruction to include regular activity resulted in inconsistencies discussed for females below.
10 Numbers calculated from a search of *all* occupational strings in censuses for those declaring 'master' or 'mistress' in their occupation and giving employee numbers; farmers excluded. Also excluding 'spurious' masters/mistresses such as station master, postmaster, drill master, paymaster, etc.
11 *Census of England and Wales, 1921, General report with appendices, Parliamentary Papers* (1927), 86.

Part 2
Overview of trends

4 Proprietor numbers, aggregate trends and sector change

4.1 Introduction

The big data extraction process from the census described in Chapter 3 allows new insights into changes of business enterprise over time. In Part 2 of this book we investigate the trends at the aggregate level (Chapters 4 and 5), and then in Part 3 at the individual level. This chapter assesses trends in entrepreneur numbers and rates of entrepreneurship as proportions of the economically active population. Sections 4.2–4.3 of the chapter show how detailed estimates can be constructed for all individuals 1851–1911, with Section 4.4 summarising the trends by sector. Section 4.5 extends the assessment to the censuses of 1921–2011. Section 4.6 compares these trends with modern estimates of the small business population dating from the 1980s up to 2017. This chapter is mainly for *non-corporate activity*; it does not cover corporate developments, which are discussed in Chapter 5. It is also restricted to England and Wales.

A key outcome from the new material developed in this chapter is the ability for the first time to assess claims about the evolution of small business numbers and entrepreneurship; for example, the claims that entrepreneurship is higher now than in previous history, or that there is a U-shaped distribution over time – with declines in small business and self-employment numbers over the mid-twentieth century being reversed by recent growth. In Britain the declining limb of the U-shape was first noted by Clark (1957), and demonstrated more fully by Bannock (1989) and later modern estimates. The U-shape has become something of an official position to support the government's statistical series that suggests that small business numbers have recently rapidly increased. The concept of a U-shape has been given wider currency by Wennekers, who extended and updated Clark's cross-sectional comparisons between countries to infer a relationship between entrepreneurship and level of economic development across countries and over time (e.g. Wennekers et al., 2010). This chapter gives insight into where these twentieth-century trends originated. There has been a tendency to assume that the position in the early twentieth century continued backwards; that is, there had been a permanently higher rate of entrepreneurship up to c. 1911 and then a steep decline (a 'plateau with cliff') before later recovery, or that there had been a steady decline up to World War I that continued until mid-century before reversing (a reverse L-shape, as claimed by Caree et al., 2007, using international cross-sectional comparisons).

This chapter provides the evidence to assess these claims. It demonstrates that the Victorian period was a 'golden age' for smaller and medium-sized business. But there was a key turning point around 1901, after which economic growth shifted towards increasing concentration in larger businesses up to the mid-twentieth century. The new estimates allow a reappraisal of the extent of modern reversals since the 1980s as the number of small firms and entrepreneurs has increased.

4.2   Estimating business proprietor numbers 1891–1911

The census provides information on entrepreneurs in two different formats: for 1851 it explicitly identifies most employers and some 'masters'; for 1891–1911 it directly provides employment status as employer, own account or worker. As noted in Chapter 3, both sources are imperfect. For the later period the data have to be screened and biases in census design and processing corrected or mitigated. For the earlier period the absence of direct data on most own account and under-recording of some employers requires a substantial process of data 'reconstruction'. Because the reconstruction of the census responses for 1851–81 requires corrected information from 1891–1911, the first stage in estimating entrepreneurship for the whole period is to start with the later censuses.

As noted in Chapter 3, the imperfect 1891–1911 census instructions and administration introduced important constraints that have to be managed when estimating proprietor numbers. All three years suffered from a lack of priority given to this question by census administrators resulting in high levels of non-response bias. As noted by Schürer (1991: 20–26) and Higgs (1988, 2005: 112), the GRO included this question only reluctantly, because of the costs of administration and processing, and because their priority lay in population counting not assessment of the economy. The GRO was forced to add the question because of sustained pressure from the Royal Statistical Society, prominent economists and social statisticians such as Charles Booth and Alfred Marshall and the Treasury (Acland and 45 others, 1888). Eventually it was only included because the Local Government Board insisted.[1] Nevertheless the GRO gave it a low priority in data collection and only published limited results. GRO administration resulted in acceptance of a high level of blank responses by householders to the question over the whole period 1891–1911 which were biased by gender, position in household, age and other factors (WP 4). Consequently, a means to correct for non-response bias is required.

In addition, the 1891 census suffered from six further defects that are unique to the instructions for that year. First, the terminology of 'Employer' and 'Employed' were so similar that it was easily misread, and resulted in a tendency to cross the wrong column; this over-recorded employers in that year. Recognising this, the GRO in 1901 replaced the term 'employed' with 'worker' and replaced columns by free text. Second, the definition of 'own account' (quoted in

Chapter 3) was confusing, long-winded and negatively phrased, making it easy to misread as defining employers as working on their own account. Third, many respondents could have read 'master', which the instructions regarded as synonymous with 'employer', to indicate that own account should cross 'employer'. Fourth, the term 'own account' was confused by many respondents to mean living on 'own means'. Fifth, the question may have encouraged respondents to inflate their importance by falsely returning themselves as employer rather than employed, or employer rather than own account. These defects all resulted in a significant danger of upward bias to misallocate some workers or own account as employers, and some workers as own account. A sixth source of bias was the instruction for wives who were assisting their husbands to be returned as employed; consequently, wives who were business partners or co-preneurs were undercounted.

Some of the defects were recognised in the 1891 census report, which seemed to vindicate the reluctant GRO who claimed the choice of columns crossed was very unreliable, and 'dictated by the foolish but very common desire of persons to magnify the importance of their occupational condition'. As a final riposte to those compelling the use of this question, the GRO stated that 'although . . . we have not considered ourselves justified, after the instructions given to us by the Local Government Board, altogether to discard the statements as to employers and employed from the Census volumes, we hold them to be excessively untrustworthy'.[2]

Although exaggerated, these difficulties cannot be ignored. As a result, an extensive process was undertaken to identify the extent of the misallocation bias between employers, own account and workers in 1891, and compensate for non-response bias in all three years 1891–1911 (summarised in Bennett et al., 2019a). The approach used was to apply to these historical censuses the sort of corrections that modern census administrators would use to make post-survey adjustments. The GRO itself made no attempt statistically to test the validity of its claims, to clean and correct data or even to report actual numbers of potentially biased responses. I-CeM now allows adjustments to be made. Modern published census tables are weighted and adjusted for significant non-response and other biases. Occupational description, which is still normally captured through open-text reporting as in the historic censuses and is our main source of entrepreneurship data, is now understood to be particularly difficult for both respondents and coders (Conrad et al., 2016: 77–80), and is especially complex and uncertain for the own account self-employed and employers in small establishments (Martin et al., 1994: Tables 1 and 2).

The 1891–1901 responses were 'edited' using standard methods of post-response processing adopted in modern surveys and censuses (see Lyberg and Kasprzyk, 1997: 355–8). Since each respondent in 1891–1911 gave two pieces of information (employment status and occupation), the tendency to cross the wrong status column, inflate status or write an incorrect status was adjusted by comparison with the occupational descriptors given. This corrected large numbers of implausible responses to employer status; for example, 'labourers' and 'domestic servants' that crossed 'employer'. Other corrections removed confusion about terminology; for example, recoding respondents 'living on own means', 'annuitant', 'living on investment income' and 'unoccupied' who crossed 'own account'. In addition, excluded from entrepreneurs were all scholars, individuals under the age of 15, all non-economically active, all own means, annuitants and retired, and all individuals whose 'main' occupation was non-business; for example, prisoners, reform school inmates, vagrants, MPs, ministers of the crown and peers, prison officers, police, military and clergy. Third, all definitive worker categories were recoded, such as domestic servants; all types of labourer, farm servants, navvies, civil servants and other government employees, and clerks; and all categories with working titles that defined an employee status, such as apprentices, journeymen, assistants or attendants.

Once the data had been cleaned, non-responses were reduced substantially, to 4.6 percent, 4.8 percent and 5.3 percent, respectively, for 1891, 1901 and 1911. However, the remaining non-respondents were not random and were particularly high for female relatives who were not heads, and in some sectors. The standard modern practice to deal with non-response bias is to estimate weights which can be used to adjust actual response numbers or proportions (Kish, 1967). The weights used here were derived from a logit regression which estimated the probability of whether an individual responded to the employment status question or not, derived from the degree to which non-response was related to gender, relationship within household and occupational sector.[3] To facilitate use by other researchers the full set of weights is available and should be used in conjunction with the database deposit.[4] The weighted estimates for 1901–11 increased estimated employer and own-account numbers by 7–13 percent; worker numbers also increased, resulting in the estimated total economically active being 5 percent higher in 1901 and 6 percent higher in 1911 than previous estimates (Bennett et al., 2019a: Table 3).

For 1891 a different approach had to be adopted because of the non-response being mixed with misallocation biases. For this a comparator source of information is needed to indicate the level of true response. The only sources available on a similar basis are for 1901 and subsequent censuses. The approach adopted used the 1901 census as the main comparator, supplemented with any trends from 1911 for each occupation category for each of the 629 of the 797 occupation categories in I-CeM that contained employers or own account. Secondary material was used to check these trends. Four methods were used, as discussed in Bennett et al. (2019a). The preferred method was to use the actual censuses responses, where it was believed responses were accurate. The second preference was a robust logit regression model based on 1901 census responses to re-allocate between employer and own account, taking account of the most significant explanatory variables for employer status in 1901. The regression method was compared with two further methods: simple linear extrapolation from 1901, and an average of the ratios between employers and own account for 1901 and 1911. In the final choice, of the 629 occupation categories with entrepreneurs, 186 were accepted as giving accurate census responses, 430 were corrected using the logit regression method, 11 used linear extrapolation, and 2 had such fractionally low estimates of potential employers that they were assigned wholly to own account. None used the average ratio. The final estimates reassigned 132,000 individuals from employer to own account to correct for misallocation biases in 1891. A further 43,000 were identified as employers in 1891 after accounting for non-response bias. Hence most corrections for 1891 derived from rectifying misallocation bias, followed by the data cleaning stages, and then non-response bias re-weighting, whereas for 1901 and 1911 data cleaning and weighting for non-response bias were more equal in effect.

4.3   Estimating business proprietor numbers 1851–81

For the earlier censuses we have to identify employers and own account by a 'reconstruction' process. The early censuses did identify many as 'employers' and 'masters', but this was only partial for most occupations, and there was no explicit identification of 'own account' or distinction from other statuses such as worker, unoccupied, etc.

The reconstruction method used follows a series of stages: (i) data preparation and cleaning; (ii) logit regression estimator for combined employers and own account using coefficients from 1891 applied to the earlier censuses; (iii) validation against the 1891 census and inspection of residuals; (iv) comparison with multinomial logit estimator of separated employers and own account; (v) estimates of reconstruction and comparisons with census extractions of 'employers' and 'masters'; (vi) final choice of reconstruction method to give reconstructed aggregate numbers; (vii) assignment of individuals to employment status as entrepreneurs or workers; and (viii) assignment of entrepreneurs as employers or own account. The details of this process are discussed at length in WP 9. Here we summarise the main elements.

There are two critical starting points. First, the known information that identifies employment status for 1891, after correction and adjustment, provides a guide to what should have been recorded in the earlier censuses. Second, the partial information that is available from the earlier censuses, once extracted, should correctly indicate many correct status responses. The process by which the early census employers and masters were extracted is described in Chapter 3. These extractions can be classified into six groups, defined from the occupational descriptor strings given and the way they were extracted:

> **Group 1:** *all employers and any others (such as masters, proprietors or owners) with stated employees;* farmers with stated employees; partners with stated employees; and the small numbers of farm bailiffs stating employees and any retired who state employees (used as surrogates for proprietors).
>
> **Group 2:** *all stating 'employer' with no employees;* 'masters' or anyone else who includes 'emp' in their occupation descriptor; and partners without stated employees.
>
> **Group 3:** *master etc.;* anyone including 'master' in their occupational descriptor but with no employees, excluding spurious 'masters' (see WP 3).

Group 4: *'farmer'* not stating 'emp' or acres.

Group 5: *farmer giving acres* but with no stated employees and having two or more acres of land (those with less than two acres with no employees were excluded; it was assumed that they worked on other farms).

Group 6: *owners or proprietors of business assets;* mine/quarry owner, ship-owner, barge owner and others with any business assets (other than land/housing).

Two additional categories were extracted for further analysis, but not included in the reconstruction:

Group 7: *'owners' with no other information*, including landowners and house proprietors with no employee information and landowners with only acres.

Group 8: *directors;* their companies are employers which are not otherwise identified in the census; however, the majority of individual directors are identified as entrepreneurs. They are included in the director analysis (Chapter 6). They are not explicitly included in reconstruction, but are included in the director analysis (Chapter 6).

No attempt was made to take account of partnership information in reconstruction, if it was given. Partners counted towards total numbers of business proprietors with no attempt to account for their combination in a firm. Also no attempt was made in the reconstruction to extrapolate portfolios; all were taken from the respondent's main occupation, except as part of the reconstruction in farming. These are the same assumptions used for the 1891–1911 processing.

The reconstruction was undertaken separately for each occupational category. I-CeM provides 797 of these, based on the actual GRO census occupational code books. We developed from these 83 additional Sub-occodes to help better identify some employment statuses, giving 880 categories in all. The additional codes were defined for sub-occupational descriptors where the internal variance of individual status was large and it was possible to reliably identify subgroups with clearly defined status as business proprietor. This was undertaken by recoding the occupational descriptor strings to either the new Sub-Occode or to the residual of the original occode. For example, for individuals in occode 473 ('earthenware, china, glass – dealers'), reconstruction was considerably facilitated by splitting it into two Sub-occodes, one with descriptors 'merchants' and 'dealers' that were highly likely to be entrepreneurs (judged by 1891 where 80 percent were proprietors) and a residual of the rest which might contain some proprietors but was majority workers. The Sub-occodes are fully listed in WP 9.

The preferred method for reconstruction was estimation of employment status using a robust logit regression model. This was based on the data contained in the 1891–1901 censuses where employment status was given explicitly. Whilst 1891 is generally to be preferred, as it is closer to the earlier censuses, it has biases noted above which may not be perfectly corrected and a large proportion of non-respondents, so that sometimes 1901 may be a preferred. The logit regression allows a wide range of the most significant explanatory variables for employer status in the later censuses to be used to identify employers in the earlier census. These logit was determined after a range of experiments with alternatives and tested to confirm it was a good and unbiased estimator for the 1891 and 1901 years themselves (see WP 9). The estimation was in two stages: first, for all employers and own account together; second, for employers only. After estimation with the 1891 and 1901 data, the model's coefficients were applied to the 1881 and earlier years to calculate the probability of being an employer.

In addition to the logit method, three other estimators were tested: (i) entrepreneurship ratios for 1891; other things being equal these will stay relatively constant in many occupational categories between censuses, especially where there is 'organic growth'; (ii) entrepreneurship ratios for 1901, preferred where the 1891 data may give less accurate measures of entrepreneurs; (iii) choices from extraction groups, accepting the actual census responses, preferred where the extractions of employers and own account are thought to be complete for all individuals, where the occupational category is clear and unambiguous and respondents are believed to have been accurate (e.g. for Sub-occodes in mining and quarrying). These three methods provide valuable baselines for comparison. A good reconstruction should be able to predict accurately the actual extracted employers and own account, even if these are not complete in including all employers and own account. Similarly, where organic growth occurred, the entrepreneurship ratios for either 1891 or 1901 should offer accurate estimators. In addition, all reconstruction estimates were compared where possible against trade directory and secondary sources to establish that the specific numbers reconstructed and any trends could be independently validated.

Each of the 880 Sub-occodes had estimates of identified employers from each of the reconstruction methods. Decisions between the methods finally adopted were based on rules that compared the variance between entrepreneurship ratios and actual extraction groups with the logit estimators. All Group 1 were accepted. For farmers an additional method was used based solely on the extraction groups. All Group 1 were accepted as definite actual employers; Group 2, which is small, was assumed to be own account since they contain an 'emp' descriptor but none list employees. Group 5 were assumed all to be farm proprietors, but their acreages were used to separate employers from own account using estimates discussed in detail in Montebruno et al. (2019a). It uses a logistic regression to assign between employer and own account for each of 630 Registration Districts separately. In the final choice of reconstruction methods for 1881, 50 percent of sub-occupation categories derived from the 1891 logistic regression, 30 percent from the 1901 regression, 13 percent from the baseline 1891 ratio, 2 percent from the baseline 1901 ratio and 5 percent were accepted responses using the extraction groups (including farmers and mining) (see WP 9). Similar proportions were used for 1851 and 1861.

4.4   Trends 1851–1911

After cleaning and re-weighting the 1891–1911 censuses and reconstructing entrepreneur numbers from the 1851–1881 censuses, we can investigate trends in entrepreneurship over time, except for 1871 where the data are not in I-CeM and the infilled S&N data do not include workers and many own-account categories. This section gives a brief overview of the main trends that are evident. These are subject to more detailed assessment in subsequent chapters.

The main trends 1851–1911 are shown in Figure 4.1. Total entrepreneur numbers as a whole increased steadily over the period, although expansion slowed 1901–11. Within these, employers increased more slowly throughout the period, and most slowly compared to all entrepreneurs between 1851 and 1861, and between 1891 and 1901, suggesting that these were periods in which there was increasing own account and slower development of concentration, two processes which may well have been connected in some sectors, notably farming. After 1901 the trends show a major reversal: own account fell absolutely and employer numbers began to increase more rapidly, resulting in the total for all entrepreneurs showing a marked slowdown in rate of growth. It is this point which we take as the turning point for the end of the Victorian 'age of entrepreneurship'. It shows a profound re-balancing after 1901 between the smallest sole proprietors with no employees in favour of those employing others. When compared with the evolution of workforce numbers (also shown in Figure 4.1) the total of all entrepreneurs tracked a similar but slower trajectory 1851–91, but after 1891 workforces increased much more rapidly than entrepreneurs, and the rates diverged after 1901. This exhibits the shift to larger firm sizes and the narrowing of scope for the individual own-account proprietor.

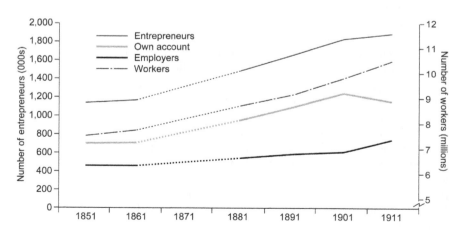

Figure 4.1 Reconstructed total numbers of own account, employers and all entrepreneurs, 1851–1911

Source: BBCE database.

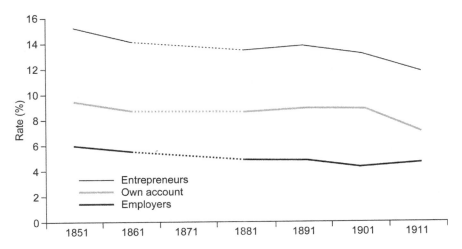

Figure 4.2 Entrepreneurship rates: total numbers of own account, employers and all entrepreneurs as percentage of all economically active, 1851–1911

Source: BBCE database.

When converted to rates, as shown in Figure 4.2, the pattern is somewhat different. The rates compare entrepreneurs to the total economically active; thus balancing the comparisons against workers in Figure 4.1. They combine changes in entrepreneurial participation and the size of the population. The economically active are calculated from the total of all those in employment for all EA17 categories, including all non-entrepreneur categories and domestic staff. The period saw a rapidly and steadily rising total population and economically active population. Demand for waged labour grew rapidly, absorbing population growth by employing people in larger factories, utilities, coal mines and transport undertakings, as discussed later. In consequence, the general rate of entrepreneurship declined across the period, steeply 1851–61, and steeply again after 1901, but with a small upturn for 1891. Viewed in terms of the type of businesses, employers steadily declined as a proportion of the total economically active for the whole period until 1901, after which there was a small increase in proportion reflecting their steeper rise in numbers 1901–11 (Figure 4.1). Own-account entrepreneurship rates, after a decline 1851–61, rose slowly over 1861–1891,[5] before falling sharply 1901–11. This was the fastest rate of change for any period or group. In relative terms there was a growing shift in the proportion of entrepreneurs towards employers (and also to corporate employers, as discussed in Chapter 5), whilst the overall rate of entrepreneurship was declining after 1891. The turning point of 1901 was, therefore, especially a turn in the fortunes of the own-account proprietor employing no one else.

The actual data for these figures are summarised in Table 4.1. At the foot of each section of the table the additional employers of domestic staff are included;

Table 4.1 Entrepreneur numbers and rates of entrepreneurship, 1851–1911

Numbers	1851	1861	1881	1891	1901	1911
All Entrepreneurs	1,151,341	1,163,966	1,489,267	1,657,094	1,829,536	1,879,445
Employers	460,744	454,658	535,810	584,258	593,111	741,718
Own account	690,597	709,308	953,457	1,072,837	1,236,425	1,137,727
Economically active	7,465,035	8,094,614	10,836,178	11,989,894	13,812,822	15,879,799
Employers of domestic staff	591,050	596,438	686,957	740,850	752,112	757,383
Rates/economically active (percent)						
All entrepreneurs	15.4	14.4	13.7	13.8	13.2	11.8
Employers	6.2	5.6	4.9	4.9	4.3	4.7
Own account	9.3	8.8	8.8	8.9	9.0	7.2
+ Employers of domestic staff	23.3	21.7	20.1	20.0	18.7	16.6
Rates/population (percent)						
All entrepreneurs	6.4	5.9	5.7	5.7	5.6	5.2
Employers	2.5	2.3	2.1	2.0	1.8	2.1
Own account	3.9	3.6	3.7	3.7	3.8	3.1
+ Employers of domestic staff	9.7	8.9	8.4	8.3	7.9	7.3

Source: BBCE database.

Note: non-corporate activity mainly; all numbers are approximate although shown as actual counts; employers of domestic staff are shown separately; 1871 not available.

these are *excluded* as entrepreneurs in the rest of our analysis but shown here for comparative purposes with some modern data, as discussed below (Section 4.6).[6] The table also includes rates calculated as a percentage of the total population, which is a commonly used index in international comparisons (such as GEM, World Bank and UN statistics). It is less satisfactory since it is biased by changes in birth rates that affect the younger age cohorts that are not yet contributing to the economically active, as well as changes in death rates and changing forms of retirement behaviour. It is included for comparative purposes, but we normally use rates relative to the economically active as the more reliable index of activity. Compared to modern entrepreneurship rates in different countries, the Victorian period was high on all indicators, but especially for the rate of employer activity. Note also that the table is mainly for non-corporate entrepreneurship; full inclusion of company directors and company businesses would increase entrepreneurship rates a little further.

Entrepreneurship trends differed by industry sector. For the total number of entrepreneurs for the 13 categories within EA17 that contain entrepreneurs (see Table 3.3), the trends are shown in Figure 4.3. This enlarges substantially on earlier understanding (e.g. Broadberry, 2014; Broadberry et al., 2010) and shows important sector contrasts within the general steady increase of numbers across the

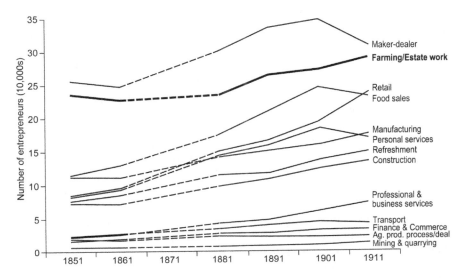

Figure 4.3 Total entrepreneur numbers, 1851–1911, for 13 aggregate business sectors

Source: BBCE database.

period. Maker–dealers were the largest group throughout this period, and by the later censuses the gap in size between those businesses and others was substantial up to 1901. But after 1901 they experienced the most marked downturn at the end of the growth period. They were experiencing competition from two directions, reflecting their hybrid status across areas of manufacturing and retail, from metal working to the very substantial numbers involved in the production of clothing. Manufacturing was experiencing considerable consolidation into larger firms as a result of increasing mechanisation of some processes requiring greater capital investment. Retail was also beginning to see expansion of the multiple stores and large operations with branches across the country. Although the sectors were not declining in total employment, the number of independent proprietors was under challenge, especially the smallest business proprietors. Similar trends also occurred in agricultural-food processing and personal services, though they were less marked than for maker–dealers. A very small contraction in proprietor numbers also affected transport. These sectors were all subject to increasing consolidation into larger businesses, with the personal services sector also showing impacts from the increasing activity of charitable, municipal and state sectors. These were expanding into large-scale provision in hospitals, state schools and other sectors that absorbed or displaced a previously buoyant area for entrepreneurship as private nursing, medical practitioners and private schools' proprietorships, which had been particularly important fields for female businesses.

In farming and the rest of agriculture the trends were more mixed. Although farm labour had been steadily declining over the century, especially after the agricultural depression in 1873, the number of independent proprietors tended to grow. New machinery made it possible to manage the land with a smaller number of labourers or as a sole proprietor with no employees. In addition, rural–urban migration and rising agricultural wages made working with fewer or no employees increasingly attractive to farmers. This was reflected in the slow growth in the number of farming proprietors throughout the period.

Retail was the most rapidly growing sector in terms of proprietor numbers across the whole period. Construction proprietor numbers also grew rapidly and consistently across the period. Professional and business services, refreshments and finance and commerce also saw continuous growth. Other sectors had more uneven profiles. For example, manufacturing had declined 1851–61, but then grew rapidly before slowing down over 1891–1901, after which the sector again expanded. Mining had very little change in proprietor numbers until after 1891.

Figure 4.4 shows the development of employer numbers for the 13 aggregate sectors (own-account development, being far more numerous, closely follows the aggregate in Figure 4.3 and is not given here). There were important differences in the trends between sectors compared to the aggregate trend for all employers in Figure 4.1. All employer sectors show an upturn in numbers 1901–11, though this is small in many cases.[7] But the downturn in numbers 1891–1901 varied. It was greatest in maker-dealers, farming, refreshment and agriculture processing. But a downturn hardly occurred in most other sectors which experienced either a still-stand, or in retail, construction, transport and food sales, continuous growth, which was particularly rapid in retail. In the earlier period there are other contrasts. Over 1851–61 most sectors grew, especially

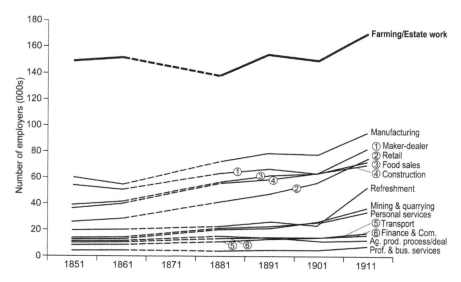

Figure 4.4 Employer numbers for 13 aggregate business sectors 1851–1911
Source: BBCE database.

retail and construction, but maker dealers and manufacturing declined before
increasing through to the 1880s. Farming decreased markedly in the period
before and immediately after the 1873 agricultural depression, but then recovered (though as shown in Chapter 10 this was regionally highly differentiated).

A valuable comparison is provided by entrepreneurship rates. These are shown
in Figures 4.5 and 4.6, respectively, for employers and own account. The rates
are overestimates because a significant part of the economically active in the
three categories EA14–EA17 (see Table 3.3: mainly general labourers) cannot
be assigned to specific sectors. The figures exhibit four important contrasts.
First and primarily, the overall aggregate trend was similar across most sectors:
there was a steady decline in both employer and own-account rates, which for
employers was steep 1851–61, and then slow for the rest of the period; for own
account the decline was slow for most of the period, but then steep 1901–11.
Second, one of the most important aspects is that changes in farming did not
share any of the declines in entrepreneurship rates; rather, farming entrepreneurship increased. For employers, farmers were an exceptional sector. Their rise in
the rate of employer entrepreneurship was a strong contrast to all other sectors.
There was no impact from incorporation in farming for this period. As a result
all changes occur between employers and own account. For the early period
up to 1881, as noted by Montebruno et al. (2019a), there was a switch from
employers to own account, mainly influenced by occasional or unrecorded use
of spouse and family to substitute for hired labour (continuing a trend noted

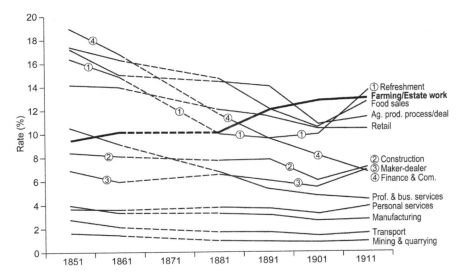

Figure 4.5 Entrepreneurship rates for employers for 13 business sectors. Note these rates
    exclude economically active that cannot be assigned to sectors, such as general
    labourers; hence, they are not quite comparable with Figure 4.2 for the aggregate

Source: author adjustments of published censuses.

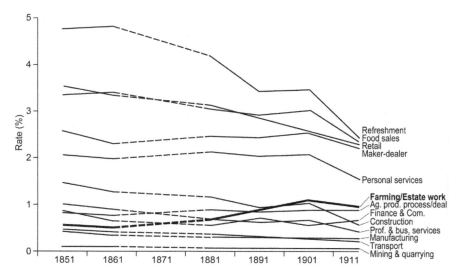

Figure 4.6 Entrepreneurship rates for own account for 13 business sectors

Source: BBCE database.

Note: as Figure 4.5

by Shaw-Taylor, 2012). However, over 1891–1911 the rate of farm employer entrepreneurship grew faster than own account, which experienced a slow rise 1881–1901, and then levelled off. Third, five sectors (food sales, and to a lesser extent agricultural produce, maker-dealers, construction and personal services) have very substantial dips in employer entrepreneurship in 1901. Some of this decline was spurious because of anomalies in the census process that affected how different occupations were recorded, and also possibly small effects of the South African War. However, over the full period 1881–1911 most sectors experienced substantial growth that negated any 1901 declines. Fourth, for own account there were only minor sector contrasts, and these were mainly in the speed of decline rather than their shape. Refreshments and retail, which were closely associated trades, both show the strongest decline. This was the main contrast with employer entrepreneurship rates: the single-person shop or refreshment hostelry was being displaced by larger establishments employing assistants and by national retailers with many branches or large-scale brewery chains for pubs. In an increasing number of these cases such chains were becoming corporate businesses.

A further indicative comparison between sectors can be made against the classification of primary, secondary and tertiary development (PST: see Wrigley, 2006; Shaw-Taylor and Wrigley, 2014). PST is an occupational classification. Here a comparison is made for PST level one, which normally has six sectors, to which we add a seventh by sub-dividing primary into agriculture and mining. The PST evolution of proprietor numbers was similar to earlier figures (and hence not displayed), though more aggregated in the seven PST categories. Rates of PST entrepreneurship also show the same systematic changes for most sectors as our sector comparisons, confirming that the definition of aggregates does not influence the main conclusions to be drawn.

The comparison is shown for the employer entrepreneurship rate in Figure 4.7, which can be compared to Figure 4.5. PST shows the same aggregate trends as the more detailed 13 sectors. However, the more aggregate classification of secondary and tertiary, and rather arbitrary distinctions often necessary between makers and dealers for PST when using census data, mask the rather distinctive evolution evident in Figures 4.5 and 4.6. Nevertheless the trends are similar. However, an important contrast to note is that the trends of entrepreneurship rates using the PST classification differ profoundly from PST trends based on the total occupied population (Shaw-Taylor and Wrigley, 2014). Entrepreneurship changes reflect shifts in numbers of firms rather than workforces, and are an important distinction between the total economically occupied and the businesses that employed them. In all the cases of major declines of rates there was a sharp contrast with their major increase in worker numbers: in all tertiary sectors, and especially in transport and mining. The contrasts reflect increasing average firm size, which became very large in transport, mining and some manufacturing (secondary sectors), as discussed in Chapter 5, and the slow increase in entrepreneurship rates in primary contrasted with its loss of workers.

This review of entrepreneurship trends shows that important insights can be achieved from the reconstructed estimates of the employment status aligned between the 1851–81 early censuses and the later censuses for 1891–1911, where employment status was explicitly identified. This will contain some inaccuracies, but at the aggregate level for 13 sectors the results are robust. The next section extends this up to the present.

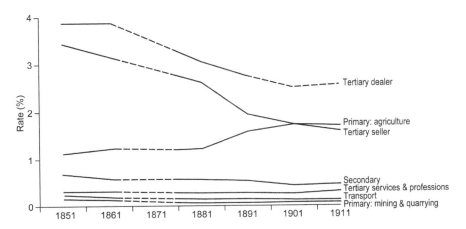

Figure 4.7 Employer rates of entrepreneurship for seven PST sectors

Source: BBCE database.

Note: as Figure 4.5

4.5   Long-term census estimates 1851–2011

This section extends the assessment of trends from the big data based on individuals up to 1911 forwards in time to cover 1921 to 2011 using published census tabulations (and special tabulations for 2011). For this later period no reconstruction of responses is required: from 1921 there is a full coverage, for all sectors, with explicit tables for own-account self-employed with no employees and self-employed who employed others. However, as noted in Chapter 3, the published tabulations require adjustments. Unfortunately published tables were often aggregated, and the aggregations were made in different ways for each census. Not all adjustments are important, particularly for the aggregate of all entrepreneurs, and for the simple differentiation of non-farm and farm, but other sector comparisons are often not possible on a consistent basis. Also to align with the rest of this discussion England and Wales must be identified. The main adjustments made are summarised in Table 4.2.

Table 4.2 Adjustments to census estimates of employers, own account and all economically active, 1921–2011. Note the 1921 adjustments are required because of the postponement of census day to June that year

Year	Adjustment to Employers and Own Account	Adjustment to Economically Active	Primary Method Used to Adjust
1921	Own account adjusted for June census date for seasonal work; employer visitors not adjusted	Exclude June seasonal workers and fruit pickers not recorded in other censuses, and exclude out of work	Reassign estimated June excess lodgings and inn keepers own account to worker; reassign farm to non-farm excess agricultural labourers, and pea and fruit pickers; both mainly female
1931	Exclude managers included with employers	Exclude out of work and part time	Rescale employers, part time and unemployed, using ratios in Chapman and Knight (1953: Table 18), with extra adjustments from 1921
1951		Exclude out of work and part time	All exclusions derived from published tables
1961	Exclude managers from employers; exclude market gardeners from farming where using detailed sectors	Exclude out of work and part time	Market gardens, part time and unemployed from published; managers rescaled using 1951 ratios
1971	Adjust agriculture from GB for E&W		Published tables for GB used to rescale E&W farming
1981	Exclude farm managers; adjust from GB for E&W		Ratios from managers in GB used to rescale E&W
1991	Exclude part time; adjust agriculture from GB for E&W	Exclude students and part time	Students in published; part time rescaled using 2001 ratios; farming scaled using 1981 E&W
2001	Adjust agriculture from GB for E&W		Farming scaled from mean ratios 1991–2011 for E&W
2011	Exclude part time	Exclude part time	Special tabulations from ONS

Source: author adjustments of published censuses.

Using these adjustments the development of entrepreneurship for the later period can be assessed, as well as extended over the whole period 1851–2011. However, it is important to be aware that the census process changed over time so exact comparability cannot be achieved. Most potentially contentious is the alignment of the censuses to full-time activity. We cannot be sure that part-time activity was excluded from the 1851–1911 censuses: undoubtedly some was included. However, we believe this was likely to be a small proportion because of the embedded concept noted in Chapter 3 that occupations were those that were 'regular' or 'main'. We also take a point of view that for many entrepreneurs their earnings-equivalent could be significant, even if the activity was not full time, including some 'marginal' or female occupations such as lodgings, refreshments and home manufactures (cf. Davidoff, 1995). But most seasonal work was excluded over 1851–1911 because of the census date. The inclusion of those that were inactive through retirement is controlled in our analysis because we calculate trends only on those aged 65 and under. The exclusion of seasonal work and the relatively limited inclusion of part-time activity make the alignment of later censuses to a full-time definition important, as summarised in Table 4.2.

With these caveats in mind, the long-term trends are shown in Figure 4.8. This exhibits a steady increase in entrepreneurship numbers up to 1911 followed by a decline up to 1951 and a subsequent increase in entrepreneurship, accelerating after 1981. The figure also indicates that the shifts between employers and own account over most of the period were relatively slow, but occur in four episodes. First, over 1881–1901 own account increased at a much higher rate than for employers, but over 1901–21 then declined steeply, initially ahead of employer numbers, but then followed by employers. This was associated with the build-up of business consolidation pre–World War I and the aftermath of war, which took so many from the labour force and stimulated large-scale industrial concentration

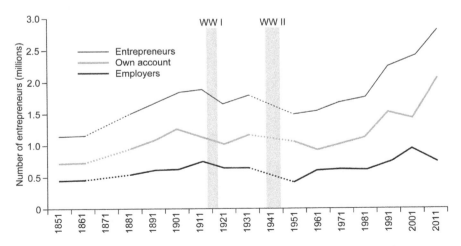

Figure 4.8 Entrepreneurship numbers of own account, employers and all entrepreneurs 1851–2011

Source: BBCE database and author adjustment of published censuses.

as a government policy. Second, over 1921–31 own account increased rapidly when employers continued to decline. This probably reflected necessity entrepreneurship during the depression. Third, over 1931–61 own account then declined, but at a slower rate than employers. Fourth, after 1951 employer numbers picked up quickly, but from 1961 own account again expanded more quickly, and this continued up to 2011 except for 1991–2001. The 1940s and 1950s reflected World War II and its aftermath, where again industrial concentration was encouraged. Employer numbers also expanded over the whole period 1951–2001, but since then have declined sharply. For the recent period, the 1991 census coincided with a deep recession which marked a setback for own account but which affected employers less; however, employer numbers registered a major setback after the onset of another deep recession in 2008. The general trends from the 1930s align with those found by Bannock (1989) for a U-shaped pattern, though we now have insight into the earlier period. The small reduction in employers in 1981, and large reductions for own account in 2001 and employers in 2011, accord with other estimates from the LFS for full-time and result from recessions in these periods (Tatomir, 2015: Chart 3).

The evolution of the entrepreneurship *rate* (Figure 4.9), as a proportion of the economically active 1951–2011, shows a U-shape over the whole 1901–91 period. But the longer-term picture is more complex, one of a slowly declining rate of entrepreneurship over the period from 1851 until 1881, a relatively short reversal 1891–1901, before an even steeper decline up to 1951/61. Over 1961–91 the pattern reversed, with a sharp increase in entrepreneurship, followed by a decline since 2001.

Rates, therefore, show a much more complex evolution than a U-shape, which seems to be relevant only for the mid-twentieth century. As noted earlier (Figure 4.2)

Figure 4.9 Entrepreneurship rates: total numbers of own account, employers and all entrepreneurs as percentage of all economically active 1851–2011

Source: BBCE database and author adjustment of published censuses.

the employer entrepreneurship rate slowly and steadily declined as a proportion of the total economically active after 1851 (except for a small upturn in 1911); now we can see it steepened its decline up to 1951. Own-account entrepreneurship rates were more responsive to short-term economic fluctuations. After a decline over 1851–81, own account increased over 1881–1901, before falling even more sharply than employer rates until 1961, before following the employer upturn that had started in 1951. The turning point of 1901 recognised in the earlier discussion was thus even more dramatic when viewed across the longer period. The rates of total entrepreneurship approximately halved from the 1901 peak by 1951–61. This was especially the turning point in the fortunes of the sole proprietor employing no one else, but employer entrepreneurship also experienced steep decline until 1951.

Moreover, despite recent claims, the modern period is not especially highly entrepreneurial, it merely has a larger population. Within the growing population, since the 1960s the proportion that is waged has continued to grow. But at the same time own account has expanded rapidly at the expense of employers. More people are therefore being employed by fewer employers. Hence, our recognition of the Victorian period as the age of entrepreneurship can be interpreted in two different ways: a peaking in numbers with an expanding population on the eve of World War I, or as a peak of entrepreneurship participation rates in the 1850s or earlier, partially revived in 1891–1901, but then declining steeply.

4.6   Comparisons with modern estimates of the business population

Census data are only one source of long-term comparisons. Another is modern small firm statistics. Whilst the early data on businesses are meagre, those for later in the twentieth century only slowly became better. As Storey (1994: 16, 21) commented, until the late 1980s there was an 'absence of any single comprehensive data base covering all firms in the UK economy' and 'our ability to specify their precise numbers remains weak'. This undermined most attempts to construct reliable counts of business by size. Bannock (1989) made the first attempt to provide a modern comprehensive count, primarily based on firms registered for VAT and estimates of self-employed in the Labour Force Survey (LFS). Bannock's series was published by government departments as *Small Business Statistics* for 1980, 1984 and 1987. This was adapted as *SME Statistics (SMES)* over 1989–2009 (DE, 1991; DTI, 2009). Bannock's method has been built upon by subsequent government official estimates, expanded to cover the income tax records of the self-employed as well as VAT using the Interdepartmental Business Register (IDBR), culminating in the *Business Population Estimates (BPE)* initiated in 2010. The current time series for *BPE* have been put on a fully consistent detailed basis only from 2012, with retrospective estimates back to 2000 solely for *aggregate* numbers (BIS, 2014; DBEIS, 2017).

All these modern estimates have important features in common: (i) they are acknowledged as estimates; (ii) they are based primarily on the formal HMRC tax records of firms using VAT, PAYE and self-employed tax self-assessment which give a good estimate of the total number of firms, but are enhanced by use of the LFS to estimate numbers of self-employed; (iii) the basic unit is the enterprise (company, sole trader or partnership) which includes separate units and subsidiaries which are aggregated for VAT or PAYE purposes, but units with greater autonomy counted separately; (iv) they all use a form of what Bannock (1989) called a 'matrix approach' to obtain estimates of the numbers of firms by size of employment and turnover; this uses scaling from other sources to translate VAT turnover data into employment data for small enterprises and to estimate the different numbers of sole traders and partnerships; and (v) estimates of private-sector businesses exclude all central and local government activity, but include public corporations and nationalised industries and some health care trusts and further education colleges for some later years. The estimates attempt to take account of most definitional changes in VAT thresholds, self-employment regulations and SIC sector classification, but ignore the scale and form of the shadow economy which particularly affects small businesses. However, despite using similar approaches, the detailed methodology has changed considerably over time which makes modern estimates difficult to turn into a continuous series.

The modern *BPE* includes many businesses that are excluded in the census and that we exclude from our estimates. First, a person running several businesses will be treated as several enterprises in *BPE*, though not in the census (or the earlier *SMES*) nor in our estimates where they are portfolio entrepreneurs, not multiple counts; this leads to approximately 0.4m more businesses in *BPE* in 2017 (where LFS data show 11.1 percent of self-employed had a second occupation). Second, all self-employment is included if possible in *BPE* ('even a small amount of business activity counts': BIS, 2014: para 20), but the modern censuses requires it to be activity over 30 hours a week, and we believe that historic censuses similarly excluded most part-time and seasonal activity. Similarly *BPE* counts self-employment even where this is miniscule and almost the whole activity is as employee or inactive (BIS, 2014: para 15). These differences (multiple counts and inclusion of part-time or miniscule activity) in the *BPE* results in an inflation in numbers compared to the historic and modern censuses.

The modern estimates of proprietor numbers for 1980–2017 are shown in Figure 4.10 superimposed over the census estimates. The modern data have been aligned between the different SME series using overlaps to rescale. This is approximate since the figures prior to 1990 are not strictly comparable with later figures, as business were counted in a different way and cannot be readily recovered. Similarly, it is not possible to be sure whether changes around 2000 following the introduction of the *BPE* data are real or due to different methods of estimation. They omit, in particular, changes in ratios between own account and employers. Hence they are only an approximation of modern trends.

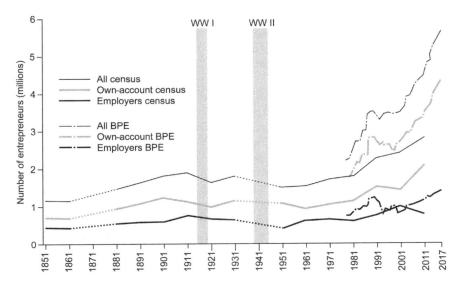

Figure 4.10 Entrepreneurship numbers for all census businesses 1851–2011 (BBCE database), and modern statistics for all employers and own account England and Wales 1980–2017 (*BPE* estimates 2001–17; *SMES* rescaled 1980–2000)

Nevertheless it is possible to grasp the broad order of magnitude of modern estimates compared to historical census data for total entrepreneurs; the modern estimates do not differentiate the gender.

Comparisons of proprietor numbers between census estimates and modern *SME* data methods are approximately aligned for employers in Figure 4.10. However, for own account the modern series show a massive increase compared to the census. Moreover, the progressive move away from Bannock's methods to include any business activity in *BPE* leads to the modern estimates becoming progressively higher and diverging further from the census, especially after 2001. This is the result of the counting of multiple businesses in *BPE*, and having no limitation for part-time inclusion.

Despite the differences, however, both series show growth in proprietor numbers 1981–91, decline or slowdown 1991–2001, and then growth again 2001–11. It is notable that in the 2001–02 recession (tech and dot.com bubble) own account were most affected (according to the census), but in the *BPE* employers and own account were more equally affected. The absence of a lower boundary for inclusion in the *BPE* and inclusion of both full-time and part-time employees probably accounts for the much more extreme fall in *BPE* numbers in 2001 as many marginal activities were more difficult to sustain. In the financial crisis and 'great recession of 2008–11', which has been compared to the Great Depression of the 1930s, the trends in entrepreneurship were different. In the 1930s employer numbers reduced, but own account increased. In 2008–11, as measured by *BPE*, growth appears to have continued for both employers and own account, and rapidly for the latter. The census can only show the early stages of any effects. It appears to confirm *BPE* in suggesting own account was little affected, but for employers indicates a decline from their 2001 peak and a relative shift to own account that conflicts with the *BPE*.

The trends in modern proprietor numbers take no account of population, which was more than twice as large in the 2000s as the early 1900s. As in the previous discussion, it is important to calculate rates that balance comparisons with changes in the numbers of workers to assess changes in entrepreneurial participation within a changing size of population. These are shown in Figure 4.11. In this figure there is an approximate match of employer rates between the census and *BPE* for employer numbers. However, own account rates and hence total proprietor numbers again show extreme divergences after 1991.

If accepted uncritically the modern *BPE* data suggest that Britain is now in its most entrepreneurial period. However, this is illusory. The two series are measuring different things. If we counted census portfolio businesses multiple times for each field of business as in *BPE*, this would increase the 1851–1911 numbers over 10 percent, increasing rates by 1–3 percent. If we also counted the part-time self-employed for the early period using a comparable method, this would increase the earlier numbers by about 30 percent, increasing rates by

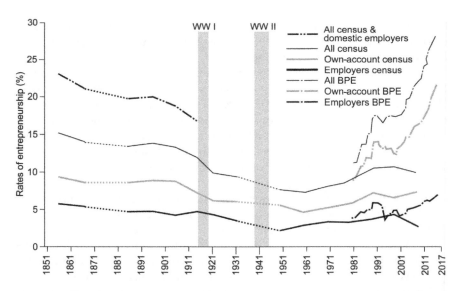

Figure 4.11 Rates of entrepreneurship calculated from the census and *BPE* as a percentage of the total economically active in England and Wales. Census calculations also shown for total 'proprietors' when the census counts include employers of domestic staff 1851–1911

Source: BBCE database and author adjustment of censuses and BPE.

about 5 percent (though this is speculative). If we included health care trusts and colleges, as partly included in *BPE*, this would increase numbers still further. Moreover, if employers of domestic staff are included in the early period, this increases proprietor numbers by approximately 591,050 in 1851, rising to 757,383 in 1911. Figure 4.11 shows the historical rate calculations including these domestic employers (see also Table 4.1).[8]

It is clear that interpreting businesses as estimated in *BPE*, so that 'even a small amount of business activity counts', is grossly misleading and the census calculations for the modern period (Figures 4.8 and 4.9) provide more useful long-term comparisons. They show that there has indeed been a very significant recovery in entrepreneur numbers and the rate of entrepreneurship since the 1950s and 1960s, but the *rates* so far achieved only just exceed that reached in 1921, and are nowhere near the levels achieved over 1851–1911. Moreover, there are indications of a levelling off of census entrepreneurial numbers and rates since 2001, and the beginnings of a downturn (especially for employers), which suggests that modern growth is much less stimulative of entrepreneurial development than often claimed. Indeed our long-term graphs tend to confirm the conclusions of detailed studies on the nature of modern self-employment: that this activity can be marginal, part time or on the fringe of the formal economy (Blanchflower and Shadforth, 2007; Meager and Bates, 2004). Hence, as Tatomir (2015) notes using LFS data, although self-employment has a large and growing component that is part-time, those who want to work more hours have increased only since the 2008 recession and is similar to that sought by paid workforces, with technical changes and age effects (older individuals seeking more part-time self-employment) also being important. The recession may explain the very large increase in *BPE* own-account entrepreneurship rates after the 2008–11 recession, but most increases were probably limited part-time hours of activity.

4.7　Conclusion

This chapter has given an overview of the main aggregate trends in *non-corporate entrepreneurship* over 1851–1911 and has extended this to cover census estimates 1921–2011 and up to 2017 from modern *SME/BPE* statistics. The analysis demonstrates that total *entrepreneur numbers* increased steadily over the 1851–1911 period, although expansion slowed 1901–11. Employer expansion was slower than own account, but after 1901 own account fell absolutely and employer numbers began to increase marginally. This marked the turning point for the end of the Victorian 'age of entrepreneurship', with a profound re-balancing after 1901 between own-account proprietors in favour of those employing others. After 1891 workforce numbers increased far more rapidly than entrepreneurs and their firms. This marks the onset of the modern period when there was a shift to larger firm sizes and a narrowing of scope for the individual own-account proprietor. However, one of the most important conclusions is that this was not driven as many have suggested (e.g. Clark, 1957) by changes in farming, where employers, business numbers and rates of entrepreneurship all increased.

Although there are many limitations to joining data over time, most trends are so large as to overwhelm data uncertainties. The changes after 1911 show that the U-shape first noted by Clark (1957) became firmly established. Whilst there had been increasing *entrepreneur numbers* up to 1901–11, there was then a steep decline until the 1960s. Rather than a long-term U-shape therefore, there was not a V- or reverse L-shape, but an N-shape: up, down and then up again; perhaps even an M-shape with a downturn evident in the twenty-first century. Hence the 1920s–1950s appear as one of the most exceptional periods where very large firms dominated, the attractions of waged employment grew with the security of large employers and their wage rates exerted increasing competitive pressures on smaller employers and the own-account self-employed, who in many sectors increasingly struggled to maintain their businesses. Within this broad trend there were major sectoral differences, with the own account and smaller firm increasingly squeezed in manufacturing, maker-dealing, transport and primary processing, but having greater opportunities in services.

For *entrepreneurship rates* there was a general decline across the period, steeply after 1851, and steeper again after 1901, but with a small upturn over 1881–91. Within this, employers slowly and steadily declined as a proportion of the total economically active for the whole period up to 1951, although subsequently expanding up to 2001. Own-account entrepreneurship rates, after a decline 1851–61, increased a little for 1881–1901, before falling very sharply 1901–61. The reversal of this trend with own account increasing more rapidly than employer entrepreneurship rates has continued from 1961 up to 2011. The turning point of 1901 was, therefore, especially a turn in the fortunes for own-account proprietors. Comparisons of numbers and rates with the alternative sector classification of PST demonstrate the robustness of the estimated historical trends irrespective of the classifications used.

Comparisons of total proprietor numbers from census estimates with *modern small business BPE statistics* demonstrate approximate alignment with our census estimates in 1981. However, for own account the modern series massively overestimate entrepreneur numbers compared to the census, especially after changes in method of calculation after 2001. This is the result of including in modern series multiple businesses, all part-time activity however small and some health care trusts and colleges. Hence the belief that Britain is now in its most entrepreneurial period is illusory. Census calculations provide a more consistent indicator. They show a significant recovery in entrepreneur numbers and the rate of entrepreneurship since the 1950s and 1960s, but the rate so far achieved is only just exceeding that reached in 1921, and nowhere near the levels achieved over 1851–1911.

The comparisons over time confirm the difficulties of how we define and measure entrepreneurship noted in Chapters 2 and 3. But the analysis in the chapter demonstrates that consistent and robust definitions can be developed from the censuses for the period since 1851 up to the present. These provide the basis for the analysis in subsequent chapters. Analysis of trends in firm size, and comparisons with corporates, is taken further in Chapter 5.

Notes

1 *Report of the Committee Appointed by the Treasury to Inquire into Certain Questions Connected with the Taking of the Census* (1890), C 6071, HMSO, London.
2 *Census of England and Wales, 1891, Vol. IV General Report, with Summary Tables and Appendices*, Parliamentary Papers, 1893–4 (CVI), 36.
3 To simplify estimation the sectors used are the 17 aggregate occupational categories derived from 797 occupational codes in I-CeM; 4 contain no proprietors, so estimates cover 13 sectors; see Table 3.3.
4 The method is described in full in Bennett et al. (2019a); weights described in WP 11, actual weights given at https://doi.org/10.17863/CAM.26376
5 Some of the very slow change over 1861–81 may be an artefact of the way the reconstruction process estimates own account, but alterative reconstruction estimates give the same change of rates over this period. Rates differ a little from using Feinstein's (1972) estimates of the working population which misallocate some self-employed to workers (see Chapter 5).
6 Employers of domestic staff include all heads of household who employed at least one and less than 10 domestic servants (where larger numbers could be dormitories or hotels, though alternative assumptions make only minor differences); they are a mix of employers, own account, workers, as well as the economically inactive (e.g. annuitants and retired).
7 The upturn in refreshments 1901–11 is partly spurious, reflecting a change in how the census recorded lodging house keepers in 1911 which is impossible to adequately correct. Figure 4.4 slightly smooths this.
8 See note on Table 4.1. There is some double counting, since employers of domestic staff are a mix of employers, own account, workers and inactive.

5 Business size and organisation

5.1 Introduction

This chapter examines trends in the distribution of businesses by employee
size and the balance between incorporated and non-incorporated proprietors
by business numbers and volume of profit. At the start of the nineteenth century almost all businesses were small. Large organisations were restricted to the
chartered companies (East India, African, etc.), the naval dockyards and military
ordnance, and a few industrial sectors of which brewing, sugar baking, cotton
textiles and some woollen manufacturers were the main examples. Some firms
in industries characterised by extensive outworking, such as glove making,
employed substantial numbers of people, but this was a markedly different form
of industrial organisation to the factory, with outworkers generally working to
piece or on their own account for each batch of produce. Factory-based production was limited, with units themselves also small (Payne, 1967, 1984). The main
exception was in cotton textiles where some units were employing hundreds of
workers, and a few had several thousand workers by the 1780s. By 1822 the average cotton mill had 100–200 workers, and by the 1830s the average was much
larger; yet the number of firms also continued to increase (Chapman, 1972: 26;
Gatrell, 1977). The other main industries with larger firms during the period up
to the 1880s were metal trades, heavy engineering, pottery, brewing, chemicals,
tobacco and iron smelting. But even in these sectors there were many small and
new firms, so that scope for market dominance and control was limited, with
'the number of small businesses constantly growing' (Marshall, 1919: 247). The
main exception to this in 1851 that had experienced considerable merger and
concentration was rail. After the early period of 'mania' up to 1840s, railways
had been increasingly consolidated into a few large companies which began to
raise concerns about monopoly pricing with increasing pressures for regulation
(Parris, 1965; Alderman, 1973). Nevertheless Hannah (1983: 13) estimates that
the largest 100 firms across manufacturing sectors controlled less than 10 percent
of the market by 1880, compared to 40 percent by the 1960s.

Getting beneath these earlier studies to give a more detailed understanding of
firm size has been previously limited by inadequate data. This chapter seeks to
overcome some of the data limitations by using the statistics on firm workforce

size in the censuses. These are mainly for *non-incorporated businesses* and to 1851–81, where there was the question for employers to give their employee numbers. Despite the limitations of these early censuses these data do provide the widest and fullest coverage of businesses by size available for this period. For 1891–1911 these data are unavailable; however, estimates can be calculated of changing *average* firm size by relating number of firms to the sector labour force.

Because the census information is almost entirely restricted to non-incorporated businesses, it is important to put their evolution into the broader context of developments of *all firms* (corporate and non-corporate) by size. Important changes of company law in 1856 and in 1862 extended the scope to incorporate as limited companies which had been previously restricted to specialist chartered, parliamentary or trust structures. The Joint Stock Companies Act (1856) and Company Act (1862) made limited liability available to all businesses if they wished to use it. This led to a rise in corporate business numbers after the mid-1850s, and especially from the mid-1860s, with the trend accelerating from the 1890s. This is a major influence on what we can observe using mainly non-corporate proprietors from census data. The development of the corporate form was to become a dominant force in the twentieth century, with non-corporate numbers steadily declining. Hence our analysis of firm size over 1851–81, and in lesser detail over 1891–1911, covers an important period of transition in the organisation of proprietorship. The assessment here shows that the corporate sector grew from an important but small component with a few thousand businesses in the 1850s, responsible for about 15 percent of output, to half of all output by 1911. Entrepreneurship thus changed fundamentally over the main period analysed: from dominantly non-corporate with a few corporate sectors, to a mixed structure where entrepreneurial opportunities were becoming more common in the corporate sector where the highest entrepreneurial incomes often increasingly lay.

Section 5.2 presents the detailed assessments possible from the census using the individual employer records of workforce size for 1851–81. Section 5.3 extends this analysis, but in less depth, by examining evolution of average firm sizes over 1851–1911. Section 5.4 compares non-corporate developments based on census data to corporate developments using tax records. The analysis allows an assessment of how entrepreneurship adjusted over the period since 1851 as reflected in business size and the balance of non-corporate and corporate business activity.

5.2 Firm-size statistics from the censuses 1851–81

The census question to employers over 1851–81 asked them to state the numbers in their workforce. It was not possible to access this major source of information for firm size for this period until the availability of e-records and the extraction of employer responses. The only major previous attempt to use these data by Clapham (1932: 35) analysed selected sectors using the one group of tables published from the 1851 census.[1] These census tables are problematic since they mostly exclude women, and it is unclear how they were tabulated, with checks against the CEB records now indicating that some large firms were left out by clerks and others are omitted from the I-CeM (WP 13). The analysis we can now undertake provides new insights into firm size. This is chiefly analysed using the categories adopted in modern small firm statistics (e.g. DBEIS, 2017): one employee, 2–4, 5–9, 10–19, 20–49, 50–99, 100–199, 200–249, 250–499 and 500 or more. These are more aggregated than the GRO table for 1851, but the database deposit can be used to create categories based on any other definitions users may desire.

There are some important issues to bear in mind for interpretation (WP 3). First, census respondents, and/or enumerators, had a tendency to provide employee numbers in rounded terms, resulting in some 'bunching' around the tens (especially) and also the fives and twelve; for example, for '10 employees', '15 men', 'a dozen hands'. Because we suspect the tendency was mainly to round up, the DBEIS categories tend to place the bunching in the upper category; that is, a firm of 'about 10' that may have actually had 9 employees will be in the 10–19 category. Second, there appears to have been some underestimation of the smallest businesses (mainly those with one employee). This is primarily due to a tendency not to include family members such as a wife, son or daughter, and also probably reflects poorer-quality returns from some of the smallest traders who took the census question less seriously or were less rigorously scrutinised by enumerators. This seems to have been more important for 1861–81, with the 1851 census more thoroughly returning one-employee firms and employers of family members (see WP 13). For this reason we mostly focus on businesses with more than one employee. Underreporting of the one-employee category is a generic issue for this period, and is also suspected in the US Census of Manufacturers (Atack and Bateman, 1999; who usually exclude it from analysis). Third, as discussed in Chapter 3, there are gaps in the data: 3–4 percent of data were lost in storage for the 1861 census; there are gaps in the coverage of some areas in the 1871 extraction, as evident in Table 5.1 (WP 12); and parts of the 1851 extractions are missing compared to the published tables for London, Cheshire and Lancashire (WPs 3 and 13). However, the manner in which these gaps occurred means that there is no reason to believe that missing data affected one firm size rather than another. Fourth, some errors of over- and underestimation may occur through erroneous treatment of partnerships. The census return for employee numbers was supposed to be given by 'the senior partner or one partner only', but it is not always clear whether this included partner(s) as employees. Since over 80 percent of partnerships had just two partners (Stamp, 1916; Bennett, 2016), this may lead to some overestimation of one-employee firms. A small level of uncertainty also results from some returns being given by multiple partners. This can affect all size categories. However, overall the gaps in responses and confusion by partners should be random by size, though not by location. These constraints are managed in this chapter mainly by restricting tabulations to proportions rather than absolute numbers, which should be representative of the real patterns.

Non-response also can lead to underestimating the total number of employers and employees. This is more difficult to manage. Whilst the total numbers of employers (and their employees) can be estimated through the reconstruction process used in Chapter 4, the employee numbers of non-respondent individual firms cannot. This is believed to be similar to the under-reporting of employer status in 1891–1911 which mainly affects employers of family and spouses (as judged by RELA codes; see Chapter 4), and thus leads to underestimation of one-employee and other micro-businesses. Hence focusing on firms with more than one employee should eliminate most biases. However, the main aspect of non-reporting in the census is the absence of some corporate employers and their workforce. We address this is in section 5.4.

Number of employees

As shown in Table 5.1 and Figure 5.1, the vast majority of firms were micro-businesses: over 60 percent had fewer than five employees. Small firms (5–19 employees) accounted for another 26–33 percent of businesses, while medium and large businesses were relatively rare. Only 157 firms in 1851 had 500 or more employees, rising to 433 firms in 1881: these were nearly all textile

Table 5.1 Percentage of firms in each size category in England and Wales, 1851–81 and 2017

Firm size (No. of Employees)	1851	1861	1871	1881	2017
1	25.5	18.9	18.6	19.0	46.2
2–4	43.0	41.1	39.4	39.8	31.7
5–9	17.3	21.6	21.5	20.9	11.1
10–19	8.8	11.3	12.2	11.3	6.0
20–49	4.0	5.0	5.7	5.9	3.2
50–99	0.8	1.1	1.3	1.6	1.0
100–199	0.3	0.5	0.7	0.8	0.4
200–249	0.1	0.1	0.2	0.2	0.1
250–499	0.1	0.2	0.3	0.3	0.2
500+	0.1	0.1	0.2	0.2	0.2
N	200,490	174,960	137,979	182,445	2,257,655

Source: BBCE database.

Note: The total numbers reflect gaps in census database coverage between years, whilst proportions should be accurate guides of distribution. Modern distribution from *BPE* 2017 for UK, private sector only (DBEIS, 2017: Table 3). One-employee directors are reassigned to one-employee businesses to align results with the much smaller corporate sector in our earlier period. If all one-employee partnerships that DBEIS also assign to no-employee businesses were reassigned then the one-employee businesses would be 52.6 percent in 2017. However, as discussed in Chapter 4, the *BPE* overestimates by multiple counting many enterprise activities that are predominantly one employee, so that these partnerships are not adjusted.

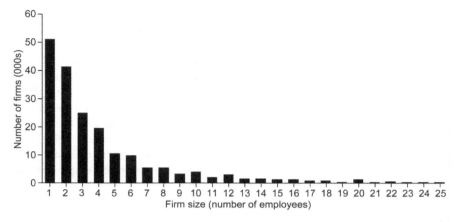

Figure 5.1 Number of firms by size for up to 25 employees in 1851. Note bunching at 10, 12 and 20

Source: BBCE database.

manufacturers or steel and coal owners who could be employing several thousand people. The general pattern is a log-normal distribution, declining steeply with increasing size, as evident in Figure 5.1; although by aggregating groups of unequal size in Table 5.1 this is obscured. The log-normal distribution, often referred to as the outcome of Gibrat's law, mirrors almost all previous firm-size analyses for historical and modern periods and is discussed further in the conclusion.

There are some important trends over time. The main pattern of almost three-quarters of firms having fewer than 5 employees and less than 2 percent of firms having more than 100 employees stayed the same over 1851–81. There was also a consistent trend across the size categories from 5–9 upwards from 1861 for the proportions to be higher than earlier, and for firms of 20–49 and larger to increase in proportion over time. Although the distribution was dominated by the large volume of the smallest firms, the rise of the larger firm was notable, with the proportion of firms over 50 employees rising from 1.4 percent in 1851 to 2.0, 2.8 and ultimately 3.1 percent by 1881: their proportion more than doubled over the course of three decades. The largest firms, over 100 employees, in 1851 made up only 0.6 percent of all firms, which rose to 0.9 in 1861, and to 1.5 percent in 1881. Although a small proportion, the firms over 20 employees employed the majority of the waged population, and the census responses clearly evidence the rise of the large firm among the non-corporate business population. For the smallest category, the difference in proportion of the one-employee firms for 1851 compared to later years must be an artefact of better census processes for that year, in particular in relation to the family firm, as noted earlier.

A comparison with the modern period is shown in the last column of Table 5.1. Although comparisons are difficult, the modern data suggest that the firm-size distribution is remarkably constant over time. However, the comparison

Table 5.2 Percentage of firms in each size category, 1851–81 and 2017, for firms with five employees and upwards; 2017 data as for Table 5.1

Employees	1851	1861	1871	1881	2017
5–9	55.0	54.0	51.1	50.7	50.2
10–19	27.9	28.3	29.0	27.4	27.1
20–49	12.6	12.5	13.6	14.2	14.5
50–99	2.5	2.7	3.1	3.8	4.5
100–199	1.1	1.3	1.7	2.0	1.8
200–249	0.2	0.3	0.4	0.5	0.5
250–499	0.5	0.6	0.7	0.8	0.8
500+	0.2	0.3	0.4	0.6	0.7

Source: BBCE database.

does suggest that if the historical patterns were at all similar to modern data then under-reporting among the very smallest firms was significant: the one-employee category as recorded over 1851–81 is perhaps about one-half of its true size. This comparability with modern data is even clearer if we omit the problematic smallest categories. As shown in Table 5.2, after excluding businesses of 1–4 employees, the 2017 distribution of small, medium and large firms very closely follows the nineteenth-century size structure, with only a slightly smaller proportion of small firms, and correspondingly larger number of medium firms. Table 5.2 also confirms the key trends in firm size. The proportion of the smallest business (5–9 employees) was declining, whilst the proportion of all size classes for 20 employees and upwards was increasing over 1851–81. The rate of change was fastest for the decline of 5–9 employee firms over 1861–71, and for the largest businesses fastest for increases of 100–199 employee firms over the same period, but for 50–99 employee firms fastest over 1871–81. The 10–19 employee category was more ambiguous, increasing in size over 1851–71, and then decreasing.

The previous tables and figures combine farm and non-farm data. Figure 5.2 splits them and also shows firm size by gender. While both genders mainly operated small firms, larger firms were much more likely to have male proprietors. Women generally had smaller firms, and were particularly concentrated in the 2–9 employee categories, whereas male proprietors had higher proportions in the larger categories. Most trends were similar between genders. For *non-farm businesses* the small-size categories of 1 and 2–4 generally declined over time (although some of this may be the result of changed census processes). However, for female businesses the trend to consolidation showed some reversal between 1871 and 1881: whilst almost all categories of male non-farm businesses of 5–9 employees and above increased in proportion over time, the proportion of female businesses declined in 1881 for most of these categories. Conversely the proportion of female 2–4 employee businesses increased more than for males. Non-farm concentration thus was predominantly a male phenomenon, but with female participation growing in the smaller (and more numerous) size categories.

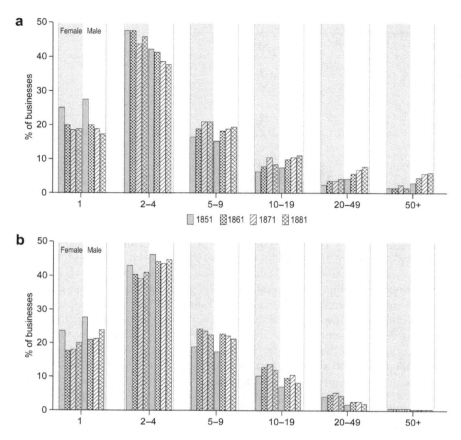

Figure 5.2 Percentage of (a) farm and (b) non-farm businesses by gender and size category, 1851–81

Source: BBCE database.

For *farm businesses*, both genders show the same trends: that is, over the first three decades there was initial growth of larger farms, those with over 10–19 workers, and a corresponding decline of smaller farms, a trend which reversed between 1871 and 1881 with an increase in proportions of smaller employee sizes in 1881. Hence, the effect of price pressures and depression in agriculture was associated with general contraction of farm size except in the 2–4 employee category and limited consolidation in a few large farms (see also Montebruno et al., 2019a). There must have also been some switching between categories, with some female-headed farms of 10–19 employees and above switching to having 10 employees or below in 1881. This is explored further in panel-tracking studies reported in later publications.

Geography of firm size

The geography of firm size was also distinctive between farm and non-farm businesses. Firms drew from the dynamics of each separate sector. While some sectors were rather generally distributed, many were highly concentrated in some parts of the country, as examined further in Chapter 9. This results in strong spatial concentrations of the largest non-farm firms. These were in the main urban areas, ports and major industrial locations, especially those with metal processing (iron and steel), textiles, coal and ship building, as shown in Figure 5.3

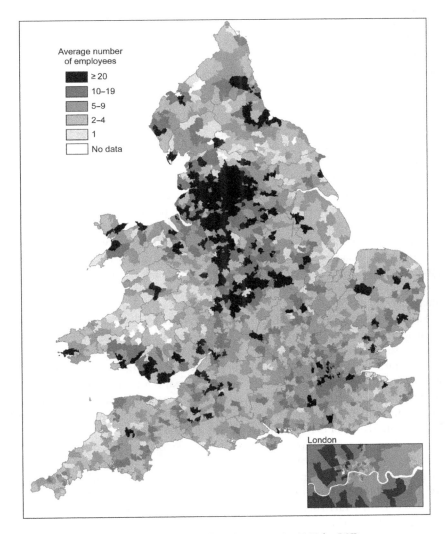

Figure 5.3 Average employee size of non-farm businesses in 1881 by RSD
Source: BBCE database.

for RSDs. Within London it was in the port areas, some central boroughs and in the fringe areas of the centre mainly to the West and North. Conversely, the places with the smallest average firm sizes were upland areas of Wales, the Pennines and South West, and the more remote rural areas of Lincolnshire and North Yorkshire. In between were areas with mixed patterns of large-medium and small firms, covering a large part of the country which had average firm size of 2–5 or at most 5–10 employees (close to the national average). This typified most rural and transition communities that were not remote or upland that had a mixture of towns and large villages with concentrations of agricultural and other primary processors, retail, professions and small manufacturing or maker-dealer industries.

It should be noted that some of the concentrations in the fringes of London and the other large urban areas may not reflect the actual locations of the businesses but rather the residences of the owners. The census records employers where they were resident on census night. As shown in Figure 5.3, this was frequently in country or suburban homes of the richer merchants and manufacturers. Whilst for industries such as coal, many large proprietors lived in another city or rural areas distant from their mines. However, this effect was fairly minor for non-farm businesses (Figure 5.4).

The average size of farms was much smaller than for non-farm businesses, as to be expected (Figure 5.4), but shows the same pattern of very small sizes concentrated in Wales, the Pennines, South West and remote rural areas. Larger farms were mainly towards urban fringes, and the better land of Southern England, to the South and East of a line from the Humber to the Severn, and in East Yorkshire and Northumberland. Land quality, and thus type of agriculture; proximity to urban markets, especially London; and the specifics of large-scale estates, explain this pattern. The map is far more detailed than the county mapping previously available (e.g. Grigg, 1989) and extends previous studies (Shaw-Taylor, 2005; 2012).

Farming was more affected by large employers that were resident elsewhere or returned in their estates on census night. This results in artificially high average sizes in some locations around London, other large cities and some areas with concentrations of country retreats favoured by absentee proprietors. This effect is, however, confused since many of these retreats also reflect the actual locations of large farms, especially where combined with sporting estates for pheasant, grouse and other game (e.g. in the Cotswolds, Hampshire Downs, Norfolk and Northumberland Cheviot; see Lawton and Pooley, 1992).

The distinction for farming between employers and own-account proprietors was very important. It depended, among other things, on the interaction between farm acreage available, land quality, market accessibility and farm labour resources available, whether from family or hired in. Unlike the non-farm sector, this can be estimated for farmers who did not respond fully to the workforce census question but did provide their farm acreage (excluding rough grazing). Acreage data can be used to correct for non-response bias to the workforce question. The method of estimation,

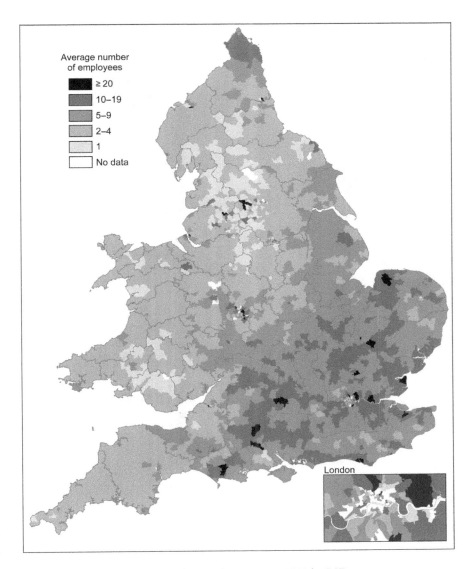

Figure 5.4 Average employee size of farm businesses in 1881 by RSD

Source: BBCE database.

described in Montebruno et al. (2019a), provides estimates for the acreage size of farms that mark the average cut-off between employers and own account in each RD.[2]

The average acreage cut-off varies widely, as shown in Figures 5.5a–d, with important changes over time. In 1851 the area covered by farms with low

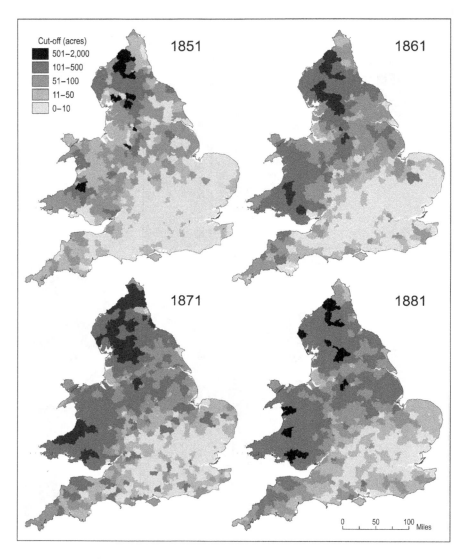

Figure 5.5 Distribution of cut-off size in acres below which it was normally possible to be an employer, RDs 1851–81

Source: Data from BBCE; maps adapted from Montebruno et al., 2019a.

cut-offs where small acreages were sufficient to support employers was much greater than in subsequent years, with a severe decrease in area of employer-run farms by 1881 after the 1873 depression. Conversely, the area where high cut-offs were associated primarily with own-account farms expanded from what were chiefly upland areas with poorer land in 1851 (the uplands in Wales and the Pennines (as in Figure 5.6a) to cover a much wider area by 1881 (Figure 5.6d),

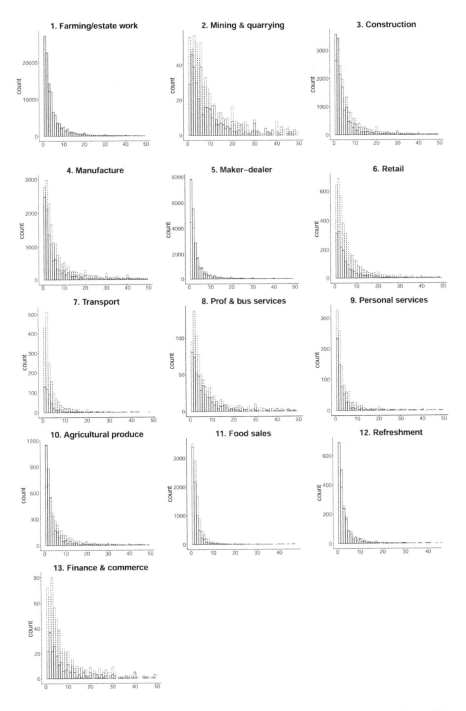

Figure 5.6 Number of businesses by size (number of employees) for 13 aggregate sectors 1851 (solid) and 1881 (dashed)

Source: BBCE database.

much of which had good quality land. Small farms of 50 or fewer acres run by employers became restricted to an area around London and South East, and the major urban centres such as the Midlands and North West. Hence, not only was farm size decreasing over time in terms of employee numbers, but the proportion of farmers that employed anyone other than themselves and immediate family was also declining.

More detailed comparison of the maps with climate, urban and transport location suggests that near urban areas employers were more common than own-account farmers, while in areas of predominantly upland and rough grazing own-account activity was more probable. In response to increasing price pressures, farmers were substituting for labour through adjustments to their entrepreneurial status, taking account of their geographical opportunities as discussed in Chapter 9 and also demonstrated by the spread of rail access summarised in Chapter 6. These effects are more fully reported in Montebruno et al. (2019a).

Sectors

Business sector is usually the most important influence on firm size, reflecting the different market and technological characteristics of different industries, as discussed in Chapters 2 and 4. Figure 5.6 shows the proportions of different firm sizes for the 13 sectors in 1851 and 1881. Relatively small changes occurred over time in only four sectors: farming, maker-dealers, food sales and refreshments. All the other sectors show an increasing proportion of larger firms, which is most marked for mining, retail, transport, and finance and commerce, and to a lesser extent in manufacturing. This trend is mainly for non-corporates. It has been previously recognised that incorporation was important for the largest mines (especially for coal) and manufacturing (which here includes utilities in our EA17 classification; see Table 3.3), but the data here show that the complete pattern of consolidation in this sector was even greater. Three sectors exhibit a more complex pattern. The first, agricultural processing, showed the most rapid increase in the medium-sized firms of 5–49 employees. This reflected the strong growth in agricultural output which stimulated some consolidation of the processing and dealing sectors at the local level rather than in very large firms, including the effect of wider local catchments for processors as transport, milling and other processing technologies developed (Grigg, 1989: 149–65; Lawton and Pooley, 1992: 153). This was observed by contemporaries such as Morton (1855, vol. 2) who viewed this as the transition to larger-scale operations, such as the 'modern four-floor mill' with large and more divided processes of cleaning, grinding, dressing and storage; and also resulting from the application of steam power which consolidated processing into larger operations for threshing and other trades such as timber processing.

The other two sectors were *professional and business services* and *personal services* where there was also a shift to consolidation in the small-medium size categories but more towards 20–99 employees. Although the number of businesses involved was small, this was consistent over time after 1851 and appears to reflect the growth of London and large-city partnership businesses that became nationally or regionally focused with branches in some parts of this sector; most often this affected engineers, but also applied to surveyors and land agents, some solicitors and architects, and for personal services in larger steam laundries.

The balance between these different sector changes by size categories is brought out in Figure 5.7 for 1851 and 1881. The sectors can be treated as three groups. First, sectors that displayed a high peak and a steep decline had many micro-firms usually and also had very few large businesses. The inter-related sectors food sales and refreshments were the extremes, with at least two-thirds of firms having 2–4 employees. Examples of businesses in these sectors include grocers, bakers, butchers, innkeepers and publicans. Because these sectors did not yet benefit from refrigeration, sales were localised to consumers who had to shop daily, whilst the dealer often acted as part of the supply chain (butchers taking in animals prior to slaughter; poulterers keeping stock; milk sellers keeping cows or goats) or needing to provide continuous fresh supplies (bakers and confectioners). This kept food sales firms small and numerous.

The next highest proportions of micro-businesses, maker-dealers, which included blacksmiths, shoemakers and milliners, and personal services such as laundresses, hairdressers and chimney sweeps, had less steep declines in size, evidencing some expansion of small-medium sized firms, but mostly those with fewer than 50 employees. Maker-dealer trades such as blacksmiths or whitesmiths usually continued to be small and operate at a predominately local scale, even though an increasing number shifted to specialist larger operations and would be recorded in ironmongery manufacture or as parts of factory,

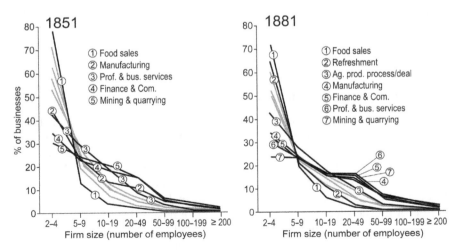

Figure 5.7 Percentage of business in aggregate sectors 1851 and 1881

Source: BBCE database.

mine or shipyard activity. In addition, highly skilled and specialised trades such as watch- and clockmakers continued mostly at small scale, though increasing sub-division of the actual production occurred in the manufacture of specialist parts. In comparison, a wide range of maker-dealer footwear and apparel trades, although remaining predominantly small scale, and often feminised, were increasingly experiencing competition. This came first from larger 'workshops' where craftwork was centralised under one roof, but then was more profoundly affected by the introduction of machine sewing in the 1870s in major factory production (Gamber, 1997; Holmes, 2009: 185–90). By the end of the period shown in Figure 5.7 this was only beginning to affect shoe, boot and clog makers; buttons; and some tailoring, shirt and textile finishing; whilst other apparel trades remained mostly unaffected until later (such as hatters, milliners, clothiers, dressmakers).

A second group of sectors were those characterised by a large proportion of small-to-medium businesses with consolidation at various scales: construction (carpenters, builders, plumbers), retail (ironmongers, drapers, booksellers), transport (carriers, fly and ship owners) and agricultural produce (millers, brewers, maltsters). Only a very small proportion of businesses in these sectors had over 50 employees, though some very large non-corporate businesses were emerging, such as W.H. Smith station bookstalls. While they, as with all businesses, still included many micro-firms, this proportion was lower, and they had a larger proportion of small-to-medium firms (5–49 employees). However, agricultural processing was beginning to see the growth of larger firms of 100 employees and upwards, mainly located in the main ports to process increasing volumes of American and Russian grain imports. Finally, there were the three sectors that had a flatter distribution, with fewer than 35 percent of firms employing fewer than five people; these sectors included almost all the large firms of 100 or more employees. These sectors all consolidated fastest: manufacturing (especially large textile firms, iron and steel, and shipbuilding, but also small-to-medium cabinet makers and coopers), mining and quarrying (especially coal) and finance and commerce (mainly banks and merchants).

5.3   Trends in *average* firm size 1851–1911

The information on workforce size for individual firms cannot be carried forward after 1881 as the data were not collected. However, to examine long-term trends we can make comparisons of firm size over time on another basis by calculating mean employees (R) using all workers in a sector compared with the total number of employers (after reconstruction, with own account excluded from both categories). This second method can be continued for the whole period of our detailed analysis 1851–1911 (once reconstructed information on employers is included); unfortunately this method cannot take account of corporate workforces, but the analysis shows how their numbers influence findings. Both methods are informative, and the comparison is indicative of differences in definitions and a check on the completeness of the census data extraction.

The mean number of workers per employer in each sector is depicted in Figure 5.8 and Table 5.3 for 1851–1911. This is those declared as workers of all firms (corporate and non-corporate), compared to non-corporate business numbers. The patterns for the early years are consistent with the extracted data discussed in the previous section and show the same general trends for the early period: mining and manufacturing had the largest firms and also experienced the fastest growth in mean firm size, while the professions had small firms but grew rapidly. The main difference between the two methods of calculation is the much larger mean firm size of transport, finance and commerce, and to a lesser extent manufacturing. The important message from Figure 5.8, however, is that for the later period non-corporate firm size growth began to slow, and after 1901 mostly went into reverse. For several sectors, particularly farming and construction, there was a dip in 1891, and in other sectors (such as transport, personal services) a slowing rate of growth, reflecting the tail-end of the depression of trade of the 1880s. There was then an important revival 1891–1901 which included almost all sectors. After 1901 the picture is less clear because the 1911 data includes an unusually large number of general labourers owing to the introduction of a new census question on industry which led more people to give generic answers to the occupation question and used the industry question to specify their sector; for example, rather than occupation as 'labourer in iron works' they might answer 'labourer' for occupation and only specify 'iron works' in the industry question. This increases the number of unspecified labourers

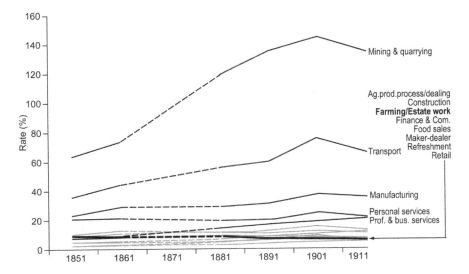

Figure 5.8 Average firm size calculated as the mean number of workers to employers in each sector. Note: 1891–1911 weighted data; 1871 information not in I-CeM; 1911 unreliable, see text

Source: BBCE database.

Table 5.3 Average firm size calculated as the mean number of workers to employers in each sector: note as Figure 5.8

Sector	1851	1861	1881	1891	1901	1911
Farming	9.1	8.4	8.3	6.7	6.07	6.07
Mining and quarrying	63.2	73.6	119.5	134.8	144.1	134.1
Construction	9.9	10.5	11.3	11.0	14.7	12.4
Manufacturing	23.5	28.6	29.3	31.0	37.1	35.8
Maker-dealer	9.8	12.0	10.7	11.6	12.5	10.5
Retail	3.6	3.8	4.8	5.3	6.1	6.4
Transport	35.1	44.6	56.8	59.7	75.6	65.7
Professional and business services	7.6	9.0	13.3	16.6	19.1	21.2
Personal services	20.7	21.8	20.3	20.7	24.5	21.3
Agricultural produce processing and dealing	4.3	5.1	5.3	5.5	7.4	7.0
Food sales	2.8	3.0	3.8	4.8	5.7	5.0
Refreshment	2.2	2.5	4.8	5.9	7.9	4.7
Finance and commerce	3.5	4.2	6.6	8.5	10.1	13.2
Total	11.0	12.1	13.2	14.8	16.8	15.8

Source: BBCE database.

in the I-CeM that are not assigned to a sector using occupations. If they were included, the decline in mean firm size in Figure 5.8 and Table 5.3 would be reduced or disappear. It is likely, therefore, that the rate of increase continued to slow between 1901 and 1911, as it had done after 1891, but the absolute decline shown is unlikely.

The method of calculating mean firm size from the non-corporate employer numbers and workforce is imprecise because (i) corporate employers cannot be easily included and (ii) the difficulties of attributing many categories of workers between sectors, especially general labourers, clerks and generic trades such as 'blacksmiths' or 'turners'. To test the robustness of the trends in Figure 5.8 we can compare it in Figure 5.9 with the mean size calculated from declared workforces of declared employers (E), as used in Section 5.2, although this covers only 1851–81. However, this method suffers from the deficiency that reconstruction attempts to overcome: under-reporting of employer status.

The comparison of methods shown in Figure 5.9 demonstrates that most sectors have very similar estimates from both calculations. There are two major exceptions, mining and transport, where the extraction underestimates firm size, and the discrepancies become larger with successive censuses. This is to be expected because of the increasing number of very large incorporated businesses in these two sectors whose workforces do not fully appear in the extracted data (E), but are included when all workers are divided by all census employers (R). Railways were the largest employers in the country, and all but a few small private lines were incorporated; large coal mine companies became dominant by the end of the century. For these two categories the comparison shows the scale of the

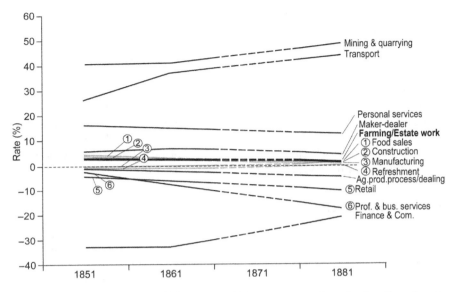

Figure 5.9 Average percentage difference, R − E, between mean firm size for all workers to employers (R) and employers declaring workforces (E) (1871 information not in I-CeM)

Source: BBCE database.

omission resulting from partial presence of corporate firms in the census data. For a third sector, personal services, the mean size calculated from workers exceeds employer declarations of workforce by a smaller amount and the difference declines over time. This arises from different circumstances where employers under-responded. First, workforce numbers were mostly missing from larger private medical institutions (with nurse and doctor proprietors) and education establishments (with school proprietors, music teachers, etc.) because of the alternative specific census instructions they received. Second, some professions included in personal services gave poor responses probably because of the peripatetic or mixed employee/proprietor status of many self-employed individuals in art, music, theatre and cinema establishments. Third, the very small numbers of large firms in personal services leads to outliers distorting comparisons. Fourth, many personal services employers did not record employees in the family leading to underestimates of E.

Conversely, there are three sectors where declared workforces (E) exceed the ratio of all workers to employers (R): finance and commerce, professional and business services, and retail. These result from two issues in census recording. First, there is the effect of the general groups of workers where sector attribution is not possible; chiefly for 'clerk' and 'general labourer'. For clerks this is the main cause of under-recording firm size in finance and commerce. Large numbers of clerks who should be recorded mainly in this sector cannot be attributed. Their non-attribution also affects retail and agricultural processing and dealing, which are also among the sectors most affected by the under-reporting small firm numbers (due to not acknowledging family assistants).

The reconstructed data we use to identify employers to overcome these sources of bias were designed to correct for these discrepancies but they cannot compensate for all census deficiencies. However, overall discrepancies are small for most sectors and confirm that the extraction and reconstruction processes that have been followed are robust when used with care, bearing in mind the constraints that affect some sectors, indicating that in general the sector trends in Figure 5.8 give reasonable indications of a period when incorporation was concentrated in a narrow range of sectors (Wardley, 1999).

5.4   Corporate compared to non-corporate developments

Business incorporation became increasingly important after reform of company laws in 1856 and 1862 offered the scope for a fairly simple process of establishing limited companies and extended the possibility of limited liability to all companies (including banks, under the 1857 and 1858 Acts, and to insurance companies under the 1862 Company Law Act). Although this was initially resisted by many individuals, it had increasing impact in some sectors, particularly mining, large-scale manufacturing and metal processing, iron and steel shipbuilding, utilities and transport. Indeed almost all major transport undertakings had been incorporated from their outset under the legal procedures available before 1856; namely Parliamentary Acts, charters or trusts (railways, canals and navigations, turnpikes), and the more restricted incorporation allowed under the Joint Stock Companies Registration and Regulation Act (1844). Previous analyses of company's numbers by Shannon (1932) and Todd (1932) suggest that early development was relatively slow. The number of new registrations after 1856 initially totalled only 200–300 per year. After the 1862 Act registrations grew more rapidly, increasing to over 500 per year 1863–65. However, business failures and lack of implementation of registration was common, with Levi (1870: 37) showing that of the first 7,056 companies to be newly registered over 1844–68, only 2,974 (42 percent) were still active in 1868 (excluding statutory and other special statuses). The next major benchmark is about 7,000 in 1877 and 7,799 in 1883 'operating' in England and Wales.[3] The *Statistical Abstract for the UK* reports 'registered companies believed to be carrying on business' from 1884 (7,580) for those registered in London and the Stannaries, which rose to 13,032 (1891), 25,574 (1901) and 47,996 (1911).[4] This is a valuable indication of the steep upward trend but includes those operating overseas, which makes comparisons difficult against non-corporate businesses from the census which were mostly domestic in activity, though many were exporters, and a few operated abroad (at least 794 in 1909: Worswick and Tipping, 1967: 118).

To overcome the lack of information on the numbers of corporate businesses for this period, and to make estimates comparable with the domestic non-corporate sector, we resort to a new approach. It is beyond the scope of this book to reconstruct the domestic corporate population at the individual level. However, it is possible to construct *aggregate numbers* of primarily domestic companies using tax data. Companies were included in tax data if they had UK domestic activity and were profitable at that time, including foreign companies for profits derived from UK domestic activity. These data have been widely used but no detailed effort has been made to process the data to provide a consistent series for domestically active business numbers. Feinstein (1972) drawing from previous methodology by Stamp (1916), Bowley (1919) and Bowley and Stamp (1927) all estimated only business incomes. Feinstein's (1972) income estimates for 1855–1965 are the benchmark for gross national income, used by almost all others for the period before the Census of Production began in 1907: for example, Mitchell (1988), Broadberry (1997, 2006), Clark (2010) and Piketty (2014). The method used here to estimate business numbers begins with the same published Inland Revenue (IR) *Annual Reports* used by Feinstein. These summarise corporate taxed income. However, there are three difficulties: first, the number of taxpayers of each type is not fully listed; second, although referred to as 'public companies', the tables also contain numerous non-corporates; and third, there are duplicate entries. These aspects of IR reporting introduce significant challenges for analysis.

To interpret and use the IR data it is necessary to 'unscramble' the reported entities, as Feinstein (1972: 157) refers to it. The largest IR entry is 'general public companies'. This includes all taxable corporations, public and private, whatever legal status, that were active and making returnable profits. This should be entirely domestic profits.[5] However, municipal trading enterprises are included, but listed separately by IR only from 1900–01; accounting for 8 percent of English and Welsh public companies in that year. They have been separated here using data in Parliamentary Papers and secondary sources. In addition there were 10 sectors separately listed by IR for historical reasons: quarries; mines; ironworks; gasworks; salt springs or works; waterworks, canals and docks; fishings and shootings; markets and tolls; cemeteries; and railways. Unfortunately this reporting contained true registered companies and also non-corporate proprietors and municipal bodies. As stated in the 1842 Income Tax Act for these concerns: 'The duty is to be charged on the persons, corporations, companies, or societies of persons, whether corporate or not corporate, carrying on the concern'. Corporate numbers can be separated by using IR *Reports* for the number of taxpayers (reported from 1871–72), and separating the different entities using other records; duplicate reporting is eliminated where different parts of the same business made returns in different places (e.g. mines). The estimates here are preliminary, particularly prior to 1871. Although the data cover Britain, analysis is restricted to England and Wales, in line with the non-corporate data.

There is some discrepancy from Feinstein because, although he used the same census sources, he had available only the published census tables plus some secondary information on unemployment. It is unclear if he made any adjustment to the 1911 published total employers and own account which excluded important sectors (notably commerce and professions). This led to an overestimate of workers, and underestimate of self-employed for 1911 by about 15 percent, excluding farmers (compare Bennett et al., 2019a: Tables 1 and 3, with Feinstein, 1972: 173, 224).[6] He also allowed for the unemployed in the working population and assumed constant employer/own-account ratios over 1851–1911.

The estimates of corporate business numbers are shown in Figure 5.10. To match the census data only 10-year census dates are estimated.[7] The non-corporates are not scaled down for any multiple counting of partners, which the census imperfectly records and might reduce numbers by perhaps 10 percent. Hence, the comparisons are approximate. The corporate numbers and ratios are exaggerated in the figure to show the trends: the actual scale of corporate sector numbers was small; the percentage of corporate compared to non-corporate employers rose from 0.2 percent in 1851 to 2.2 percent of all businesses by 1911. Even excluding own account, corporate compared to non-corporate employers were only 6 percent in 1911. There was a take-off over the period, however. After the slow start for incorporation in the 1850s, numbers accelerated over the 1860s and 1870s, but after 1881 began to take off steeply, with the trend continuing to steepen up to 1911. This is particularly evident in the ratio of corporate to non-corporate numbers shown in Figure 5.10. This upturn occurs well after the main data uncertainties before 1871. Within this trend municipal corporate numbers also grew more rapidly after 1891, but decreased compared to the total of all companies (about 14 percent in 1871, declining to 6 percent in 1911).

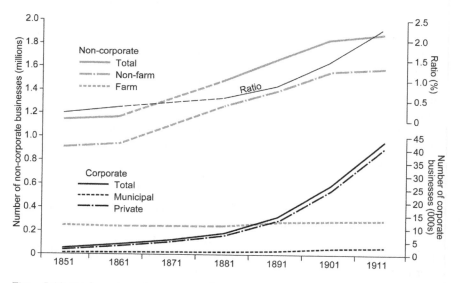

Figure 5.10 Total number of corporate and non-corporate businesses 1851–1911 in England and Wales, and ratio between the two (1871 not available for non-corporate and hence ratio)

Source: BBCE database.

In comparison, non-corporate numbers grew steadily over the period, but at a slower rate than corporations in the later part of the period. The slowdown in non-corporate numbers 1901–11, as previously indicated from Figure 4.1, can now be seen as coinciding with the most rapid period of growth in corporate numbers. The comparison is particularly stark for farming (which had no significant domestic corporate activity), which stagnated in business numbers over the whole period whilst non-farm non-corporate numbers grew rapidly, and remained strong up to 1911. These estimates confirm that far from declining over the Victorian era, entrepreneurship remained buoyant, but its form was beginning to change fundamentally as corporate numbers began to take off.

Trends in business incomes, however, show an entirely different picture. Figure 5.11 shows the level of gross profits based on adjusted Feinstein estimates from 1855 to 1938 for the UK. From Feinstein's (1972: Table 1) estimates we already know that total UK self-employment income (which was Feinstein's definition of non-corporate entrepreneurial income) continued to grow up to World War I (except for cyclical fluctuations), but reduced relatively: from 70 percent of all business income for the earliest year Feinstein was able to estimate in 1889, to 58 percent by 1900, and 53 percent by 1913. Figure 5.11 now allows this trend to be taken back to 1855 and non-corporate components to be seen. It shows an important contrast between the early and later parts for our main period of analysis. For 1855–71 the growth of the non-corporate sector was more buoyant than the corporate sector. For the later period, however, the economic downturn of the 1870s and 1880s, as well as other drivers, triggered a steep change in market dominance towards the corporate sector. The key shift in entrepreneurship over the Victorian era was thus less about entrepreneurial

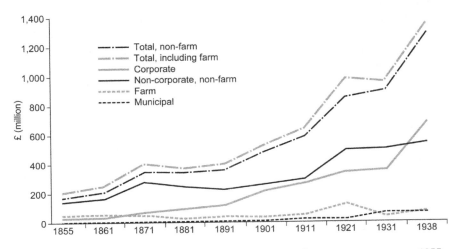

Figure 5.11 Incomes (gross profits £m) in the corporate and non-corporate sectors 1855–1938 in the UK. 1871 interpolated

Source: Adjusted from Feinstein (1972).[8]

numbers, than changes in the incentives towards the higher average earnings possible in the corporate sector from a small but increasing number of companies that were able to grow into major concerns.

The non-corporate sector experienced a steady decline in gross profits in the slowdown from the 1870s up to 1891; incomes then slowly increased 1891–1911, before experiencing a period of more rapid growth 1911–21 (mainly a result of abnormal farm payments). In contrast, the corporate sector showed no major decline after 1871 measured at the points of the 10-year time slices of the census dates (although declines for individual years occurred, e.g. in the 1870s). Corporate incomes also increased more rapidly after 1891 and again after 1931. Although non-corporate incomes grew again after the 1890s, the ratio of non-corporate to corporate profits showed a long-term decline over the whole period 1855–1938. The level of non-corporate profits (non-farm) within the economy fell from about 85 percent of total output in 1855 to 71 percent in 1881, 51 percent in 1911 and 42 percent in 1938. Even including farming, non-corporate income fell from 87 percent in 1855 to 45 percent in 1938. Hence whilst non-corporate numbers continued to dominate (as shown in Figure 5.10), profits had to be shared between a larger population of non-corporate businesses whose incomes were growing at a slower rate. Figures 5.10 and 5.11 confirm that the depression of industry in the 1880s did mark the acceleration of a shift to corporate control. This would have also shifted more businesses towards hierarchy and reduced the role of craft masters, as suggested by Landes (1969) and Littler (1982), but the earlier discussion of this chapter shows this would have been slow compared to the continued growth of small and own-account non-corporate businesses until World War I.

The information now available on corporate and non-corporate business numbers could allow calculations of profit per firm; this is a different way to compare firm size that is comparable between non-corporate and corporate (where workforce data are not available). However, the preliminary estimates here require adjustment: to disaggregate the UK and to allow for many non-corporate incomes not recorded as exempt under the personal threshold for taxation (whereas all corporate profit was taxed whatever level). Further research is needed to make these adjustments. However, crude comparisons show the stark contrast: corporates had average incomes 100 times larger than non-corporates and, even excluding own-account entrepreneurs, had average incomes 10 times larger than non-corporate employers. Hence, whilst non-corporate numbers continued to dominate and indeed increased, firm size (measured as profits per firm) was being increasingly concentrated within the much smaller corporate sector.

5.5   Conclusion

This chapter has examined trends of firm size and the balance between incorporated and non-incorporated proprietors. It has allowed for the first time a whole-population tracking of the transition from a restricted pattern of limited numbers of large firms in a few sectors to more widespread large firm development, and also greater concentration within the small-medium size categories. Against this, firms run by small employers contracted, although own-account activity remained expansive before showing the first evidence of contraction over 1901–11. The small firm remained dominant, as observed by Marshall and others, but we can now examine the changes within the firm-size distribution. Further analysis using the database created can be developed to expand the analysis to test Gibrat effects which show expansion of the upper tail (e.g. Montebruno et al., 2019b), and to trace how individual firms evolved over time using record linkage. These are parts of future research. But the key conclusion of this chapter is that over the Victorian era entrepreneurship did not see a decline as often claimed, but it did see a major shift in the form of entrepreneurship fuelled by the incentives towards the higher average earnings possible in the corporate sector from the increasing number of companies able to grow into major concerns, and pressures on the smallest employers (mainly under 10 employees), and own-account operators that began to experience significant declines. This shift to more 'modern' forms of business organisation contrasts with the traditional picture of the Victorian and Edwardian entrepreneur failing to adapt to new conditions and adopt new practices (Chandler, 1990).

Our earlier conclusions in Chapter 4 about the period up to 1901–11 marking the 'age of entrepreneurship' allow shifts in firm size to be compared with the rapid changes in corporate activity. The comparison of corporate and non-corporate developments in Figures 5.10 and 5.11, set against Table 5.2 and Figure 5.2, show the non-corporate sector accommodating to pressures on profits by a decline in the smallest employer businesses (under 10 employees), increases in small-medium businesses of 10–19 employees, and after 1871 for firms with more than 20 employees, with many of the smallest operators becoming own account. The overall pattern therefore shows a three-way strategy: shifts in non-corporates towards larger sizes where expansion was possible, reductions in the smallest employer business numbers and a shift to own account (perhaps using increasing proportions of part-time family and spouse inputs). These were different ways to cope with pressures from the growing competition from large corporate and non-corporate firms, and the alterative attractions of waged employment.

The shifts in firm size for different parts of the non-corporate sector evident in Figures 5.6–5.8 can now be seen in the wider context of the whole business population. The growing impact of business incorporation fits the expected sectors of mining, large-scale manufacturing, (mainly in textiles and metals processing, iron and steel shipbuilding), utilities and transport. The effect of incorporation on firm-size analysis based solely on the census removes an increasing number of businesses from the calculations (by dividing workers by underestimated employer numbers, it overstates mean size in sectors where incorporation was important). Nevertheless the trends were similar. This is partly because the number of corporations was still small and hence in most sectors they were swamped by the large number of micro-businesses, and also because the actual trends by firm size were in many sectors similar for both corporates and non-corporates. Non-corporates as well as corporates were capable of achieving Chandlerian economies of scale, at least into the immediate period before World War I (Hannah, 2014).

However, the analysis in Figures 5.9 and 5.11 reinforces the observation by Hannah and Kay (1977) and others that although the non-corporate sector was able to continue to act as a major part of the economy up to and after World War I, the corporate sector increasingly dominated, with growing business concentration among the largest firms (Hart, 1960; Prais, 1964, 1981; Wardley, 1999; Hannah, 2014). The period after the 1870s thus appears to evidence the start of the take-off in the benefits of Chandlerian management hierarchy within corporate organisational models. For the 1870s–1911 this was mainly evident in coal, steel, major manufacturing and utilities, shipbuilding, and small parts of a few other sectors.

The turning point for the end of the Victorian 'age of entrepreneurship' we recognise for 1901 was thus a combination of major shifts towards concentration in larger firms both corporate and non-corporate, but more dispersion in the non-corporate sector towards a growing proportion of medium-sized and large, rather than very small firms. The trends we recognise confirm previous analyses that the corporate sector was now beginning to dominate among large firms, especially after 1891. The turning point over 1901–11 re-balanced the economy towards growing numbers of large and increasingly corporate proprietors, a trend that was going to continue through most of the twentieth century; this ran concurrently with rebalancing after 1901 towards reduced own-account proprietors with no employees, a trend that was to accelerate after World War I. The rest of this book analyses these trends in more detail at the level of individual entrepreneurs.

Notes

1 Employers (with number of men) – 1851 Census England & Wales, General Report 1852–53 [1691-I], Vol. LXXXVIII Part I, pp. cclxxvi–cclxxix.
2 RDs are used because the small size of RSDs is insufficient for stable estimation. Like firm size, farm size is a truncated log-normal distribution (Allanson, 1992), with estimates based a logistic (Montebruno et al., 2019a).
3 Report from Select Committee on the Companies Acts, 1862 and 1867 (1877), *Parliamentary Papers*, VIII, 419; Statement of the number of banking and other registered joint stock companies . . . , 1883, Command Papers 3542, *Parliamentary Papers*, LXIV, 489; Todd, 1932: 51.
4 e.g. *Statistical Abstract of the United Kingdom*, Cd. 7875 (1895) Table 76, Cd. 4805 (1909) Table 84, Cd. 1774 (1922) Table 78.
5 Foreign earnings and dividends were reported under other elements of Schedule D, or were taxed separately abroad.
6 There is also discrepancy with Worswick and Tipping's (1967) 1909 estimates, as they included some foreign receipts, and some financial entities that were employees, which are excluded here.
7 Tax years used are those best aligned to census years, which are two years following the census; e.g. 1883–84 for the 1881 census. This is the same as Worswick and Tipping (1967) and Feinstein (1972).

8 The incomes in Figure 5.11 are based on Feinstein (1972) with adjustments. Feinstein Table 29 is used from 1889, supplemented with Table 23 for farm income; estimates for 1855–81 are from Feinstein Table 1 (and farm incomes from Table 23), but self-employment non-farm and corporate incomes are separated within Feinstein's aggregate using the new census estimates of non-corporates and IR tax tables scaled from external data as discussed in the text, using England and Wales ratios applied to the UK (these are preliminary estimates but any subsequent adjustments would not change the trends visible in Figure 5.11). In Feinstein the UK estimates include Southern Ireland up to 1920 and exclude thereafter (but this has small effect except on farm incomes); all his methods and adjustments apply, including ignoring the small number of farms that were corporate; public corporations which enter Feinstein's tables in 1932 are excluded as small (only £10m in 1938); farm incomes 1916–22 include abnormal payments that make 1921 aberrant.

Part 3

Understanding entrepreneurship at the individual level

6 Explaining entrepreneurship
Correlates and decision choices

6.1 Introduction

In Chapters 4 and 5 we looked at aggregate trends. In Part 3 of this book we move to a series of chapters that look at the individual entrepreneurs. This chapter gives an overview of the key factors characterising entrepreneurism and develops the choice framework introduced in Chapter 2. We identify the different types of entrepreneurs in each period, compare them with non-entrepreneurs and estimate the influence of different factors and opportunities on the choices that individuals made or were forced to pursue. The development of more detailed understanding of the main factors (demography and family, gender, geography, migration and portfolio activity) is investigated in Chapters 7–11. This chapter is chiefly a statistical analysis. This allows all factors available in the historical data that influence decisions to be *included together*, and their *relative* importance to be evaluated. The advantage of this approach is the capacity to measure the role of one factor whilst taking account of others. This is not usually possible in simple multi-way tabulations because the marginal effects of one factor, after controlling for others, cannot be easily evaluated. This chapter therefore provides the underpinnings for the following chapters by confirming the main dimensions of entrepreneurship for the period. This approach allows an historical assessment of the question raised by Parker (2004) and Blanchflower (2000) of the factors behind entrepreneurship. As this chapter relies on individual-level data, analysis is restricted to the historical censuses for which such data are available: 1851–1911, and at this stage to England and Wales.

The chapter falls into five sections. Section 6.2 develops the main choice framework outlined in Chapter 2: the decision between employer, own account and worker status for non-corporate business proprietors. This provides the 'base model' and its statistical interpretation. It identifies the central role of age, gender and marital status, and relationships within households, as the key generic factors associated with different levels of individual entrepreneurship. These form the foundation for Chapters 7 and 8. The following sections of this chapter then develop the base model for the specific analysis of locational opportunity (Section 6.3), portfolio businesses (Section 6.4) and portfolio in relation to firm size (Section 6.5) which provide the foundations for Chapters 9–11. The base model is extended in Section 6.6 to include the distinctive characteristics of company directors.

6.2   Base model: age, gender, marital status, household resources

As noted in Chapter 2, sole proprietors with no employees are a base case of zero agency costs (Jensen and Meckling, 1976; Ang et al., 2000). Taking on employees allows business expansion, but incurs higher management trans-action costs, bonding costs and the challenges of managing agency effects. The modern literature on the choice between sole proprietorship and being an employer is relatively limited, compared to that between corporates and non-corporates. A recent review by Evert et al. (2016) has almost no studies of the choice between sole proprietorship and being an employer. However, co-preneurship studies have investigated some of the key characteristics, with Mohr and Spekman (2006) and Zona (2015) showing the strong interaction of business and household decisions between marital and cohabiting partners, as well as with others within family or social networks. Other modern co-preneurship investigations show that mutual supports between husband and wife are usually most important, that wider family relationships and networks extend resources available and that formality and informality interrelate, leading frequently to blurred boundaries between personal and business ties (Fitzgerald and Muske, 2002; Muske et al., 2009). However, the empirical questions exam-ined in co-preneurship have not in general been extended to other businesses, although they form part of the broader literature on family firms in modern (Ang et al., 2000) and historical studies (Colli, 2003; Colli et al., 2003). Similarly, for corporates, family and kin have been found important to networks of director control and succession planning, and an important debate has developed over how to measure and compare different legal forms of close control by directors (La Porta et al. 1998, 2008; Ang et al., 2000). Concerning gender, some of this literature suggests significant differences between male and female proprietors, such as a preference for single-gender over mixed-gender partners (Mukhtar, 1998). However, most gender research for the UK suggests few differences between businesses by gender (Rosa and Hamilton, 1994; Marlow et al., 2009; Howorth et al., 2010).

Previous historical studies tend to be smaller scale. For non-corporates, family and wider networks have been found to be important for profit sharing, entry and exit by family members, expansion of capital using close kin and wider networks of trust relationships and facilitating succession planning (Pollard, 1968: 150–5; Harris, 2000; Lamoreaux and Rosenthal, 2005: 41–2). Family and kin networks have been mainly examined in business histories of individual firms, and in the larger scale *Dictionary of Business Biography* (see Jeremy, 1998; Jeremy and Shaw, 1984–6). Family structures have been noted as strong sup-ports to smaller nineteenth-century businesses, especially when female headed (Anderson, 1971, 1988; Malcolmson, 1986; Crossick, 1978, 2000; Davidoff and

Hall, 1997; Davidoff, 2012). In the nineteenth century the transition from non-corporate to corporate is often important for individual case studies.

Constraints on women's opportunities in businesses were important in the historical period. Even through there were various practical ways through which women could be involved as owners and employers, these were often special cases (e.g. through inheritance of investment assets or through taking over a business through widowhood), and progress remained slow even after the reforms of the Married Women's Property Act (1882). However, we find that many women did operate businesses, especially married women. This confirms the findings of Davidoff (2012) that businesses were a route to greater independence, though she believed this was mainly important for single women and widows, and for wider kin (nieces, cousins, aunts), which she assessed using the same census data used here for 1881. In addition we expect to find age important as a measure of life cycle effects. We also expect the dimensions highlighted in Chapters 4 and 5 of firm sector and size to interact with gender and marital status, age and position within households as key variables in estimation at the individual level.

Our estimates construct a base model to compare different types of entrepreneurs (employers and own account) with each other, and with waged workers (economically active, but not entrepreneurs at that point of time). These are category distinctions which are extended to include corporate entrepreneurs in Section 6.6. To estimate the effects of multiple variables on the category distinctions between entrepreneurs we use discrete choice estimation based on logit and multinomial logit models. These estimate the probability of being an employer compared to an own-account sole proprietor, and the probability of both types of entrepreneur compared with waged employment. Estimation of decision choices is undertaken at the level of each individual, controlling for interaction with other factors, through two models. In *Model 1*, which is the core decision model between organisational choices, the dependent variable is a multinomial indicator in three categories: employer, own account and worker. Explanatory variables include age, population density and number of servants as continuous variables. Age is measured as both a linear and squared term to capture expected nonlinearities. Population density is measured per acre for each RSD to assess effects of level of urbanisation, as well as to control for potential nonlinear relationships as density squared to indicate changing opportunities at different levels of localised market potential. The model also includes a variable to capture effects of number of servants. This acts as a proxy for wealth and other resources available that may release entrepreneurs' time as well as in some cases contributing to the business (as in many shops and on farms). Note that employment of domestic staff alone does not mean the individual was an entrepreneur: the census and our analysis exclude this as employer status. This differs from some modern studies. The same 13 sectors within the EA17 categories are used, as in Chapters 4 and 5, estimated as dummy variables.

Model 2 seeks to interpret the relation between family and intra-household structures in more depth. It includes additional variables for household relationships using dummy variables for various family and non-family connections identifiable from the census. Because of the overlap of these categories, gender and marital status are now estimated separately between the different household relationships. Relationships are measured relative to the 'head' of the house, who was most commonly the husband in a married household with children. Other explanatory variables correspond to Model 1.

In both models, because our unit of analysis is individuals, we take into account that people in the same cluster (the same parish or RSD) have the same spatial measures (such as population density or urban/rural classification). This leads to common cluster-level effects or level-2 errors, which have to be controlled for in the estimation process. Given the constraints of the data, as discussed in Chapter 4, we allow for non-response and misallocation biases in the later censuses using weighted estimates. For the earlier censuses we use the reconstructed data described in Chapter 4.

Model 1: Estimates for joint categories of marital status and gender

In Model 1, as well as other variables, marital status and gender are combined to create six dummy variables to compare against married men (the base category). The results are reported in Table 6.1 for 1901, with estimates for 1891 and 1911 given in WP 15. Logit and multinomial models estimate the probability of being in one state compared with a base category. In our case the base category is worker; hence we assess the probability of being an entrepreneur compared with being a worker. In the table two versions of the estimates are compared: in column 2 the weighted logit model gives the probability of being *either* an employer or an own-account self-employed; that is, all entrepreneurs compared to workers. Columns 3 and 4 give the *separate* probabilities of being an employer or an own account compared to workers using a multinomial logit estimator. The estimation in column 2, by combining employers and own account, overcomes any errors in classification of entrepreneur categories.

Focusing initially on the impact of gender and marital status on the probability of being an *employer* (column 3), the estimates suggest that all categories were less likely to be employers than married men (the base category): with single women the least likely of all to be employers, followed in declining rank order by married women, and then single men, widows and widowers. This strongly confirms the dominant role of the Victorian marital unit as a major advantage in mutual resource support: freeing the husband to develop the business whilst wives and family provided household support and other unpriced inputs to the family business. However, when death of the spouse occurred, women as widows show higher probability of maintaining or initiating employer status than men as widowers. Such widows may have already been de facto partners in the business, but this was not recorded in the census responses.

For *own account* (column 4) the pattern is very different. Married men no longer had the highest probability of entrepreneurial activity; instead it was married women, followed by widows and single women, each of which were more probable to be own account than married men. Single men were less likely to be

Table 6.1 Estimates of the coefficient probabilities of the weighted logit model for the probability of being an entrepreneur (col. 2), and weighted multinomial logit model for the probability either employer or an own account (cols. 3 and 4), compared to being a worker (omitted base category) in 1901

	All Entrepreneurs	Employers	Own Account
Density	−0.00946	−0.00825	−0.00993
Density^2	0.0000279	0.0000249	0.0000291
Age	0.157	0.189	0.146
Age^2	−0.00124	−0.00160	−0.00111
Single men	−0.610	−0.887	−0.463
Widowers	−0.326	−0.467	−0.228
Single women	−0.0268	−1.433	0.277
Married women	0.167	−1.030	0.472
Widows	0.222	−0.284	0.400
Number of servants	0.941	1.369	0.553
Mining and quarrying	−2.689	−2.582	−2.841
Construction	−0.398	−0.374	−0.432
Manufacturing	−1.183	−1.091	−1.220
Maker-dealer	0.973	0.388	1.314
Retail	1.104	0.598	1.436
Transport	−1.441	−1.963	−1.108
Professional and business services	−0.793	−1.346	−0.432
Personal services	0.285	−0.697	0.693
Agricultural processing and dealing	0.113	0.0391	0.154
Food sales	1.671	0.890	2.079
Refreshment	1.097	−0.321	1.646
Finance and commerce	−0.0181	−0.561	0.333
Constant	−5.454	−6.835	−5.923
Observations	10,637,079	10,637,079	
Pseudo R^2	0.279	0.264	

Source: BBCE database.

Density at RSD level; married include spouse absent; base categories omitted are: worker, male, married, and farming/estate work (for 13 sectors). All coefficients significant at $p \geq 0.01$, except finance and commerce (col. 2) where $p \geq 0.1$.

own account than widowers, who were both less likely to be own account than married men. This is a striking and significant comparison not previously noted in nineteenth-century studies. It confirms the general and dominant status of the so-called 'male breadwinner family' as waged labour, and also the dominance of married males among employers. But it also demonstrates that women were important complementary supports to the male waged breadwinner, developing income opportunities through their own entrepreneurial activities. It has often been observed that women 'earned a bit on the side'; see for example the case studies of Davidoff and Hall (1997); Davidoff (2012), Samuel's (1975, 1977) ethnographic studies, and Benson's (1983) 'penny capitalists'. However, rather than being a minor occupation that wives and other women engaged in, the census indicates that it was a major contribution to family incomes for many married women. It also confirms the argument from case studies that widows and single women used own–account self-employment as a major way to maintain their independence. In contrast widowers and single men were much more likely to be waged workers.

With regard to *all entrepreneurs* (column 2), there is an averaging, with the higher numbers of own account than employers weighting the estimates to the greatest extent. But the surprising result is that the highest probability of being an entrepreneur was for widows, then married women, which were all greater than for married men. Single women had almost the same probability of being an entrepreneur as married men, followed by widowers, and lowest of all for single men. Modern data show growing levels of entrepreneurship among women, but it is clear that this was a phenomenon of long-standing, and that modern trends may be only recovering levels of female self-employment that were much more widespread in the 1891–1911 period. Although many would be survival and necessity entrepreneurs, the estimates confirm that entrepreneurial spirit existed strongly among women as well as men at this time, and that the dominant pull of the higher wages and greater security of wage employment frequently tilted towards recruiting males. It is also to be borne in mind that with the dominance of males in the waged labour market the main alternative for women was domestic service which was either unattractive to many or was biased towards younger single women and relatively closed once women were married. Note that the estimation covers only those sectors with entrepreneurs, focusing on the sectors where there was a choice. Well-paid categories of male employment in public administration, and the most frequent category of female employment in domestic service, are excluded. The results are the more remarkable since, as noted in Chapter 3, there was a systematic tendency in the census to under-record female occupations in general, and especially those of wives. Further discussion of this important finding is carried out in Chapter 8.

Turing to the sector variables in the model we would expect important differences due to differing market conditions for waged labour. There were strong contrasts between mining, heavy manufacturing and transport (dominated by large railway companies and dock enterprises) that employed large numbers of waged personnel on the one hand, intermediate sectors such as construction, and commerce that had a mix of large businesses and smaller traders, and on the other hand sectors such as maker-dealers, refreshments and retail that were predominantly small traders. This is indeed the case. For *employers* (column 3) the lowest probability of being an employer is in mining, followed in rank order by transport, professional and business services (because of the high level of clerical activity), and then manufacturing. In contrast the highest probability of being an employer is in food sales, followed by more general retail, and then maker-dealers. A similar general grouping of sector probabilities also characterises *own account* (column 4), but there are important contrasts, where the highest probability is in food sales, followed by refreshments, retail, then maker-dealers and personal services. These all reflect ease of market entry and the influence of gender: they are all sectors that were accessible to all and often especially useful for women. The overall pattern of entrepreneurship (column 2) also reflects the greater own-account opportunities and high female participation. The sector estimates therefore demonstrate how different market conditions with varied levels of business concentration interacted with gender as key drivers of choice between employer, own account and worker status.

The remaining three variables in the estimates (number of servants, density and age) show a generally strong positive and highly significant interrelationship of entrepreneurship with the *number of household servants*, as expected, which had much higher impact for employers than own-account proprietors. Servants released time and may have contributed to an entrepreneur's business, especially in shops and on farms, although termed servants in the census. This is borne out in the estimates: employers are the most strongly differentiated by servant numbers from workers; and own account, although having a much lower probability of having servants than employers, were still strongly differentiated from workers.

Age is estimated as a nonlinear effect as both a direct and squared term. The estimates show that this fits the model found in most literature (e.g. Rønning and Kovereid, 2006; Westhead and Howorth, 2007; Lévesque and Minniti, 2006): that the probability of being an entrepreneur increases with age until a certain point where it levels off and then declines. This differs significantly from worker status: probability of being an employer rises faster than being a worker with early age, stabilises for most of the working life, but then declines more quickly than workers at the oldest ages. The propensity of being an employer also rises more steeply with age than for own account, but the differences are small and declines at higher ages are similar. Age effects are discussed further in Chapter 7, which shows contrasted gender patterns.

Population density is also estimated as a nonlinear effect. The relationship with entrepreneurship is complex. There is generally a declining propensity to be either an employer of own account as density increases, but this is attenuated by the effect of the positive coefficient on the squared term which increases entrepreneur propensity at higher densities. This indicates behaviourally that much entrepreneurship is highly localised and serves immediate market opportunities, especially at very low population densities in rural areas. But as density increases the opportunities of wider markets beyond the locality, especially in higher density urban areas, the propensity to be an entrepreneur increases. As with age, the differences between employers and own account are small. Own account propensity is slightly higher at both lower and higher densities reflecting their generally greater numbers, but also reflecting the easier market entry for own account in both rural and urban conditions especially by women.

The estimated patterns of relationships were remarkably consistent across the years 1891–1911 (WP 15). However, there are four indications of trends.

First, there is a steady downward trend in the size of coefficients from 1891 to 1911 suggesting that differences in marital status and gender were diminishing compared to married men, though differences remained highly statistically significant and in essentially the same rank order. The marital unit continued to offer the dominant advantage for employer probability. Among women, the difference between own-account single and married women diminished to a very small factor. Second, between sectors the trends reflect patterns shown in Chapter 4: the probability of being an employer in mining, processing agricultural produce, food sales and refreshment increased; while it decreased in maker-dealing, retail and professional services, and the probability became even more negative in manufacturing, construction, transport, personal services and finance and commerce where consolidation into larger firms reduced the scope to develop as independent employers. At this stage these changes were gradual, though their trend is clear. Third, the probability of being an own-account proprietor declined in most sectors compared to farming (the base category) as consolidation squeezed out scope for easy market entry for entrepreneurs of both genders. Only construction and processing of agricultural produce had higher probabilities in 1911 than 1891. The general declines of own account are again in line with Chapter 4, indicating increasing consolidation as scale economies shifted the balance towards larger plants and organisation in most sectors. Fourth, the role of the other variables tended to shift in a reinforcing direction. The number of servants was less important by 1911 for both employers and own account, as the consolidation at the more micro level provided less scope to use domestic supports as a competitive resource. Age tended to increase the probability of operating as entrepreneurs in middle and later years. The negative influence of density generally increased over time as a result of the expansion of urban areas to cover a larger proportion of the population that facilitated agglomeration economies. This was consistent with, and underpinned, business concentration more generally.

Model 2: Estimates for interactions of marital status, gender and household structure

Model 2 presents a different approach where the composite categories of gender and marital status are separated between different household relationships using a fully interacted model between gender and marital status (i.e. five levels and six single interactions) for various family and non-family connections identifiable from the census. The estimates are shown in Table 6.2 for 1901, with the arrangement as in Table 6.1. Apart from the family relationship variables, the other variables are the same as in Table 6.1, have similar estimates and are reported in WP 15 for 1891–1911.

The separation of the different effects draws out even more clearly the greater probabilities in general of women being entrepreneurs (once those of servant status are removed), with own account much more probable for women than men. But this is now tempered by being able to see separately the interaction effects

Table 6.2 Estimates of the coefficient probabilities of the weighted logit model (col. 2) and weighted multinomial logit model (cols. 3 and 4) in 1901, as in Table 6.1; only gender, relationship status and interaction between gender/marital status shown; base categories omitted are worker, male, married, household head; all significant at p ≥ 0.01

	All Entrepreneurs	Employer	Own Account
Female	0.715	0.0424	0.870
Single	0.0929	0.178	0.151
Widowed	−0.0323	−0.134	0.0540
Female # Single	−0.213	−0.699	−0.223
Female # Widowed	−0.317	−0.00207	−0.403
CFU member	−0.694	−1.464	−0.493
Older generation	−1.265	−2.066	−1.084
Siblings	−0.744	−1.249	−0.572
Other family	−1.069	−2.378	−0.767
Servants	−4.226	−3.863	−4.374
Working title	−2.676	−1.378	−3.106
Lodgers/boarders	−1.256	−1.644	−1.154
Non-household	−1.625	−2.321	−1.481
Unknown	−0.597	−0.179	−0.727
Observations	10,637,079	10,637,079	
Pseudo R^2	0.294	0.278	

Source: BBCE database.

with marriage and household status. Being single for men (the base) increases the probability of entrepreneurship once household position is controlled for, but for single women greatly reduces it. Widow- or widowerhood in general reduces the probability of being an employer, but increases the probability of own account. This extends the interpretation of Model 1 by indicating that own account was particularly strongly developed by married women, which was in turn a reflection of their labour market opportunities within the marital unit where husbands were predominately waged workers. This in turn indicates a strong necessity motivation; that wives were seeking to supplement household income.

Within the rest of the household, compared with heads (the base category) all other within-household relations had much lower probabilities of being entrepreneurs. As expected this is lowest of all for servants and those with a working title (usually 'assistants' in the business), followed by boarders and lodgers, and then those with various levels of family and non-family interrelationship. For *employers* the highest probability of entrepreneurship among relatives is for siblings of the head: brother–brother, sister–sister and brother–sister sometimes operate in partnership, or operate as heads of different businesses, and cohabit the same household. Indeed analysis of 1881 census data on partnerships for the period shows that siblings constituted 28 percent of all recognisable partnerships in non-farm businesses, and 42 percent on farms, with brother–brother partnerships most frequent (Bennett, 2016: Tables 6 and 7). However, sibling's probabilities of entrepreneurship were still much lower than for heads, and all other household relations had even lower probabilities. This indicates that employers were the dominant entrepreneur figures in their households: all others are part of domestic support that released resources for them to focus on business, confirming that in general entrepreneurs tended to reduce the involvement of other household members as independent entrepreneurs. Of course those family members not resident in the same household may have been partners or run independent businesses but are not included in this analysis.

Tuning to *own account*, although again there were no types of individuals within a household that have a higher probability of entrepreneurship than the own-account head, and the range of negative probabilities is similarly wide to that of employer-headed households, some within the household have less negative probabilities than for employers. Among these, other members of the nuclear family (conjugal family unit of children and spouses) were the most likely to be also own account, followed by siblings and other family (which included grandchildren, cousins and other relatives). These relatives all had higher probability of being an entrepreneur than similar relatives in an employer-headed household. The relationship of the household to entrepreneurship is discussed at greater length in Chapter 7.

All these results confirm the role of family resources, especially from wives, but also from sons and daughters, in facilitating increased household income either by supporting the head through domestic duties, pursuing external waged employment and, especially for wives, by developing own-account activity. Over 1891–1911 the household unit became slightly less important to supporting the activities of household business heads, as urban dominance and business concentration steadily ate into the opportunities for smaller firms. But this remained the period where domestic supports were critical to non-corporate business activity.

6.3   Locational opportunity

Responsiveness to opportunities was one of the key characteristics of entrepreneurship, as discussed in Chapter 2. Following Knight (1921) and Kirzner (1979) entrepreneurism is understood as 'alertness' to hitherto unexploited opportunities for arbitrage. Among the many drivers of change in entrepreneurship for the Victorian era that opened scope for opportunity-based entrepreneurship was the urbanisation (which increased from 54 to 79 percent 1851–1911 of England and Wales: Lawton and Pooley, 1992), and improved transport from roads, waterways and especially railways. These developments increased potential business scale and access. They modified market opportunities in two directions: they opened up opportunities for existing firm expansion or new firms, either locally or from outside a locality, and they eroded the power of local firms that had previously held a local monopoly in production or services. Increased market opportunities thus should have led entrepreneurs to a wide range of responses that increased competition, reduced previous deadweight and increased overall economic growth. But this would have differed significantly by location and business sector. To assess these potential effects here, we extend the previous models of discrete choice discussed above to estimate the effect of different locational opportunities.

Three forms of opportunity are tested in this analysis:

- *Market potential and distance decay*: the distance (km) from the centre of the RSD or parish polygon to the nearest population centre (Pop: population size). The population centres are defined from the Law (1967) and Robson (1973) classification for the 934 towns/cities of over 2,500 population. The combination of population and distance give a form of gravity model estimate.
- *Type of parish within which the entrepreneur was located*: urban (base category), rural or one of the two transition categories of hinterland defined in WP 6 for towns over 10,000 population.
- *Distance to nearest rail line (km) at the census date*: rail lines are used because they capture all the main effects of alternatives (distance to rail stations, roads, waterways); see Bennett et al. (2019b).

The rest of the estimates use a slight simplification of Model 1, with age, age squared, gender, number of servants, relationship to head in six categories and marital status. The model is then estimated separately for each of the 13 sectors. The logit estimates for the probability of being an employer compared to own account are shown in Table 6.3 for 1851.

We might expect an increasing population to increase the probability of being an employer relative to own account since this increases market potential for large businesses. But Table 6.3 shows the reverse is generally true: the larger the population centre nearest to the entrepreneur, the lower the probability of being an employer and the greater the chance of being own account. This is most significant for farming, construction, manufactures, agricultural produce, food sales, refreshment and commerce. Distance has a uniformly negative effect: the larger the distance to a centre the less impact it has on the probability of being an employer. This effect is most highly weighted by distance for farming, manufactures, retail and personal services. These effects vary slightly by year, but the general pattern is stable, that where population potential is significant it depresses the probability of being an employer. However, the urban classification, where significant, is predominantly positive: the more urban the location, the higher the probability of being an employer, with significant negative coefficients compared to the urban base for hinterlands and rural areas: especially for construction, manufactures, maker-dealers, retail and commerce. The exception is farming where rural areas and hinterlands are significantly more likely to support employer than own-account businesses.

Table 6.3 Estimates of the coefficient probabilities in 1851 of the weighted logit model for the probability of being an employer compared to own account; separate estimates for each sector, clustered at continuous parish level, rail derived from WP 16; reconstructed data; base categories omitted: own account, urban, male, head of household, single

Sector	Pop (000s)	TC (km)	Urban Class		Rail (km)	Age	Age²	Gender	Servants	Relationship to the Head				Marital status	
			Hint	Rural				Female		CFU	Older	Sibling	Other Family	Married	Widowed
Farming	−0.0115‡	−0.024‡	1.00‡	1.07‡	−0.01‡	0.036‡	−0.00032‡	−0.14‡	0.80‡	−1.15‡	−1.14‡	−1.20‡	−1.48‡	−0.24‡	−0.30‡
Mining etc.	−0.0113	−0.018	0.12	0.04	−0.02‡	0.024*	−0.00037‡	−0.50‡	0.61‡	−0.82‡	−0.57	−0.31	−0.77‡	0.35‡	−0.09
Construction	−0.0105‡	−0.011*	−0.31‡	−0.37‡	−0.01‡	0.126‡	−0.00134‡	−0.38‡	1.96‡	−0.68‡	−0.61‡	−0.70‡	−0.94‡	0.39‡	−0.13‡
Manufacture	−0.0094‡	−0.034‡	−0.45‡	−0.39‡	−0.00	0.026‡	−0.00041‡	−1.05‡	1.52‡	−0.79‡	−0.47‡	−0.81‡	−0.87‡	0.22‡	−0.08*
Maker-dealer	0.0009	−0.011†	−0.13‡	−0.06	−0.00	0.032‡	−0.00046‡	−1.08‡	1.20‡	−0.43‡	−0.32‡	−0.52‡	−0.73‡	0.29‡	0.10‡
Retail	−0.0043*	−0.028‡	−0.13‡	−0.34‡	−0.00	0.022‡	−0.00023‡	−0.82‡	1.35‡	−0.35‡	−0.17	−0.52‡	−0.54‡	0.18‡	0.09
Transport	−0.0045	−0.013	0.06	0.08	0.00	0.028‡	−0.00026‡	−0.63‡	1.49‡	−0.22‡	−0.49*	−0.06	−0.25	0.08	−0.05
Professional and business services	−0.0039	−0.037†	0.02	0.32‡	−0.00	0.035‡	−0.00028‡	−0.34‡	2.97‡	−0.36‡	−1.04‡	−0.49‡	−0.30	1.73‡	−0.11
Personal services	−0.0012	−0.032‡	0.05	0.03	−0.00*	0.031‡	−0.00029‡	0.32‡	0.65‡	−0.24**	−0.73‡	−0.30‡	−0.28	0.25‡	0.17‡
Agricultural processing	−0.0180‡	0.015	−0.05	0.33‡	−0.00	0.016*	−0.00040‡	−1.38‡	1.34‡	−1.10‡	−1.39‡	−0.97‡	−1.39‡	0.07	−0.03
Food sales	−0.0048‡	−0.001	−0.00	0.05	−0.01‡	0.006	−0.00011†	−0.51‡	1.65‡	−0.71‡	−0.77‡	−0.59‡	−0.75‡	0.08‡	−0.03
Refreshment	0.0103‡	0.011	0.08*	0.07	0.00	0.016‡	−0.00017‡	−1.13‡	1.47‡	0.15*	−0.43	0.00	0.11	0.55‡	0.29‡
Finance and commerce	0.0134‡	−0.038‡	−0.47‡	−0.32†	0.01†	−0.016	0.00004	−1.66‡	1.69‡	−0.24‡	−0.53	−0.11	−0.14	0.72‡	0.27‡

Source: BBCE database.

* p < 0.10, † p < 0.05, ‡ p < 0.01.

The impacts of rail lines generally increased the probability of employer status compared to own account: this was most significant for farming, mining, construction, food sales and commerce. In later years manufacturing (from 1871), retail (from 1881), and personal services and agricultural produce (from 1901) were also affected. The most affected sectors suggest that rail made market entry for own account more difficult, and it increased the scale of businesses mainly where more significant capital investment was needed (especially in mining, construction, commerce, manufactures and agricultural produce). Rail had less effect on sectors where market entry costs remained low: retail, services and refreshments, but the increase in employer probabilities for personal services from rail from 1901 was a sign of the increasingly difficult future in store for own-account entrepreneurship.

The rest of the estimates in Table 6.3 follow Tables 6.1 and 6.2. Age, gender, marital status, number of servants and relationship to the head of the census household unit are significant for almost all sectors. These are separate estimates for each sector and show weaker significance for mining, transport, agricultural produce, refreshments and commerce than the pooled estimates in the earlier tables, but in general the same conclusions apply.

We can also now see that these personal characteristics were mostly more significant, across more sectors, than were measures of locational opportunity. Locational opportunity (measured by the size of the nearest population centre, its distance away, urban location and distance for rail lines) generally significantly increased employer probabilities over own account in sectors where investment, premises and scale were needed: for most of the locational measures used here this was most apparent for construction, manufactures, retail and commerce. The same was true for farming, where almost all locational measures favoured employers over own account. In contrast, areas classified as rural or hinterlands significantly favoured own account. However, since all sectors were significantly affected by demographic factors, locational opportunities were mainly an extra factor for only some sectors significant. Opportunity-led entrepreneurism was thus important for the period, but the benefit of statistical estimates is to show that, after taking other major factors into account, the role as head, especially for married men of young to middle age, and support from family members and servants were among the most important influences on being an employer. This reflects the dominance of the non-corporate sector by small business where resources and personal support from the family played a major role.

The relatively secondary role of locational opportunity in some sectors is in some ways a surprise. However, it is explained by well-developed transport network present in England and Wales during the period examined. As shown in Table 6.4, although railways were the most significant transport innovation of the period, diffusing to cover more parishes over the 1851–1911 period, almost all parishes were already easily accessible by roads, and many also had waterway access before railways arrived. Because rapid industrialisation had been occurring since the eighteenth century, a well-developed transport system existed before the railways, and most railways followed previous transport-lines to connect existing centres (Mitchell, 1964). Consequently, rail mainly sped up existing access, rather than changing its geography.

Table 6.4 Number of continuous parishes that had rail lines, stations, turnpike, main road and waterway in 1851, 1881 and 1911 censuses; turnpike data are only available for 1851 and roads for 1900 (WP 16)

Transport Access	1851	1881	1911
Rail line in parish	3,018	5,857	6,691
Rail line in parish or ≤ 7.5 km	7,927	11,850	12,308
Rail station in parish	1,127	2,694	3,372
Rail station in parish or ≤ 7.5 km	7,171	11,459	12,156
Turnpike in parish	7,811	7,811	7,811
Turnpike in parish or ≤ 7.5 km	12,189	12,189	12,189
Main road in parish	8,575	8,575	8,575
Main road in parish or ≤ 7.5 km	12,522	12,522	12,522
Waterway in parish	2,783	2,546	2,306
Waterway in parish or ≤ 7.5 km	7,910	7,441	6,865

Source: BBCE database and Satchell et al. (2019) database (WP 16).

In addition, by the start of the analysis in 1851 the main national trunk railway network was complete so that the rail development we observe mainly connected more rural areas. However, even if we had a longer period of rail development, its effect on entrepreneur categories was probably relatively limited. Estimates of the effect of rail on the aggregate UK economy by Hawke (1970) and Mitchell (1964) suggest that in the early years the effects of rail on freight, and hence directly on business costs (rather than on passenger transport), were relatively small. Hawke (1970: 392) concluded that up to the 1870s rail caused 'no large or dramatic change' except for the transport of coal and iron ore and brewing (sectors we find among the most significantly affected by location in Table 6.3). Hawke also claimed 'the basic distribution of industry established before the arrival of the railways' was maintained: a claim we largely confirm in Chapter 9. Our finding is thus in line with more general evaluations of transport impacts, that the effect of the locational opportunities was focused on only some sectors, did not change accessibility for most places radically, but mainly reduced costs and speeded communications. It was mainly a support to other factors influencing entrepreneurial choice or a generic fillip to most businesses. It tended to increase the total volume of entrepreneurism: a rising tide lifting all ships. There were some significant effects on increasing firm size, with rail links showing direct casual effects on firm size after 10 or 20 years in differences-in-differences estimates for, in rank order, manufacturing, farming, agricultural produce, construction, retail and maker–dealers (Bennett et al., 2019b). However, it was generally most significant in parishes that had pre-existing turnpikes, roads or waterways (i.e. were pre-treated by earlier forms of transport access). This is in line with findings by Hawke (1970) for Britain, and Fogel (1964) and Atack et al. (2011) for the US, that railways made significant but relatively constrained contributions mainly in previously well-connected locations.

Similarly the effects of rail improvements on business choice were important but more marginal up to 1911. They contributed to patterns shown in Chapters 4 and 5: the relative increase in employers over own account after 1901, the radical increase in waged employment deriving from the growth of very large firms and the shift in the sectoral structure of the economy towards large manufacturing and extraction industries and towards the distribution and service sectors. But major locational impacts were sector and firm specific.

6.4 Portfolio businesses

As well as the distinction between employer and own account, a proprietor could also develop more than one business at the same time – acting as a portfolio entrepreneur. This could be important both for large-scale businesses to diversify into new markets and for small-scale operators to supplement low or insufficient earnings in a first business. In the census portfolio proprietors are identified as individuals listing more than one business in response to the occupation question (see Chapters 3 and 11). The analysis differs between the period 1851–81, which is restricted to extracted Groups 1–6 as listed in Chapter 4, and 1891–1911, where the portfolios are those responding as employers or own account. It should also be noted that the data for 1871 as in other chapters is less complete, but is reported here for comparison purposes. The results are reported in Table 6.5, but with a dividing line between 1881 and 1891 to highlight the difference in portfolio identification method. To save space only the coefficients estimated for portfolios are shown; the rest of the coefficients are very similar to those in Table 6.3.

Table 6.5 Estimates of the portfolio coefficient probabilities in 1851–1911 of the weighted logit model for the probability of being an employer compared to own account (base category); reconstructed data, 1851–81; all other definitions as in Table 6.3

Sector	*1851*	*1861*	*1871*	*1881*	*1891*	*1901*	*1911*
Farming	−0.63‡	−1.14‡	−0.25‡	0.27‡	0.28‡	−0.00	0.03
Mining and quarrying	0.29	0.38†	0.35	0.24†	0.03	−0.18†	0.07
Construction	1.25‡	1.36‡	0.71‡	1.08‡	0.03*	0.62‡	0.64‡
Manufacture	1.71‡	1.62‡	0.92‡	1.64‡	0.04†	0.30‡	0.29‡
Maker-dealer	2.10‡	1.96‡	1.19‡	1.90‡	0.26‡	0.32‡	0.17‡
Retail	3.46‡	2.40‡	0.75‡	2.58‡	0.26‡	0.40‡	0.56‡
Transport	1.27‡	1.34‡	0.77†	0.80‡	0.41‡	0.86‡	0.50‡
Professional and business services	0.00	1.71‡	1.01‡	3.60‡	0.18‡	0.35‡	0.11‡
Personal services	3.22‡	3.23‡	1.55‡	3.63‡	0.13†	0.26‡	0.21‡
Agricultural processing	3.97‡	2.70‡	1.42‡	1.81‡	0.17‡	0.45‡	0.01
Food sales	2.09‡	1.37‡	1.53‡	1.38‡	0.12‡	0.57‡	0.62‡
Refreshment	3.05‡	1.57‡	0.87‡	1.92‡	0.15‡	1.06‡	0.29‡
Finance and commerce	1.72‡	1.66‡	1.35‡	2.62‡	0.14†	0.38‡	0.02

Source: BBCE database.

Table 6.5 estimates the difference in probability of employer status compared to own account as a result of being a portfolio business rather than not having a portfolio. In all but a handful of sectors, where significant, portfolio businesses are much more likely to be employers than non-portfolios. This applies to all sectors in almost all years, except farming and mining. Moreover the discontinuity in method of identifying portfolios and source of the census question between 1881 and 1891 has little effect on significance, though it changes the scale of the coefficients estimated. This encourages us to conclude that the estimates are robust enough to be confident about the conclusions. The estimates also indicate a trend to a generally decreasing probability for portfolios to be employers over 1851–91 (with 1871 uncertain); that is, the scope to develop portfolios was becoming less important to employer decisions over time, with employers concentrating more resources into single sectors. This is interrelated with the general trend to increasing firm size over time, and the reduction in proportion of businesses under 10 employees observed in Chapter 5. However, after 1891 portfolios show a more diversified trend. The general trend of declining relevance of portfolios to employer status is shown for three to four sectors. However, portfolios were associated with increasing probability of being an employer in construction, retail and food sales. There were also more unstable results for 1911 that probably reflect the different way the census records survive (drawn from household returns rather than enumerators).

The exceptions to the general pattern were agriculture and mining. Farms generally had a negative relationship between employer status and portfolios, indicating that portfolios were more important to own account and thus evidence of an effect of survival entrepreneurship on marginal farms where farm income alone was insufficient. However, this relationship changed in 1881 and 1891, and became insignificant thereafter. The agricultural depression after 1873 appears to have forced employers to diversify into portfolios for a period, but after 1891 farms tended to separate into the two types of employer or own-account businesses with scope for portfolios playing little role in choice of entrepreneur status. Mining and quarrying, the other exception, had a significant positive association between employer status and portfolios in two years (1861 and 1881), and a small negative association in 1901. It is well-known that some mines and quarries did diversify: into related industries such as metal, clay or stone processing and construction, and for coal into smelting and metal refining; and for others into unrelated sectors, mainly the smallest businesses diversifying into carting or using the land for farming, and even retail and refreshments (see Chapter 11). However, the instability of the results in mining suggests that there may be data recording or other factors that restrict interpretation.

6.5   Corporate proprietors: company directors

To create a parallel analysis of incorporated businesses we use information on company directors who can be linked to the census. As explained in Chapter 3.4, we use company directors as the nearest equivalent to the non-corporate business proprietors who were the responsible individuals bearing the risks of running the enterprise; we do not directly consider other risk bearers such as shareholders, lenders and managers. The information is derived from the *Directory of Directors* linked to the 1881–1911 censuses, plus directors identified in the census itself. The latest year, 1911, is used here as this has the largest sample size which is most equal between the two sources: 6,990 directors who had census records identified from the census directly but not in the *Directory*, and 7,041 identified in the *Directory* and matched to the census; see Table 3.2. This sample size is large enough to give a robust analysis of the main differences between corporate and non-corporate entrepreneurs.

As argued in Chapter 2, the advantages of the corporate form favoured businesses that had greater opportunities for internal economies of scale and scope, and where externalisation of risk to a wider body of shareholders and larger financing was needed. This tended to be concentrated in larger firms, and some sectors rather than others. Comparison with workers is not a relevant base category for directors. Instead, we compare the corporate choice against all other proprietors (employers plus own account), and also directors against employers and own account separately. We expect the probability of a proprietor being a director to vary by business size, sector, location of main business activity, as well as demographic and other characteristics. The estimates of the choice model are made in the same way as the earlier parts of this chapter, with the variables defined identically. However, because of the very large number of companies that were utilities, these were separated from the rest of the manufacturing category in which they are included in the rest of this book; thus there are 14 sectors rather than 13, but farming remains the base. Although there were virtually no corporate farms in Britain, there were many companies involved in agriculture overseas.

The results of the estimates are shown in Table 6.6. The logit model for the probability of being a director (column 3) compared to all entrepreneurs produces similar results to that for employers against workers. Gender and marital status, however, are different, all categories were less likely to be directors than married men (the base category), but now with married women rather than single women the least likely of all to be directors. This is reverse of employers and own account where married women were more likely than single women to be entrepreneurs. However, it fits the nature of the very small number of female directors: they were mostly single and either inherited their position on the board from their father or were active in a sector dominated by single women. For density there is also a very different estimate than for other entrepreneurs. As they were very highly concentrated in London and the large cities, the probability of being a director compared to other entrepreneurs increased with density, with only a minor slowdown in this effect for very high densities; also density of the location is one of the least significant features of being a director. The other variables produce more comparable estimates. Director age effects are similar to other entrepreneurs, but strong age compared to age squared indicate that director probabilities increased more rapidly with age, and tailed off more slowly: they

Table 6.6 Estimates of the coefficient probabilities of the logit model for the probability of being a director (col. 2), compared with all employers and own account; and multinomial logit model for probability of being a director and employer, compared to own account (cols. 3 and 4), in 1911; other variables defined as in Table 6.1

	Directors	*Directors*	*Employers*
Density	0.0144***	0.0154***	−0.000255*
Density²	−0.000124***	−0.000127***	−0.00000131*
Age	0.0960***	0.108***	0.0254***
Age²	−0.000801***	−0.000946***	−0.000285***
Single men	−0.251***	−0.457***	−0.335***
Widowers	−0.362	−0.538	−0.391
Single women	−2.936***	−3.158***	−1.141***
Married women	−7.470***	−7.568***	−1.070***
Widows	−3.047***	−3.066***	−0.528***
Number of servants	0.418***	1.371***	0.987***
Mining and quarrying	4.231***	4.451***	0.301***
Construction	0.900***	1.043***	0.0533***
Manufacturing	3.537***	3.645***	0.144***
Maker-dealer	0.981***	0.687***	−0.608***
Retail	1.187***	0.787***	−0.788***
Transport	2.489***	2.309***	−0.434***
Professional and business services	2.161***	1.548***	−0.630***
Personal services	0.854***	−0.251*	−1.559***
Agricultural processing and dealing	3.696***	3.586***	−0.0877***
Food sales	−0.730***	−1.118***	−0.881***
Refreshment	−0.469**	−0.682***	−0.858***
Finance and commerce	3.001***	2.510***	−0.441***
Utilities	4.170***	4.116***	−0.0486*
Constant	−10.13***	−10.04***	−0.807***
Observations	1,672,122	1,672,122	
Pseudo R^2	0.308	0.161	

Source: BBCE database.

***$p \geq 0.01$, ** $p \geq 0.05$, * $p \geq 0.1$.

were older but had the same overall inverse U-shape. The number of domestic servants is an even stronger indicator of director status than of employer status. This surrogate income effect reflects the generally higher earnings to be obtained in companies compared to non-corporate businesses.

Sector differences strongly reflect both size/economy of scale effects, and the use of incorporation most frequently for more risky ventures. The highest probabilities of being a director compared to non-corporate status and compared to farming (the base case) were (ranked downwards): mining, utilities, agricultural processing, manufacturing, and finance and commerce. Being a director was unlikely in food sales and refreshment, where own-account ownership was dominant and there was very little market entry by corporates. The probability of being a director was also low in personal services, construction and maker-dealing: again, sectors where corporates had made few incursions. These were sectors where own account or small employers could continue to compete by being prepared to accept low or survival incomes.

The multinomial estimates of directors and employers are compared to own account as the base case in Table 6.6 (columns 3 and 4). The comparisons of employers with this own-account base are very similar to those in Table 6.1. The most important issue is the different factors influencing the distinction between the probability of being directors and employers. These two categories are the most comparable, as in some sectors there was a real choice between corporate and non-corporate form. Age, gender and marital status variables all operated in the same direction, with employers much closer in probability levels to directors than entrepreneurs as a whole (which are normally dominated by the more numerous own account). They were closest for single men and widows, and most distinct for all the female categories: bringing out how the few directors who were women were truly exceptional. Non-corporate male employers and directors of companies were therefore much less distinct from each other in gender and marital status than they were from female employers and directors. A similar closeness between employers and directors is reflected in the coefficients for age, age squared and number of servants.

For three sectors, personal services, food sales and refreshments, directors and employers were most similar to each other and distinct from own account. These sectors had negative probabilities of director and employer involvement, reflecting the willingness of own-account proprietors to operate in them on low incomes. Employers and directors have the same positive sign as the logit estimates in only three sectors: mining, construction and manufacturing. However, in each of these cases the employer probability was markedly lower. These were the sectors where many corporates were gaining considerable advantages of economies of scale and more profitable organisation than non-corporates; whilst traditional employers were still highly probable in these sectors compared to own account, directors were now significantly more frequent. Seven sectors have contrasted signs of positive for directors and negative for employers: maker-dealer, retail, transport, professional services, agricultural processing, finance and commerce, and utilities. In each of these sectors traditional employers were less likely to operate than own account, and also less likely than corporates: they were being squeezed from both sides. This is most surprising for maker-dealers, which was a small sector for corporates, but it shows some important development of corporate market entry by the time of these 1911 estimates.

Knight, Marshall and most contemporaries writing in the early twentieth century saw entrepreneurship increasingly favouring large corporations. The estimates here confirm that by 1911 this was certainly true in the main sectors requiring significant capital: mining, construction and manufacturing, in each of which traditional employers also remained strong. But it also shows that corporates were moving into seven sectors where traditional employers were suffering strong competition from own-account proprietors. Only in three sectors with low entry costs and willingness to operate on low incomes (personal services, food sale and refreshments) did employers and directors show similar negative probabilities, indicating less capacity to compete with own account. The results confirm that corporations were most common in sectors with high risk or where high degrees of division of labour were possible, favouring large-scale factories.

6.6 Conclusion

This chapter opens a new avenue of understanding on how an entrepreneur's organisational choice between employer and own account, choice between entrepreneurship and waged employment and the distinctiveness of directors was influenced and constrained by different factors. This seeks to answer the question 'what makes an entrepreneur' at the scale of the whole population for the historical period. The central focus has been on how the non-corporate population of own account and employers was distinguished from workers, but we have been able to extend analysis to corporate directors. For non-corporates we demonstrate that decisions between being employers or own-account proprietors interacted with the individual's age, gender, marital status, household and family relationships and locational opportunity. We also show how all these characteristics interacted with portfolio proprietorship. The estimates indicate that the choice between business forms (own account and employing others) varied significantly by age, income (through the surrogate variable of number of servants) and sector, and was heavily influenced by gender, marital status and family/household relationship structures.

Locational opportunity was also important, and most significant in some specific sectors, but even this was also strongly influenced by household and personal characteristics. Generally we confirm the findings of Hawke (1970) that railways contributed to a general rise in business activity, but mainly in previously well-connected locations which were chiefly urban. For the first time we have been able to estimate the effect of improved rail access on entrepreneurial choice between employer and own-account status. Its effects were important in some sectors but in conjunction with personal characteristics. As we have seen from earlier discussion, the relative share of employers over own account increased after 1901, but the most important changes were usually the radical increase in waged employment, sectoral shifts towards large manufacturing and extraction industries and an increasing presence of distribution and service sectors.

Portfolios interacted with personal and locational factors. The probability of being an employer increased for portfolio businesses in all sectors in almost all years, except farming and mining, though this trend decreased over time up to 1891. Portfolio concentration among own-account farms appears to have had a strong necessity driver in 1851–71, where farm income alone was insufficient, but portfolios then became less significant as farmers became more focused on their single business or moved out of the sector altogether. The results for mining and quarrying are unstable which suggests that there may be data recording or other factors that restrict interpretation in this sector.

One of the most important conclusions from the results of the base model is to strongly confirm earlier historical and modern studies that marital status, family relationships and gender were (and are) key influences on business involvement. The Victorian married couple offered an efficient means to share resources, with men either being freed for wage employment, employer or own-account activity (e.g. Anderson, 1971; Davidoff, 2012) with the family unit offering resources from in-household labour and other inputs, as found in modern studies (Carter, 2001; Carter and Ram, 2003; Fairlie and Robb, 2007). The estimates strongly confirm that the scope to share human and other resources was of central importance to entrepreneurship, with having a spouse one of the most important characteristics that increased the likelihood of entrepreneurship compared to being unmarried. This applied to both men and women, and to corporates and non-corporates. However, the base model also confirms that within the household the head as employer was the most advantaged by the marital relationship in terms of recognised entrepreneur status. Since heads were predominantly men, the support of the household to entrepreneurship in the nineteenth century was chiefly for their benefit. Where women were involved in entrepreneurship, and were most numerous, was in own-account activity. The nature of the sectors and form of activity suggests this was often a strategy for survival or necessity to increase family income.

Relative to the base category of married, all other marital status-gender were significantly less likely to engage in entrepreneurship. This is in line with wider findings of the role of gender and marriage in the family economy. But there was an important contrast. Married men certainly emerge as the leading employers, as to be expected from their generally socially privileged status in Victorian England, and also in the emphasis of the census on the activities of the head of household which could reduce recording of the occupational activities of wives and daughters. As a result, the results indicate something of a composite of the real social advantages of the married male, and the advantages of the married couple. However, in contrast to the conclusions of most previous historical studies, married women were also very entrepreneurial, mainly running own-account businesses, chiefly in sectors with easy market entry in dressmaking, millinery, laundry, lodging houses, innkeeping and shops; and chiefly to supplement family incomes. The major exception was for companies, where single women were much more likely than married women to be directors, though at this stage very few women were involved: this was a very rare phenomenon.

The investigation of the corporate sector has been more limited than non-corporates because of the much smaller number of people involved as directors, the small number reporting director status in the census and the level of record linkage possible with the *Directory of Directors*. Nevertheless the analysis of directors indicates that many corporate entrepreneurs were very similar to non-corporate employers, distinct from many categories of own account, and all were very different from workers. Directors had similar though slightly older age profiles as employers, and were similarly of higher income (as measured by the surrogate of number of servants). However, as well as having an exceptional gender pattern with single women more likely than married to be directors (the reverse on non-corporates), locational effects also differed, with probability of being director increasing with density whereas it declined for non-corporates (for both employers and own account). This reflects both the urban concentration of the directors of limited companies, especially in London, but also the prevalence of traditional employers and own account in rural areas where entrepreneurship was often the only option: there were few opportunities for waged work. This means that whilst rural and fringe urban areas had high rates of entrepreneurship (see Chapter 9), corporate entrepreneurs were essentially urban because economies of scale required for the large workforces by many corporations depended on the large populations available in urban locations, as well as the other externalities available only there. All these features are examined in more depth in the following chapters, but because the number of directors is small, in most cases we limit attention in the subsequent discussion to non-corporate businesses.

7 Demography, the household and entrepreneurship

7.1 Introduction

This chapter expands the analysis of entrepreneurship at the individual level begun in Chapter 6, focussing on one of the key aspects of the Victorian entrepreneur: the demographic characteristics and structure of the families and households that helped to resource and support them. The chapter considers the relationship between gender, age, nuptiality, fertility and household structure and business proprietorship. It also examines the issue of the family firm and other forms of household entrepreneurship. Historians and economists have long argued for the centrality of the family to entrepreneurship. Family involvement in businesses can take many forms, from formal partnership, to formal and informal labour, to the provision of capital. Consequently, this chapter encompasses not just family businesses, but a range of ways in which family structure can affect the choices made by the business proprietor. Gender and its interaction with other features is examined further in the following chapter.

7.2 Family structure and business proprietors

Previous historical commentary on the role of family involvement in business has taken two forms. First, studies of middle-class family structure, and particularly the role of women in businesses. Second, studies of family businesses which have been particularly concerned with the efficiency or otherwise of that particular type of firm. Historians and others commenting on the nineteenth-century middle class have stressed the importance of family structure to business creation. They emphasise that the nature of the family economy promoted entrepreneurial behaviour. Thus, business creation was driven by the need to either maintain a particular form of lifestyle as part of a mixed strategy to prevent economic ruin or to cope with situations in which family members could not enter the waged workforce. Such enterprises were central to many nineteenth-century middle-class families; even when other resources such as annuities, trusts and property were available, the firm run by and sometimes employing family members remained the main source of income and economic stability, especially when the family was relatively young (Davidoff, 2012: 57–65; Morris,

2005: 148–9, 170–7). In contrast, the family could also push more precarious individuals into entrepreneurship. An example of this is discussed at length in the Chapter 10, which stresses the importance of family needs in driving international migrants to set up businesses in this period.

More generally entrepreneurs could attempt to avoid the transaction and agency costs of becoming employers by utilising inputs from their spouse or family when they required labour. Such employment, formal or informal and sometimes unwaged, could draw on the social hierarchy that was especially important in Victorian and Edwardian gender relations and the role of patriarchy and matriarchy. For large firms use of family resources could help avoid the transaction and agency costs of incorporation, and possible loss of direct control; but even for incorporated businesses, family networks could hold shares that allowed an entrepreneur to retain control and keep their company effectively 'private'.

Whether the business proprietor was entering trade to preserve their accustomed manner of living or to provide for a family in the absence of readily available wage labour, the family provided similar benefits to the prospective entrepreneur. Given the limited availability of capital from Victorian banks, the family and familial contacts were essential for raising capital (Cottrell, 1980: 236–44; Davidoff, 2012: 57–8). This could come through informal contacts and loans or through formal arrangements, including share-holding. Crossick has suggested that marriage was the moment at which the most significant property transfers occurred among members of middle-class families, some of which were specifically aimed at business goals (Crossick, 2000: 70). In addition to capital, family members and contacts provided labour and networks for any family business (Casson, 2003: 169–70).

In this context much discussion has focused on the role of women and, to a lesser extent, children in family businesses run by a male head of household. Davidoff and Hall argued that even as it became harder for women to be active economic agents across the nineteenth century they remained central to the economic activity of their husbands, sons and brothers through the provision of capital and labour. The labour they provided came in two forms, either direct work in firms or domestic labour, which enabled others to run their businesses without the burden of having to cook, clean and care for children (Davidoff and Hall, 1997: 272–315). While there has been much criticism of their argument that female economic activity declined in the early nineteenth century, their argument about the unseen contribution of female and other family members to all types of family enterprise stands.[1]

The place of children and other relatives in family businesses has received less attention and has usually been considered in the context of succession. It seems to have been rare for a business to last more than one generation in this period, although the precise nature of this issue is hard to judge because of the difficulties associated with conducting large-scale studies of business continuity in this period. First, it is hard to track individuals through record linkage across the multiple sources required to reconstruct biographies of businesses on any scale

(Nenadic et al., 1992: 170–3). This leads to a tendency to concentrate on large businesses as well as spectacular failures and successes (Owens, 2002: 23; Nicholas, 1999b). Second, scholars have focused on wills as evidence of succession, when the business may have been transferred before death (Owens, 2002: 27–9; Morris, 2005: 79–141). However, while the mechanisms of business transfer remain unclear, most previous analyses suggest that businesses lasting more than one generation were uncommon (Nenadic, 1993: 86; Owens, 2002: 30).

Even if they rarely inherited the business, it is clear that children often worked in their parents' businesses, although their contribution was in tension with the increasing desire for children to attend school regularly (Humphries, 2010: 202–7). As they grew older some children remained in the family home, working in their family's business, others left home but remained involved in such enterprises, while others left to start their own firms or enter waged labour. The literature on leaving home has shown a relationship between socio-economic context and the age at which children left home, with children remaining in wealthier households longer than in poorer ones. However, this relationship was complicated by spatial and occupational variation; poorer households in the south-east were more likely to retain male children than those in the rest of the country, while richer households in the south-east were less likely to have co-resident adult male children than the equivalent households elsewhere (Pooley and Turnbull, 1997: 400–6, 418; Day, 2015: 90–153). Yet, such studies remain focused on the population as a whole and little has been written on the specific nature of leaving home for the children of business proprietors or of the middle class in general.

The historical literature discussed here implicitly stresses the importance of the life cycle to individuals' business activities, yet few address the issue explicitly. Indeed, historians have tended to examine the life cycle as something which happens to particular groups such as the middle class, rather than as something which affects an individual's chance to be part of a group. Thus, Morris' discussion of the property cycle argues that members of the middle class moved from earning income and loan repayment as a young adult, to earning income and receiving dividends and other interest-based payments in later adulthood, to living off rentier income in old age (Morris, 2005: 148–9). Our concern here is with how an individual's chance of being a business proprietor varied with their life cycle stage; this is related to Morris' property cycle, but is concerned with a wider section of society than the established middle class which formed the basis for his study.

The efficiency of family firms

Similar topics have been approached from a rather different angle by scholars primarily concerned with business history and economics. The long-running debate over whether family firms damaged the British economy has asked: were the needs of the family a source of conservatism among British business proprietors? Alfred Chandler argued that the 'personalised capitalism' of the nineteenth-century family firm detrimentally affected Britain's economy

(Chandler, 1990). This promoted a particular interest in succession, with a number of scholars arguing that finding competent heirs to inherit businesses was a major problem in the nineteenth-century economy (Nicholas, 1999b: 707; Lazonick, 1991: 48). Connected to this has been a flimsy argument that British business proprietors were too concerned with securing the trappings of gentility for their families to be successful entrepreneurs (Wiener, 1981; comprehensively critiqued in Rose, 1993: 129–32). Such interpretations partly reflect a neoclassical argument that family firms reduce the flexibility of the market economy, promoting inefficiency by, for example, forcing individuals to obtain capital within the family rather than from supposedly cheaper outside sources (Casson, 1999: 13). It also stems from a focus on big business where the issues of succession and managerial competence have been dominant. However, as stated above and demonstrated elsewhere in this volume, most nineteenth-century businesses were small and short-lived; consequently, the issue of succession was less important. Indeed, some scholars have suggested that the fact that most nineteenth-century firms ended with the death of the proprietor may have promoted entrepreneurial activity because this freed capital for children to invest in their own businesses (Owens, 2002: 38–41). Others have suggested that the family firm was the rational response to the uncertainty of the Victorian and Edwardian economy or that the object of such firms was to support the family, not to grow the national economy (Nenadic, 1993: 88; Owens, 2002: 39–40; Popp, 2013: 2; Fernández Pérez and Colli, 2013: 2–3; Colli, 2013). As we have little data on success or firm growth, at least in terms of turnover or profits, this literature on the efficiency or otherwise of the family firm cannot be directly addressed; however, this chapter provides a discussion of the context from which family firms emerged: the life cycle of business proprietors and their household structure.

7.3   Life cycle

The first aspect of the life cycle to examine is the effect of age on the chances of owning a business. The models estimated in Chapter 6 show that older people were more likely to be entrepreneurs, but that this diminished somewhat as people grew older. Figure 7.1 illustrates this relationship for entrepreneurs as a proportion of the economically active in 10-year groups. However, the relationship between business proprietorship and age was not as simple as it seems as it was closely related to gender and marital status. For male business proprietors the life cycle is usually couched in terms of a move from generating income actively through business activity to the passive generation of rentier income from property, investments and sometimes continued business activity in older age (Morris, 2005: 142–77). For women, in contrast, the life cycle is usually couched in terms relating to marital status. Thus it is argued that women moved through life starting as a wage-earning single young adults, then they married and left paid employment to care for young children, later having older children living at home contributing to the household, and ended being older,

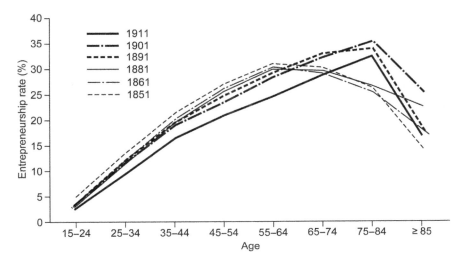

Figure 7.1 Entrepreneurship rate by age, 1851–1911
Source: BBCE database.

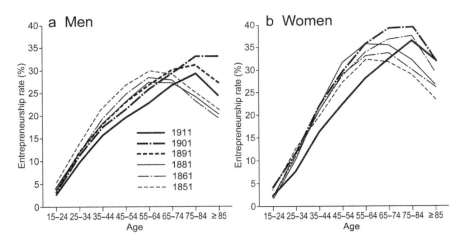

Figure 7.2 Male and female entrepreneurship rates by age, 1851–1911
Source: BBCE database.

often widowed, in the household of one of the adult children (Roberts, 1988: 13; Wall, 2002; Kay, 2009, 121).

Entrepreneurship by age trends remained remarkably stable over the course of the census period, and at first sight seems similar between the sexes, albeit with slightly higher entrepreneurship rates for women. However, the data behind

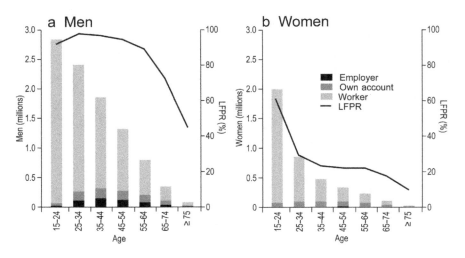

Figure 7.3 Employment status and labour force participation rate by sex, 1901
Source: BBCE database.

these figures reveal important differences in entrepreneurship rates throughout the life cycle. Figure 7.3 shows the employment type broken down into
employer, own account and workers for 1901, a typical year, for both men and
women. In addition, the figure shows each sex's labour force participation rate
(LFPR): the percentage of the total population that was economically active.
For men, the proportion of people working declined gradually with each age
group, with the LFPR remaining over 90 percent up until age 65. The overall
decline in the economically active population was driven by worker numbers,
with numbers of entrepreneurs increasing both absolutely and proportionally,
until they declined together with the LFPR. Numbers in the highest age groups
were small, but show how the entrepreneurship rate slightly declined, meaning
that the few older people who were still economically active were more likely
to be workers again.

A similar analysis for women looks completely different. A substantial number of the economically active were only found in the youngest age band, with
both the numbers of workers as well as the LFPR dropping steeply by the age of
25, showing the importance of the life cycle to patterns of female work as well
as entrepreneurship. The LFPR then remained relatively stable at 22 percent of
the population between 35 and 65, after which it dropped further at old age.
The number of female employers is too small to be discerned in this graph or
to affect the overall trends. However, the number of own-account proprietors
stayed remarkably stable, with a slight growth until the 45–54 group after which
it declined. As this graph shows, therefore, the seemingly higher entrepreneurship rates of women were mainly due to patterns in workers and women's overall

labour participation rate. Many women, particularly workers, left the economically active population during their 20s, in order to get married and start a family. For those who remained, age had little effect over the years 25–64, and was less important to determining their entrepreneurial status than it was for men.

There were other important variations. Table 7.1 shows the average age of business proprietors in different sectors. Mean ages were relatively consistent across all sectors, with the exception of farming where business proprietors were consistently older than those in other sectors. The other two different sectors were refreshment, where entrepreneurs were older than usual, and maker-dealing, where they were younger. In both sectors, it was female business proprietors which drove the different age structure. For example, in 1891 male entrepreneurs were on average 47 years old in maker-dealing and 46 in refreshment, similar to the mean age in all other sectors; however, female entrepreneurs were on average 37 years old in maker-dealing and 51 in refreshment. This reflected the importance of maker-dealer occupations to younger female business proprietors, dressmaking being particularly important; and of lodging houses, as well as hotel and innkeeping, for older women (Davidoff, 1995).

It is also worth noting the large numbers of older business proprietors. The proportion of workers aged over 65 was only 3–4 percent, whereas for business proprietors it was 9–11 percent. As shown in Figure 7.1 a quarter or more of the economically active population aged between 65 and 85 were business proprietors. These participation rates were dropping towards the end of period, in line with the general decline in the participation of those over 65 in the economy (Johnson, 1994: 111). Entrepreneurs over the age of 65 were found throughout every sector of the economy. However, they were particularly prominent in farming (in 1891 18 percent of farming entrepreneurs were

Table 7.1 Mean age of business proprietors by sector, 1851–1911

Sector	1851	1861	1881	1891	1901	1911
Farming	49.5	49.9	50.2	49.8	49.6	49.4
Mining	42.2	42.2	41.8	45.3	44.5	43.2
Construction	41.7	42.3	41.3	45.9	45.7	46.0
Manufacture	39.6	41.1	40.2	44.8	44.8	44.7
Maker-dealing	39.6	43.3	44.7	40.5	40.2	41.3
Retail	44.9	45.5	46.2	44.3	44.5	44.8
Transport	40.0	38.1	38.7	44.1	43.8	44.2
Professional and business services	45.5	46.9	45.6	43.0	43.7	44.4
Personal services	48.6	49.7	47.3	43.2	42.6	42.7
Agricultural produce processing and dealing	45.3	47.5	45.0	45.4	46.0	46.8
Food sales	45.4	46.3	45.9	44.3	43.9	44.1
Refreshment	47.0	47.6	47.6	46.9	47.2	48.3
Finance and commerce	44.3	44.5	45.8	44.1	44.3	44.8

Source: BBCE database.

over 65); agricultural produce production and distribution, construction and manufacture (each had 11 percent over 65 in 1891); and mining and retail (both 10 percent over 65 in 1891). In a period before the widespread existence of pensions, continuing to work was important for workers and entrepreneurs alike (Thane, 2011: 14–17; Hannah, 1986, 5–14). While it is likely that many middle-class business proprietors were able to make greater provision for their old age than workers, through the purchase of property and other investments, many clearly still had to continue working in order to survive (Morris, 2005: 142–78; Green et al., 2009). Business proprietors had the considerable advantage that they primarily used their own labour, and were less likely to be involved in the kind of manual labour that was less feasible later in life; both these factors may have encouraged people to continue running their business into old age (Baines and Johnson, 1999: 950). Unlike manual labour, many entrepreneurs could also continue in their original sectors with less need to change their type of activity. This is suggested by the very high age-specific entrepreneurship rates seen in sectors such as maker-dealing (55 percent of the economically active population aged over 65 were business proprietors in 1891), retail (72 percent), food sales (80 percent) and refreshment (69 percent). In all of these sectors it was more likely for an entrepreneur to continue in business after the age of 65 than it was for a worker in the same occupation.

7.4   Marital status

Marital status also played an important role that interacted with gender. Figure 7.4 shows the LFPR and entrepreneurship rates of men and women compared with the percentage of the population who were married for 1901. The effect marriage had on women's work is clear, and especially pronounced by this date following a halving since 1851 in married women's LFPR. Marriage played an important role in removing women from the labour force (as defined by enumerated census occupations), most comprehensively in non-textile or clothing-related sectors where married women's waged work was most concentrated, but it had a lesser effect on their levels of entrepreneurship, which did not show a similar decline. The effect of marriage on entrepreneurship is not evident from these graphs; however, as Figure 7.5 shows, marriage was clearly advantageous for entrepreneurship, and this effect was greater for women. There are several aspects to this. Partly this was an artefact of better census enumeration of female business owners compared to female workers, particularly when it comes to married women, but this only explains a small part of the difference. More important were the more limited opportunities for married women in terms of waged work, as both domestic service and certain professions placed limitations on married women's employment. However, that does not offer a full explanation, since marriage made men more entrepreneurial as well, and they were less affected in terms of restrictions in waged work after marriage. It is likely therefore that the added resources and opportunities that came with marriage and the extra incentives of setting up a joint household played a role for both sexes.

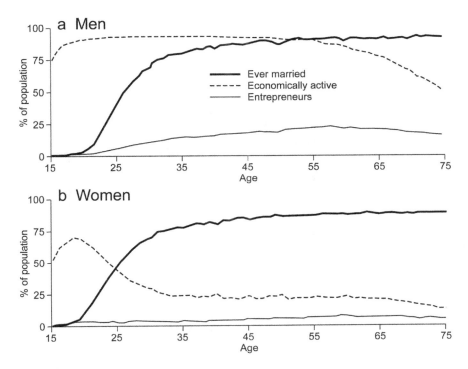

Figure 7.4 Labour force participation rate, entrepreneurship rate (owners and own account) and marriage rate for women and men by age, 1901

Source: BBCE database.

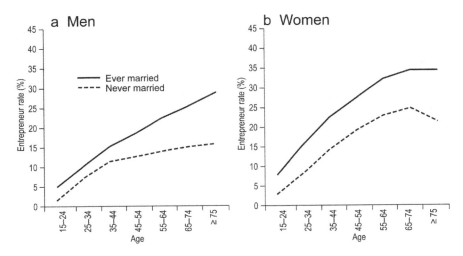

Figure 7.5 Entrepreneurship rates by marital status and sex, 1901

Source: BBCE database.

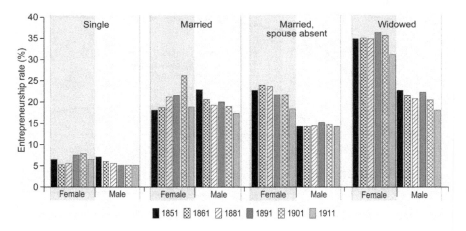

Figure 7.6 Gender-specific entrepreneurship rates by marital status, 1851–1911
Source: BBCE database.

Figure 7.6 shows how these gender- and marital status–specific entrepreneurship rates changed over the period of analysis. For married women, it
is evident that from 1851 to 1901 entrepreneurship increased steadily even
though LFPR for this same group declined over the same period, perhaps suggesting that restricted opportunities led to entrepreneurial activity. The lower
entrepreneurship rate for women in 1911 aged between 15 and 54 is because
in 1911 there were 90,000 fewer female self-employed sole proprietors than
in 1901. The main drops were in textile/clothing-related maker-dealers,
where the number of self-employed dressmakers fell by nearly 30,000, and
personal services, where there were 24,000 fewer own-account laundresses in
1911 than 1901. In both cases these were industries undergoing significant
concentration in these periods, which restricted opportunities for female self-
employment, as noted in Chapter 8 (Malcolmson, 1986: 127–9).[2] Beyond this
specific issue, it is clear that business proprietorship among men and women
increased substantially upon marriage. There was a decrease in ever-married
male and female entrepreneurship ratios in 1911 which reflected the decrease
in the overall entrepreneurship rate from 13.0 to 11.3 percent between 1901
and 1911.

The effect of marriage can be illustrated more precisely using the fertility data
included in the 1911 census. The 1911 census contained information for each
couple on the length of their marriage. These data allow us to examine both
the chance that recently married individuals were business proprietors and the
more general nuptial activity of entrepreneurs. There are a number of problems
with the data on the length of marriage, notably that people tended to round
reported duration. Consequently, there was an excess of marriages reported as
having lasted 10, 20, 30 years and so on. Additionally, there were too few very

recent marriages reported, shown by a shortfall in the numbers of marriages with a duration of less than one year (Garrett et al., 2001: 86–7). Furthermore, there is no way to tell if the marriage reported was a first marriage or not. Additionally, as a retrospective survey, the 1911 census provides no information on marriage ages, duration or fertility of couples where one of the partners had died. As mortality rates fell over the course of the nineteenth century, the chance of both spouses surviving and hence their marriage duration being reported in 1911 increased. Consequently, the behaviour of different cohorts cannot be readily compared (Garrett et al., 2001: 220–2). Finally, some of the data provided was inconsistent either in the original or in the transcribed version. For example, some individuals gave marriage durations too long for their ages. Such individuals are dropped from the analysis. These problems mean that the number of observable recently married individuals is lower than in reality and mean ages at marriage calculated from the data tend to be higher than in reality.

Table 7.2 shows the numbers of male and female employers, own account and workers in 1911 aged 25 who were either unmarried or had been married less than a year. Although the entrepreneurship rate of both groups was fairly low (a function of their young age), the recently married were substantially more likely to have been business proprietors than unmarried people of the same age. As noted above, there were a number of reasons why recently married individuals were more likely to be business proprietors than the unmarried. First, marriage brought with it added resources; marriage settlements and access to new social networks made raising capital easier and provided a new pool of readily accessible labour – a new spouse could work in the business and their extended family potentially increased the number of possible workers. Second, the additional costs incurred after marriage provided an incentive for one or both of the couple to start their own business. This could take many forms, not just the husband starting a new firm, but also wives engaging in entrepreneurial activity (particularly as own-account proprietors) while their husband continued in the waged labour market. Third, as marriage and starting a business both required certain levels of capital, an individual might have delayed both marriage and starting a

Table 7.2 Entrepreneurship rates of 25-year-old males and females, recently married and unmarried in 1911

Employment Status	Male		Female	
	Newly Married	Unmarried	Newly Married	Unmarried
Worker	11,087	168,749	1,784	135,380
Employer	471	3,342	22	690
Own account	517	5,480	146	5,992
Total	12,075	177,571	1,952	142,062
Entrepreneurship ratio	8.2	5.0	8.6	4.7

Source: BBCE database.

Table 7.3 Average age at marriage of economically active men and women (under 35 years of age at time of marriage) by employment status in 1911

Marriage Date	Male			Female		
	Employer	Own Account	Worker	Employer	Own Account	Worker
1876–1880	24.9	24.6	23.8	22.6	22.2	22.0
1881–1885	25.3	24.9	24.2	23.2	22.8	22.3
1886–1890	25.7	25.3	24.6	23.6	23.3	22.7
1891–1895	26.2	25.6	24.9	24.3	23.8	23.2
1896–1900	26.6	25.9	25.1	24.8	24.1	23.4
1901–1905	27.1	26.3	25.4	25.3	24.6	23.7
1906–1910	27.7	26.8	25.7	26.0	25.3	23.9

Source: BBCE database.

business until a similar point in their life cycle (Garrett et al., 2001: 429–30). It is likely that all three factors were operating in this period.

The fertility data can also be used to compare the age at marriage for men and women of different employment statuses. Table 7.3 shows the mean age at marriage of men and women who were aged between 15 and 35 when they married, broken down into 5-year intervals and by employment status in 1911.[3] Although it uses employment status in 1911 to examine marriage behaviour in previous years, the consistency of the pattern for each cohort suggests that pattern is real. For both men and women, across each cohort, employers married at an older age than own-account entrepreneurs, who in turn married later than workers. The gap widened across the period, but this was likely to be due to the fact that some employers in 1911 who married in the 1870s or 1880s were workers at that point, lowering the employer mean marriage age.

The pattern of age at marriage by husband's occupation was consistent across all marriage cohorts. The general pattern is shown in Table 7.4 using the example of the 1896–1900 cohort. In all categories, employers married later than workers, except for personal services, where the age at marriage was similar across all three groups. Employers were also generally older than own-account business proprietors, except in mining and personal services. It is notable that the age at marriage, in general, of each employment status group followed the same pattern in each occupation category. Thus, employers, own account and workers in mining all married at a younger age than their counterparts in professional and business services or finance and commerce, but the pattern of employers marrying later than own account, who in turn married later than workers, also held true across each sector. This supports arguments made by others that nuptiality did not vary simply by class, but interacted also with occupation and other factors (Garrett et al., 2001: 213–33).

There was, however, considerable variation between sectors in the proportion of business proprietors who were never married as shown in Table 7.5 for those

Table 7.4 Average age at marriage of men aged between 15 and 35 married 1896–1900, by employment status and occupational category in 1911

Sector	Employer	Own Account	Worker
Agricultural produce processing and dealing	27.2	25.9	25.1
Construction	25.9	25.4	24.9
Farming/estate work	27.4	26.6	25.6
Finance and commerce	27.5	26.7	25.9
Food sales	26.1	25.5	24.9
Maker-dealer	26.2	25.9	24.9
Manufacturing	26.5	25.8	24.9
Mining and quarrying	26.0	26.0	24.3
Personal services	26.2	26.4	26.2
Professional and business services	27.9	27.3	26.2
Refreshment	26.4	26.2	25.5
Retail	26.8	25.3	25.6
Transport	25.7	25.4	24.9

Source: BBCE database.

Table 7.5 Percentage of business proprietors over 45 never married by sector, 1851–1911

Sector	1851	1861	1881	1891	1901	1911
Farming	8.0	7.7	7.5	7.7	7.9	9.3
Mining	9.4	9.7	6.2	6.3	6.5	8.9
Construction	4.3	5.1	4.3	3.8	4.3	5.0
Manufacture	7.5	7.7	6.9	6.9	7.7	9.5
Maker-dealing	11.5	13.6	14.9	15.2	18.6	23.6
Retail	10.0	9.4	9.2	9.7	10.2	12.0
Transport	8.3	9.9	6.3	4.8	5.5	6.6
Professional and business services	12.4	11.5	10.5	10.1	10.3	11.8
Personal services	9.6	9.8	10.4	13.4	17.1	21.8
Agricultural produce processing and dealing	8.0	7.6	5.6	6.3	7.3	8.5
Food sales	7.2	6.9	6.0	6.5	7.3	8.7
Refreshment	6.7	7.0	9.0	8.8	11.6	15.4
Finance and commerce	12.3	11.3	11.3	8.3	9.9	11.0

Source: BBCE database.

over 45 years old. This seems to have been driven by capital requirements and gender. In sectors characterised by higher initial capital requirements, farming, mining, construction, transport and manufacture, the proportions never married were low. A similar picture emerges for many of the sectors which required permanent premises from which to operate, such as food sales, refreshment and, to a lesser extent, retail. These often had high proportions of female business proprietors but were the kinds of businesses typically carried on by married or widowed women, notably lodging houses, innkeeping and other forms of food and drink retail. The sectors with high proportions never married were either those involving large numbers of single women, such as dressmaking among the maker-dealers, or were professions in which several factors combined to reduce the rates of marriage. For men, professional careers were less reliant than other occupations on the capital and labour resources provided by marriage; the professional training which was prior to starting a legal or medical business, for example, generally occurred early in life, before marriage. For women, similar issues applied but were exacerbated by the growing cultural pressure on women to leave teaching when they married (Copelman, 1996: 190–3).

Age and marital status both reflected the general trend that people were more likely to start a business once they had accumulated capital and other resources, either through marriage or through waged work. Furthermore, older people and married people were more likely to need to start a business, some to support their family or themselves, and some driven by necessity because other means of making a living were unavailable to them. The exceptions to these trends were those areas of the economy which were open to people otherwise economically marginalised, most notably the large number of young unmarried women who ran businesses in industries characterised by small-scale production and retail such as dressmaking, millinery, and other kinds of clothing manufacture.

7.5   Fertility

There is extensive literature that examines the relationship between social class and fertility during the late nineteenth century (Woods, 2000: 114–22). However, it has proved difficult to establish any clear narrative about the connection between social class, nuptiality and fertility. This has reflected difficulties with defining social groups (Szreter, 1996: 285–309). However, the 1911 fertility data included in I-CeM allows us to examine in detail the fertility behaviour of employers, own-account proprietors and workers in the late nineteenth century (Garrett et al. 2001: 85–9). In 1911, in addition to the data on the length of marriages noted above, respondents were also asked to state the number of children ever born, the number of children who had died and the number still living. These new questions were part of the long-running battle between environmental and hereditarian views of population change that dominated much medical, economic and political debate in the early twentieth century (Szreter, 1996: 69–75, 256–62). In addition to the problems noted above about the marriage date information, the data on children born were concerned only with live births, thus any miscarriages, stillbirths or abortions were not usually counted, and there are issues concerning how accurately the census question was answered. Despite these drawbacks, the 1911 data offer a useful source with which to compare the fertility of employers, own account individuals and workers.

Fertility had a similar gradient across the three categories of employer, own account and worker as nuptiality, though with less separation between own account and employer. If we consider women aged over 45 in 1911, who married between the ages of 20 and 24 (in other words who married in the years 1876–80), we see that male workers and their wives had, on average, 6.2 children, and couples that included male own-account individuals or male employers both had 5.6 children. Once again, this varied between different sectors, as Table 7.6 shows. In all cases, except retail and transport, worker couples had the most children; and in all cases, except farming and transport, employers had the fewest children, although for some sectors the differences between employers and own account was very narrow or they were identical. However, there was considerable variation between occupation groups, with the largest difference coming in mining, in line with much scholarship on the high fertility of the wives of miners. The lowest fertility (in increasing rank order) was for employers in finance and commerce, personal services, professional and business services and refreshment.

This brief analysis provides support to Szreter's supposition from the published results of the 1911 fertility census that employers were more likely to postpone marriage and have smaller families, partly as a consequence of those later marriages (Szreter, 1996: 348–51). However, questions as to causation remain. Were these late-marrying business proprietors born into the entrepreneurial classes simply following the mores of their families and peers? Or did late marriage allow individuals from the working classes more time to raise capital, make contacts and acquire skills that allowed them to start their own business? Or did later marriage and smaller families free individuals from the necessity of seeking

Table 7.6 Average number of children born to women aged over 45 who married 1876–80, by husband's employment status and occupation category in 1911

Sector	Employer	Own Account	Worker
Agricultural produce processing and dealing	5.5	5.7	6.4
Construction	5.8	6.1	6.3
Farming/estate work	6.1	5.9	6.6
Finance and commerce	4.3	5.0	5.1
Food sales	5.6	5.6	5.9
Maker-dealer	5.5	5.9	6.2
Manufacturing	5.3	5.7	6.1
Mining and quarrying	5.1	5.5	7.1
Personal services	4.8	5.1	5.3
Professional and business services	4.8	4.8	5.0
Refreshment	5.0	5.0	5.5
Retail	5.1	5.4	5.3
Transport	6.2	6.1	6.2

Source: BBCE database.

wage labour to support larger families and consequently allow individuals more scope to experiment as business proprietors? Presumably some combination of all three processes were occurring; however, future panel work is required to shed light on where the balance of causation lay.

7.6   Household structure

Most business proprietors were heads of households. Table 7.7 shows the relationship to the head of household for business proprietors and workers for each census year.

Whatever the contribution of other household members to businesses, it was rare for a business proprietor to be anything other than a head of household. However, there was considerable variation by sector. For example, in 1911 over 90 percent of farming business proprietors were heads of household; in construction, agricultural produce processing and dealing, and refreshment the figure was over 80 percent; and in mining, manufacturing, retail, transport, professional and business service, food sales, and finance and commerce it was over 70 percent. In the remaining sectors the proportion of heads of household was 57 percent of maker-dealers, and 60 percent of business proprietors in personal services. These two sectors were characterised by high levels of female business proprietorship, and women were far less likely to be the head of a household. Households in which at least one business proprietor resided were more likely to be extended family households than those which included only workers, as Table 7.8 shows.[4]

Extended families were more common in some parts of England and Wales than in others (Schürer et al., 2018: 387–8); however, the tendency for employers

Table 7.7 Relation to head of household for business proprietors ('Ent': employers and own account) and workers (W), 1851–1911

Relation	1851 Ent	1851 W	1861 Ent	1861 W	1881 Ent	1881 W	1891 Ent	1891 W	1901 Ent	1901 W	1911 Ent	1911 W
Head	74.5	37.6	77.1	41.4	74.4	38.7	74.8	39.0	72.9	38.6	73.4	39.0
CFU member	15.8	28.6	15.4	29.0	16.3	29.9	16.6	32.0	18.2	32.6	17.1	34.6
Older generation	0.4	0.6	0.4	0.6	0.60	0.66	0.6	0.5	0.53	0.54	0.49	0.51
Sibling	1.7	2.3	1.6	2.0	1.86	2.26	2.0	2.3	2.40	2.72	2.38	2.75
Other family	0.7	2.0	0.5	1.7	0.54	1.71	0.7	1.9	0.72	1.82	0.77	1.98
Servant	0.4	14.1	0.5	12.8	0.18	11.8	0.1	10.8	0.06	10.0	0.05	8.13
Working title	0.3	1.0	0.1	1.0	0.12	0.76	0.1	0.8	0.11	0.58	0.11	0.71
Lodger/boarder	3.1	7.8	2.5	7.4	3.78	9.57	3.2	6.7	3.02	8.75	3.25	7.78
Non-household	0.4	1.0	0.4	1.5	0.74	1.98	0.6	2.0	0.68	2.17	0.74	1.97
Unknown	2.7	5.0	1.4	2.6	1.41	2.70	1.3	2.0	1.39	2.16	1.73	2.57

Source: BBCE database.

Table 7.8 Extended family households as a share of all employer, own account and worker households, 1851–1911 (%)

Year	Employers	Own Account	Worker
1851	19.7	16.9	13.0
1861	17.9	14.8	11.8
1881	18.6	16.5	12.2
1891	18.5	17.3	12.9
1901	18.5	15.8	12.7
1911	16.9	15.3	12.8

Source: BBCE database.

Note: Employer households are those which include at least one employer, own-account households include at least one-own account individual but no employers, worker households contain only workers among the economically active members.

Table 7.9 Extended family households as a share of all employer, own account and worker households by division, 1891

Division	Employer	Own Account	Worker
London	16.4	14.6	10.3
South Eastern	18.9	17.3	12.8
South Midland	17.9	17.2	12.9
Eastern	18.3	17.1	13.0
South Western	19.7	18.0	13.1
West Midland	18.7	17.8	13.5
North Midland	18.5	17.9	13.1
North Western	18.6	17.9	14.0
Yorkshire	18.1	17.4	12.7
Northern	20.6	18.9	13.9
Welsh	19.6	18.3	12.9

Source: BBCE database.

and own-account individuals to live in extended family households was greater than workers throughout all parts of the country, and was not an artefact of the geography of household structure, as Table 7.9 shows for 1891. Even where extended families were uncommon, such as in London, employers and own-account individuals were still more likely to live in such households. This pattern was remarkably consistent across all sectors, occupations and years. Even in low-status occupations employers were more likely to live in extended family households. For example, in 1891, 18 percent of employers and 18 percent of own-account proprietors working in laundry lived in extended households, compared to 10 percent of workers.

These data support the suggestion made by Davidoff that aunts, uncles, brothers, sisters and other extended family members were particularly important for middle-class families (Davidoff, 2012: 78–107). The precise reasons for this varied with each family's circumstance, as Davidoff shows though case studies, and are difficult to untangle, but they reflected a combination of different economic, demographic and cultural factors. Part of the explanation relates to the changing proportion of the population who never married and by the protracted nature of marriage during this period. The proportion of the population aged over 45 who were never married rose from 10.6 to 12.4 percent between 1851 and 1911, leading to considerable concern during the nineteenth century regarding what to do with unmarried individuals of both genders (Anderson, 1984: 378–9; Garrett et al., 2001: 214–16). Additionally, for those who did marry, the *range* of ages at which people married in the nineteenth century was considerable: in 1851, 80 percent of women married for the first time over a range of about 20 years; in 1911, this became only slightly more concentrated into a range of 17 years (Anderson, 1990: 67–8). Consequently, there were a great many single men and women in Victorian and Edwardian England and Wales who had to live somewhere and had to support themselves in some way. For families in which someone owned a business, having extended family members living in the household and contributing to the business either through direct labour or domestic labour was a viable way to help sustain these unmarried individuals, the family and its enterprise. This can be seen in the data; for example, in 1911, 7.5 percent of people in households which contained at least one employer were unmarried extended kin; this was 12.1 percent of people in own-account households, and just 4.9 percent of people living in worker-headed, worker-only households. The extra flexibility available to households who included a business owner of one kind or another, the fact they were less reliant on the fluctuations of the wage-labour market, as well as the advantages in terms of access to labour, capital and connections that extended family members provided, seems to have contributed to the relative abundance of extended-family households among entrepreneurial families. For similar reasons, employer and own-account households were more likely than worker-only households to contain no conjugal family unit. In other words, entrepreneurs were more likely to reside in households consisting of co-resident siblings or co-resident relatives who were not spouses or children. In 1901, 5 percent of employer and 6 percent of own-account households were so constituted, compared to just 3 percent of worker-only households.

Own-account individuals were far more likely than either workers or employers to head single-person households. For example, in 1851, 10 percent of households headed by an own-account individual consisted of just one person compared to 2.5 percent of employer-headed households and 6.6 percent of worker-headed households. In the absence of familial or household-member support, own-account occupations provided a means of supporting individuals, whether they were single or widowed (the two main categories of single-person households). Thus, in 1851, 18 percent of widows and 16 percent of widowers who were running own-account businesses lived in single-person households, in 1901 these figures had risen to 23 and 25 percent respectively.

Beyond kin, the households of business proprietors were more likely to contain servants than worker-only households, and they employed more servants on average than heads of worker-only households that employed servants. For example, in 1891, 46 percent of households in which at least one employer lived had at least one resident servant. The figure for own-account households was 15 percent and for worker-only households just 5 percent. The average number of servants employed in a house in which an employer was resident was 0.9, in a house containing an own-account individual it was 0.2 and in a worker-only household it was 0.1. Resident servants were common in the households of business proprietors for two reasons. First, many resident servants were employed not just in domestic tasks, but also in the family's enterprise. This was especially true of businesses that were carried on in the residence such as hotel keeping, farming and much shopkeeping (Smith et al., 2018: 591–2; Higgs, 1983). Second, employment of a servant freed up family members to work exclusively in the family business, sparing them the necessity of domestic labour. Finally, while employing resident servants was not a simple indicator of middle-class status in Victorian England and Wales, the employment of male servants was a more reliable sign of bourgeois status. Employers were more likely to employ male servants than either own-account individuals or workers. In 1911, although the number of households including male servants was small, households including employers were four times more likely to employ resident male domestic servants compared to own-account households, and almost nine times more likely than worker-only households. The employers with male servants were a mixture of substantial manufacturers, professionals, and hotel, inn and lodging-house keepers.

In all the aspects of household structure discussed so far, the particular economic needs and characteristics of business proprietorship have been seen to interact with the social and cultural factors affecting family life. However, the precise direction of causation is hard to identify. Did people start businesses when they got married because their new status required them to provide for their new partner? Or, did their new status bring with it capital and labour which enabled them to start a business? Or, were marriage and starting a business activities which occurred at a certain moment in individuals' life cycles and caused by something else entirely? Such questions are difficult to answer from the data available. However, it is clear that the family and the enterprise in the nineteenth and early twentieth centuries were closely intertwined in ways which went beyond the close identification inherent in the family firm. These patterns of demographic and household behaviour distinguished employers and own-account proprietors from workers, and provided sources of difference within the wider group of business proprietors.

7.7 Household and family firms

As noted above, there has been considerable debate about the efficiency or otherwise of family firms. However, such debates have tended to focus on large enterprises, debating issues of succession, insider trading and crony capitalism

(Church, 1993; James, 2013: 58–66). While interesting, such scholarship ignores most family firms, which were small and short-lived. Indeed, the 'family firm' is a rather broad category covering everything from a mother and daughter-run grocer to a multi-national entity such as the Rothschild's bank. Much of the disagreement about the malign or otherwise influence of family firms on national economies stems from the fact that concept is too broad. Some nuance is required; we need a typology of the different kinds of family businesses which is alert to historical as well as geographical differences (Colli and Rose, 2008: 197; Jones and Rose, 1993: 14; Colli et al., 2003: 30; for a contemporary typology see Westhead and Howorth, 2007; Bianchi and Milkie, 2010. A full typology is not attempted here; rather, attention is drawn to one particular kind of family firm that can be identified from the census.

As has been noted elsewhere, the historical study of family businesses lacks an adequate quantitative basis (Fernández Pérez and Colli, 2013: 3). Definitions are often broad, for example one definition of a family firm is one in which a family 'owns enough of the equity to be able to exert control over strategy *and* is involved in top management positions' (Colli and Rose, 2008: 194; Casson, 1999: 10). Statistics on ownership and control based on stock ownership are hard to come by on a large scale for nineteenth-century Britain. Consequently, definitions based on family shareholders are difficult to use and usually incomplete (Colli, 2003: 15). Hence most scholarship on historical family firms has been based on case studies. It is likely that the majority of businesses in nineteenth- and early twentieth-century England and Wales were family businesses of one kind or another. From the census it is possible to assess one particular type of family firm: one in which an employer was living with family members working in the same occupation, which we assume to mean they were working together in the same business in most instances. There were other types of family businesses: ones run by a family member for the benefit of the family but in which no other members were involved, ones in which non-co-resident family members were involved and partnerships between family members, to name a few. However, the focus here is on what can be identified from the census on businesses in which family members co-resident in the same household were explicitly involved. Table 7.10 shows the number of such businesses identifiable in each census.

It is difficult to judge trends over time across the entire period because comparable data using reconstruction cannot be easily utilised, and enumerator practices varied: some enumerators were more assiduous than others in recording the occupations of individuals other than the head of household.[5] Furthermore, the incidence of particular kinds of family business is related to household structure; notably the size of employers' households. Household size did not change much over this period (Schürer et al., 2018: 376), but to be check whether there was any effect the final column gives the standardized rate of co-resident family businesses, this gives the percentage of all employers who headed co-resident businesses standardized to the distribution of household size in 1911.[6] This shows that although the magnitude changes the pattern across years is the same. It might also be suggested that if children were leaving home earlier, then the

Table 7.10 Co-resident family businesses, 1851–1911

Census	Co-Resident Family Businesses	% of All Employers	Standardized % of All Employers
1851	62,423	31.1	47.2
1861	44,593	25.3	38.6
1881	47,869	26.0	36.7
1891	79,377	14.7	22.5
1901	104,859	18.9	27.2
1911	103,619	15.2	23.1

Source: BBCE database.

Note: For the earlier censuses only extracted data are used, not reconstructed results. This leads to significant underestimation of such businesses for 1851–81, but those identified were certainly proprietors. For similar reasons unweighted data are used for 1891–1911.

number of this kind of family business would fall; however, the age of leaving home was rising in this period (Day, 2015: 8–9; Schürer et al., 2018: 399–400). Although the differences between the early and late censuses mean that they cannot be directly compared, it appears that the incidence of these co-resident family businesses was falling in the period 1851–81. The later period is harder to interpret, but it may be that 1891 was a dip, with 1901 representing a partial return to the norm, before a drop 1901–11 which signalled a slow decline driven by the increasing popularity of new forms of business organisation, most obviously the corporation (Hannah, 1983: 8–28).

This particular kind of business was more likely to be headed by a woman than businesses in general, as Table 7.11 shows. This interacted with the familial relationships involved in these businesses. Female employers were much more likely to be involved in a business with their daughter than male employers; for example, in 1901, 17 percent of female employers in these businesses were working with their daughter compared to just 4 percent of men. Women were similarly more likely to be working with their sisters than men were, again in 1901 the figures for female employers were 9 percent compared to 1 percent for male employers. Furthermore, while men numerically dominated other co-resident businesses where the relationship was either with male relatives or a mixture of male and female relatives, female employers were numerically much more important to daughter- and sister-only businesses, as Figure 7.7 shows. Some constraint on cross-gender business formation may be expected from lack of opportunity for women to pursue some occupations and conversely female dominance in others. Nonetheless this particular kind of business was an important area for female entrepreneurship entirely separate from male activity. In part, this approach to identifying a particular kind of family business merely makes explicit what was often hidden in other firms, the contribution of wives, daughters and other female household members. It also interacts with marital status to reveal an interesting picture. Thus, most sister-only businesses were headed by a single

Table 7.11 Gender of co-resident family business employers and all employers, 1851–1911

Census Year	Co-Resident Family Business		All Employers	
	Female	*Male*	*Female*	*Male*
1851	10.5	89.5	7.9	92.1
1861	11.9	88.1	7.4	92.6
1881	10.9	89.1	6.6	93.4
1891	9.5	90.5	11.6	88.4
1901	14.2	85.8	10.5	89.5
1911	13.1	86.8	13.5	86.5

Source: BBCE database.

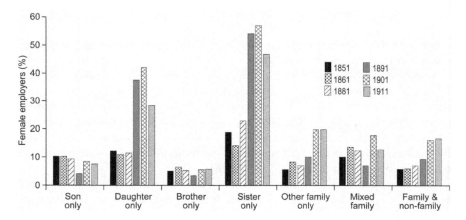

Figure 7.7 Female employers by family business type, 1851–1911
Source: BBCE database.

woman; in 1901, 81 percent of women who were running a business employing at least one sister were single. For daughter-only businesses, the female employers were most likely to be widows, but a significant minority were run by married women. Again taking 1901 as the example, 62 percent of women running these businesses were widowed, but 35 percent stated that they were married.[7] These sister–sister and mother–daughter businesses were mostly in maker-dealing, food sales and personal services, areas in which female entrepreneurship was common, however, they were missing from one key areas, farming; in 1901, 6.8 percent of mother–daughter and 9.8 percent of sister–sister businesses were in agriculture, as opposed to 21.5 percent of all female employers.

Figure 7.8 shows the distribution of co-resident businesses by RSD, for the proportion of employers in each district in 1901 that were running this kind of family firm. These businesses were most prominent in Wales, northern England

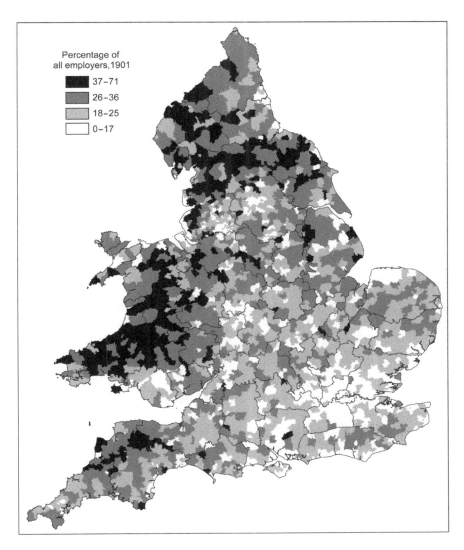

Figure 7.8 Co-resident family businesses as a percentage of all employers by RSD, 1901
Source: BBCE database.

and Devon; 46 percent of these businesses were in urban RSDs, 17 percent in
transitional RSDs and 37 percent in rural RSDs (see Chapter 3 and WP 6 for
definitions). This is a different distribution to that of all employers, where, in
1901, 64 percent were in urban RSDs, 15 in transition RSDs and just 21 percent
in rural RSDs. Therefore, this type of business offered a useful model for rural
entrepreneurship where the supply of labour may have been scarcer.

Table 7.12 Co-resident family businesses by occupation category (percentage), 1851–1911

Sector	1851	1861	1881	1891	1901	1911
Farming/estate work	75.6	74.3	73.5	51.7	50.0	58.8
Mining and quarrying	0.1	0.0	0.1	0.3	0.2	0.3
Construction	4.6	5.1	4.8	5.5	6.5	5.3
Manufacturing	3.7	4.3	5.4	8.1	7.6	5.4
Maker–dealer	9.1	8.3	5.3	9.0	10.0	7.7
Retail	1.3	1.9	3.3	6.2	5.7	4.5
Transport	0.1	0.1	0.1	0.6	1.0	0.9
Professional and business services	0.0	0.0	0.1	0.4	0.3	0.5
Personal services	0.2	0.2	0.4	2.6	3.7	4.1
Agricultural produce processing and dealing	1.5	1.2	1.2	1.4	0.9	0.6
Food sales	3.7	4.4	5.7	13.1	13.0	10.6
Refreshment	0.1	0.1	0.2	0.9	0.9	1.1
Finance and commerce	0.0	0.0	0.0	0.3	0.2	0.2

Source: BBCE database.

Table 7.12 shows the occupational breakdown of the co-resident family businesses for each census year. This shows that, even with the difficulty of comparing the early and late censuses, farming was always an important sector for this
kind of business. Furthermore, this form of business structure was particularly
important for farming; in 1851, 73 percent of all employers in farming were
living with a worker involved in the farm. By 1901 this proportion had fallen
but was still significant, with 58 percent of all farm head employers running a
co-resident family business.[8] Beyond agriculture, it is clear that this kind of business suited certain sectors and not others. Thus there were significant numbers
in maker-dealers (particularly tailors, blacksmiths, shoemakers, dressmakers and
chemists) and food sales (notably grocers, butchers, bakers and cowkeepers). In
other words, sectors characterised by small-scale, often home-based economic
activity. For example, in 1901, 43 percent of employer blacksmiths, 30 percent
of dressmakers, 32 percent of grocers and 44 percent of bakers were running co-
resident family businesses. Unsurprisingly this kind of business was less common
in mining, the professions and in finance and large-scale commerce. The larger
numbers involved in construction and manufacturing is more surprising. Many
of these were in small manufacturing or, for construction, were often carpenters,
plumbers and housepainters; in other words, the aspects of construction where
small employer-led businesses were most likely. However, this kind of business
was not entirely absent from large-scale businesses; for example, 14 percent of
employers in iron founding in 1901 were running this kind of family business.

Table 7.13 shows the firm-size data for these businesses for 1851–81. For the
majority of occupational categories in each year the co-resident family businesses had smaller declared workforces than other businesses. Of the categories for which there were more than 50 co-resident family businesses, only in

Table 7.13 Firm size of co-resident family businesses, 1851–81

Sector	1851		1861		1881	
	Family Business	Others	Family Business	Others	Family Business	Others
Farming/estate work	5.0	6.1	5.9	6.4	5.2	9.5
Mining and quarrying	22.0	23.4	*32.3*	32.5	*39.4*	73.3
Construction	4.6	6.9	6.1	8.6	8.3	12.4
Manufacturing	15.0	26.3	16.3	33.4	27.3	35.5
Maker-dealer	3.2	5.1	3.9	6.0	5.0	6.8
Retail	6.4	8.6	7.1	10.5	11.2	16.8
Transport	3.4	9.3	4.1	7.6	6.8	13.5
Professional and business services	*4.3*	10.4	*58.8*	15.8	*68.4*	28.3
Personal services	2.7	5.0	4.6	7.5	4.0	8.3
Agricultural produce processing and dealing	4.3	5.5	5.4	7.8	7.8	11.0
Food sales	2.8	2.8	3.4	3.5	3.3	3.5
Refreshment	4.2	3.4	*6.9*	4.0	5.8	4.7
Finance and commerce	*236.7*	29.7	*47.6*	36.5	*20.1*	27.8

Source: BBCE database.

Note: Figures in *italics* are based on fewer than 50 businesses.

refreshment in 1851 and 1881 were the family firms larger on average that the other kinds of businesses. It is unclear whether all employers included familial employees when reporting the size of their workforce. Where commented on, it has generally been assumed that family members were not included in employer's workforce returns (Mills, 1999: 60). It is possible that many omitted them. If this is true, then these co-resident family firms may have been larger on average than other firms in their sector once familial labour was added. In such cases, family members replaced workers that would otherwise have to be paid a wage. However, it is also possible that the declared workforces included family members. If so, then the majority of sectors that have smaller sizes indicate that co-resident family firms were either more marginal or were more reluctant to take on staff; perhaps because family commitments or other non-business activities restricted choice. It is likely that there was a mixture of the two: under-reporting that indicates unwaged family inputs, as well as family firms in more marginal sectors or niches or with constraints on following opportunities such as limited markets (as indicated in the geography of entrepreneurship discussed in Chapter 9). This fits with the analysis offered throughout this section which shows that this kind of business was characterised by more marginal employers; this is reflected in their smaller size, their concentration in rural areas, their occupational concentration in smaller-scale trades, and in the fact that women seem to have been more frequent as employers in these kinds of enterprises than in businesses with different structures in other locations.

Table 7.14 Employment status of spouses, 1901, from the perspective of economically active (a) men and (b) women

Wife	Employer	Own Account	Worker	Non-Economically Active
(a) Male economic actor				
Employer	0.8	0.7	1.5	97.0
Own account	0.1	3.7	2.4	93.7
Worker	0.1	1.4	5.8	92.7
Husband	Employer	Own Account	Worker	Non-economically active
(b) Female economic actor				
Employer	39.3	8.3	50.3	2.1
Own account	3.6	25.3	69.5	1.7
Worker	2.5	5.1	91.6	0.9

Source: BBCE database.

The co-resident family firm is not the only entrepreneurial relationship that can be identified in households in this period. Table 7.14 shows the relationship between the employment statuses of economically active men and women and that of their spouses in 1901. The low level of female proprietorship among the wives of entrepreneurs is unsurprising and represents both the low rate of formal labour force participation by married women (as defined by the census) and the stark problem of under-recording of the economic contribution of wives in the census. However, women, whether workers or entrepreneurs, were likely to be married to an economically active man. While over 90 percent of worker women were married to a male worker, the marriage behaviour of entrepreneurial women was more varied, with both employer and own-account women being more likely to be in marriages where their husband's employment type matched their own. The presence of dual-entrepreneurship marriages has previously been identified for eighteenth-century London as well as for mid-nineteenth-century Albany, New York. While some of these constituted partnerships, in many other cases these were two people running separate businesses (Erickson, 2008; Lewis, 2009: 40).

A small percentage of entrepreneurial women had husbands who were not economically active in 1901, 2.1 percent of female employers and 1.7 percent of own-account women, implying an inversion of the male-breadwinner/female-homemaker ideology. While this did not necessarily make the women sole breadwinners of their household – there could have been contributing children or parents – the fact that this dynamic was more than twice as likely to occur if the woman was an employer rather than a worker points to the possibility that her business was able to support both spouses. In addition, in the majority of married female entrepreneurs' households, the women were more entrepreneurial than the men; 50 percent of employer women (almost 3,000 women) had a worker husband. Over two-thirds of these were laundresses ($N = 1,162$) and dressmakers or milliners ($N = 1,097$ and 179). The difference in occupations between these groups of female employers and their husbands reveals a lot about their status in society: while the most common occupations for husbands of employer laundresses included general labourers, agricultural labourers, gardeners and construction workers, the husbands of employer dressmakers and milliners were generally clerks, company agents, drapers and shoemakers, as well as construction tradesmen.

We can also link parents to their children and examine the impact of starting a family on parents' entrepreneurship rates. Table 7.15 shows ever-married women who had children under age 5 by age group for census year 1901. Ever-married women who had no children under 5 either had no children (yet) or had older children who had aged out of this group. The former is more likely amongst the younger age groups in Table 7.15, while the latter is more likely for the older groups. Up to the 35–44 age group, entrepreneurship rates increased with the arrival of one child and continued to increase as more children were added to the family. At later age groups this difference disappeared, probably as the no-child category here is a mix of women who never had children and those who only had older children. The entrepreneurial relationship with having young children appears in the 1891 census as well; however, by 1911 it only held true for the youngest two age groups, whereas for women over 35 there was no notable entrepreneur relationship with having small children. Early fatherhood, on the other hand, did not relate to entrepreneurism at all. In fact, having young children had a negative relationship with male entrepreneurship rates compared with being married and having none; and adding multiple children under 5 years showed no discernible pattern.

The final form of household firm considered here is that in which non-family members were employed by a family member. Table 7.16 shows the proportion of these in different sectors in each census year. There are three different kinds of business with resident non-family member workers: those with boarders or lodgers working for them, those with a mix of family and non-family employees

Table 7.15 Entrepreneurship rates for ever-married women with children under 5, by woman's age group, 1901

Number of Children Under 5	15–24	25–34	35–44	45–54	55–64
0	8.5	15.9	25.9	33.4	39.0
1	10.4	21.8	30.9	35.3	37.7
2	14.5	22.9	32.2	33.2	n/a
3	14.7	26.9	34.3	n/a	n/a

Source: BBCE database.

Note: A few single women recorded with children have been excluded.

Table 7.16 Co-resident businesses including non-family members by sector, 1851–1911

Sector	1851	1861	1881	1891	1901	1911
Farming/estate work	80.7	78.9	81.1	61.6	63.4	71.3
Mining and quarrying	0.0	0.0	0.0	0.1	0.1	0.1
Construction	2.3	2.7	1.6	1.5	1.5	1.0
Manufacturing	2.0	2.3	1.6	2.3	2.0	1.4
Maker–dealer	7.6	7.2	4.1	8.2	7.5	5.3
Retail	1.5	2.3	3.5	6.6	5.2	3.1
Transport	0.1	0.1	0.1	0.3	0.7	0.6
Professional and business services	0.0	0.0	0.0	0.1	0.1	0.2
Personal services	0.3	0.2	0.4	2.5	3.9	5.2
Agricultural produce processing and dealing	1.4	1.0	0.8	0.7	0.4	0.2
Food sales	4.2	5.1	6.6	15.5	14.5	10.5
Refreshment	0.0	0.0	0.2	0.5	0.7	0.9
Finance and commerce	0.0	0.0	0.0	0.1	0.0	0.1

Source: BBCE database.

and those with just non-family-member workers who were not lodgers or boarders, namely apprentices, assistants, farm servants and so on.

It is clear that this mode of business organisation was most common for farmers. This was common throughout the period and substantial numbers of farmers had co-resident non-family members who worked on their farms. In 1851, 58,731 farmers had such individuals in their household, 38 percent of all farmer employers. By 1911, the number had fallen to 42,358, but this was still 31 percent of all employers in farming. Clearly suggestions that resident farm employees were in terminal decline by the mid-nineteenth century are incorrect (Kussmaul, 1981: 120–34; although she and her critics do not consider Wales). Furthermore, even in 1911 the practice was not just found in northern counties as Table 7.17 shows. While it was common in the northern counties, it was also found in the South West (particularly in Devon), the West Midlands (especially Shropshire and Staffordshire), the north Midlands (notably Lincolnshire) and Wales, where it was most common in west Wales (Cardiganshire, Carmarthenshire) and Montgomeryshire. However, it is clear that it declined in the south and east, as historians have suggested; in the South Eastern division the proportion fell from 9.2 percent in 1851 to 2.7 percent in 1911, in the South Midlands from 7 percent to 1.8 percent and in the Eastern division from 6.6 percent to 1.5 percent. This decline was not sudden, but instead gradual, the proportion of such farmers fell from 9.2 percent in 1851 to 6.7 percent in 1861, 5.1 in 1881, 3.5 in 1891, 3 percent in 1901 and 2.7 percent in 1911. In the South Midlands and Eastern divisions the decline occurred more suddenly between 1861 and 1881, with drops in this period from 6.9 percent to 3.9 percent in the South Midlands and 7.1 percent to 3.7 percent in the Eastern division. Even with these provisos, it is clear that live-in non-family labour was important to

Table 7.17 Proportion of farmers with co-resident non-family workers by division, 1911

Division	% of Farmer Employers with Co-Resident Non-Family Workers
London	0.01
South East	2.7
South Midland	1.8
Eastern	1.5
South West	12.7
West Midland	12.7
North Midland	10.8
North West	10.8
Yorkshire	14.8
North	10.1
Wales	22.1

Source: BBCE database.

many farmers into the twentieth century in the north and west of England and Wales, and into the later nineteenth century for the arable south and east, this is in line with more recent studies of the issue (Goose, 2004; Goose, 2006). Given the pressure on farming caused by the agricultural depression, the migration of workers away from agricultural areas to towns and the rise in farm workers' wages, offering accommodation may have helped farmers continue to be able to continue to employ people despite those growing pressures (Howkins and Verdon, 2008: 473–6, 480–1).

Table 7.16, however, not only shows the continued significance of live-in non-family workers for farming, it also shows that it was an important form of business organisation in maker-dealer trades and increasingly important in food sales. In maker-dealing employers in shoemaking, blacksmithing, tailoring and, later in the century, dressmaking, all employed live-in workers. In food sales the practice became increasingly common among bakers, butchers and grocers. There were several reasons why these trades were more likely than others to adopt this practice. These were trades in which informal or formal training was important, and the presence of apprentices or assistants in the employer's household reflected this fact. Furthermore, some of these trades were characterised by high levels of immigrant labour, such as tailoring and baking in London; in 1901, 78 percent of tailors in London with resident non-family workers were immigrants, the figure for bakers was 44 percent. In such cases offering accommodation as well as employment was an important factor in employing immigrant labour.

7.8 Conclusion

This chapter has shown how important family and household structure was for business proprietors. This importance went beyond the formal employment of family members in the family business. Marriage, size of household, fertility and age all interacted with business proprietorship in ways indicating that entrepreneurship and the decision to operate a business rather than to enter waged labour was bound up with family strategies. The analysis offered in this chapter, therefore, supports the long-standing historiography which has stressed the close relationship between family and business in nineteenth- and twentieth-century England and Wales (Davidoff and Hall, 1997; Nenadic, 1993; Barker, 2017; Colli, 2003). However, it also suggests that authors who move from that position to one which argues that this close link explains British economic performance are wrong to do so (Chandler, 1990). Whilst the family and the business were closely linked, the relationship between the two areas could take many forms. This is clear from the consideration of the concept of the family firm. Given the relative scarcity of non-family businesses in this period, arguing that the family firm was central to the Victorian and Edwardian economy is correct but relatively uninformative. There were firms which were run by and employed family members, firms which were run for the benefit of the family, firms that were owned by a single family but were managed by non-family members and so on. All these were 'family firms', yet they were structured differently, were of different sizes, had different lifespans and contributed to the national economy in different ways. We cannot interrogate all these types of family firm here, although future enrichment of the BBCE database with family history and other information would allow this to be done. This would allow a fuller assessment of the impact of family structure on economic performance, using much firmer and clearer definitions and more comprehensive descriptions of the precise relationship between the different demographic aspects of family life and business proprietorship; this chapter has begun to provide just such a starting point.

Notes

1 The claim of a declining rate of female proprietorship appears incorrect: see Chapter 8; review in Honeyman, 2007: 479–82; importance of female labour see Gleadle, 2001; Nenadic et al., 1992: 174–7, 184–7.
2 *Annual Report of the Chief Inspector of Factories and Workshops for the year 1907. Report and Statistics, Parliamentary Papers*, XII (1908), 148.
3 This age range is used to minimise the distortion caused by remarriage. In 1876, the mean age of re-marriage for widowers was 43.1 years and for widows 39.5; in 1910, it was 45.9 for widowers and 41.3 for widows. The problem becomes less important over time as the incidence of remarriage fell: in 1876, 14 percent of men marrying were widowers and 10 percent of women were widows; in 1910, 8 percent of men were widowers and 6 percent of women were widows. See *Thirty-ninth Annual Report of the Registrar-General (1876), Parliamentary Papers*, XXII (1878), xvii; *Seventy-third Annual Report (1910), Parliamentary Papers*, XI (1911), xiii, xviii–xix.
4 Extended family households are those containing a conjugal family unit and one or more relatives living together; see Laslett, 1972: 29–31.
5 For example, in 1901 over half of the male residents of the parish of Kenton in Devon aged 15–65 (normally expected mostly to be occupied) and not heads of households, had no occupation. In contrast, all but 35 of the 7,267 men with the same characteristics in the parish of Portland had occupations. This indicates that variation in the presence of co-resident family businesses was partly due to enumerator variation.

6 The household includes all relatives of the household and all servants, but not lodgers, boarders, visitors or other non-familial residents.

7 Ten percent of these women were married with their spouse absent, an ambiguous marital condition as discussed above.

8 These numbers are not strictly comparable because some employers are missing in 1851. The reconstruction process adds an additional 28,900 farm employers; of these, 23,965 were living with a worker employed in agriculture. If these were included then 75 percent of farmer employers would be running a co-resident family business. However, the nature of the reconstructed farmers renders this calculation tentative, but provides support for the importance of this business structure to agriculture.

8 Gender

8.1 Introduction

The conventional image of a Victorian entrepreneur is a captain of industry, heading a steel or engineering factory employing hundreds of workers, and generally an older male. Previous chapters have already shown that this type of entrepreneur was the exception; the majority of firms were small businesses and their owners either employed only a handful of people or worked on their own account. This chapter focuses on gender, revealing the population of female entrepreneurs in nineteenth- and early twentieth-century England and Wales, and showing how the incidence of female entrepreneurship changed over the course of our period. However, gender influenced all aspects of business proprietorship, and thus comments and analysis of the gendered aspects are to be found throughout the other chapters; in particular, the interaction between gender, age, life cycle and other demographic issues in Chapter 7. Our analysis draws on the expectations outlined in Chapter 2 and the statistical patterns evidenced in Chapter 6 that demonstrate gender combined with marital status as among the most important factors in entrepreneurship of the period. This reflects the major difference between genders in levels and forms of entrepreneurship, and in access to the alternatives of waged work. Also, because of the interdependence of many female opportunities with networks dominated by men, especially their husbands if married, the level of access in different sectors, and between being employers and own account, differs markedly for women. Generally women had less flexibility of choice than men, and this is reflected throughout the following analysis.

Historians have depicted the rate of female entrepreneurship, as well as women's waged employment, as following its own U-shaped curve, like that discussed in Chapter 4. However, the female curve started to decline during the nineteenth century, earlier than for male entrepreneurs, and remained low from the late Victorian period until after World War II (Craig, 2016: 1; Richards, 1974: 337). This has often been interpreted as the solidifying of gender roles during the second half of the nineteenth century, with women withdrawing from business to become homemakers and 'angels of the house', increasingly constrained by laws of coverture and social conventions (Seccombe, 1993;

Davidoff and Hall, 1997; Honeyman and Goodman, 1991: 615, 618; Vickery, 1993: 412–3). In many readings of the late nineteenth century, those left in the workforce were working-class women struggling to make a living, with impoverished widows or single women in feminised industries eking out a living from micro-enterprises. More recent research, however, shows that in North America as well as in several European countries there is no evidence of women withdrawing from the world of business until the early twentieth century (Craig, 2016: 99–100). In Britain several case studies of female entrepreneurship in urban areas have shown that women continued to conduct business throughout the nineteenth century, in similar numbers as they had done during the eighteenth century (Kay, 2009; Aston, 2016; Phillips, 2006; Barker, 2006; Burnette, 2008).

Women have been shown to have had more economic opportunities than previously assumed, and were often able to act independently regardless of legal constraints. Although important, coverture was not as strict as the legal system demanded, with many legal devices available to enable married women to act as independent business owners (Finn, 1996; Erickson, 1993). The 1882 Married Women's Property Act was a major reform, but may have been less important for entrepreneurs because the courts could treat a married woman as 'feme sole' for business purposes (Phillips, 2006: 24–30; Kay, 2009: 20–4). Indeed married women's business independence was confirmed in 1877 as a 'pure personalty', establishing trade earnings as separate property (Ashworth v. Outram: Law Reports 1877, 5 Ch. D. 923 at 941). As argued by Bennett (2016: 1198), the 1882 Act to some extent codified previous case law and business practice. Hence, although it was of enormous significance for women, it may not have affected entrepreneurship as much as might be expected. Indeed, we find only slowly changing married women's participation rates in entrepreneurship over the period. Moreover, the chapter shows that the number of female entrepreneurs was generally much larger than has hitherto been estimated.

Female entrepreneurship was a varied experience. Mary Ann Bennett, for instance, from Newport Pagnell in Buckinghamshire, was a dressmaker who never married. After serving an apprenticeship, she developed her business working from home, first in 1881 employing her younger sister Caroline, and then in 1891 entering a partnership together until Caroline married. By 1901 Mary Ann headed her own household, and in 1911 owned a millinery and drapery shop, employing a shopkeeper and a dressmaker assistant; in contrast, Caroline dropped out of the economically active population after marriage.[1] Other female-run businesses were more precarious. Emma Smith was a widowed laundress in Cheam, Surrey, with five children in 1901. After her husband's death she moved back with her mother, and drifted in and out of running her own laundry business, sometimes recorded as a worker and at other times as an own-account proprietor.[2] A very different experience was that of Rosa Gatti, who came from Switzerland to London as a widowed mother of small children to join her father's ice cream and cafe business. By 1871 she appeared in the census as the co-proprietor of a music hall.[3] She later married fellow Swiss Giovanni (or James) Corazza, and inherited one-third of her father's business (her mother and one of her sisters received the other thirds). Her father's will made explicit that his bequest was 'for her sole and separate use, independent of her husband and not subject to his debts, control or engagements' (Kinross, 1991: 45). Indeed, Rosa Corazza, by then living in Italy, is listed in the 1901 and 1911 *Directory of Directors* as a director of United Carlo Gatti, Stevenson & Slaters Limited, without any mention of her husband.

While Corazza was an exceptional example, many women actively continued businesses set up by male as well as female family members, and so operated in diverse sectors, many of which are often thought of as 'typically masculine'. But alongside this diversity, there were some distinct patterns in the population of female business owners. While *the* 'female entrepreneur' may not have specifically existed, certain demographics clustered in specific trades and, as with general employment, there was a distinct gendering towards the types of businesses men and women owned. More than was the case for men, women's life cycle events such as marriage, motherhood and widowhood played an important role in the work available to her, and the entrepreneurial choices she could make; and more than was the case for men, these choices were embedded in household and family life, as Chapter 7 has shown. While it is often shown that many female entrepreneurs were single or widowed, it is important to note that neither marriage nor motherhood was an insurmountable obstacle to involvement in business, whether on their own or as a joint partner with their spouse or others. Indeed, sometimes the necessity of providing for a family may have induced entrepreneurial activity.

Locating female entrepreneurs is extremely source dependent, and there are huge variations of how fully what is recorded reflected the actual activities of women. The evidence is further complicated by the fact that many women's business activities took place within the same space as domestic activities, and were often seen as extensions of these activities. Taking in boarders, for instance, provided additional household income for many women, but not all would have been described as boarding-house keepers (Lewis, 2009: 21). Other businesses may have been occasional when spouses were unemployed or during slack periods in the male seasonal labour cycle (Malcolmson, 1986: 15). Many shops were in the same building as living spaces, allowing work and domestic functions to interchange depending on whether customers were present or not. Many women advertised their business through trade cards or were listed in trade directories, but cultural values regarding women and the public sphere led to others relying on word-of-mouth networks as a way of attracting customers, which do not survive in the historical record. The data underlying our study, the UK census, have often been criticised for under-recording female employment. While some of this criticism is valid, the use of the Census Enumerator Books (CEBs) overcome many shortcomings, and recent research has shown that enumeration of female employment was not as bad as often thought; indeed it provides wider coverage than most other sources.

8.2   Gender, entrepreneurship and the census

As discussed in Chapter 3, there were deficiencies in the enumeration of female employment in the census. As Higgs and Wilkinson argued, the process of census-taking was 'a predominantly male affair'. A household's information was collected via its head, with all members defined through their relationship to this head. Most heads of household were male, and married women in particular were rarely if ever recorded as heads of household when their husband was present. In addition, the census enumerators who copied the schedules into the CEBs, the General Record Office (GRO) clerks who processed and tabulated the information and the officials who issued the instructions were almost exclusively male (Higgs and Wilkinson, 2016: 17). Against a background of the gender relations in the Victorian age, it has been argued that these men had certain preconceptions about a women's place in society, and that this biased the instructions, the recording of responses and the enumeration of women in the census (Higgs, 1987: 60). As a result, women's work was often under-represented in the census, with married women's work particularly under-enumerated (Humphries and Sarasúa, 2012). This view has been challenged by the findings that in areas where many women were enumerated as working, such as in Lancashire textile factories, married women had high labour force participation rates, particularly married women who did not yet have children (Anderson, 1999; McKay, 2007; Shaw-Taylor, 2007). As Higgs and Wilkinson (2016: 22) have pointed out, many of the reservations over using census data are only relevant for the tables *published* in the Parliamentary Papers, which had been processed by the GRO, and that many of the usually cited issues with women's enumeration disappear when looking at the original CEBs. Scholars who have performed nominal linking of other records on female economic activity, be it owners of businesses listed in trade directories or workers recorded as employees in a mill, show that women who were known to be economically active from these sources were usually accurately enumerated in the census (Higgs and Wilkinson, 2016: 27; McGeevor, 2014).

While this offers confidence in using the I-CeM data, which are derived from the original CEBs, for the study of female employment and entrepreneurship, limitations have to be recognised. Although CEBs are an accurate source for full-time, regular employment, seasonal or part-time work was mostly not recorded (Shaw-Taylor, 2007; McGeevor, 2014). While this holds for men as well, whose seasonal agricultural work during harvest time was one of the reasons for the census being undertaken in spring, it is likely that women, and married women in particular, would have been more heavily affected by the implicit focus on 'regular' employment contained in the instructions. However, there is reason to believe that female entrepreneurs were better enumerated than female workers. An own-account lodging-house keeper who only had to spend a few hours a day running her business was likely to have been enumerated as such, while a woman spending the same number of hours working in a family member's business was probably more often missed, perhaps being considered as part time.

Another issue pertinent to female entrepreneurship concerns their contribution to running a small business from home, such as a grocery or an inn. Here, the production of goods and services was naturally part of the household setting, and wives and other female family members acted as co-workers in many occupational tasks with husbands or other family members. In family businesses they were often de facto partners, even if this was not frequently recorded as such (Bennett, 2016). Hence the wife's work could be hidden under the occupational descriptor of 'grocer's wife', which could be used as much as a social status descriptor as an occupational title. This practice varied considerably between enumerators, with some recording all married women as wives of their husband's occupation, and others only a small selection of women (You, 2014: 216). In other cases, the enumerator applied the same occupation to all members of the household which may have over-recorded the extent of female contribution (Higgs, 1987: 68). There may be a disconnect between the early censuses and the later censuses in the extent to which ever-married women's occupations were enumerated, given that later censuses show considerable falls, of up to 10 percentage points fewer, in ever-married women being economically active in the higher age groups. This was probably due to a combination of real factors, and the way that women were recorded. Women who were only described as 'wife of [husband's occupation]' or '[husband's occupation]'s wife' have been excluded from the analysis in this chapter. While we acknowledge that this removes some genuine female partners in the family business, the irregularities of recording these occupations between and within censuses made this necessary to avoid distortion. It is therefore important to remember that for ever-married women, this analysis represents the lower boundary of business participation, which in reality was most likely higher.

Our understanding of women's enumeration in the census is still continuing to develop, and these are issues that should be kept in mind while looking at interpreting the census data. However, the data derived from the CEBs is one of the better sources for female entrepreneurship we have for the nineteenth century, and despite its gaps it captures a far larger number of female business proprietors than any other large-scale source available.

8.3   Female entrepreneur numbers

Table 8.1 shows the numbers of male and female entrepreneurs throughout 1851–1911. The proportion of female entrepreneurs remained fairly constant at around 30 percent of the total business-owning population throughout the second half of the nineteenth century, before dropping slightly in 1911. This drop in female entrepreneurship in the early twentieth century was part of a wider trend towards business consolidation as discussed in Chapter 4, and was mainly due to mechanisation in some of the main occupations in which women were predominantly active, such as dressmaking and laundries.

These numbers are much higher than previous estimates of female entrepreneurship in England and Wales. While a small but thriving literature on

Table 8.1 Numbers of entrepreneurs by gender, 1851–1911

	Male	*Female*	*Total*	*% Female*
1851	820,718	320,027	1,140,745	28.1
1861	812,092	348,652	1,160,744	30.0
1881	1,035,503	453,763	1,489,266	30.5
1891	1,164,821	481,965	1,646,786	29.3
1901	1,286,513	530,833	1,817,346	29.2
1911	1,377,382	502,065	1,879,447	26.7

Source: BBCE database.

female entrepreneurship has emerged in the past decade, most of this is based on urban case studies, and few have tried to quantify the proportion of female entrepreneurship. Estimates of female business ownership range between 3 and 12 percent of the total entrepreneurs (Aston, 2016: 67; Kay, 2009: 52; Burnette, 2008: 32; Craig, 2016: 99–100). These studies have been mainly based on trade directories and insurance records. Trade directories are problematic for several reasons. First, they systematically under-recorded married women and property owners who were also entrepreneurs. Second, certain sectors, as well as multiple entrepreneurs in a single household, were often underrepresented in directories. Finally, many trade directories often only stated an owner's first initial rather than a full name, which inhibits the identification of women. Joyce Burnette's work on mid-nineteenth-century trade directories in Birmingham shows that while 11.8 percent were identifiably female, another 8.9 percent were of unknown gender, meaning that the potential population of listed women could be over 20 percent. Similar figures for Manchester (9.3 percent female, 15.0 percent unknown) and Derby (12.1 percent female, 6.6 percent unknown) show the difference these unknowns can make (Burnette, 2008: 32). Record linkage between the census and trade directories in Devizes and Idle have shown that many of the unknown gender in directories were women. This explains some of the discrepancy between Jennifer Aston's estimates of female entrepreneurship in Birmingham and Leeds based on trade directories of between 3.3 percent and 8.2 percent, and the census-based 26 percent and 35 percent for Birmingham and Leeds respectively, although the comparative difference between these two cities, and the downward trend in female entrepreneurship in Leeds, match similar trends observable in census data (Aston, 2016: 67).[4]

Alison Kay's study on female entrepreneurs in London between 1800 and 1870 is based on fire insurance records, and does not state explicit proportions of women as business owners apart from stating that they were unlikely to account for more than 10 percent of the total (Kay, 2009: 52). Fire insurance records have their own inherent bias: businesses with higher capital needs were more likely to be insured, and businesses taking place at home with few additional business assets were less visible in the policies. Men often owned the first kind of business, while women dominated enterprises of the second kind. In addition, some trades would have been more vulnerable to fire, and more likely to appear in the records. For instance, chandlers (who made or sold candles, perhaps among other household goods) appear in Kay's top 10 businesses for both men and women in 1861 (and are second most frequent for women in 1851) but do not make the top 100 of entrepreneurial occupations in the census, accounting for less than 0.1 percent of both male and female entrepreneurs in both census years (Kay, 2009: 46–7).[5]

International studies based on census records show a much closer similarity to the proportion of female entrepreneurs to the numbers derived from the census. In the 1880 US census, between 25 percent and 40 percent of economically active women in seven cities were running a business (Sparks, 2006). Similarly, in Canada, when including boarding-house keepers, the 1901 census showed that 30 percent of business owners were women (Craig, 2016, 101). In Belgium, census data between 1880 and 1910 showed that 34 percent of businesses were female owned, while German official statistics reveal that women owned around 25 percent of businesses between 1882 and 1907 (Craig, 2016: 118, 122). In addition, if we look at the population of shareholders in England and Wales, who effectively owned part of an incorporated business, we find similar proportions of female involvement as in the census. Female shareholdership in a range of businesses rose from 24 percent to 34 percent between the 1880s and the 1910s, while similar numbers were found for shareholders in various banks (Rutterford et al., 2011: 169; Turner, 2009: 179–80).

8.4   Long-term trends

Figures 8.1 and 8.2 show the total numbers of female employers, own-account proprietors and workers, and their rates. These figures are equivalent to Figures 4.1 and 4.2 for the whole population, and reveal how female entrepreneurs differ from the total population. First of all, female entrepreneurship consisted predominantly of own-account businesses. Only 2 percent of women who were economically active employed workers, against overall figures of 6 percent. This number rose in 1911, both in terms of absolute numbers and rate, in line with overall trends that favoured larger firms with employees instead of own-account businesses. Indeed, the drop in own-account entrepreneurship between 1901 and 1911 was even more evident for women than for the total population, and led to a drop in the total number of female entrepreneurs as well as a fall in the rate of female entrepreneurship. For women therefore, the decline in entrepreneurship that set in after 1901 was more severe than for men. However, entrepreneurship, and particularly own-account proprietorship, had been fairly stable during the second half of the nineteenth century, meaning that women entered the downward curve of the N-shape at the same time as men and not before, although their decline was then steeper.

Figure 8.3 shows the number of female entrepreneurs (a) and their rates (b) by marital status. The 1882 Married Women's Property Act, which allowed married women to own property, such as a business, in their own right and separate

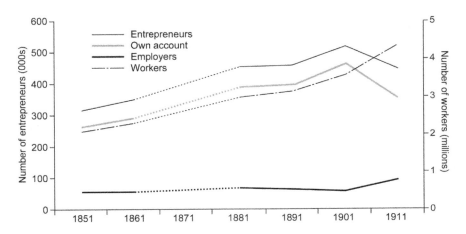

Figure 8.1 Reconstructed total numbers of own account, employers and all entrepreneurs, 1851–1911, women only

Source: BBCE database.

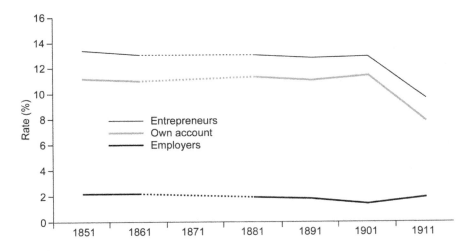

Figure 8.2 Entrepreneurship rates: total numbers of own account, employers and all entrepreneurs as percentage of all economically active, 1851–1911, women only

Source: BBCE database.

from their husbands, does not seem to have had any significant positive impact on either the numbers of married women who owned businesses recorded in the censuses, or their entrepreneurship rates. Unfortunately, interpretation is made difficult by the Act's timing, as it came into force nine years before a census was taken, and shortly after the break between the early and later censuses that

Figure 8.3 Entrepreneurship (employer and own account) numbers and rates by marital status, 1851–1911, women only

Source: BBCE database.

affects how we can measure women's employment and own account status (see Chapter 4). Figure 8.3 actually shows a slight decline in the rates of married business-owning women between 1881 and 1891, particularly for those women whose spouse was not present on census night; however, their number was relatively small. Single women showed a gentle rise in terms of entrepreneurship rates; however, a demographic sex imbalance and a shift towards later marriage during this time caused there to be an overall increase in the number of single women, many of whom were workers (Anderson, 1990: 67–8; Woods, 2000: 82). These workers hide the dramatic increase in the number of single female entrepreneurs: from 128,000 in 1881 to 176,000 in 1891, on to 226,000 in 1901, before dropping back in 1911 to 217,000. The drop in business ownership from 1901 onwards affected women of all marital statuses.

Figure 8.4 breaks down male and female entrepreneurs by sector, and this reveals some further differences. The maker-dealer sector was by far the most common sector for women, followed by personal services, whereas for men it was farming, followed by food sales. When combined these graphs produce the graphs shown in Figure 4.3, which had maker-dealer as most numerous followed by farming. This gendered aspect of entrepreneurship is further illustrated by the fact that while there were thousands of male business owners in all of the 13 main sectors, the numbers of female entrepreneurs in the construction, transport, professional and business services, mining, finance and commerce, and agricultural produce processing and dealing sectors were so low as to be almost invisible in Figure 8.4a.

The gendered aspect of entrepreneurship can also be expressed as the percentage of female entrepreneurs in the whole business population by sector, shown in Table 8.2. While, as shown in Table 8.1, the overall female entrepreneurship share hovered around 30 percent, this varied considerably between sectors.

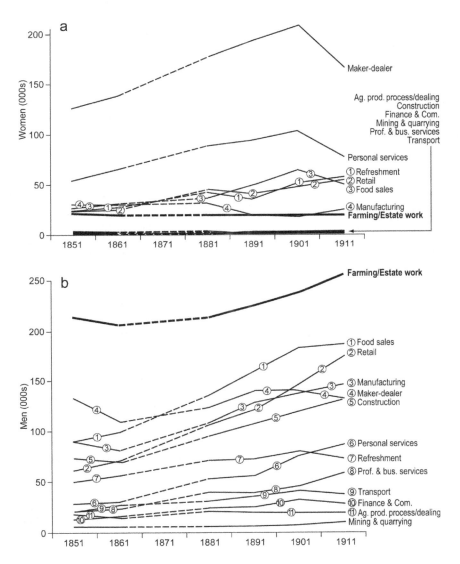

Figure 8.4 Reconstructed total entrepreneur numbers, 1851–1911, for 13 aggregated business
  sectors by gender

Source: BBCE database.

Table 8.2 shows the sectors identified above as being mostly composed of male
business owners. While farming was a male-dominated sector as well, due to its
overall size this was still a relatively significant sector for women, as shown in
Figure 8.4. In personal services and maker-dealing, on the other hand, and in
refreshment in 1911, women actually constituted the majority of entrepreneurs

Table 8.2 Percentage female entrepreneurship by sector, 1851–1911 (1871 not in I-CeM)

Sector	1851	1861	1881	1891	1901	1911
Farming	9	9	9	9	8	8
Mining	10	10	7	4	4	6
Construction	2	3	2	1	1	2
Manufacturing	25	27	22	14	13	16
Maker-dealing	49	56	59	58	60	57
Retail	29	27	29	25	25	25
Transport	6	5	3	3	3	3
Professional and business services	6	6	6	3	3	5
Personal services	66	69	63	62	57	48
Agricultural produce processing and dealing	9	9	7	8	7	8
Food sales	22	23	22	24	27	22
Refreshment	33	33	38	39	42	48
Finance and commerce	7	6	9	2	3	4

Source: BBCE database.

for most census years. They also formed a significant minority in refreshment, retail, food sales and manufacturing.

The high numbers of female entrepreneurs in these sectors means that they were responsible for some of the overall trends identified in Chapter 4. The 1901 dip in employer rates for food sales, for instance, was mainly driven by female employers, whereas male employers only experienced a gentle decline. Similarly, the upturn in employers' rate for refreshment as noted in 1911 was more strongly pronounced for women than it was for men. Overall, however, entrepreneurs and employer rates followed similar trends between the sexes.

Within the 13 main sectors there was further variation. The high proportion of women in personal services was predominantly caused by large numbers of laundresses, an occupation that was over 90 percent female. Other personal services occupations were much more male dominated; hairdressing, for instance, was over 95 percent male. Masculine industries such as construction were also not uniformly male, and included occupations such as whitewashing, where almost a quarter of entrepreneurs were female. Retail is often considered a sector that employed many women; however, it was a diverse sector that offered female entrepreneurs opportunities in some, but not all sub-sectors. Most women were, unsurprisingly, concentrated in clothing-related retail, but general shopkeeping, hawking, stationers and artificial-flower shops were often headed by women as well. Raw material textiles, on the other hand, were often sold by men, as were skins, leather and metal. Food sales saw a similar divide between male and female occupations, with butchers being over 90 percent male, while confectioners were predominantly female. An example of an extreme gender split can be found within the refreshment sector, where women made up almost 90 percent of all lodging-house keepers, but less than 20 percent of inn and hotel keepers.

It is evident from Figure 8.4 and Table 8.2 that compared to men, business-women engaged in a much more limited field of sectors. In the census, the two most feminised sub-sectors, clothing manufacturing and personal services, together accounted for over half of all female entrepreneurs.[6] Kay's study of London insurance records in the mid-nineteenth century finds that around 15 percent of female entrepreneurs owned businesses in the more 'masculine' production trades, which included the non-retail manufacturing trades outside textiles and food (Kay, 2009: 43). In the census, however, non-retail female entrepreneurs not in textile or food-related sectors comprised no more than 3 percent of the total. This difference is, once again, explained through the difference in data sources: some of these masculine trades would have had higher capital needs, and as such were more likely to obtain an insurance policy, whereas some of the most numerous female occupations in the census, dressmaking and laundry, would have required very little capital and consequently had little need or ability to take out insurance.

Table 8.3 shows the top 10 occupations by census year, based on the most detailed level of occupational codes. These occupations together consistently

Table 8.3 The top 10 female entrepreneurial sectors by census years and their percentage of total female entrepreneurs for that year, 1851–1911

1851	1861	1881	1891	1901	1911
Dressmaker	Dressmaker	Dressmaker	Dressmaker	Dressmaker	Dressmaker
Laundress	Laundress	Laundress	Laundress	Laundress	Lodging/boarding-house keeper
Farmer	Farmer	Lodging/boarding-house keeper	Lodging/boarding-house keeper	Lodging/boarding-house keeper	Laundress
Milliner	Shirt maker/Seamstress	Shirt maker/Seamstress	Grocer	Grocer	Shopkeeper
Shirt maker/Seamstress	Lodging/boarding-house keeper	Farmer	Farmer	Farmer	Farmer
Lodging/boarding-house keeper	Grocer	Grocer	Shirt maker/Seamstress	Teacher	Grocer
Grocer	Straw plait manufacture	Shopkeeper	Milliner	Confectioner	Teacher
Shopkeeper	Milliner	Hawker/huckster	Hawker/huckster	Shirt maker/Seamstress	Confectioner
Straw plait manufacture	Shopkeeper	Milliner	Shopkeeper	Music teacher	Music teacher
Innkeeper	Innkeeper	Innkeeper	Schoolmistress	Innkeeper	Milliner
71%	**73%**	**71%**	**72%**	**73%**	**69%**

Source: BBCE database.

accounted for over 70 percent of female entrepreneurs, apart from 1911, which showed a slight increase in diversification, although this might be partly due to the use of the household responses rather than CEBs in I-CeM in 1911. Some sectors remained important throughout the period: dressmakers were consistently most common, with the related clothing manufacturing occupations milliner and shirt maker/seamstress also listed in the top 10 in most years. In fact, dressmaking alone accounted for around 30 percent of the total number of female entrepreneurs in every year, showing the extremely skewed nature of the female business population. In comparison, the most common male occupation, farming, only accounted for 15–21 percent of all male entrepreneurs. This was partly driven by demographics; as shown below, dressmakers were overall younger than some of the other entrepreneurial professions. If we break down the top 10 by age group, by the age of 55 laundresses were more numerous, and dressmaking was further down the top 10 in the highest age groups.

Over the course of the period, laundresses accounted for 14 percent of female entrepreneurs. Grocers and shopkeepers also consistently made the top 10. Other sectors were subject to some change: the straw plait manufacture industry, still solidly in the top 10 in 1851 and 1861, collapsed towards the end of the century, and accounted for less than 0.1 percent of female entrepreneurs by 1901. The declining size of the agricultural labour force during this time can be seen in the relative decline of farm entrepreneurship, which dropped from being the third most common occupation down to fifth. Education, in the form of schoolmistresses or music teachers, crept into the top 10 by the second half of the census period, highlighting the opportunity of setting up schooling or private tuition as an entrepreneurial choice. Lodging- and boarding-house keeping increased in importance over time, and while some of this is an artefact of differing ways of recording occupations in the census, the continuous trend is nevertheless obvious.[7]

8.5   The angel of the hearth? Home and the family

The previous section has shown how women operated in a narrow selection of occupations compared to men, who were relatively numerous even in the most feminized sectors of making and dealing. Cultural factors played an important role here. Female-run business sectors, as well as women's work, were often seen as an extension of domestic work. Doing laundry and boarding-house keeping relied on skills that were used in the household that easily adapted to business, and while dressmaking was a skilled job with an apprenticeship, most women would have been taught basic sewing skills as part of their domestic responsibility to make or maintain clothing for the family, and fancy or decorative needlework was seen as an acceptable pursuit for women of higher social status. Another aspect of respectability was remaining in the private sphere of the home. The 1901 and 1911 censuses included a question on whether an individual worked at home.[8] Table 8.4 shows male and female percentages of working at home for 1901, demonstrating that women were more than twice as likely to work at home as men.

Table 8.4 Percentage working at home, 1901

Age Group	Female			Male		
	E	OA	W	E	OA	W
15–24	37.0	80.1	4.6	18.5	36.4	2.6
25–34	56.6	76.9	7.5	22.9	42.6	2.0
35–44	55.5	73.9	10.5	21.9	45.1	1.6
45–54	51.7	72.8	12.5	22.1	46.3	1.7
55–64	43.2	71.4	14.3	22.3	48.2	2.2
65–74	35.4	70.1	16.0	21.3	49.2	3.0
75+	27.0	65.7	14.0	20.3	51.0	3.7
Life average	47.9	74.5	7.0	22.0	45.3	2.1

Source: BBCE database.

The possibility of working at home was largely sector dependent, with the majority of entrepreneurs in maker–dealing, personal services, food sales and refreshment working in the same place they lived, and the lowest rates were in the mining and quarrying sector. Dressmakers and laundresses had particularly high rates of working at home at close to 90 percent, and the opportunity of being able to work from home may have contributed to the popularity of these professions for women. There were also stark differences between employment types. Workers of both sexes were least likely to work where they lived, while the majority of female own-account business owners worked at home. For women in particular, this was subject to change over the course of the life cycle, with female workers increasingly more likely to work at home as they aged. Own-account women followed a contrasting trend with declining percentages working at home for the higher age groups. Employers fell somewhere between the two groups. Both male and female employers were most likely to work from home between 25–34 years old, with lower rates in later years. This was likely related to the setting up of a business during these years, and then expanding to separate premises as the business grew.

Marital status was another influence, particularly for women. Married female workers were twice as likely to work from home as single workers, a trend that held up throughout the life cycle. In addition, if they had children under 5 years old they were more likely to work at home as well: 18 percent of worker women with one child under 5 worked at home, going up to 24 percent for worker women who had two children, and 29 percent for worker women who had three children under 5. For own-account women, on the other hand, the story was less straightforward. While in the younger age groups 81 percent of single own-account women worked at home, against 72 percent of married own-account women, this flipped at higher ages as the proportion of single women working at home gradually declined to 69 percent for the over 75s, while 77 percent of married own-account women worked from home by the age of 25, which then stayed consistently high. However, these results are mainly due to the demographic characteristics of entrepreneurs in different sectors: dressmakers, for instance, who were very likely to work from home, were overall a younger and unmarried group. Demographic characteristics and sector were strongly related, and given that female work and entrepreneurship was so skewed towards a few occupations, the demographics of these key occupations drove much of the trends that can be identified for female entrepreneurs as a whole. Different sector markets presented major constraints and opportunities that were highly gendered. It is therefore necessary to pick out the specific driving forces for different sectors that influenced different groups of women, to reveal the varied experience of female entrepreneurial life in Victorian Britain.

8.6   Sector, employment type and the life cycle

Figure 8.5 contrasts employment type over the course of the life cycle for the main female occupations in which they were entrepreneurs, and shows the diversity of employment status breakdowns over the life cycle. Dressmaking was a trade dominated by young workers, but with a core of own-account work that could solidly sustain a woman throughout her life. Contrast this with lodging-house keepers, on the other hand, where very few women were either young or workers. The industry was dominated by women in middle age, the vast majority were working on own account, and there were substantial numbers of women still running a lodging house at advanced age. Both female laundresses and grocers show a large contingent of workers at a young age. However, while, similar to dressmakers, the workers disappear in higher age groups, for laundresses and female grocers a second peak in numbers is driven by an increase in entrepreneurs. While entrepreneurial rates by age were similar between dressmakers and female grocers, the driving forces behind these rates were very different. Dressmaker women were able to start a business at a young age, but as they aged, absolute numbers of dressmakers dropped. Young grocers were likely to have been employed in a family business, and dropped out of the economically active on marriage. Grocer proprietors, on the other hand, entered the business at a later age as businesswomen in their own right. Farmers, finally, displayed an age and employment pattern seen by female entrepreneurs in the 'traditionally male' industries: a large proportion of employers at higher age. Blacksmithing, the occupation most skewed towards men, showed a very similar distribution for the few women active in this industry who were mostly older and likely to employ others. For both farmers and blacksmiths this was mainly driven by widows, who likely continued a business after their spouse died. These were the only groups with a significant proportion of employers. As mentioned in Chapter 7, farmers were most likely to employ household members in their business, which accounts for most of these employers.

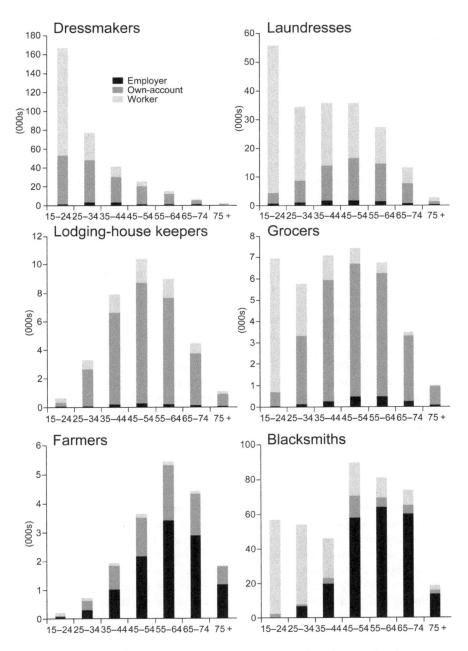

Figure 8.5 Employment types for women in 10-year age bands in the main female entrepreneurial sectors, 1901

Source: BBCE database.

Of the other top 10 occupations, those that were in the same sectors often followed similar trends. Not surprisingly, milliners looked like dressmakers, although their entrepreneurship rates were much lower: overall, 77 percent of milliners were workers, versus only 49 percent of dressmakers. This difference was particularly stark in the youngest age groups, with only 10 percent of young milliners being entrepreneurs, while over 30 percent of dressmakers owned their own business. Seamstresses and shirt makers were even less entrepreneurial at a young age; while their overall percentage of workers was the same as for milliners, only 3 percent of seamstresses in the youngest age band were entrepreneurs. Dressmaking therefore stands out as a trade that allowed women to set up their own business from a young age, even compared to other parts of the clothes-making sector. The reason for these dynamics can be found in the structure of the trade. Dressmaking required an apprenticeship, after which they could run their own businesses. The poor working circumstances of milliner and dressmaking apprentices in the mid-nineteenth century was a strong cause of this; the young and single female who was desperate to earn a wage was more prepared to endure these working conditions than others. However, their employers, who were often successful businesswomen, have received less attention in the historiography on women's work, which tends to focus on the workers (Phillips, 2006: 232).

As a sector, dressmaking increased in importance between 1851 and 1901, driving an expansion of female business opportunities, before numbers declined in 1911. The reasons for this were complex, and can be found in a combination of the availability of sewing machines at home, leading to a rise in amateur dressmaking for the family, new systems that transformed dressmaking from a craft industry to an increasingly factory-based one and the rise of the department store (Gamber, 1997: 158–228; Nenadic, 1998: 628). It should be noted that milliners, whose craft could not be so easily mechanised, did not experience a similar drop in numbers in 1911.

Table 8.5 shows the marital status breakdown by 10-year age bands and employment type for women in key female sectors in 1901. With a few minor exceptions, these trends echoed the breakdowns in 1891 and 1911, the years for which the best data are available, although over the course of the period the proportion of single women increased across all age groups and occupations, due to the increase in age at marriage and the general increase in the proportion of never-married women in the population during this time (Anderson, 1990: 67–8; Woods, 2000: 82). Of these main female occupations, dressmaking was most dominated by never-marrieds. However, in the younger age bands, both employers and own-account dressmakers were slightly more likely to be married than worker dressmakers, a difference that was at its greatest between the ages of 25 and 34 and then declined, to almost disappear in the older age bands. Clearly, for young dressmakers, marriage either enabled them to set up their own business or made it more difficult to work for someone else. This could follow two directions: either the additional resources of marriage allowed them to set up a business or difficulties in committing to long working days acted as

Table 8.5 Marital status by 10-year age band and employment type for key female occupations, 1901; MAS, married, absent spouse

	Dressmakers			Laundresses			Lodging-House Keeper			Grocer			Farmer		
	E	OA	W	E	OA	W	E	OA	W	E	OA	W	E	OA	W
15–24															
Single	95.6	96.2	99.2	78.2	86.7	91.1	87.5	76.8	90.6	71.0	65.1	98.7	81.6	80.6	98.9
Married	3.2	2.6	0.5	17.6	9.1	5.9	12.5	10.0	4.2	22.6	30.4	0.8	10.5	11.9	0.0
MAS	0.9	1.1	0.3	2.5	3.1	2.6	0.0	8.4	3.9	3.2	2.9	0.4	0.0	4.5	1.1
Widow	0.3	0.2	0.1	1.8	1.1	0.4	0.0	4.8	1.3	3.2	1.5	0.1	7.9	3.0	0.0
25–34															
Single	77.7	78.7	87.8	34.1	46.3	48.5	54.7	49.9	61.7	38.3	31.4	83.0	48.3	60.1	79.8
Married	16.9	14.0	6.5	50.1	30.7	30.5	18.8	16.2	10.7	30.0	48.3	12.0	6.6	10.7	8.3
MAS	2.9	4.1	3.4	7.7	9.7	12.0	14.1	12.6	11.6	5.0	6.4	2.6	8.3	12.0	7.1
Widow	2.5	3.1	2.3	8.0	13.3	9.0	12.5	21.3	16.0	26.7	13.9	2.4	36.8	17.2	4.8
35–44															
Single	60.3	57.3	62.2	24.6	23.9	21.1	35.9	40.9	42.4	23.6	25.9	57.1	31.0	40.2	52.0
Married	24.6	23.3	17.4	47.1	35.3	36.9	24.2	13.5	15.7	24.8	38.5	27.8	3.3	9.1	10.8
MAS	5.2	6.4	7.2	9.6	9.9	13.6	14.1	12.9	13.6	7.7	7.1	5.4	7.0	12.5	10.8
Widow	9.9	13.0	13.2	18.8	31.0	28.4	25.8	32.8	28.3	43.9	28.5	9.7	58.7	38.2	26.5
45–54															
Single	48.7	42.7	41.5	13.4	14.1	13.0	32.1	34.6	35.0	16.7	18.6	34.5	17.4	27.4	26.8
Married	25.1	24.1	22.1	43.6	33.0	31.8	16.0	11.3	11.9	18.3	29.9	39.0	2.7	3.5	18.9
MAS	5.4	7.0	8.4	9.2	8.4	10.7	12.7	11.0	9.6	7.0	8.1	5.3	4.4	7.6	5.5
Widow	20.8	26.2	28.1	33.8	44.6	44.5	39.2	43.1	43.5	58.0	43.4	21.2	75.5	61.5	48.8
55–64															
Single	34.9	33.0	31.5	10.1	10.7	10.0	28.7	26.4	26.8	7.0	13.8	19.2	9.3	13.6	14.7
Married	22.1	20.3	19.2	35.7	25.2	24.5	7.6	8.4	8.3	11.6	19.0	34.3	1.1	2.3	11.6
MAS	5.9	5.3	6.5	7.2	6.2	8.0	4.1	7.5	8.0	5.6	6.5	6.1	3.0	5.2	9.3
Widow	37.1	41.3	42.9	47.0	58.0	57.6	59.6	57.7	56.8	75.9	60.6	40.4	86.7	78.9	64.3

a barrier to waged employment that pushed young married workers into self-employment, which could be precarious. The 1911 marriage and fertility data shows that dressmakers who married did so at a later age than the average shown in Chapter 7, for all age cohorts.

Dressmaking businesses varied from London society showrooms to smaller establishments where clients brought in their fabrics – or even pre-made department store dresses that had to be altered – and had different associated start-up costs. Many young dressmakers set up businesses together as partnerships in order to share these costs (Ingram, 2000: 90–4). The example of Mary Ann Bennett at the start of this chapter shows how a career in dressmaking allowed a single woman some independence – 13 percent of single entrepreneur dressmakers were heads of households, while worker dressmakers often depended on others, with only 3 percent heading their own household. This opportunity of an independent life was deemed one of the more compelling reasons to choose a dressmaking apprenticeship over other occupational options, as indicated by the introduction of a contemporary Guide to Trade (1843: 5–6) for dressmaking, which also mentioned that a dressmaker would be able to have a house of her own.

Laundry work was considered a lower-class occupation and often seen as one of the sweating trades (Malcolmson, 1986: 5). Charles Booth (1902–03, 2nd ser. IV: 266) noted the large proportion of laundresses that were married women, and indeed, in contrast to the dressmakers, laundry business proprietors were the group most likely to have been married. Laundry workers were reported by their employers often to be the main wage earner, who supported their families when their husbands were (temporarily) out of work (Malcolmson, 1986: 13). Many of these laundry workers were reportedly married to manual labourers, often active in seasonal building trades. Marriage was even more common for business-owning laundresses than for workers, but, as shown in Chapter 7, entrepreneurial laundresses had a similar domestic setup as workers, and were predominantly married to general labourers, agricultural labourers or those active in the building trades. Employer laundresses were particularly more likely to be married than own-account laundresses, whereas for dressmakers this difference was negligible for all age cohorts. This is partly explained by these employers being particularly reliant on in-house workers: over 40 percent of the married laundress employers had laundry workers living with them in their household in 1901, over half of whom were daughters, meaning that many of these were family businesses.[9]

Running a laundry business was evidently a good opportunity for a married woman from an early age. It required little additional skills and equipment beyond what was already required for the household, and the work could be fitted into the domestic routine, was often available all year round and offered a degree of flexibility. Laundry proprietors were said to complain about the irregular hours worked by their employees, who worked around their home duties (Booth, 1902–3, 2nd ser. IV: 266); setting up a small business would allow a woman to maintain these hours without having to negotiate with employers.

Female-run laundry businesses were particularly concentrated in places containing many temporary residents, such as spa towns, sea resorts and university towns. Areas with the highest proportions of female-run laundries by population included Poole, Bath and Cambridge. While London has been identified as an area with many laundresses as well (Malcolmson, 1986: 7), it was less entrepreneurial for this trade, with a higher proportion of worker laundresses, which reflected the large scale of the market. The higher visibility of employee laundresses in the metropolis may have contributed to the image of laundresses as one of the sweated trades, exploited by (male) business owners as presented by Charles Booth and the *Royal Commission of Labour*.

The most entrepreneurial occupation for women, with almost no workers, was lodging-house keeping, which was almost entirely own-account work. As a profession, lodging-house keeping accounted for between 4 and 6 percent of entrepreneurs over the period, with a rise to 14 percent in 1911. The key requirement was some business capital in the form of a house, which was often only achieved at middle age groups, and there were very few young lodging-house keepers of any employment type.[10] In contrast to laundresses, it was an occupation typically undertaken by women who lived without a man. It had the second highest rate of never-marrieds after the dressmakers, as well as some of the highest rates of being married with an absent spouse. This was an ambiguous term. While in many cases it indicated a married woman whose husband was somewhere else on census night (such as military, visiting elsewhere), it also included single or separated women, perhaps with children, who stated 'married' as a mark of respectability. Young widows were also unusually common among lodging-house keepers. Renting out rooms provided a vital form of entrepreneurial income for women who otherwise might have struggled to support themselves and their families through waged labour.

The demographic profile of lodging-house keepers can be contrasted with innkeepers. As mentioned above, this was a much more male-dominated profession, although also a sizeable one, meaning that the 20 percent of innkeepers who were women accounted for a small percentage of the total female entrepreneur population, and innkeeper appeared in the top 10 of female business owners' occupations most years. In terms of age, female innkeeper-business proprietors followed a similar curve as lodging-house keepers, although they were more likely to be employers. However, innkeepers rarely remained single throughout their lives, with only 5 percent of innkeepers in the 55–64 age group never having been married. They were often widowed, at even higher numbers than the lodging-house keepers by their mid-30s. Single and widowed innkeepers under the age of 35 were most likely to be employers; presumably they were pushed into hiring a workforce as running an inn required more labour than they could source within their own household, while lodging houses could be kept more easily with a limited labour force, as also indicated by the higher proportion of own-account lodging-house keepers. The difference between these related professions was even more pronounced in their geographies. Boarding-house keepers had clear concentrations in similar areas to those where laundresses were prominent: spa towns such as Bath and Buxton, and university towns like Cambridge, and seaside resorts such as Blackpool, where 7 percent of all female boarding-house keepers were concentrated. Innkeepers, on the other hand, had particularly high concentrations in Wales and the north, where travel distances were higher.

Grocers made up between 3 and 5 percent of all female entrepreneurs, and their characteristics reveal some of the largest differences between entrepreneurs and workers. Entrepreneurial grocers were much more likely to be married, and while the most numerous occupation of their husbands was a grocer as well, suggesting a de facto partnership, there were substantial numbers of female grocers married to farmers, coal merchants and other food sales occupations. This presence of dual-entrepreneurship marriages has previously been identified for eighteenth-century London (Erickson, 2008: 267–307). Further indication of the importance of families in running a food sales business was the fact that employer grocers were more likely to be widowed than own-account grocers, suggesting that these own-account grocers had access to some unenumerated labour from within their households or wider networks, while after the death of a spouse the remaining one running the business had to employ help. Indeed, of the 1,565 female grocer employers in 1901, over half employed at least one person from their household, with widows being the most likely to do so. The vast majority employed their own children. The other food sales occupations, such as bakers, butchers, fishmongers and confectioners, all appeared in the top 50 of female occupations, although together only accounted for a few percent of the female entrepreneur population. Their demography was similar to that of the grocers.

Farming, while a large sector that consistently appeared in the top 10 female entrepreneurial occupations, was a very male-dominated sector. As shown in Table 8.2, well over 90 percent of farming entrepreneurs were male, and it was the most entrepreneurial occupation for men throughout the period. However, as noted in Chapter 3, a lot of female involvement in farming was hidden due to census questions explicitly asking for returns of occupations such as 'farmer's son' or 'farmer's daughter' for relatives of farmers, even if they worked on the farm. A farmer's wife was included in the 1851–81 example household schedules although wives were never named as a specific sort of farmer relative in the instructions to householders, but later censuses dropped farmer households from the example schedule. It is clear however, that many were actively involved in the farm. As Montebruno et al. (2019a) have shown, married male farmers were more likely to be own-account rather than employers, since they could rely on labour from their household. In addition, very few of the female entrepreneurial farmers were married. Unlike the grocers, where both spouses stated their entrepreneurial role, farm businesses seems to have mainly been listed under the men only.

As Chapter 7 has shown, farming was the sector in which the family household firm was most prevalent, and the majority of female farmer employers had farm workers living in their household. Female farmer demographics displayed a pattern usually observed in male-dominated trades, in that the women were mostly older, and often widowed. It seems probable that they had been involved in the farm business throughout most of their marriage and continued to run their late husband's business. Many of them were widowed from a young age: almost 40 percent of female employer farmers were widows by the age of 35. Other male-dominated occupations show a similar distribution of female entrepreneurs as farmers: usually comparatively older and often widowed, such as the blacksmiths shown in Figure 8.5. As mentioned previously, compared to Kay and Aston's studies their numbers were low, at 3 percent of the total. However, in correspondence with such studies, these women were more likely to be in the middle age groups, peaking at 45–55, and with a larger likelihood of being an employer than any of the other groups apart from farmers.

The average age difference between male and female entrepreneurs in a given occupational sector offers a good proxy for the level of female business ownership in a sector, with large positive age differences indicative of a paucity of opportunities, and hence a lower level of female business ownership, and small or negative age differences indicative of wider opportunities. Female blacksmith entrepreneurs, for instance, were more than 10 years older than male blacksmiths across all census years and females headed only around 1.5 percent of blacksmith businesses. Road and rail transport entrepreneurs had a similar age gap of 9 to 15 years, while construction operatives showed average gaps of 5 to 10 years. The gender age gap in farming was consistently between 8.3 and 8.8 years. Conversely, in clothing manufacturing, as well as several textile manufacturing sectors, men were on average older, showing the business opportunities for young women in these sectors. Finally, while most sectors showed a consistent age pattern over 1851–1911, some sectors showed change. For instance, in the professions, which included teaching, a consistent age gap of over 10 years is evident in the earlier decades, but this gap disappeared by the early twentieth century, reflecting the new opportunities open to women in teaching.

Although Kay (2009: 85) found that female entrepreneurs in her 'masculine trades' sectors were on average older, she stressed that this did not have to mean that they inherited their business, just that there were limited options for young women to enter trades like these. Conversely, she suggests that the more popular trades, such as dressmaking, were both easier to enter in terms of low capital requirements, but also that women were likely to follow others into these professions (Kay, 2009: 46). Rosa Corazza, the company director introduced at the start of this chapter, had inherited her business from her father, as opposed to Mary Ann Bennett and Emma Smith, who both seem to have been self-made businesswomen without a parent or spouse in the same profession. However, Rosa was an active entrepreneur, helping to expand the family business horizontally from ice cream cafes to music halls, and a company director in a time when only a handful of women were included on corporate boards (Kinross, 1991). Many male entrepreneurs then and now would also have benefitted from having a family member setting up a business, and as Chapter 7 shows, there were many co-resident sons collaborating with older family members in their businesses. Women, often outliving their spouses, in whose business they were likely to have been involved as a hidden partner for at least some part of the marriage, would have been the ideal person to continue to run it.

8.7   Firm size

As previously discussed, the census was a population rather than a business census and did not record a business's turnover, capital or valuation. However, the distinction between own account and employers gives some indication of business size and organisation. This varied by sector as it was feasible in certain industries for a single individual to run high-value enterprises, while others needed multiple people even at quite small scales. The employee numbers provided by employers in the early censuses, as reviewed in Chapter 5, can be used to probe the different company sizes by gender further. These data are based on the extracted sample only. As already shown in Chapter 5, firm size was extremely sector dependent, and the fact that sectors were very gender-specific accounts for most of the gender gap in firm size. When women were in charge of a firm belonging to a more male-dominated industry, they could have very large businesses as well. For instance, in 1871 Eliza Tinsley, a widow, ran a nail and chain manufacturing firm employing 4,000 people in Dudley, Staffordshire.[11] Table 8.6 shows that average firm size in sectors where there were many female entrepreneurs, such as making-dealing, was often very similar between the sexes. Conversely, the largest differences were in sectors that were very male dominated,

Table 8.6 Average number of employees by gender of business owner, 1851–81, based on extracted data. Figures based on fewer than 50 people have been italicised

	1851		1861		1871		1881	
	F	M	F	M	F	M	F	M
Farming	4.1	5.5	4.9	6.2	5	6.4	4.6	6.1
Mining	7	23.9	*18.5*	33.3	*19.8*	53.5	*6.3*	103
Construction	5.2	6.3	5.9	8	9.6	9.4	8.8	11
Manufacturing	12.1	24.7	18.9	31.1	21.4	37.9	12.9	38.3
Maker-dealing	4.6	4.2	4.6	5.2	5.5	7.1	5.7	8.4
Retail	4.9	8	6.7	9.6	6.5	11.2	5.6	11.7
Transport	*5.8*	8.7	*4.5*	7.4	*6.1*	8.8	6.3	14.8
Professional and business services	*5.8*	10.2	*13.5*	17.3	7.9	26	*17*	41.7
Personal services	3.8	4.4	3.8	6.4	4.4	5.5	7.2	6.5
Agricultural produce processing and dealing	3.8	5.2	4.6	7.4	6.2	9.2	6	9.9
Food sales	2.3	2.8	2.5	3.5	3	3.6	3	4.4
Refreshment	3.2	3.6	2.6	4.2	4.5	5	3.2	4.7
Finance and commerce	*8.4*	36.8	*5.9*	38.1	*4.4*	24.6	7.2	32.4

where male businesses were more than twice the size, particularly in mining and finance and commerce. Only in maker-dealing in 1851, and personal services in 1881, did women have a higher average firm size than male employers.

In all years for which marital status data were available, married women reported more employees than single and widowed employers, again showing the added value of marriage in growing a business, whether in partnership with their husbands or not. While for single and widowed women business size was at its largest around the age of 45–54, for married women this peak was a decade later, but after that there was a steeper decline than for others, although numbers at that age were small. Of the key female professions, dressmakers stand out as a sector where women continued expanding their businesses until later in their lives. They employed their highest number of employees between the age of 55 and 64, even though this was a sector dominated by single rather than married women. Laundresses, on the other hand, show a very stable number of employees over their life cycle, an indication of the ease of entry in this profession and the lack of career progression as opposed to dressmaking, something which is illustrated by the contrasting experiences of Mary Ann Bennett and Emma Smith in the introduction.

8.8 Conclusion

Horrell and Humphries (1995: 113) have argued in a context of female labour force participation that there was no uniform female experience, and that nineteenth-century industrialisation opened some doors while closing others. Although they were mainly writing about worker women, their emphasis on how industrialisation's impact on female employment depended on individual situations is applicable to entrepreneurial women as well. This chapter has shown the variation of female entrepreneurship, and the different populations that owned businesses in different trades. While women tended to be found in a relatively small number of sectors compared to male entrepreneurs, within those sectors employers and own-account proprietors in different occupations had strikingly different age, marital status and household profiles. Furthermore, while female entrepreneurs were concentrated in certain sectors, these were increasingly important sectors where they were vital and played a central role, notably the production and retail of consumer goods and the provision of food and accommodation.

The census data confirm many of the findings from recent case studies of female entrepreneurship, and affirm that women had greater economic opportunities than was legally thought to be open to them. Indeed, the 1882 Married Women's Property Act appears to have had no significant effect on married women's participation in the business population. However, census data also show that the size of the female business-owning population compared to males has been significantly underestimated. Women in business were as numerous in England and Wales in the second half of the nineteenth century as they were in North America and Europe, and any decline in numbers or proportion took place during the early decades of the twentieth century, rather than during the Victorian period. Rather than following a U-curve that dipped in the late nineteenth century, female entrepreneurship followed a similar N-shaped curve to that of the men. It also had a steeper decline, which was not caused by cultural factors but rather by economic change; women were more likely to possess businesses on own account, rather than employing others, and as such were more affected by trends that consolidated business in fewer, but larger, firms. This trend continued after World War II, as the proportion of self-employed started to rise again. Women's proportion of the self-employed, and thus of the business population, increased between 1956 and 2001 (Honeyman, 2009: 103).

The evidence in the chapter also amply illustrates the theoretical discussion found in Chapter 2 about the nature of entrepreneurship in nineteenth-century England and Wales. Many women ran their own businesses during this period, but their choice to do so, and their choices about the kind of business they ran, were constrained by a series of factors. Some of these constraints can be observed in the census data: age, marital status, sector and the choice between employing others and working on one's own account; however, others are invisible, in no small part due to the nature of the census as a source, most notably the impact of cultural norms about gender roles and relations. However, it is clear that entrepreneurship was an important choice for many women, even if that was sometimes a choice thrust upon them both by necessity and the increasingly gendered nature of the waged labour market. Hence there were opportunities for those who had the entrepreneurial capacity. Their entrepreneurship was thus in many ways similar to that of men, but more constrained, especially with regards to sector and working at home.

Notes

1 TNA, manuscript CEB, 1881, Mary Ann and Caroline Bennett, RG11/1481; TNA, manuscript CEB, 1891, Mary Ann and Caroline Bennett, RG12/1151; TNA, manuscript CEB, 1901, Mary Ann Bennett, RG13/1362; TNA, manuscript CEB, 1911, Mary Ann Bennett, RG14/7992.
2 TNA, manuscript CEB, 1891, Emma Smith, RG12/543; TNA, manuscript CEB, 1901, Emma Smith, RG13/578; TNA, manuscript CEB, 1911, Emma Smith, RG14/2943.
3 TNA, manuscript CEB, 1871, Rosa Gatti, RG10/651.
4 This is partly due to Aston's (2016: 66) method of only including women who 'registered their firms using names that were clearly identifiable as female'.
5 Chandlers do not appear in the top 10 occupations in similar studies based on trade directories, see e.g. for Midlands cities: Burnette (2008: 36–8).
6 Numbers from 1901, sub-sector here is the EA51, where clothing manufacturing and personal services are the only sub-sectors where female entrepreneurs outnumber male ones. Of all economically active women, a third were working in domestic service.
7 In 1911 census reports all married women who gave no occupation that were living in houses with more boarders than family members were classed as boarding-house keepers by the census clerks, *Census of England and Wales, 1911, Vol. X. Occupations and Industries, Part I, Parliamentary Papers*, LXXVIII (1913), cxviii.
8 The data suffer from non-response problem bias: it is unclear if those not reporting work from home definitely worked elsewhere or simply did not answer the question. Therefore,

the results given in Table 8.4 are likely to be underestimates; however, they are probably representative.

9   A further 20 percent were other younger female relatives, and another 20 percent were live-in servants and boarders, the remainder was made up by older female relatives and the very occasional male householder.

10 The house used need not have been owned by the lodging-house keeper themselves; many were rented given that the majority of people rented accommodation, see Daunton (1983: 198).

11 TNA, manuscript CEB, 1871, Eliza Tinsley, RG10/3004.

9   The geography of entrepreneurship

9.1   Introduction

The range of choices and opportunities available to existing or potential entrepreneurs was constrained by their social context and the externalities and opportunities of their geographical milieu. Over time the constraints, contexts and milieu changed, leading to new opportunities and different incentives for different choices of status between entrepreneurship as own account or employers and waged employment. We focus in this chapter on how the geographical context interacted with different types of entrepreneurship, and how the overall rate of entrepreneurship varied between locations and changed over time.

Behind this analysis is the theoretical context in Chapter 2. All early writers, such as Cantillon and Say, recognised location as offering market constraints and opportunities, with the contrast of rural and town locations often seen as most important. The integration of these ideas by Lösch into a general location theory argued that substitution between factor inputs and locational costs was considered by entrepreneurs at each stage of their decision making. Lösch considered that entrepreneurs could compare locations, and that 'in any given locality everything is produced for which neighbouring competition leaves room' (Lösch, 1952: 249), but that actual decisions contained considerable inertia due to personal preferences and threshold costs underpins how the Victorian economy evolved. The result was that different locations depended on economic history, with the most profitable often those that were already the best located, 'the accident of an early start', and demand and suppliers that had adjusted to them. Interrelated with this inertia were the advantages of existing locations in providing externalities to an entrepreneur in the form of available labour, capital and other factor inputs; though these stabilising influences could be upset by innovation and especially be transport developments.

The result of these underpinnings was the dominant characteristic of nineteenth-century Britain as a network of 'industrial districts', as Marshall termed them. As noted in Chapter 2, districts offered the advantages of clustering: both through agglomeration effects and localised sector specialisation. These were the micro and local mechanisms underpinning endogenous growth. District industrial clustering increased external economies of scale derived from knowledge and other spillovers between firms, thick markets of wider externalities allowing easy matching of business needs, such as available capital and workforces, and collective sharing of infrastructure and communication investments.

The interaction of industrial districts with entrepreneurship has, however, been little considered in longer-term historical studies. This chapter undertakes the first large-scale analysis of how districts and entrepreneurship interacted over the 1851–1911 period. It first considers how the census geography can be used to analyse entrepreneurship, focusing on the RSD as the main spatial unit. The chapter then considers how rates of business proprietorship varied by location, and how this can be best measured. The chapter then analyses sector markets and occupations to investigate levels of geographical specialisation and diversity, and how this interrelated with changing firm size and the increasing industrial concentration shown in Chapter 5. Finally the chapter moves beyond RSDs and 'districts' to the functional units of towns and cities. The chapter interrelates with Chapter 6 which shows how transport interacts with entrepreneurial choices.

9.2   Previous literature

There has been considerable research on the economic geography of eighteenth- and twentieth-century England and Wales (Hudson, 1989; Langton, 1984; Martin, 1988). However, there has been little consideration of the spatial distribution of entrepreneurship in the nineteenth century. Recent work on the census and other sources has argued for a long-standing north-west/south divide, with the counties of Cheshire, Lancashire and the West Riding dominated by manufacturing occupations from the early nineteenth century onwards, and the southern counties of Bedfordshire, Buckinghamshire, Cambridgeshire, Huntingdonshire, Northamptonshire, Oxfordshire, Rutland and Wiltshire initially focused on agriculture, but with industry and, especially, services playing a more important role as the nineteenth century progressed (Lee, 1984; Shaw-Taylor and Wrigley, 2014: 64–5). This literature has touched tangentially on business proprietors when discussing the supposed divide between a metropolitan and southern middle class based on finance and an affinity with the aristocracy, and a northern industrial and poorer middle class (Anderson, 1988; Anderson et al., 1979; Rubinstein, 1977). Others have pursued more sophisticated approaches. Clive Lee's factor analysis of the published census data suggests that during the nineteenth century the country was split into four regions: a textile production area, a mining and metal working region, a metropolitan area (which grew substantially during the second half of the century) and a rural region. His account presents a rather stark distinction between the manufacturing centres and the growing, service-based economic region centred on London and most of the Home Counties (Lee, 1981).

These approaches use occupational structure. However, other measures also suggest a division between London and the South East, and the rest of the country, with London in particular having a much larger share of GDP. Within the rest of the country, the North West had a higher share than other areas (Geary and Stark, 2015: 130–1; a different trend but similar regional pattern is given in Crafts, 2005: 58–9). Similarly, geographical variation in wages shows that the north of England and London had high wages in the second half of the nineteenth century, while southern England was characterised by low wages (Hunt, 1986). The continued existence of wage differentials and significant regional differences indicates that labour markets were not strongly integrated (Boyer and Hatton, 1997). Indeed Crafts (2005) and Crafts and Mulatu (2005) demonstrate that internal *within* region characteristics of Britain were most critical in explaining economic growth and competitiveness up the 1940. Between-region differentiation, 'industrial districts' and local diversity were key characteristics of the nineteenth century.

These discussions have concerned the overall economic geography. There has been little discussion of the geography of *business proprietors* or different *environments of entrepreneurship*. This is surprising, since the development of the economy into differentiated local industrial districts had been well-understood since Alfred Marshall (1919, 1961) introduced the concept, and the dominance of local market demand and supply opportunities was embedded in all the early writers on entrepreneurship reviewed in Chapter 2. Moreover the census administrators drew attention to the 'classic' industrial districts with a commentary and large-scale foldout map showing these districts, which was prominent in the GRO's 1851 census report.[1] These show the key industrial districts that were significant throughout our period of analysis: the Staffordshire Potteries; Sheffield cutlery and steel; Coventry bicycles; Manchester cottons; Darlington, Blackburn and Derby engineering; Worcester gloves; Birmingham and West Midlands small metal trades, buttons, jewellery and guns; Birmingham jewellery; Dudley, Wolverhampton and Walsall metal industries; Nottingham and Leicester knitwear, lace and hosiery; Kidderminster carpets; Northwich and Widnes salt and chemicals; Cardiff, Swansea and Newcastle-upon-Tyne coal and shipping. Some previous literature has analysed entrepreneurship in these districts, but this has been almost entirely through case studies (Wise, 1949; Checkland, 1964; Popp and Wilson, 2007; Wilson and Popp, 2003; Carnevali, 2003; Becattini et al., 2009). Many of these had already established these characteristics in the eighteenth or early nineteenth centuries (Goose, 2014; Smith et al., 2018). In addition there were new areas of economic specialisation, such as the chemical trades in Cheshire; resort and tourist industries around the coast and specialist inland resorts; and new trades in old centres, such as the growth of the car and electrical industries in Birmingham, Coventry and the Midlands which drew on local skills in metal and engineering industries (Warren, 1986: 118; Scott, 2007: 42–3; Gilbert, 1975: 9–32).

However, case studies can give no sense of the distribution of business proprietors throughout the country, how districts differed in level and form of entrepreneurism, how male and female participation differed nor how different sectors interacted across and between districts. We are now able, using the BBCE database, to begin to examine these features in a systematic way.

9.3   Census geography

Each individual in the I–CeM is coded to their parish of residence. In the census these civil parishes were organised into Registration Sub-Districts (RSDs). One or more RSDs made up a Registration District (RD). The RDs were organised into Registration Counties which in turn were aggregated into Divisions, 11 of which covered mainland England and Wales. Since the I–CeM data are coded at the parish level, individuals can be aggregated at any of the different levels of census geography, from the RSD to the nation. It is possible to aggregate census units to re-create other forms of geographical organisation, but this is difficult and remains approximate. For example, we use an urban aggregation based on the parishes that constituted the largest towns in each census year to allow large urban places to be distinguished from rural areas and other areas that had a mixture of small towns and rural environments (WP 6).

Mapping entrepreneurship

The *entrepreneurship rate* is the measure most commonly used in modern studies: the number of entrepreneurs as a percentage of either the population or of the economically active population, as in GEM (2018: 21–3) comparisons between nations, albeit modern studies often distinguish between the proportion of recently created businesses and long-established businesses. This measure can be readily used to assess more localised geography of entrepreneurship at parish, RSD or other levels. However, it is not as simple to interpret as often assumed. Even assuming the spatial units contain both the business owners and workers of the same firms, it is heavily affected by the number of workers in the geographical unit under consideration and, therefore, by the firm size distribution in different locations. If an area has many large businesses then it is likely to have a low entrepreneurship rate, not necessarily because of any inherently non-entrepreneurial characteristics, but simply because large firms mean that there will be many workers and consequently a high ratio of workers to businesses proprietors. In contrast, areas where the economic activity is characterised by large numbers of small businesses will have a high entrepreneurship rate simply because the employers and own-account proprietors are not swamped by workers. This can be illustrated by example for two areas which each have 10 employers. If one area has 10 mines or textile mills that employ the total economically active population of 1,000 persons, and the other area has a total working population of 20 employed in a typical mix of 5 farms, 2 food shops, 1 blacksmith, 1 inn and 1 doctor, the entrepreneurship rates radically differ. Discounting any own account or other activity, the first has a 1 percent rate and the second 50 percent. Yet they both have the same number of entrepreneurs and firms.

This is a particularly important when comparing urban with rural areas. Rural areas with large agricultural sectors have limits on the size of farm workforces due to land availability and its capacity to produce at different levels of intensity. Consequently, areas dominated by agriculture tend to have small total workforces and high entrepreneurship rates; something which looks odd considering the historical and contemporary emphasis on urban locations as the most entrepreneurial. This is not to say that the results produced by mapping the entrepreneurship rate are 'wrong', but rather that they reveal only one aspect of the geography of business proprietorship. This issue becomes more significant the smaller the geographical units that are used. Large units, such as counties used in many modern studies of the geography of entrepreneurship in the UK, tend to average out extreme urban–rural divides, and areas tend not to be dominated by industries characterised only by large or small firms. In those cases the entrepreneurship rate is more readily interpretable (Keeble and Walker, 1994). But when this measure is applied at smaller scales such as the RSD, other measures may be preferable to help interpret entrepreneurship.

To overcome some of these difficulties we use two alternatives, in addition to the normal entrepreneurship rate. First, a *weighted entrepreneurship rate*: the rate for a particular geographical unit weighted by that unit's share of the total economically active population in England and Wales. Second, the *entrepreneurship share*: the number of business proprietors in a unit as a percentage of the total number of proprietors in England and Wales. These measures avoid some of the difficulties with the entrepreneurship rate, but they are both strongly associated with population size. However, when these measures are put together they reveal different and complementary pictures of the geography of entrepreneurship in England and Wales which allow a better understanding of different entrepreneurship environments than using one measure alone.

9.4   Geographies of entrepreneurship

Figure 9.1 shows the entrepreneurship rate as defined above for 1851 and 1911, the start and end of our period, mapped at RSD level. These maps suggest that in most of England levels of business proprietorship declined between 1851 and 1911. In particular, the area where Buckinghamshire, Bedfordshire and Hertfordshire meet showed high levels of entrepreneurship in 1851, but this had collapsed by 1911. This shift reflects a number of changes. First, the decline of straw plaiting from the 1870s onwards, an industry which had supported a large number of self-employed women. Straw-hat making was still important in these counties, even in 1911, but was far more concentrated than straw plaiting had been (Goose, 2007). Second, other industries and services underwent concentration. For example, milliners in these counties both declined in number (from 3,784 in 1851 to 1,532 in 1911) and concentrated (the entrepreneurship rate for milliners fell from 32.7 to 13.6). Finally, employment in agriculture fell significantly while employment in domestic service rose. This meant that the number of workers in these counties rose faster than the number of employers, and consequently the ratio of business proprietors to workers fell.

Firm size change towards larger units was a general tendency across most sectors, as shown in Chapter 5. This led to significant decreases in the

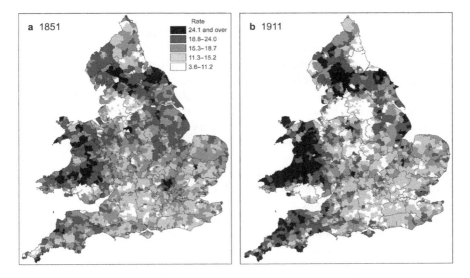

Figure 9.1 Entrepreneurship rates in 1851 and 1911 by RSD (entrepreneurs as percentage of economically active)

Source: BBCE database.

entrepreneurship rate between 1851 and 1911 occurring in the West Riding of Yorkshire, Nottinghamshire and Derbyshire. This change was driven by the expansion of coal mining in Derbyshire and the West Riding, and increased concentration into larger firms of the lace industry and dressmaking in Nottinghamshire. The growth of coal mining, an industry generally characterised by large numbers of workers and few employers, also induced the drop in the entrepreneurship rate in Staffordshire. The drop in Warwickshire was caused by the growth of the brass industry which also underwent concentration. The area around Newcastle-upon-Tyne saw a drop in the entrepreneurship rate driven by a large increase in the concentration in machinery and engine manufacturing, especially in large-scale shipyards.

Two areas witnessed an increase in their entrepreneurship rates: the South West and Wales. The decline of copper mining in Cornwall and Devon removed a highly concentrated industry from these locations, causing the overall rate of business proprietorship to rise. The case of Wales is more complex. South Wales follows the trajectory of much of England; indeed, it looks similar to the North East, which is unsurprising given the importance of mining and heavy industry in both areas. However, the rest of Wales had an unusually high entrepreneurship rate in both 1851 and 1911. This was caused by the different structure of agriculture. In England farming underwent continued consolidation during this period, with farms increasing in size. The entrepreneurship rate for farming in England did increase in this period, from 13.8 to 20.9, but this was caused by the decline in the overall number of farm workers. In Wales, the entrepreneurship rate was higher, in 1851 it was 24.9 and in 1911 it was 33.5. Farming in Wales was characterised by small-scale farming, and consequently there was a much higher ratio of farmers to farm workers (Moore-Colyer, 2000: 429–35). This is to a lesser extent true of the Pennines, North Yorkshire Moors and rural Devon and Cornwall.

Figure 9.2 shows the alternative entrepreneurship measure using the *share* of the total number of business proprietors in each RSD. This reveals a different pattern, one where the major urban areas appear as centres for entrepreneurship. In 1851, London, Manchester and Liverpool had large shares of the total number of entrepreneurs. The map for 1851 also suggests that Cheltenham in Gloucestershire, Luton in Bedfordshire, Preston in Lancashire, Leicester, Brighton in Sussex and Southampton in Hampshire had high levels of business proprietorship. Many of these were major centres of population with their own economic significance, Brighton was an important resort town and Southampton a port, but others are more surprising. Cheltenham was a spa town which had grown 12-fold between 1801 and 1851; resorts and spas offered plenty of opportunity for people to open small businesses in accommodation, retailing and other service provision. In Leicester the hosiery and other clothing industries were important sources of self-employment as well as providing opportunities for employers. Preston appears to have a larger share of entrepreneurs than other cotton towns, because Preston had a more vibrant professional, retail, construction and service sectors with more lodging houses, builders, barristers and

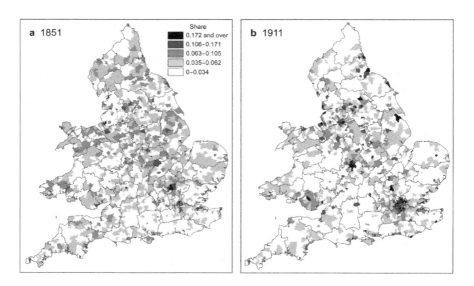

Figure 9.2 Entrepreneurship shares in 1851 and 1911 by RSD (entrepreneurs as percentage of all entrepreneurs for England and Wales)

Source: BBCE database.

solicitors, and timber and coal dealers than other towns of a similar size such as Bolton or Oldham which were increasingly dominated by large textile mills with large numbers of workers. Preston was, historically, a market town; this function and the fact that it was further from Manchester than many of the other cotton towns encouraged it to retain a larger service sector, functions which otherwise may have been fulfilled by Manchester. Luton and its vicinity had a large share of business proprietors because of its importance to the straw-plaiting industry, which provided very considerable work for a large number of self-employed women, as noted above; although it declined significantly by 1911.

Figure 9.2 also shows that between 1851 and 1911 business proprietors became more concentrated in the larger urban areas. The locations which were important in 1851 were all still significant in 1911 but these were joined by large towns such as Birmingham and Newcastle and smaller urban locations. These small towns had various functions. Scarborough, Southport, Blackpool, Southend, Bournemouth and Eastbourne were resorts, and their entrepreneurial presence reflects the abundant small-business opportunities which tourism presented. Others were port towns, such as Grimsby, Hartlepool, Newport and Folkestone, where shipping stimulated businesses based around commercial activity (and for Hartlepool and Newport a rapidly expanding local coal output), as well as ancillary services such as lodging and refreshment.

Other significant entrepreneurial centres reflected specific shifts in local economic structure. Norwich, for example, recovered from the decline of the worsted industry at the end of the eighteenth century through the emergence of a strong shoemaking industry, which involved significant numbers of own-account business proprietors. The emergence of shoemaking, combined with other new industries, notably mustard production, led to strong population growth and a generally buoyant Norwich economy in the nineteenth century (Goose, 2014: 162–3). Derby also stands out as town with abundant opportunities for business ownership. Derby and similar rail manufacturing centres seem to have promoted wider entrepreneurship; Derby was home to many lodging-house and hotel owners and innkeepers, and many retailers catering to the needs of a growing permanent population as well as visitors.

It is notable that when using the entrepreneurial share shown in Figure 9.2 the mining areas of England and Wales do not appear notably unentrepreneurial, giving a different view of the effect of coal mining compared to recent studies that have stressed the long-term negative impact of mining on entrepreneurship in the US and the Great Britain (Glaeser et al., 2015; Stuetzer et al., 2016). Figure 9.1, however, shows that the coalfields in South Wales and Lancashire/Yorkshire had low entrepreneurship rates. This reflects the different measures, rather than a simple objective difference in entrepreneurial behaviour or potential. When using entrepreneurship rate, business proprietors were far outweighed by the large number of workers employed in coal mining and attendant heavy industries, resulting in low entrepreneurship rates; however, the share measure makes clear that the rate gives a misleading impression and that the coalfields were likely to have fairly high levels of entrepreneurship, unsurprising given the concentration of large populations in such locations, populations that needed retail and other suppliers, and the relatively high wages in such locations during this period (Hunt, 1973: 72–3).

The geography of *female entrepreneurship* is shown in Figure 9.3. Comparing Figure 9.3 with Figure 9.1 enlarges the interpretations of gender developed in Chapter 8. In both 1851 and 1911 most RSDs had lower female entrepreneurship rates than overall entrepreneurship rates, suggesting that female entrepreneurship was heavily concentrated in a small number of areas. In 1851 the most striking concentration was in Bedfordshire, Buckinghamshire and Hertfordshire where the straw plaiting industry was concentrated; as noted above and in Chapter 8, this provided many opportunities for female business proprietorship. There were also clusters of high female rates in Braintree and Sudbury on the Essex–Suffolk border, Whitby in Yorkshire and Berwick in Northumberland. Braintree and Sudbury were centres of silk production, an industry in which female proprietors were significant; Whitby was a resort and fishing town with extensive lodging and refreshment trades which were common trades for women; Berwick's entrepreneurship rate was driven by an unusually large number of dressmakers. The reasons for this concentration are unclear, but may relate to the hosiery or woollen cloth industry in the adjacent Scottish Lowlands.

What is perhaps more striking, however, are the large areas of the country in 1851 where female entrepreneurship was rare: Lancashire, much of the West Riding of Yorkshire, much of West Wales and large parts of Wiltshire, Gloucestershire and Berkshire. In these areas there were extensive opportunities for

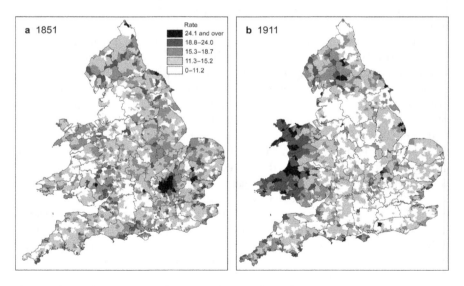

Figure 9.3 Female entrepreneurship rates in 1851 and 1911 by RSD (entrepreneurs as percentage of economically active)

Source: BBCE database.

female waged labour. In Lancashire and the West Riding this was in textiles, in the other counties domestic service was a significant source of female employment, but in these counties other sectors provided unusual amounts of waged labour employment: in parts of Gloucestershire this was in gloves and clothing production, and in the other counties in farming. These waged labour options meant that women had less need to be entrepreneurs than elsewhere.

By 1911 the situation had changed substantially. The cluster of female business proprietorship in Bedfordshire, Buckinghamshire and Hertfordshire had almost disappeared after the straw plaiting industry collapsed in the 1870s and 1880s, as had the smaller concentration based on the silk industry in Essex and Suffolk. However, female entrepreneurship rates in Wales were substantially higher, driven by an increase in female activity in maker-dealing, refreshment and retail, and a decline in female employment in agriculture. As women moved from sectors in which they tended to be workers to ones in which they were often business proprietors the entrepreneurship rate rose. Beyond Wales female entrepreneurship showed a similar contraction to that seen in Figure 9.1, with more areas of low entrepreneurship in 1911 than there had been in 1851.

Figure 9.4 for entrepreneurship shares shows a different aspect of female entrepreneurship. As with male entrepreneurship, this was more concentrated in urban areas between 1851 and 1911. By 1911 there were important clusters of female business proprietors in London, Birmingham, Manchester, Liverpool, Newcastle, Middlesbrough, Bristol and other towns. These figures also show the disappearance of straw plaiting and the consequent collapse of female

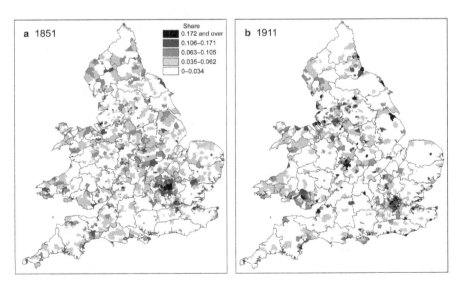

Figure 9.4 Female entrepreneurship shares in 1851 and 1911 by RSD (entrepreneurs as percentage of all female entrepreneurs for England and Wales)

Source: BBCE database.

entrepreneurship in Bedfordshire, Buckinghamshire and Hertfordshire. The cluster of female entrepreneurs in Glamorgan is somewhat surprising given the emphasis in the literature on the poor opportunities for economic activity available to women in mining and heavy industry areas; however, the range of female business activities was narrower than elsewhere and concentrated in a few occupations. For example, Glamorgan had an unusually large proportion of dressmakers, 11.4 percent of the female economically active compared to 6.4 percent in England and Wales as a whole.

How do we explain the distribution of entrepreneurs? Chapter 6 has investigated this question using statistical estimation. Here we enlarge on the findings using a more interpretative approach. First we note that there was no simple relationship with many of the normal measures of economic performance. Thus, the areas with the largest regional shares of the UK's GDP (London, the South East and the North West) had low entrepreneurship rates at the beginning and end of our period (Geary and Stark, 2015: 130–1). This is perhaps predictable as both London and the North West had very large workforces as well as a great many entrepreneurs. For similar reasons, there is also no obvious relationship between population and entrepreneurship rate: locations with large populations tended to have many workers which consequently lowered their entrepreneurship rate. Figure 9.2 is closer to the geography of GDP and population, unsurprising given that the measure used is itself partly determined by population. However, the match is far from perfect, with the importance of resorts and ports complicating any simple relationship between entrepreneurial activity and GDP.

Other measures also fail to fully fit the distribution of entrepreneurs. Figure 9.5 uses data on Poor Law rental valuations as a proxy for income, on the basis that the rent people pay is related to their income. The data are available at RD level and has had London removed as an outlier due to the high presence of state-owned property and the uneven distribution of population within London that significantly distorts RSD data. Figure 9.5 shows that there was a positive relationship between entrepreneurship rate and rental value per capita in 1891, but the relationship was weak. When plotted against the entrepreneurship share, weighted by each RD's share of the total economically active population, there is little evidence of a relationship, as shown in Figure 9.6. Although there is some connection between the rate of entrepreneurs per head of the economically active and property values, this was not a simple or strong.

Chapter 6–8 have demonstrated the importance of demographic factors such as marital status and household structure. Figures 9.7, 9.8 and 9.9 take this analysis one stage further for one illustrative year (1911) by assessing the relationship between the economically active sex ratio in each RSD and the entrepreneurship rate (Figure 9.7); the relationship between the proportion of each RSD's population aged between 35 and 84 and the entrepreneurship rate (Figure 9.8) and the percentage ever married (those married, widowed and divorced) in each RSD compared to the entrepreneurship rate (Figure 9.9). In each case the results are inconclusive. In Figure 9.7 there is a somewhat negative relationship between sex ratio and business proprietorship: as the number of economically active

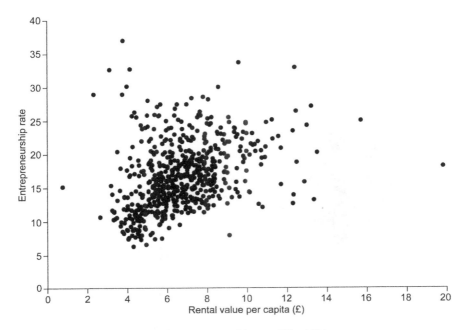

Figure 9.5 Rental per capita and entrepreneurship rate, RDs, 1891

Source: Rental valuations: *Local taxation returns (England). The annual local taxation returns. Year 1891–91,* Parliamentary Papers, LXXVI (1893–4), 67–84. *Note*: Valuation made at Lady Day 1891.

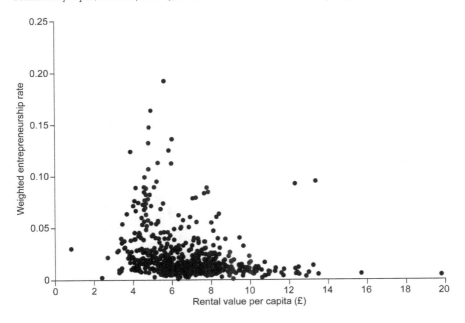

Figure 9.6 Rental per capita and weighted entrepreneurship rate, RDs, 1891

Source: Rental valuations: *Local taxation returns (England). The annual local taxation returns. Year 1891–91,* Parliamentary Papers, LXXVI (1893–4), 67–84. *Note*: Valuation made at Lady Day 1891.

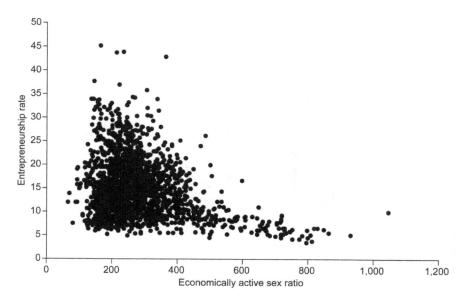

Figure 9.7 Economically active sex ratio and entrepreneurship rate, RSDs, 1911

Source: BBCE database.

Note: Economically active sex ratio calculated by dividing the number economically active men by the number of economically active women.

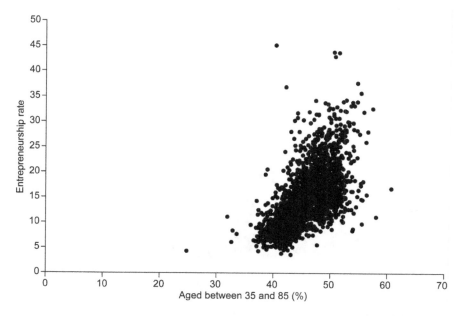

Figure 9.8 Age and entrepreneurship, RSDs, 1911

Source: BBCE database.

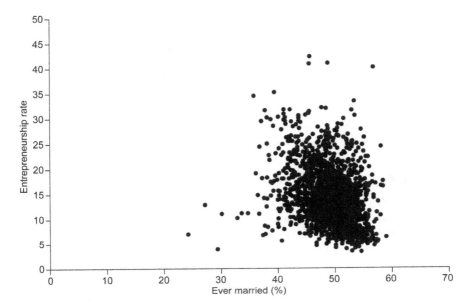

Figure 9.9 Percentage ever married and entrepreneurship rate, RSDs, 1911
Source: BBCE database.

women in an RSD decreased the entrepreneurship rate fell. However, this was strongly affected by RSDs with small numbers of economically active women. In Figure 9.8 there is the expected positive relationship between age and entrepreneurship, but this relationship is weak. Figure 9.9 also shows a weak negative relationship between the proportion of an RSD's population that had ever been married and the entrepreneurship rate. Thus, while demography explains some of the geographical variation evident, it is not a sufficient explanation. As shown in Chapter 6, many other factors need to be controlled. Critical among these was the sector market that businesses operated in and the local geography of occupations that reflected the importance of industrial districts in determining business opportunities.

9.5   Sector markets, occupations and entrepreneurship

Entrepreneurship is strongly influenced by how local market conditions interact with specific sector markets. These affect the size and diversity of local opportunities, how well the opportunities match the skills and resources of different individuals and the extent of openings or barriers that allow market entry or underpin scope for competition and business development. Sector markets condition the context of different industrial districts: Marshall's *externalities of place*. Sectors are one of the main contexts in which opportunities are opened (or closed), as Knight (1921) and Kirzner (1973) argued, and hence the dominant industries in different 'districts' are one of the main influences on the levels of entrepreneurship we can observe. As noted in Chapter 3, information on industry sector was not gathered directly by census processes; instead the aim was collection of information on social rank and occupation. However, the aggregations into EA17 and EA51 groups allows approximate sectoral analysis as a mix of occupations, sectors and entrepreneurial status. In this section we combine analysis at the EA51 level with the 797 I-CeM occupation categories, or occodes.[2] This is a starting point to examine the extent of local *specialisation* in industrial districts and local *diversity* as indicators of cluster effects.

Industrial districts and sector specialisation

Turning first to specialisation in industrial districts, one way to collapse the complexity of the full range of census occupational descriptors is to group common patterns into a more limited number of categories based on their shared variance. Following previous studies requiring similar classifications by Lee (1981) and Moser and Scott (1961), we use factor analysis based on the EA51 classification. This measures the degree of closeness of pairwise correlation coefficients between each sector for all RSDs and then classifies each RSD into its most similar group. Factor analysis assesses whether the sectors have common concentration between sectors in groups of locations; that is, they form an 'industrial district'. We use a form of exploratory factor analysis.[3] The loadings on each factor classify RSDs by their similarities across different sectors. Many RSDs have high scores on several factors. The assignment chosen is the primary loading on one factor. This classification of RSDs is largely automated but, because we follow an exploratory methodology, automatic assignment is checked at the margins where RSD allocations are ambiguous. The method follows three stages (see WPs 7, 8 and 10): (i) each RSD is classified to the factor on which it has the highest score, (ii) those RSDs with highest score on any factor below 0.5 were reallocated to a group with 'no strong loadings' and (iii) RSDs with scores over 0.5 were checked for alternative classifications to different factor(s). The third stage resulted in a few RSDs being reallocated, but was primarily used to reduce the number of factors by combining those that were similar. The 'no strong loading' category indicates that RSDs have no high concentrations in any sector and are close to the general average across the country, with no dominant spatial concentration. We focus on long-term entrepreneurship, and therefore exclude visitors, lodgers and those in institutions or ships.[4] Because of the complexity of factor calculations, there was no attempt to weight the data as discussed in Chapter 4. The results were calculated for 1891, which is the closest to the midyear of our period that has the explicit census identification of employers and own account.

Figure 9.10 shows the results of the factor analysis for employers in 1891.[5] The final classification produced 10 groups, with 574 of the 2,110 RSDs showing no strong factor loading. Of the other nine factors, the first factor (retail, lodging,

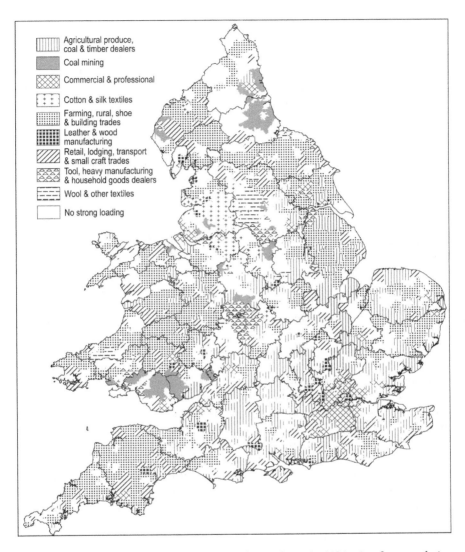

Agricultural produce,
coal & timber dealers

Coal mining

Commercial & professional

Cotton & silk textiles

Farming, rural, shoe
& building trades

Leather & wood
manufacturing

Retail, lodging, transport
& small craft trades

Tool, heavy manufacturing
& household goods dealers

Wool & other textiles

No strong loading

Figure 9.10 Classification of industrial districts for employers in 1891 using factor analysis
Source: BBCE database.

transport and small crafts) mainly applied to small towns in a wide range of locations such as Oxford, Maidenhead, Harrogate and Salisbury. Factor 3 (commercial
and professional) was concentrated in London and the South East, but was also in
Liverpool, Bristol, Hull and other ports. The majority of rural England and Wales
were covered by factors 2 (farming, rural, show and building trades) and 5 (agricultural produce, coal and timber dealers), which between them contained 719

RSDs and encompassed both wholly rural areas and county towns. Lancashire and the West Riding were mainly characterised by factors 6 and 7 which were focused on wool and cotton production, respectively. Heavy and light manufacturing, factor 4, was concentrated in Birmingham and the Black Country, parts of South Wales near Swansea, around Sheffield and isolated centres such as Warrington and Middlesbrough. Factor 8 (leather and wood manufacture) covered just 65 RSDs near the border of Bedfordshire and Buckinghamshire, a long-standing location for textile and apparel production as noted above. The other main concentration was in East London and Southwark, areas where clothing and furniture manufacture had long been important (Field, 2018), and places such as Burton-upon-Trent and Northampton. The final factor covered coal mining and was strongly concentrated in South Wales, the north-east of England, Derbyshire and the south and north Staffordshire coal fields.

Lee's factor analysis (Lee, 1981) of the county occupation statistics in the nineteenth-century censuses produced five main factors. These overlap with our analysis; however, as he used counties and we use RSDs, we inevitably have more detail and variation. Nevertheless, Lee's textile, mining and metropolitan factors covered much of the same areas as our, respective, factors 7 and 8 (wool, and cotton), 9 (coal mining) and 3 (commercial and professional), as well as 2 (farming, rural, shoe and building trades) which includes many small commercial and retail centres. The main way our analysis differs is the treatment of rural England. Whereas Lee had 18 rural counties in one factor, we have a mix of two factors: 1 (retail, lodging, transport and small craft trades) and 5 (agricultural produce, coal and timber dealing and other small-scale manufacturing trades). We also have factor 2 which covers many semi-rural areas with important market centres. This gives a more nuanced picture of economic activity than Lee's rural counties; county towns remained important centres of commerce, administration and manufacturing. This suggests that his argument that agricultural counties formed a single, homogeneous region was too generalised. Also important is our identification of manufacturing areas outside the textile and coal mining factors isolated by Lee. Indeed, his analysis has little to say about the Midlands, where the mixture of heavy and light manufacturing for both home markets and abroad disrupts his tidy distinction between export-oriented manufacturing and extraction in the textile and mining areas, and the home–oriented service and consumer goods manufacturing in the metropolitan factor that covered London and the South East. Our analysis suggests that England and Wales were much more variegated with a large number of industrial districts based around a wider range of distinct sectorally grouped economic activities: much closer to the situation understood and observed by Marshall for the 1890s, and as also suggested by the GRO's more descriptive analysis in the 1851 census report.

Table 9.1 shows the entrepreneurship rates of the RSDs for these 10 factors. Two figures are given, first for all business proprietors and, in brackets, the result when farmers are removed. The farming factor had the highest entrepreneurship rate; however, this is misleading because, as noted earlier, it is caused by the large number of farmers and the relatively small number of workers in these

Table 9.1 Entrepreneurship rate of total entrepreneurs for each RSD by employer factor, 1891

Factor	Entrepreneurship Rate	Total Economically Active Population
1 Retail, lodging, transport and craft trades	16.9 (16.5)	1,728,323 (1,573,853)
2 Farming, rural, shoe and building trades	22.2 (20.4)	636,220 (351,659)
3 Commercial and professional	14.8 (14.8)	1,567,753 (1,475,769)
4 Tool and heavy manufacturing, and household goods dealing	12.0 (11.6)	969,558 (933,370)
5 Agricultural produce, coal and timber dealing	16.3 (16.6)	1,100,589 (844,537)
6 Wool and other textiles	12.3 (11.7)	798,237 (772,563)
7 Cotton and silk	10.2 (9.5)	1,206,522 (1,166,978)
8 Leather and wood manufacture	12.6 (12.4)	747,804 (725,851)
9 Coal mining	8.5 (7.7)	635,081 (608,375)
10 No strong loading	12.5 (11.3)	2,601,667 (2,253,236)

Source: BBCE database.

Note: Figures in brackets exclude farmers.

RSDs. The 400 farming factor RSDs contained just 4.7 percent of all workers but 11.6 percent of all employers and 6.9 percent of all own-account individuals. After the farming locations, the highest entrepreneurship rates were found in RSDs classified to factors 1, 3 and 5, namely the retail and commercial sectors. As noted above, factors 1 and 5 contained a considerable number of county and other smaller towns, settlements which acted as service and retail hubs for surrounding areas, as well as transport hubs. Both these economic functions tended to promote business proprietorship: service and retail businesses were usually small but numerous, and while transport itself was characterised by large businesses with many workers and few employers, the presence of transport tended to promote other kinds of business, notably accommodation and refreshment. Factor 3, which covers much of London and the South East, as well as other ports, had high rates of business proprietorship for similar reasons, namely the presence of many highly entrepreneurial occupations because commerce and the professions often interrelated with retailing, service and transport functions. Although some professionals were employed by the state in this period, many were own-account proprietors, such as lawyers, estate agents and auctioneers. Furthermore, some professions straddled the boundary between employment and self-employment; for example, doctors who were employed as Poor Law physicians but also ran their own private practice (Digby, 1994: 117–27). Thus, professionals generally raised the entrepreneurship rate in a similar manner to other services or retail businesses.

As noted in the discussion of business size in Chapter 5, manufacturing firms tended, on average, to have larger workforces than retailing or professional businesses. Consequently, any location where manufacturing played an important role in the economy was likely to have a lower entrepreneurship rate than places that were mainly service focused, as can be seen in Table 9.1. Within manufacturing, there was a contrast between those factors in which small businesses predominated and those where large businesses were more common. Thus, factors 4 and 8 had higher entrepreneurship rates than factors 7 and 9. Factor 4 included heavy manufacturing, but also the more numerous small-scale metal-working employers: toolmaking, nail and pin production, toy making, cutlery manufacturing and so on. These smaller industries were numerous enough to outweigh the effect heavy manufacturing had on the entrepreneurship rate. Factor 8 (leather and wood industries) was more straightforwardly characterised by small-scale businesses and self-employment. In contrast, places covered by factor 9, coal mining, were dominated by large businesses and consequently low entrepreneurship rates, as many workers were employed by relatively few employers. Factor 7, cotton and silk manufacturing, was somewhere in between the small manufacturing factors and coal mining. As noted by Gatrell (1977), textile sectors remained highly competitive, with even large and long-established Lancashire textile firms under continual pressure from small firms and start-ups. Textile firms were also generally much smaller than coal mines. Many textile areas also contained a number of settlements which were commercial as well as manufacturing centres, most notably Manchester, Stockport and Bolton. The pattern was similar for factor 6, which also had a high entrepreneurship rate for a manufacturing factor. The woollen factor contained a number of large towns with significant retail and service sectors, such as Leeds, Bradford, Halifax and Huddersfield. Furthermore, in general, woollen manufacturers, while large employers in comparison to industries such as cutlery or shoemaking, had smaller businesses than cotton manufacturers.

Sector and occupational diversity

To examine sector diversity it is useful to use a more fine-grained classification. As in the previous discussion, we primarily focus on 1891 as the midpoint where entrepreneur status is explicitly given in the census. The 797 I-CeM occupations (occodes) are imperfect indicators of sector markets, but allow occupational indicators to be interrelated with entrepreneurial status to guide understanding of different market opportunities. Figure 9.11 shows the number of employer occodes out of the maximum of 797 in each RSD in 1891. The most diverse areas are dominated by the large cities, especially London, Birmingham and Manchester. These were complex economies that had significant manufacturing sectors as well as numerous retail, transport, commercial and professional businesses. Much of the rest of England and Wales is covered by the two smallest categories. Although these were much less diverse, nevertheless even rural locations and small towns had a significant range of occupations when measured at the RSD level. This suggests that there was generally a wide range of different market opportunities available. This widens the observation by Payne (1988: 42–4) that market entry and adequate profits were usually possible in most industries,

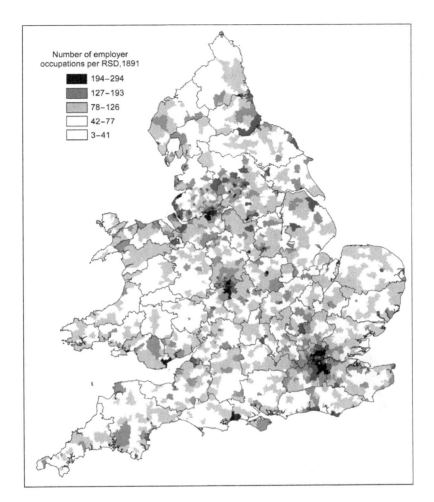

Figure 9.11 Number of sectors for employers in each RSD, 1891; sectors based on 797 I-CeM
occupations codes

Source: BBCE database.

allowing small businesses to proliferate in the Victorian period. The map of
occupational diversity suggests that diverse entrepreneurial opportunities were
available in all except the most rural areas, but they were certainly largest in the
larger cities and towns, generally scaling downwards with settlement size.

Figure 9.12 shows the relationship between population size and occupational
diversity. As expected the relationship was positive. However, the relationship
levelled off as population reached 80,000–100,000, suggesting that in even the
most populous locations there was a limit to diversification: the large urban
centres also had a degree of economic specialization.

Table 9.2 gives the entrepreneurship rates in the five categories (shown in Figure 9.11), with the results when farmers are removed in brackets. The relationship between entrepreneurship rate and occupational diversity is somewhat surprising. The least occupationally diverse locations had the highest entrepreneurship rate, it then decreased with rising diversity before rising again. This reflects two factors. First, that even the most basic of settlements required a number of businesses to function; that is, to provide services (primarily retail but also small-scale manufacturing of tools and building trades). This was a further characteristic of markets that were not yet fully integrated nationally or regionally, in which much

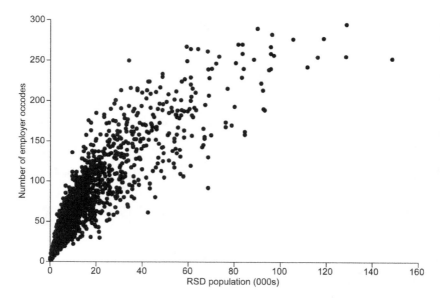

Figure 9.12 Population and occupational diversity, RSDs, 1891

Source: BBCE database.

Table 9.2 Entrepreneurship rate and share by occupational diversity, RSDs, 1891

Number of Employer Occodes	Entrepreneurship Rate	Share of Entrepreneurship	Total Economically Active Population
3–41	17.5 (15.4)	14.7 (9.6)	1,388,008 (871,126)
42–77	14.5 (13.1)	22.0 (19.4)	2,511,809 (2,058,081)
78–126	12.5 (12.0)	21.7 (23.2)	2,862,549 (2,681,143)
127–193	12.7 (12.6)	24.9 (28.4)	3,241,613 (3,149,150)
194–294	14.0 (13.9)	16.8 (19.4)	1,990,776 (1,946,691)

Source: BBCE database.

Note: Figures in brackets exclude farmers.

demand and supply was still local. Also many communities with small populations had relatively few workers per employer simply because of their small size.
Second, the relatively small differences in entrepreneurship rates for each diversity
category (especially when agriculture is removed) suggest that other factors must
be considered. Partly this is provided by the share of entrepreneurs also given
in the table, which shows that the least occupationally diverse category had the
smallest share of the total number of business proprietors in England and Wales.
However, this measure is strongly affected by the population contained in each
category (as suggested also by Figure 9.12); this explains why the most occupationally diverse category has a rather low entrepreneurship rate.

Urban structure and occupational diversity

There were important urban–rural differences in these patterns. We define an
urban location as one where the RSD contained a town or at least part of a town
with a population greater than 10,000 in that census year. Rural areas are defined
as RSDs with no town or part-town over 10,000 and population densities less
than 0.3 people per acre.[6] Using these two categories we can compare RSDs
which were definitely urban with those which were mainly rural but may have
included small towns.

For *rural RSDs*, Table 9.3 shows the percentage of rural RSDs that contained at
least one employer occupied in the 15 most common employer occodes. It shows
that entrepreneurial behaviour occurred in even the most basic rural RSDs; all

Table 9.3 Presence of most common employer occodes, rural RSDs, 1891

Occode	% of Rural RSDs
Farmers, graziers	100
Blacksmiths	91.8
Carpenters, joiners	87.9
Grocers, tea dealers	84.3
Shoe and boot makers	83.4
Corn millers	82.1
Innkeepers, hotel keepers and publicans	80.8
Builders	80.1
Butchers and meat salesmen	77.2
Tailors	77.1
Dressmakers	69.6
Clothiers and outfitters	65.3
Wheelwrights	63.2
Bakers	60.8
Carmen, carriers, carters, and draymen	56.7

Source: BBCE database.

settlements required a number of services, and that even in small rural locations there were both opportunity and necessity entrepreneurs. The dotted lines in this table show two breaks in the distribution where the frequencies drop more markedly. After the initial drop from farmers to blacksmiths, these breaks suggest that among rural RSDs there was a selection of 8–10 occodes which were present in most RSDs. These cover the basic functions required for any settlement: farming, providing employment and possibly food; carpenters and builders, required for both construction and maintenance of buildings; grocers, corn millers, butchers and innkeepers, needed for the production and distribution of food and, in the case of innkeepers, leisure; and the manufacturing occupations of blacksmiths, shoemakers and tailors providing local necessities required by any community and not manufacturing for export or other distant markets (shoemakers and tailors providing clothing, blacksmiths for various metal goods that were important for maintenance of farm implements in rural locations but also needed for the ubiquitous use of horses in agriculture and transport). If we use the presence or absence of tailors to distinguish between more and less sophisticated rural, the entrepreneurship rate for RSDs which had at least one tailor who was an employer was 20.2 while that for rural RSDs with no tailor was 18.1. There were 199 rural RSDs without a tailor employer in 1891 and 669 with one.

The *urban RSDs* are much more complex. The entrepreneurship rate increased as occupational diversity rose, from 10.5 for the least complex urban areas to 14.0 in the most complex. For *employers*, Figure 9.13 shows the percentage of

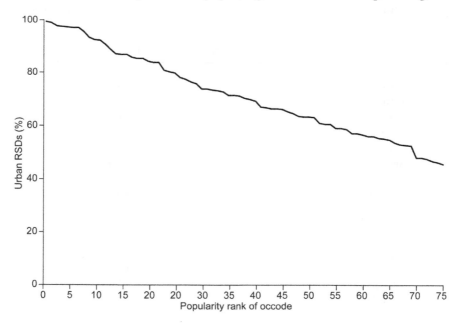

Figure 9.13 Presence of the most common employer occodes, urban RSDs, 1891
Source: BBCE database.

urban RSDs with at least one employer in each occode, for the 75 most common occodes. It is clear from this figure that urban RSDs were considerably more complex in terms of occupational diversity than rural RSDs. In rural RSDs the 18th most common occode (masons) appeared in just under half of all rural occodes; in urban RSDs the equivalent was the 70th most common occode (shirt makers). The decline shown in Figure 9.13 is fairly smooth, albeit with small breaks at the 9th, 14th, and 23rd occodes, followed by a series of small drops before a larger drop after the 69th occode. This breakpoint divides the urban RSDs into two groups, those which included a shirt-maker employer which had a higher entrepreneurship rate than those RSDs without one: 13.0 compared to 11.6.

The occodes found in all urban RSDs included all those common to rural RSDs, even farmers were fairly common, appearing in 634 of the 728 urban RSDs. However, urban RSDs contained a wide range of additional occupations: food retailers (bakers, confectioners, fishmongers, wine merchants and milk sellers); clothes makers and sellers (dressmakers, drapers, milliners and clothiers); building trades (painters, and plumbers); other retailers (ironmongers, coal and corn dealers); service providers and professionals (hairdressers, chemists, solicitors, schoolmasters, auctioneers, house agents and laundry owners); transport occupations (carmen and livery stable owners); and also more specialist goods manufacturers who were locally focused (printers, cabinet makers, saddlers and watchmakers). These occupations were all found in at least 70 percent of urban RSDs in 1891.

There were fewer urban RSDs than rural ones in 1891, 728 compared to 868, but as the previous discussion suggests, they had a far larger population and greater degree of economic complexity and diversity. To understand this diversity, it is useful to compare the urban RSDs with their factor classification, as discussed earlier. Beyond the core group of occupations common to urban RSDs, each individual factor had certain common occupations which were not in other factors. This was particularly true of specialist manufacturing occupations. Whilst most urban locations had manufacturing occupations, these tended to be makers who produced goods for local markets: clothes, furniture, carts, etc. Specialist manufacturing trades were only found in the urban RSDs with manufacturing factors. Thus, iron founders were present in 53 percent of all urban RSDs, but in 82.3 percent of RSDs in factor 5, which covered heavy and metal manufacturing. Woollen cloth manufacturers were only in 23.9 percent of all urban RSDs, but in 74 percent of RSDs in factor 6, wool and other textile manufacturing. Likewise, cotton manufacturers were present in just 20.8 percent of all urban RSDs, but in 88 percent of all cotton manufacturing RSDs, those in factor 7. This comparison reinforces the conclusions from the factor analysis: the concentration of specialised, large-scale manufacturing RSDs explains much of their relatively low entrepreneurship rates, while also emphasizing how distinctive the presence of such manufacturing businesses was when compared to the majority of the country (where manufacturing was still mainly for local markets producing everyday items that all communities required). The inclusion of manufacturing occodes in urban locations that are not classified to manufacturing factors reflected not a growing focus on industry, but instead an increasingly sophisticated local economy with a market for a wider variety of goods.

For *own-account business proprietors*, in rural RSDs the distribution and frequency was similar to that of employer occodes. There was the same breakpoint after the top 10 occodes, and many of the same occodes were included: farmers, shoemakers, blacksmiths, grocers, innkeepers, carpenters, tailors and butchers. However, the most common own-account occodes included two not found among employers: dressmakers and laundry workers. These were occupations required in all communities, providing clothes and cleaning. However, they were occupations in which female business proprietors were prominent, demonstrating that even in the most basic rural communities there were opportunities for female entrepreneurship. In urban RSDs there was a break after the 58th occupation, dealers in sundry materials. Many of the most common occodes were the same for both employers and own account; however, some were missing from the own-account individuals, such as wine, corn and other merchants, and manufacturers such as printers, coach makers and brewers. Common occodes amongst own account but uncommon among employers included hawkers, musicians, physicians, beer sellers (all present in over 90 percent of urban RSDs), lodging-house keepers, charwomen, tobacconists (present in over 80 percent), newsagents and photographers (present in over 70 percent). These were trades characterised by high proportions of own account, but they ranged from the very precarious (hawkers) to the more economically stable higher professions (physicians). They tended to be in services and retail, with relatively few own-account manufacturers common in urban RSDs; the exceptions were small-scale local manufacturers who often did repairs as well as producing goods, such as shoemakers, blacksmiths, milliners, dressmakers and wheelwrights.

Trends over time

The situation in 1891 represents the midpoint of our period. When we look earlier in the century, in 1851, there was a similar breakpoint after 10 occupations in rural RSDs; in 1851 the drop between the 10th and 11th occodes was 15 percent; in 1891, it was 8 percent. However, for urban RSDs the breakpoint came after 51 occupations rather than 69 as in 1891, suggesting urban locations were economically less complex in 1851 than in 1891; the drop in both years was 4 percent. In 1911, the breakpoint for rural RSDs came after seven occodes, a drop of 11 percent, and for urban RSDs after 72 occodes, a 3 percent drop, suggesting a slight decline in the economic complexity of the most-basic rural RSDs since 1891, but a similar economic structure between 1891 and 1911 in urban RSDs. The change in rural locations may reflect the spread of improved transport, which allowed people either to travel to purchase goods, which previously they had obtained from a local supplier, or a greater diversification of the goods suppliers, particularly grocers, that took on much wider stocks as the century progressed. In rural areas the occupations involved were very similar, as Table 9.4 shows. The most notable change between 1851 and 1891 was the

Table 9.4 Presence of 10 most common employer occodes in rural RSDs in 1851, 1891 and 1911

Occode	1851	1891	1911
Farmers, graziers	98.1 (1)	100	100 (1)
Blacksmiths	91.8 (3)	91.8	91.2 (2)
Carpenters	90.8 (4)	87.9	83.2 (6)
Grocers	79.5 (9)	84.3	85.3 (5)
Shoemakers	88.1 (6)	83.4	53.0 (13)
Corn millers	86.5 (7)	82.1	60.9 (9)
Innkeepers	90.5 (5)	80.8	86.0 (4)
Builders	48.1 (13)	80.1	86.1 (3)
Butchers	82.4 (8)	77.2	79.2 (7)
Tailors	91.9 (2)	77.1	58.6 (10)

Source: BBCE database.

Note: Percentage of all rural RSDs; rank in 1851 and 1911 shown in brackets.

spread of builders, as well as a steady increase in grocers. There were declines in a number of occupations involved in making or dealing in food, drink and clothing: tailors, millers, butchers and innkeepers. The increase in builders suggests that rather than relying on the local carpenter, people were turning to builders to co-ordinate their construction needs. The decline in some retailing industries, which for tailors continued until 1911, suggests that people were either travelling to purchase food and clothing or having it delivered, something which the improving transport networks enabled. These trends continued to 1911, although innkeepers rallied somewhat, which may have also resulted from the expansion of transport networks that stimulated expansion of refreshment and accommodation providers.

Many of the same occupations appeared in the urban RSDs in each year. However, a number of occupations before the breakpoint in the distribution in 1891 were absent in 1851, such as contractors, schoolteachers, stationers, coffee-house keepers, accountants, architects, furniture dealers, jewellers, physicians and photographers. These occodes are indicative of an increase in the sophistication of urban economies between 1851 and 1891 with an expansion in the provision of services, professions, luxury-goods dealers and more advanced construction provision. For the occodes that were common in both 1851 and 1891, many retained a similar frequency; for example, auctioneers and house agents were in 70.7 percent of urban RSDs in 1851 and 70.3 percent in 1891. However, some changed significantly: carmen, clothiers, fishmongers, hairdressers, livery stable keepers, painters, saddlers, watchmakers and wheelwrights all increased by at least 10 percent. These occodes were either associated with transport, luxury good manufacture or more specialised retail; again, suggesting an increase in sophistication between 1851 and 1891. By 1911 a number of new occodes were among the most common: lodging-house keepers, newsagents, hay dealers, surveyors, bicycle dealers and dentists. These new occodes represented a growing sophistication and specialisation, such as among professions (dentists) and newly emergent industries (bicycle dealers). Likewise, a similar spread occurred in some of the more specialised occupations common in both periods: agricultural machine and toolmakers, coffeehouse keepers, furniture dealers and tobacconists all increased by more than 10 percent. In both rural and urban locations, therefore, there was change in the occupational diversity of employers, driven by growing economic sophistication and transport connections. This was also reflected by a fall in the proportion of employers living in rural RSDs from 34 percent in 1851 to 19 percent in 1911.

Female entrepreneurship trends over time

Turning to female business proprietors, in urban locations in 1891 the rate of decline in frequency of occodes was steeper for female employers than total employers: dressmakers (95.5 percent), laundry workers (88.3 percent), grocers (83.4 percent) and innkeepers (75.8 percent) all appeared in more than three-quarters of urban RSDs. After this the decrease was rapid, with the 7th occode (confectioners) appearing in less than 60 percent of all urban RSDs, and the 11th (fruiterers and greengrocers) in less than half. There were only 11,767 female employers in rural RSDs in 1891, and of these 35 percent were farmers and 70 percent were in just five occupations: farmers, dressmakers, laundry workers, grocers and innkeepers. In terms of their distribution, there was a sharp decline: 84 percent of rural RSDs had female farmer employers, 70 percent had dressmakers, 53 percent had grocer employers and 52 percent had laundry workers. These were the only four occodes present in more than half of the rural RSDs. In urban RSDs the decline in ubiquity was slower for female own-account business proprietors than for female employers, in contrast to the total entrepreneurial population, where the break in ubiquity came sooner for own account than employers. Many of the female employer occodes were also common for female own-account proprietors, but some were distinct: musicians, charwomen and drapers. The fact that urban female own-account entrepreneurs came from a larger group of occodes than female employers reflects the importance of own-account work for women, as discussed in Chapter 8. In rural RSDs the break came slightly later than for female employers, after 6 occodes, including dressmakers, farmers, laundry workers, grocers, innkeepers and shirt makers, but as with the employers female own-account business proprietorship was far less common than in urban centres. Consequently, although even the most basic locations offered opportunities for entrepreneurship, these opportunities were gendered, with significantly more male business proprietors. Only in farming were female employers fairly common in rural RSDs. The range of occodes was also narrower for female own-account individuals (dressmaking, farming, laundry and grocery), reflecting a more restricted set of opportunities than for male counterparts, especially in rural areas.

These patterns changed over time. In 1851 the rate of decrease in urban areas for female employers was even steeper than in 1891. Only two occupations appeared in more than three-quarters of urban RSDs: dressmakers (93.9 percent) and laundry workers (90.7 percent). Only four more occupations appeared in more than half of the urban RSDs: milliners (72.5 percent), grocers (69.6 percent), innkeepers (64.2 percent) and general shopkeepers (57.9 percent). In rural RSDs the picture was similar to that in 1891: 94.8 percent of rural RSDs had at least one female employer in farming; however, after that there was a steep drop to the next most common occupation, with dressmakers present in just 74.1 percent of RSDs and laundresses in only 59.1 percent. The change between 1851 and 1891, therefore, for female employers was similar to the general pattern for all employers. Rural areas had similar levels of sophistication, but urban areas became more complex over those 40 years.

The change between 1891 and 1911 for female employers in rural areas was similar to that seen in total employer population, albeit the change was starker. By 1911 rural RSDs were less complex; only farmers appeared in more than half of the rural RSDs (96.2 percent). The next most common female employer occupations were innkeeper (46.3 percent) and dressmaker (41.1 percent). The decline in diversity of entrepreneurial opportunities by 1911 in rural areas highlighted above clearly impacted women particularly strongly. In urban areas, however, the change was different. In 1911 the picture for female employers was similar to that in 1891; four occupations were found in more than three-quarters of urban RSDs: dressmakers (93.0 percent), innkeepers (83.8 percent), milliners (76.0 percent) and lodging-house keepers (75.0 percent). However, there were some notable changes as well: laundresses, which had been found in 88.3 percent of urban RSDs in 1891, were now only found in 69.4 percent of RSDs. Less precipitous declines occurred in school teaching, which fell from 65.9 percent to 58.6 percent, and grocers decreased from 83.4 percent to 72.3 percent. In contrast, some occupations were more common, most notably lodging-house keepers which were present in just 31.0 percent of urban RSDs in 1891 but in 75 percent in 1911; part of this was caused by a recording change (as noted in Chapters 4 and 8) but it also reflected a genuine change in the kind of businesses female employers ran between 1891 and 1911. Therefore, while female rural entrepreneurship followed a similar, albeit harsher, decline than exhibited by the wider population, female urban employers remained concentrated in the same kinds of occupations across the period 1851–1911.

This discussion suggests that, because firms are the means by which resources are extracted, goods produced and distributed and services provided, a basic level of entrepreneurship will be found in every community, from the smallest village to the largest city. However, beyond this base level for essentials, the analysis reflects local opportunity and specialisation in industrial districts as strong influences on the level of business proprietorship in any location. In particular, places with specialised manufacturing industries or mining tended to have lower per capita levels of business proprietorship than areas focused on distribution, professional services or transport. This was not necessarily because such areas were lacking in innovation or risk-taking, which have been the traditional explanations for entrepreneurial distribution, but because the structure of those industries and their relatively large workforces meant that the ratio between workers and employers was higher. In contrast, we find as wide a range of opportunities in specialised urban areas as in other urban areas, but they show up less well as measured by the entrepreneurship rate. In other words, regional economic geography mattered as much as the personal characteristics of the men and women who ran businesses.

9.6   Towns and entrepreneurship

The urban classification used above also allows us to examine the entrepreneurial characteristics of particular towns. Table 9.5 shows the entrepreneurship rates of 25 towns in 1851, 1891 and 1911. These towns include the 10 largest towns in 1851 and a selection of other locations, including settlements of different sizes and economic functions. These towns reinforce the conclusions already

Table 9.5 Entrepreneurship rates of selected towns, 1851–1911

Town	1851	1891	1911	Population in 1911
London	15.6	13.2	10.6	6,417,581
Liverpool and Birkenhead	13.2	12.1	10	1,092,549
Manchester and Salford	11.2	11.5	9.3	1,018,640
Birmingham and Smethwick	14.6	12.7	9.9	911,097
Sheffield	14.1	11.4	9.9	468,830
Leeds	14	11.8	10.3	448,655
Newcastle and Gateshead	14.6	10.4	8.4	422,995
Bristol	15.9	13.5	11.6	373,012
Bradford	10.2	11.7	10.4	267,769
Plymouth	14.5	14.6	11.3	211,671
Cardiff	16	12.6	11.4	191,401
Brighton and Hove	16.6	17.3	16.9	179,864
Oldham	7.6	8	7.2	175,782
Southampton	15	15.1	11.8	129,270
Norwich	17.4	14.7	11.8	123,844
Merthyr Tydfil	8.8	9.7	8.2	80,990
Lincoln	18.9	13.4	10	57,285
Cheltenham	18.1	18	15.5	53,437
Luton	23.4	16.9	11.8	52,220
Worcester	17.6	12.4	12.4	48,011
Torquay	17.7	19.8	17.7	38,771
Ramsgate	21.7	23.7	19.5	29,603
Wednesbury	10.4	9.7	7.9	28,103
Whitby	20.6	27.3	25.8	11,139
Penzance	21.9	21.6	24.1	9,492

Source: BBCE database.

reached: entrepreneurship rates were primarily driven by the economic activities of each town. Thus, Merthyr Tydfil, dominated by large manufacturing and mining firms, had a consistently lower entrepreneurship rate than a resort town like Ramsgate where tourism promoted the development of a great number of small businesses in refreshment and accommodation: hotels, coffeehouses, pubs, lodging houses and so on. But towns also had nuance. For example, Manchester's entrepreneurship rate was consistently higher than Oldham's, despite both places being characterised by a similar primary economic function: cotton manufacturing. However, Manchester was also a centre for retail, commercial and service activity, all of which tended to be characterised by smaller businesses, hence increasing entrepreneurs as a proportion of Manchester's population compared to Oldham where manufacturing was dominant. In 1891, for example, 63 percent of Oldham's economically active population was involved in manufacturing, but only 33 percent of Manchester's. We can also see the effect of particular local characteristics; Oldham was characterised by a large number of joint-stock companies (Smith, 1961: 35). Non-corporates were also larger than cotton spinning firms elsewhere in Lancashire; in 1881 the mean firm size reported by employers in the census in cotton manufacturing in Oldham was 198, in contrast in Manchester and Salford it was 144, in Rochdale 173 and in Bolton 122.

Table 9.5 also sheds light on change over time. During this period, the entrepreneurship rate fell in many of the towns shown. At the national level we have seen elsewhere how 1901 marked a turning point, with a downturn in the numbers of own-account proprietors. Many towns were following this national trend. In London, the decline was mainly driven the drop in own-account entrepreneurship, especially amongst maker-dealers. In trades such as dressmaking, tailoring, blacksmithing and others, own-account proprietors became less common, and employers and workers more so; in 1851, 20.8 percent of people involved in maker-dealer trades in London were own-account proprietors, 5.2 percent were employers and 74 percent were workers; by 1911, 14.9 percent were own-account individuals, 7 percent were employers and 78.1 percent were workers. Thus, maker-dealers were concentrating with more workers per entrepreneur. Similar changes occurred in other sectors; refreshment underwent much the same process as maker-dealing, and the professions and manufacturing saw large increases in numbers of workers.

All of these changes increased the size of the worker population more rapidly than the entrepreneur population, which caused the entrepreneurship rate to fall. Birmingham is an interesting example where scholarship has tended to stress the dominance of small workshops, often contrasted with Manchester's factory-based economy (see Smith et al., 2019). However, Table 9.5 suggests that waged labour was increasingly important to Birmingham's population, and it is likely that large employers were more and more common in Birmingham, contrary to the general account of Birmingham's history (Briggs, 1990: 184–240). Indeed the increase in waged labour continued throughout England and Wales over the period up to and after 1911, as shown in Figures 4.1 and 4.2. Elsewhere some declines in rate of proprietorship were precipitous; for example, Luton's rate halved between 1851 and 1911, reflecting the decline of the straw plaiting trade. However, other towns' entrepreneurship rates remained fairly stable across the period, such as Brighton and Hove, Bradford and Oldham, reflecting that such towns had balanced economies between the push towards consolidation in larger firms and the maintenance of own-account activity. In Brighton, provision of accommodation and refreshment continued to be characterised by high levels of own-account and small-employer activity; in Bradford and Oldham entrepreneurship remained low throughout the period as the size structure of the wool and cotton industries in those two towns changed little between 1851 and 1911. Other locations saw rises in business proprietorship between 1851 and 1891, followed by falls between 1891 and 1911. For example, the resort towns of Ramsgate, Torquay and Whitby had a rise of tourism in the second half of the nineteenth century as wages rose, holidays were institutionalized and transport improved. But they declined 1891–1911, in contrast to Brighton's stability, reflecting loss of non-tourist activities, their smaller size, and relative isolation, which gave a smaller population base to sustain businesses outside the tourism season. Penzance had yet another pattern; its rate was stable between 1851 and 1891 before rising considerably by 1911 due to a large expansion of the number of own-account fishermen from 1891 to 1911. Analysis of towns therefore reveals how shifts in locally important sectors affected levels of business proprietorship. If the dominant sector grew or declined, or if it changed structure, then the entrepreneurship rates changed as well.

These trends are reinforced by considering how entrepreneurship characteristics evolved for different groups of urban locations. Table 9.6 shows this for a factor analysis of towns classified using the 1891 census, this time using the entire economically active population to calculate entrepreneurship rates. This combination was then adjusted to take account of the town classifications produced by Moser and Scott (1961: 84–8) and Welton (1911: 598–603) and the classification in the 1851 census report.[7] The resulting classification places the 147 towns with populations over 10,000 in 1851 into 14 categories based on their economic structures and their entrepreneurship rates (Smith et al., 2018).

The general trend was for entrepreneurship rates to decline across the period for all kinds of town. The largest declines were in light manufacturing towns, county towns (those included in the agriculture, small manufactures, transport and professions factor), agricultural produce towns, and London, with smaller but still significant declines in ports, earthenware production centres and gas and chemical towns. In general, this fall was caused by a combination of industrial concentration into larger firms and increased integration into national markets. For example, in Northampton, one of the light manufacturing towns, the entrepreneurship rate dropped by more than 9 percentage points between 1851 and 1911. This was due mainly to the increased concentration in the shoemaking industry in which factory production became the norm and own-account businesses became increasingly rare; these changes arose from the increased mechanization of the trade, the pressures of international competition and growing

Table 9.6 Entrepreneurship rates of urban classes, 1851–1911

Category	1851	1891	1911
Agricultural produce manufacturing	17.8	15.7	12.6
Agriculture, small manufacturing, transport and professional centres	18.5	15.4	13.1
Coal and diversified trades	10.2	9.7	8.6
Commercial centres	14.9	13.2	12.0
Cotton and silk manufacturing	9.4	9.2	8.5
Earthenware manufacturing	13.1	10.8	8.9
Gas and chemical manufacturing	12.1	9.3	8.1
Light manufacturing	16.4	11.9	10.5
London	15.7	13.2	10.6
Metal and heavy manufacturing	13.5	11.2	9.4
Ports and shipbuilding	15.5	13.2	10.6
Regional centres	13.1	12.0	9.9
Resorts	18.4	19.1	17.7
Wool and other textile manufacturing	12.8	12.1	10.5

Source: BBCE database.

opposition to outwork from the shoemakers' unions (Bythall, 1978: 111–15; Church, 1968). In Exeter, one of the larger county towns, the drop was driven by a decline in maker-dealer trades, particularly shoemaking. In 1851 there were 875 people in total in Exeter engaged in that trade; in 1911 there were just 209 people left. The growth of mass-produced, nationally mass-marketed footwear in Kendal, Northamptonshire and Leicestershire meant that it was increasingly difficult for small proprietors to compete, and it was no longer necessary for other locations to have their own shoemaking industry for the local market. This was also reinforced by the increasing spread of large retailers, especially branches of chain stores which reached most market towns by the 1890s (Jefferys, 1954; Shaw, 1982; Shaw and Tipper, 1997; Winstanley, 1983). Instead, the local shoe-makers in places like Exeter had to make do mainly from the trade generated by repairs. This reinforces the view that increasing regional and national integration was occurring. Given that shoemaking, and other maker-dealer trades, had high ratios of entrepreneurs to workers, their decline meant that entrepreneurship rates in places like Exeter fell. Similar declines affected locations relying on agricultural produce manufacturing in semi-rural centres. But for towns with earthenware manufacturing, gas and chemical manufacturing, metal and heavy manufacturing and ports and shipbuilding centres, these effects of consolidation were also important, though at this stage less marked than for the more tradi-tional county and semi-rural centres.

Only one urban category saw the entrepreneurship rate increase over this period: resorts, where rates increased from 1851 to 1901 before falling slightly to 1911. In these locations the high rate was based on a very large number of own-account proprietors, which was highest of any of the urban categories by 1891. Furthermore, their specialisation in maker-dealing, refreshment (hotels, inns, coffeehouses) and food sales meant that the employers in these towns tended to run firms with small workforces. Consequently towns like Brighton, Bath or Margate had relatively few workers and many entrepreneurs. This was also indicative of the seasonal or weekend focus of the resort market, which left greater scope for smaller traders who were prepared to operate either on lower incomes or had other activities in the off-periods. Whilst these locations also saw the spread of retail branches and consolidation within maker-dealer and smaller manufacturing, this was more than offset by the numbers catering for the expanding tourist trade.

A longer-term comparison can be made against the Moser and Scott (1961) classification for 1951 of towns with populations over 50,000 in England and Wales. Their principal complement analysis was based on published census occupational data, and led to 14 categories. Again there is a remarkable continuity over time for many of the categories. Although they analyse only occupations and not businesses, and five of their categories include many towns that were too small in our earlier period to be included (what they called 'suburban' towns cover settlements not included in our classification), there is a strong overlap for most other categories. Moser and Scott's six categories which cover industrial production are mainly found in our heavy manufacturing group in Table 9.6; the exceptions were Liverpool and Birkenhead which appears in our regional centre category and Stockport which is in our commercial centre category. Their resort category is identical to ours, but their spa and professional centre group covers both our resorts and county towns. There is most difference with their commercial centre category, which covers towns as varied as Bristol, Northampton and York. In our classification these towns are more likely to appear in manufacturing categories or as ports, in large part reflecting their stronger industrial base in our period, which was superseded by a shift away from manufacturing and the continued rise of services in England and Wales in the first half of the twentieth century. But nevertheless the comparison demonstrates that the industrial districts of the mid-nineteenth century (which in most cases reflected even earlier industrial structures), had remarkable continuities into the mid-twentieth century.

As with the analysis of England and Wales as a whole, analysis of individual towns demonstrates the centrality of sector markets to the entrepreneurial character of different locations. This in turn reflected the occupational structure of the wider workforce, with changes in firm size becoming increasingly important to local entrepreneurship rates. These rates were always lower in coal, other mining and textile areas because of the large size of many of the businesses whose large workforces tended to swamp recognition of the small businesses in their areas. By the 1890s and accelerating thereafter, increasing concentration of businesses also in the maker-dealer, smaller manufactures sectors and a wide range of other industries, combined with the spread of national retail chains where branch managers were employees, led to decreases in the entrepreneurship rates of almost all areas by 1911.

9.7 Conclusion

There was considerable variation in the geographical distribution of business proprietors in England and Wales in the nineteenth and early twentieth centuries. This chapter has assessed these patterns. The distribution bears little resemblance to measures of income, and while demographic characteristics explain some of the variation, they do not tell the whole story. Moreover the pattern of entrepreneurship also differs in important respects from the distribution of occupations; particularly where occupations reflect the dominance of large employer industries such as mining, textiles and heavy manufacturing. These places do not appear as low in entrepreneurship as many previous studies have assumed. This extends the comparison of occupations with entrepreneurship rates summarised in Chapter 4.

The key conclusion of the chapter has been the persistent character of the British economy as a network of industrial districts that Marshall had observed at the turn of the century, and indeed was reflected in the map and commentary in the 1851 census report. However, the occupational structure of the locations in question and the relationship between these features was complex. Furthermore, even if the distribution of industry changed relatively little between 1851 and 1911, or indeed in many cases into the 1950s (as indicated by comparisons with Moser and Scott, 1961; and as Crafts, 2005 has observed), the sophistication and character of those locations changed, as the discussion of occupational diversity has demonstrated.

Relatively high shares of entrepreneurship were usually associated with towns, and in particular towns which were either commercial or tourist centres. However, entrepreneurship also depended on the particular structure of trades in different locations. Thus, Huddersfield had a higher level of business proprietorship than somewhere like Bradford because the wool trade there was organised on a smaller scale than in Bradford. In general, places characterized by small businesses always have higher rates of business proprietorship than places dominated by large employers because there are necessarily fewer workers per entrepreneur in a location with fewer large businesses. However, modern scholarship has suggested that the nature of small businesses may themselves encourage entrepreneurship. There are several reasons for this: first, that people in locations with a plethora of small businesses are likely to experience working in multiple firms and that this experience increases the chance of an individual starting their own business; furthermore, high density of entrepreneurship may improve the reputation of entrepreneurship as an alternative to waged labour. Second, areas with many small firms are likely to have a larger pool of individuals who have started a business at some point in their lives. Third, the short-lived nature of many small firms means that resources are continuously being released back into the local economy, and consequently accessing labour and capital is usually easier in such areas (the most important externalities noted by Marshall), especially given that the businesses being started tend to have lower capital and labour requirements. Fourth, geographically concentrated small businesses can be argued to contribute to the easy flow of information, which in turn encourages further firm formation; an argument by Marshall and supported in the historical literature on industrial districts (Sorenson, 2017; Mason, 1994; Acs and Armington, 2009; Popp and Wilson, 2007). It is not possible to directly test such arguments using these data. However, the distribution of entrepreneurs does suggest that such factors were at play in the nineteenth century.

The analysis also confirms the importance of local market conditions in determining entrepreneurial activity; in general, levels of business proprietorship were determined not just by personal and cultural factors often associated with entrepreneurship, but rather by the market opportunities available locally, and the economic conditions in which individuals lived. For our historical data we have no information on the personality and cultural differences which are often a focus of the modern entrepreneurship literature. But even if we had, it is unlikely that personality or cultural differences 1851–1911 would be sufficient to explain the geographical variation between places in the levels of entrepreneurship shown in this chapter. Cultural and behavioural factors may affect whether an individual starts a business or not. However, they could have had little effect on the overall distribution of entrepreneurs throughout England and Wales. Instead, the geography of entrepreneurship was driven by local sector market conditions discussed here and in Chapter 6: the occupational and industrial structure and its history of businesses and skills, the transport infrastructure and the available local externalities.

Notes

1 *Census of Great Britain, 1851, Population Tables, II. Ages, civil conditions, occupations and birth places of the people with the numbers and ages of the blind, the deaf-and-dumb, and the inmates of workhouses, prisons, lunatic asylums, and hospitals, Vol. I, Parliamentary Papers*, LXXXVIII (1852–3), cxx, foldout.

2 Occodes are the 797 occupational categories to which each individual in I-CeM is coded; they are based on a modified version of the published 1911 census occupational classification to give a complete list of all occupational categories used by the census over any of the years 1851–1911.

3 This retains those factors that have eigenvalues greater than one, with orthogonal varimax principal component factor rotation where each factor has a correlation of exactly zero with all the others (Goldberg and Velicer, 2006; Osborne and Costello, 2005). The resulting factor loadings determine how much each sector contributes across all RSDs to a given factor from the aggregation of different sectors. Although any value that differs from zero is potentially of interest, we focus on those where the loading is greater than ± 0.5, with inspection of ± 0.2 as a check. Sectors load strongly where closely related to a factor; positive or negative depending on direct or an inverse relationships; for example, finance and commerce will have a negative relation to farming.

4 Lodgers were important parts of local economies in some locations; however, few were entrepreneurs, as shown in Chapters 6 and 7.

5 The results quoted are for one of a number of analyses carried out. Further details of the method and alternative trials are given in WPs 7, 8 and 10; see also Smith et al., 2018.

6 See Chapter 3. For full details of the classification and data download see WP 6.

7 *Census of Great Britain, 1851. Population Tables, I: Number of the inhabitants in 1801, 1811, 1821, 1831, 1841 and 1851. Vol. I, Parliamentary Papers*, LXXXV (1852–53), xlix.

10 Migration

10.1 Introduction

There has been little previous research on the relation between migration and entrepreneurship. Most work concentrates on migration by workers to find employment. However, two recent reviews of modern patterns offer useful guides to how entrepreneur migration is defined (of people vs. businesses), and distinguishes migrant entrepreneurship (which is our main focus in this chapter) from ethnic entrepreneurship (Levie, 2007; Koster and Venhorst, 2014; Niedomysl et al., 2018). Migration between locations is one means to search for new opportunities, as outlined in Chapter 2. For entrepreneurs it could be driven by *push factors*: the origin location did not have the facilities, workforce or other externalities needed, at the right price, for a given business to be established or flourish. Migration also occurs out of necessity because people have no opportunities in their origin locations or because they are fleeing economic or political turmoil, which occurred in parts of continental Europe in the 1840s, 1870s and 1880s, or famine, which drove most of the emigration from Ireland in the 1840s. Migration is also be driven by *pull factors*, where the greater opportunities of other places attracts an existing or potential entrepreneur to move. The factors influencing push from origin locations and pull to destinations normally differ profoundly: one set of factors are predominantly negative that discourage or create barriers to entrepreneurship; the others are mainly positive attractions that provide easier market entry or opportunities for growth that encourage entrepreneurship. Analysis of migration therefore requires assessment of the different locational opportunities and barriers of different places.

Migration is also individually selective. Under negative pressures the people who move for entrepreneurial reasons and those who stay usually differ substantially. Modern studies find that demographically the movers are usually younger, more likely to be single, often the most skilled or highly educated, have previous entrepreneurial experience that match expanding opportunities elsewhere and often have backing from family supports and capital (Levie, 2007; Niedomysl et al., 2018). Those who stay are more likely to be older, married, less skilled or adaptable, as well as those with greater family of other assets that are difficult to transfer or lose. Gender plays a role chiefly between access to opportunities:

generally males are more likely to move for entrepreneurial reasons and females for reasons of labour force opportunities (historically primarily in domestic service; Day, 2015). However, gender is not usually found to be a significant factor on migration among entrepreneurs themselves (Niedomysl et al., 2018). But much depends on family and social context, experience of family business background, existing or potential networks that facilitate market entry elsewhere and previous history with one person following another after an initial move has taken place, with multiple generational factors identifiable in modern Swedish micro-level data (Andersson and Hammarstedt, 2010) or the US (Fairlie and Robb, 2008). Of course those who move may not have had a tradition of entrepreneurship but moved from necessity and became entrepreneurial because they had no alternatives. Our analysis shows that such necessity-driven migration differed profoundly between origin areas, which reflected differences in the sort of skills and cultural background of origin areas and type of origin family structures.

Entrepreneurial migration is also selective between business sectors. As recognised in Chapter 2, entrepreneurs are usually more 'sticky' to location than workers. First, they have higher risks, higher start-up and transfer costs, longer lead times to get activity underway and sometimes more to lose than workers. Second, entrepreneurial profits are often argued to be more sensitive to location than wages (Knight, 1921). Third, opportunity costs are usually far higher for employers who might obtain good or adequate returns without moving to make a small marginal gain. Fourth, existing firm size and complexity is negatively related to potential mobility. The larger the firm and its premises, the more difficult it is to move, and if a move occurs, the more likely it is to be relatively local so that it can draw on its existing workforce and established supply chain, markets and externalities. Hence sectors where business proprietors have more fixed and less mobile assets are less likely to move (manufacturing, construction, retail and transport); whilst entrepreneurs in service sectors, especially business services, are more likely to move (Koster and Venhorst, 2014; Niedomysl et al., 2018). They are also less likely to move from a large more urban location which already has high levels of market potential; almost all business migration is up the urban hierarchy or from regions with lower to higher GDP (Keeble and Walker, 1994; Keeble and Tyler, 1995).

Most historical research has used cases studies. These have provided rich detail because many of nineteenth-century Britain's most famous entrepreneurs were migrants or related to recent migrants. For example, Michael Marks, the son of a Russian tailor, arrived in England in 1882, fleeing anti-Semitic pogroms in Russia. He started out running market stalls in Leeds, Castleford and Wakefield selling clothing, household goods and toys. Over the next decade this expanded into a business with multiple 'penny bazaars' in towns throughout Lancashire. In 1894, he entered into a partnership with Thomas Spencer, creating the firm Marks and Spencer which continues to this day (Shaw, 2004). Others moved around within the British Isles. Andrew Leslie, born in the Shetland Islands in 1818, initially started work as a boilermaker in Aberdeen, setting up his own business there before moving to Hebburn in 1853 and founding a shipyard and boiler works. This business grew, with output rising from an average of 2,000 tons a year in the 1850s to 23,500 tons in 1881, when he was returned in the census as employing 'about 2,700' men.[1] The company he created merged with R. and W. Hawthorn when Leslie retired in 1885, and the resulting firm continued to build ships until the 1970s (Baker, 2004).

Other historical studies have focused on particular migrant communities associated with certain economic activities; for example, the strong association between London's Jewish population and tailoring (Godley, 1996). In the context of late nineteenth-century Jewish immigration and the intricacies of London trade union politics, contemporaries debated the influence of immigration on costermongers (Brodie, 2004: 159–98). Henry Weston Blake, a prominent costermonger penned anti-Semitic tracts against Jewish costermongers and gave evidence to the Royal Commission on Alien Immigration about their influence on the state of trade in London. His evidence was fiercely contested by Benjamin Davis, secretary of the Whitechapel and Spitalfields Costermongers' Union.[2] For more major businesses, scholarship on the Germans in London has highlighted their dominance of the sugar baking trade, something upon which contemporary commentary agreed (Panayi, 1995: 120–4), and in the London merchant and banking community (Chapman, 1984).

The association between migrants and entrepreneurship, however, goes beyond noting the tendency of migrants to dominate or affect particular industries. There is an argument that many of the qualities which are associated with immigrants overlap with those required to be a successful entrepreneur: an ability to judge risk successfully and evaluate market opportunities and access to personal capital and to networks that could provide both labour and capital (Aldrich and Waldinger, 1990; Levie, 2007). Furthermore, it has been argued that migrant communities can create their own markets or 'ethnic economies' based on demands specific to that community; the market for kosher food created by Jewish migrants in the East End of London in the nineteenth century is a classic example (Panayi, 2010: 107).

The analysis of migration in this chapter considers employers and own-account proprietors together, using the records of residence at the census date and the birthplace of each individual. The chapter examines the characteristics of migrant entrepreneurs in England and Wales over 1851–1911 and provides the first large-scale analysis of their international and internal migration. The first part of the chapter covers the activities of immigrant entrepreneurs and the second addresses the relationship of internal migration, including that from Ireland, to entrepreneurship.

10.2   Quality of the data

The examination of migration in this chapter is based on the birthplace data given by all individuals in the census. The 1851–1901 censuses asked individuals for different information depending on where they were born. Those born in

England and Wales were to give their county and town or parish of birth; those born in Scotland or Ireland were to give the county; those born somewhere in the British Empire had to give the name of the colony or dependency; and those born in any other foreign country were to give the name of the country and whether they were a 'British subject', 'naturalised British subject' or 'foreign subject' followed by their nationality ('French', 'Russian', etc.). In 1911 this changed, and two columns were provided, one for birthplace and one for nationality.

The accuracy of birthplace data is unclear. Studies of Preston, Llangefni, Colyton, Bethnal Green and six Kentish parishes comparing individuals' birthplaces across more than one census have found error rates ranging from 4 to 17 percent (Higgs, 2005: 88–91). Many of these were minor errors; but some, in Preston, for example, transformed migrants into non-migrants and vice-versa (Anderson, 1972: 75). Part of this is explained by the apparent tendency for residents to adopt their place of residence as their place of birth, which reduces the level of migration shown in the census, and tends to change the scope for recognition of a migrant the longer they have been resident (Wrigley, 1975: 300–1, 306). There is further doubt, expressed by the GRO in the nineteenth century and by modern scholars, about the accuracy of the reporting of foreign birthplaces, particularly with regard to the issue of British subjects born abroad (Higgs, 2005: 91).[3] Foreign birthplaces also suffer from the same problem of inconsistency across censuses as individuals adopt their new residence as their stated birthplace. Furthermore, the birthplaces given by individuals are heterogeneous in descriptors used and have to be related to contemporary geographies which are often different from modern states.

The example of Nathan Shonman illustrates both issues. Shonman ran a bazaar and in 1891 returned himself as being born in Iceland, but in 1901 he reported his birthplace as Poland.[4] In his naturalization certificate his birthplace was stated as Płock, which is in modern Poland, but at that date was part of the Russian Empire.[5] These issues are important, but little can be done to correct them given that the analysis in this chapter is based on cross-sectional, not panel data. However, in order to reduce the issues associated with individuals recording different birthplaces the categories used for analysis have been kept large. Thus, internal migration is measured between counties or from Ireland and Scotland, and international migration is examined using 14 categories which cover large geographical entities.[6] Assuming that any error is likely to be mainly caused either by shifts between different locations within counties or between different countries within larger geographical entities (continents, regions), the chance of an individual being in the wrong category is reduced, and is far lower than them returning the wrong parish or town of birth.

There are other issues with using census data to study migration. Census data will only identify first-generation migrants and thus underestimates the size of migrant communities. For example, the children of migrants born in the UK will not be recognisable as from a migrant parentage unless they are still cohabitant with them. Furthermore, birthplace can give only limited information about the characteristics of individual migrants at the moment of travel as well as limited information about whether they were newly arrived or long-term residents at the moment of the census in question (Pooley, 1977: 368; Tabili, 2011: 42; Day, 2015). However, in the absence of large-scale panel data on migrants, the census provides the most complete large-scale dataset for examining the characteristics and behaviour of migrant entrepreneurs available.

'Immigrant' is taken in this chapter to refer to any individual who was born outside the United Kingdom and moved to England and Wales. Consequently, British subjects born elsewhere who moved to England or Wales will appear as immigrants. The majority are included in the British Empire category used below, but all categories included a certain proportion of British subjects born abroad. The census data, as noted above, is inadequate to fully capture this phenomenon. However, the laissez-faire approach to immigration adopted by the British state from 1850 until 1905 means that the non-British subjects faced no additional obstacles compared to these hidden British subjects (Porter, 1979: 3–5). Thus, the factors affecting British subject immigrants and non-British immigrants were more similar in the nineteenth century than at other points in Britain's history.

10.3   International immigration and Irish migration

The UK has long been a country characterised by high levels of migration with historians documenting extensive internal and international migration at least as far back as the Black Death (Whyte, 2000: 5–7). Between 1851 and 1911 the number of overseas-born migrants rose from 599,701 to 980,412, broken down as shown in Table 10.1. This table shows steady increases in the German, French and Northern European populations across the period. The population of migrants from Southern Europe, Central America and the Caribbean, Africa and the Middle East remained relatively stable, though African, Middle Eastern and Southern European migrants increased in the 1870s. Migration from Italy, Central Europe and South America is fairly stable until the 1890s, when it increased significantly. Migration from the US peaked in the 1880s before declining slowly over the next 30 years. Russian migrants increased slowly between 1851 and the 1870s before taking off in the 1880s. This reflected the movement of Jews out of the Russian Empire, driven partly by the anti-Semitic pogroms and partly by the changing economic situation in Russia which caused the proletarianisation of the Jewish population (Feldman, 1994: 147–55). The increase in migrants from Asia was driven by a significant rise in the numbers coming from China after 1871. However, as John Seed points out, many of those born in China were the children of British merchants, soldiers and missionaries (Seed, 2006: 62–3). This also applied to individuals born in Japan, who also increased after the 1870s. The large and rapid increase in the numbers of migrants from the British Empire after the 1860s is something that has gone unexamined by historians, who tend to characterise immigration to Britain as dominated by arrivals from Ireland and continental Europe (Panayi, 2010: 23–4, 39–40; Webster, 2011: 122–3; Harper and Constantine, 2010: 184). Much of the

Table 10.1 Migration to England and Wales, 1851–1911

Origin	1851	1861	1871	1881	1891	1901	1911
Ireland	505,871	584,392	566,540	563,909	459,502	427,301	422,439
Germany	14,322	22,360	32,823	49,304	55,826	65,926	64,348
Russian Empire	3,541	5,907	9,569	19,904	46,742	93,026	106,844
France	16,983	19,028	17,906	25,919	33,306	39,566	45,529
British Empire	30,273	38,889	70,812	91,411	103,784	136,085	172,841
Italy	3,334	3,857	5,063	8,413	10,588	22,695	21,807
US	2,982	4,829	8,270	26,020	15,180	16,200	40,986
South America	4,252	5,883	1,642	3,578	16,948	29,241	8,303
Northern Europe	7,116	10,850	19,592	26,951	31,009	43,341	45,223
Southern Europe	3,021	3,220	2,246	6,645	5,386	7,694	8,663
Central Europe and the Balkans	604	1,053	1,802	3,892	6,781	16,257	20,521
Central America and the Caribbean	295	321	108	780	766	1,029	1,232
Africa	526	718	685	1,188	1,109	1,106	1,588
Middle East	253	408	565	1,841	1,814	3,275	4,329
Asia and the Pacific	639	722	323	2,385	2,761	3,882	5,616
Total foreign-born population	88,141	118,045	171,406	268,231	332,000	479,323	547,830
Total	594,012	702,437	737,946	832,140	791,502	906,624	970,269
Net change in total		108,425	35,509	94,194	−40,628	115,122	63,645
% change		18.25	5.06	17.76	−4.88	14.54	7.02

Sources: 1851–61, 1881–1911 from I-CeM; 1871 from *Census of England and Wales, 1871, Population Abstracts. Ages, civil condition, occupations and birth-places of the people, Vol. III, PP*, LXXI (1873), l–li.

Notes: Data for 1871 contain ambiguous 'other states' category in America – put into South America, but likely to be Central America or the Caribbean.

change between 1861 and 1881 was driven by a large increase in the numbers coming from India, Australia and Canada, which rose from 17,702 people in 1861 to 52,775 in 1881. The next large increase, between 1891 and 1901, was also caused by increases in migration from India, Australia and Canada; however, there was also significantly more migration from South Africa, with almost twice as many South African residents present in 1901 as there had been in 1891 (partly as a result of the South African War at the time). Much of the migration from India was individuals born there but who were British subjects. These are hard to assess as many did not follow the census instructions to specify their nationality if born abroad. However, in 1891, 35 percent of those born in India declared they were British subjects; the 1911 census report stated that just 4,067 of those born on the Indian sub-continent were not of European parentage, 7 percent of the total migrant population.[7] The Australian, Canadian and South African migration, however, goes unmentioned in many histories and represents a pre-history to twentieth-century migration from what would become the Commonwealth to the United Kingdom.

Throughout this period the Irish were the largest group of migrants to Great Britain. They were not of course 'international', since Ireland continued as part of the UK until 1922, but they can be tracked in the same way as international. The beginning of this period was dominated by post-famine migration, which drove the large increase in 1851–61. While the rate of migration declined after this, emigration from Ireland remained high for the rest of this period and Britain remained a popular destination, reflecting both the long-established patterns of migration from Ireland to Britain and the more general factors that promoted high emigration from Ireland throughout the nineteenth century (Ó Grada, 1995: 224–35; Swift and Campbell, 2017: 515–16; Fitzpatrick, 2010: 606–9).

Numerous specific push and pull factors drove migration to England and Wales in this period. First, changes in the economic and demographic structure of Europe and the wider world promoted migration: population growth and the slow decline of agriculture created structural conditions in countries in Europe conducive to emigration. To take one example, Germany in the nineteenth century experienced rapid population growth, which created pressure on agricultural land; this combined with periodic agricultural downturns and fragmented land ownership to promote emigration. Added to this was the decline of some industries in Continental Europe; for example, the effect of cheap textile production in Manchester on the rural cottage textile industry in Westphalia prompted some individuals to consider emigration as a solution to unemployment or underemployment (Baines, 1995: 17–18). Such issues also explain shifts in the rates of emigration; for example, in Germany emigration declined as the country industrialised and the economy was able to absorb the growing population, reducing the need to emigrate (Panayi, 1995: 35–40).

If these factors help explain why people left countries, other factors explain why they chose England and Wales as their destination. This was a combination of economic and social factors. The British economy was characterised by relatively high wages, a comparatively fragmented labour market, apprenticeship was declining and there were few other access restrictions which reduced entry barriers to finding employment, although other difficulties remained as discussed later in this chapter (Feldman, 2000: 193–4; Panayi, 2010: 58–61). Such economic enticements were enhanced by the presence of pre-existing networks and communities of migrants. It is notable that many of the largest migrant communities had long histories of immigration into England and Wales. This could take a supportive form, whereby existing migrant communities created business and employment opportunities which were communicated back to the home country (Panayi, 1995: 99). However, it could also create opportunities for exploitation; for example, young boys sent from Italy to London to work as street musicians were a cause of considerable concern for British authorities and the Italian community (Zucchi, 1999: 76–110).

There was considerable variation in the characteristics of these migrant communities in terms of their demographics, location and occupations, and such characteristics varied not just between and within nationalities but also over time. For example, the German migrant population ranged from street musicians to merchant bankers. However, there were some concentrations in terms of occupation, and Table 10.2 shows the most common occupational category for the economically active members of each migrant group for each census year. There was considerable stability in the most common economic activities of many immigrant communities. Within this general picture, there were some occupations which were particularly associated with certain nationalities. For example, there were 12,716 immigrant tailors in 1891, 2,369 of these were from Germany and 8,139 were born in Russia, which was a quarter of the total Russian-born occupied population in that year. These immigrant tailors were 7 percent of the total number of tailors in England and Wales, but the majority lived in London, where they made up 19 percent of all tailors. There was also an exceptional group of immigrants who were employers and own-account proprietors of high status, notably foreign-born merchants and bankers resident in England and Wales. The determinants of their location and employment status were different from other entrepreneurs, they were driven less by previous factors and more by multinational expansion and opportunities (Buckley, 1989; Koster and Venhorst, 2014; Chapman, 1984, 1992). In 1891 there were 2,345 immigrant merchants, 1,269 of whom were employers, 685 own account and 391 workers; 42 percent of these were from Germany, with smaller groups from France, Switzerland, the Netherlands, Italy, Turkey and the US, reflecting the growing attraction of the UK, and especially London, as a centre for international business.

Table 10.3 compares the demographic characteristics of the immigrant and native-born populations. The immigrant population was, on average, younger than the native population, and the high sex ratios show that they consisted of more men than women. The sex ratio is even more imbalanced if it is restricted to the economically active population; for example, in 1891 the immigrant economically active sex ratio was 296 while the same value for the English and Welsh population was 227. The proportion never married was higher for immigrants, although the gap between the two communities closed across the period. The higher proportion of never married immigrants was driven by single men; for example, in 1891 it is 32 percent for immigrant men, compared to 25 percent for the native-born population. The uneven sex ratio, younger mean age and higher rates of never married for men suggest that, despite the undoubted importance of family migration, many migrants were working-age single men.

The geography of migrant residence was characterised by a wide dispersion of the migrants from the British Empire. However, non-British Empire immigrants lived almost exclusively in large towns; indeed, in each census year 44 to 48 percent of the non-British Empire migrants lived in London. The history of immigration in nineteenth-century England and Wales is one dominated by London. There were also other smaller concentrations in Lancashire and Yorkshire, in the cities of Manchester, Liverpool and Leeds. In London itself, migrant

Table 10.2 Migrant occupations, 1851–1911

	1851	1861	1881	1891	1901	1911
Germany	Maker–dealer	Maker–dealer	Maker–dealer	Maker–dealer	Maker–dealer	Refreshment
Russian Empire	Maker–dealer	Maker–dealer	Maker–dealer	Maker–dealer	Maker–dealer	Maker–dealer
France	Personal services	Personal services	Personal services	Personal services	Personal services	Personal services
British Empire	Public admin, military and clergy	Public admin, military and clergy	Public admin, military and clergy	Public admin, military and clergy	Personal services	Personal services
Italy	Manufacturing	Manufacturing	Personal services	Personal services	Food sales	Refreshment
US	Transport	Transport	Manufacturing	Manufacturing	Manufacturing	Manufacturing
South America	Manufacturing	Manufacturing	Professional and business services	Manufacturing	Manufacturing	Professional and business services
Northern Europe	Maker–dealer	Maker–dealer	Transport	Transport	Transport	Transport
Southern Europe	Manufacturing	Manufacturing	Transport	Transport	Transport	Transport
Central Europe and the Balkans	Manufacturing	Manufacturing	Maker–dealer	Maker–dealer	Maker–dealer	Maker–dealer
Central America and the Caribbean	Finance and commerce	Manufacturing	Professional and business services	Professional and business services	Professional and business services	Professional and business services
Africa	Domestic service	Domestic service	Manufacturing	Manufacturing	Personal services	Personal services
Middle East	Finance and commerce	Finance and commerce	Finance and commerce	Finance and commerce	Manufacturing	Manufacturing
Asia and Pacific	Manufacturing	Domestic service	Transport	Manufacturing	Personal services	Personal services

Source: BBCE database.

Table 10.3 Demographic characteristics of immigrants, 1851–1911

Year	Mean Age		Sex Ratio		Age Standardized Never Married (%)	
	Immigrant	England and Wales	Immigrant	England and Wales	Immigrant	England and Wales
1851	35.29	36.49	107	94	29.76	25.18
1861	34.35	36.74	121	95	29.15	24.56
1881	34.44	36.45	118	94	28.72	24.37
1891	35.06	36.27	105	93	28.02	25.43
1901	35.18	36.26	109	93	27.65	26.12
1911	36.79	37.2	112	94	28.55	27.13

Source: BBCE database.

Notes: Never married rate standardized to 1891 age structure; age and never-married rate aged 15 and over.

communities were concentrated in the East End, with smaller communities in Westminster, Marylebone, Hampstead and St Pancras. Irish migration is similarly an urban story with significant communities in Manchester, Liverpool and London, but Irish migrants were more widely dispersed, settling in towns such as Bournemouth, Bradford, Newcastle, Portsmouth and others.

10.4 Immigrant entrepreneurs

As with the immigrant population more generally, the numbers of migrant entrepreneurs increased across this period, as Table 10.4 shows. However, while the absolute numbers increased, the overall proportion of entrepreneurs among the immigrant economically active population remained stable. The immigrant entrepreneurship rate was considerably higher than for those born in England and Wales, roughly 20 entrepreneurs per hundred economically active, compared to 13 per hundred for the English and Welsh born population.

This table hides considerable variation between migrants born in different locations, as Table 10.5 shows. Some communities were fairly stable across the period, such as those born in Germany or the British Empire. However, others changed significantly. Thus, those born in the Russian Empire, the Middle East or Asia all became more entrepreneurial towards the end of the period, while entrepreneurship rates of immigrants from France, Italy, Northern Europe, and Southern Europe declined. There was variation in the level as well as the pattern; those immigrants from Germany, Russia, France, Italy, the US, Southern Europe, Central Europe, Central America, Africa and the Middle East all had entrepreneurship rates that were consistently higher than those of the English- and Welsh-born population. Those from the British Empire were less entrepreneurial between the 1860s and 1890s, which is unsurprising given that most were older colonial civil servants and merchants retiring to Britain. People

Table 10.4 Migrant entrepreneurs, 1851–1911

Year	Entrepreneurs	Workers	Entrepreneurship Rate
1851	8,945	31,356	22.2
1861	9,684	41,198	19.0
1881	23,576	112,679	17.3
1891	35,632	131,589	21.3
1901	53,730	196,182	21.5
1911	62,281	225,534	21.6

Source: BBCE database.

Table 10.5 Immigrant entrepreneurship rates, 1851–1911

Origins	1851	1861	1881	1891	1901	1911
Germany	24.5	19.9	21.6	27.3	26.4	25.3
Russian Empire	25.3	20.7	19.9	26.3	27.6	32.2
France	20.4	19.1	18.3	20.0	18.7	16.4
British Empire	16.8	14.8	12.3	13.6	15.5	14.3
Italy	32.8	28.0	23.2	34.8	29.4	29.0
US	18.5	15.9	13.4	15.8	20.0	16.4
South America	16.8	14.0	18.0	14.7	15.9	19.0
Northern Europe	25.2	18.8	14.3	15.1	12.7	13.2
Southern Europe	25.3	23.5	16.2	20.9	16.9	15.0
Central Europe and the Balkans	28.3	23.6	19.1	28.6	23.7	26.8
Central America and the Caribbean	*23.3*	*18.6*	19.8	27.2	19.0	16.6
Africa	19.9	17.3	16.1	16.5	24.8	18.9
Middle East	*26.9*	*37.4*	25.7	31.3	36.7	34.8
Asia and the Pacific	11.0	10.3	10.0	12.9	13.3	15.0
English and Welsh	15.4	14.4	13.6	13.8	13.2	11.6

Source: BBCE database.

Note: Figures in *italics* calculated from fewer than 200 people.

born in Northern Europe were initially more entrepreneurial than the native population but this declined, and in 1901 they had lower entrepreneurship rates. The entrepreneurship rate for migrants from Asia and the Pacific went in the opposite direction, starting lower and ending up higher.

As with the general immigrant population, immigrant entrepreneurs were heavily concentrated in London. It might be argued that London, as a wealthy population centre, was likely to promote unusually high levels of business ownership because the wealth and size of it increased the scope for businesses. However, as Table 10.6 shows the entrepreneurship rates for immigrants was higher than the rates for English- and Welsh-born individuals resident

Table 10.6 Immigrant and London-based entrepreneurship rates, 1851–1911

Year	Immigrant London Residents	English- and Welsh-Born London Residents
1851	22.2	15.6
1861	19.0	13.5
1881	17.3	12.2
1891	21.3	12.6
1901	21.5	10.7
1911	21.6	9.6

Source: BBCE database.

Table 10.7 Estimates of the logit model for all entrepreneurs compared to workers, 1911; England and Wales birthplace base; all other variables as in Table 6.1.

Ireland	−0.338***	South America	0.735***
Scotland	−0.0470***	Northern Europe	0.338***
Germany	0.591***	Southern Europe	0.773***
Russian Empire	0.974***	Central Europe and the Balkans	0.966***
France	0.539***	Central America and the Caribbean	0.691***
British Empire	0.289***	Africa	1.001***
Italy	1.100***	Middle East	1.819***
US	0.656***	Asia and the Pacific	0.919***

Source: BBCE database.

*** $p \geq 0.01$.

in London; as indicated below, this was mainly a result of high numbers of migrant workers.

While entrepreneurship rates are a simple way to compare levels of business ownership between different populations, the migration birthplaces can be added to the base model discussed in Chapter 6 to assess how far origins differ significantly when other variables are controlled for. The results are shown in Table 10.7 for 1911, with English- and Welsh-born residents as the base; estimates for the other variables are similar to those in Table 6.1. The estimates show that all foreign-born groups were more entrepreneurial than individuals born in England and Wales. However, there was variation between locations: those people born in the Middle East, Italy, Africa, Russia and Central Europe appear most entrepreneurial; an intermediate group, including Southern Europe, South America, Central America, the US, Germany and France; and finally, those born in Northern Europe and the British Empire were the least entrepreneurial.

The entrepreneurship rates and the entrepreneurship model both suggest that immigrant communities were generally more likely to operate businesses than the general population born in England and Wales. Historical and contemporary studies of migrant entrepreneurship have suggested a number of reasons why immigrants were more likely to start businesses than native populations (Foreman-Peck and Zhou, 2013; Levie, 2007; Panayi, 2010: 107–14). First, some immigrants faced difficulties entering wage labour markets and consequently they started businesses out of necessity. Second, many migrant communities had strong networks that allowed capital to be raised and provided ready labour to help compensate for the disadvantages faced by immigrants in accessing resources. Third, it has been suggested that immigrants, having already taken one bold decision, to migrate, were more likely to take another, starting a business. Fourth, the culture of migrant communities affected their propensity to start businesses; it is argued that immigrants often came from places which were more entrepreneurially minded than the host country. Fifth, it is also argued that immigrants could have a better perception of market opportunities than life-long residents. Finally, immigrant communities, in part, generated their own new markets through the creation of markets which are run by a particular community solely for that community, such as kosher food production. Assessment of these different possibilities is necessarily limited by the information provided in the census data; for example, while the model controls for the effects of age, gender, marital status, occupational sector and location it does not include other issues which affect the likelihood of an individual starting a business: other personal attributes, such as available capital, or wider structural factors, such as the openness of the labour market. However, a number of these factors can be examined by other means.

Labour market

The difficulties facing immigrants in entering the labour market arose from a variety of causes. First, they might lack the relevant language or other skills. Thus, entry into many of the older London trades was restricted by trade bodies or more informal mechanisms. For example, throughout this period, coopers in London had to serve an apprenticeship; each cooper could take on one apprentice who had to be the son of a cooper (Booth, 1902–3, I: 255; Stedman Jones, 2013: 142–4). Second, their own skills might not match the available jobs. For example, Morris Cohen, a naturalized mantle manufacturer from the Russian Empire interviewed by the Royal Commission on Alien Immigration related how when he arrived in London in 1877 there were few ladies' tailors in England. He set up a successful business based on his own experience as a ladies' tailor, one which employed several other migrants who had been ladies' tailors before migrating to London. Some of his employees later left and set up their own ladies' tailoring businesses. By 1903 his business employed over 180 people, of which, according to Cohen,

> 50 of these are English Christians, about 50 English Jews, and the remainder are aliens who do the principal parts of the work, such as basting and fitting, and which I cannot get done by English workers. These English

workpeople have all learned their trade from the original foreign workmen, who brought the new manufacture into this country.[8]

He later commented, 'an English tailor is unfitted for fancy needlework such as is required for the mantle trade'. In this case, immigrant tailors could find no work in such fields because no such English or Welsh businesses existed; consequently they had to start their own enterprises. Third, immigrants might face discrimination such as that suffered by West African sailors in early twentieth-century Liverpool (Frost, 1995: 26). These reasons suggest that some immigrants may have struggled to enter the labour market and consequently saw starting their own business as the best or only option.

One measure of a community's ability to access the labour market is the unemployment rate. Unemployment is difficult to measure using census data; however, we can identify men of working age who reported no occupation or explicitly stated they were unemployed and compare them as a proportion of the total employed population for the immigrant population and those people born in England and Wales. This can be only an approximate indicator of labour market stress, but as Table 10.8 shows, in each year the unoccupied rate was higher for immigrant communities than for the population born in England and Wales, suggesting that immigrants did indeed find it harder to enter the labour market.

The activities in which migrants most frequently developed businesses were also indicative of the balance between necessity and opportunity-driven entrepreneurship. Table 10.9 shows the proportion of immigrant workers in each census year in the 10 most common occupations in London in 1891.[9] Table 10.10 shows the 10 most common immigrant occupations in 1891 and the share of immigrants in those professions.

There is some overlap between the two tables, thus tailors, servants, commercial clerks and shoemakers were occupations that employed significant proportions of the immigrant workforce and were also common occupations among the entire London population; although only in tailoring, and later in

Table 10.8 Unoccupied rates, men, aged between 15 and 65, 1851–1911

Year	Immigrant Unoccupied Rate	England and Wales Unoccupied Rate
1851	3.81	2.55
1861	3.38	2.36
1881	2.53	2.12
1891	3.18	2.01
1901	2.98	1.86
1911	1.90	1.36

Source: BBCE database.

Note: Wildcard occupation string search for *unemploy* and ' – '. 'Unoccupied' does not measure unemployment, but declared lack of occupation. The industrial unemployment rate for 1870–1913 was 5.8 percent (Boyer and Hatton, 2002: 667).

Table 10.9 Most common London occupations, 1851–1911, immigrant share of workforce

Occupation	1851	1861	1881	1891	1901	1911
Servant	1.0	1.3	2.4	2.6	3.6	3.4
General labourer	0.8	0.6	1.1	1.1	1.3	0.9
Commercial clerk	3.2	4.1	5.5	4.7	4.8	4.4
Dressmaker	1.2	1.5	2.6	2.8	4.2	4.9
Laundry	0.7	0.6	1.1	1.2	1.3	1.3
Tailor	3.8	6.2	12.0	19.4	30.7	34.7
Carter	0.4	0.4	0.3	0.5	0.6	0.6
Shoemaker	1.3	2.1	4.2	7.1	12.8	11.6
Messenger	0.7	0.8	1.2	1.2	1.3	1.2
Painter	0.8	0.9	1.1	1.1	1.8	1.6

Source: BBCE database.

Table 10.10 Most common London immigrant occupations, 1851–1911; immigrant share of workforce

Occupation	1851	1861	1881	1891	1901	1911
Tailor	3.8	6.2	12.0	19.4	30.7	34.7
Servant	1.0	1.3	2.4	2.6	3.6	3.4
Commercial clerk	3.2	4.1	5.5	4.7	4.8	4.4
Baker	4.5	9.1	16.9	18.0	20.3	17.3
Shoemaker	1.3	2.1	4.2	7.1	12.8	11.6
Hotel waiter	2.5	5.4	16.6	19.3	28.7	30.2
Dressmaker	1.2	1.5	2.6	2.8	4.2	4.9
Cabinet maker	1.7	4.1	6.1	13.6	22.8	24.6
Hairdresser	3.2	5.4	18.9	26.7	37.2	40.1
Other clothing manufacture	1.5	2.5	7.4	14.8	26.8	26.8

Source: BBCE database.

the period shoemaking, did immigrants constitute a substantial share of the total workforce. The other occupations in Table 10.10 were relatively insignificant in the total London economy, although bakers, hotel waiters and cabinet makers were fairly large groups. The occupations in Table 10.10 are a mixture of old declining industries (cabinet making), new trades (hotel waiters and hairdressers) and trades in which the cost of entry was low and immigrant entrepreneurship was high (tailoring and baking).[10] In other words, all fields in which entry to the labour force was likely to be easier than into either older London trades that were still relatively strong or more general occupations where competition from English- and Welsh-born people was fiercer. There were few immigrants in trades dominated by London-born individuals such as bookbinding, printing and other paper trades, leather or silk working, ship building or dock labouring (Stedman Jones, 2013: 145). Nor were immigrants able to enter trades dominated by internal migrants such as the building trades. The restrictions that prevented immigrants from freely entering all parts of the labour force increased the likelihood that immigrants would choose business proprietorship instead of wage labour, especially given that the highest-paid occupations, such as the building trades, coopering or printing, were often those closed to them (Booth, 1902–3, V: 16, 273–4). The ability to earn a high wage was important because of the particular household structure of immigrant families.

Family structure and capital

There is ample testimony about the importance of the family to entrepreneurs in Victorian and Edwardian England and Wales. It provided labour and capital to businesses, and the needs of the family often determined the nature of the firm. As shown in Chapters 6–8, the chances of becoming an entrepreneur were increased when an individual was married. Table 10.11 shows the proportion of immigrant entrepreneurs aged between 20 and 24 who were married to people from the same birthplace compared to internal migrants.

Except for 1851, the proportion of immigrants with a spouse born in the same birthplace as themselves was significantly higher in all census years than

Table 10.11 Birthplace of immigrant and internal migrant entrepreneurs' spouses, aged 20–24, 1851–1911

Year		Immigrant 20–24		Internal Migrant 20–24	
		% Same Country	% Different	% Same County	% Different
1851	W	20.9	79.1	28.9	71.1
	E&OA	22.4	77.6	26.7	73.3
1861	W	35.0	65.0	28.2	71.8
	E&OA	27.8	72.2	25.5	74.5
1881	W	32.8	67.2	26.0	74.0
	E&OA	38.4	61.6	26.0	74.0
1891	W	47.9	52.1	24.4	75.6
	E&OA	49.4	50.6	22.9	77.1
1901	W	56.7	43.3	24.7	75.3
	E&OA	61.8	38.2	23.6	76.4
1911	W	38.2	61.7	24.4	75.6
	E&OA	50.1	49.9	22.9	77.1

Source: BBCE database.

Note: Figures in *italics* are calculated from fewer than 100 individuals.

for internal migrants. As these figures are for immigrants aged 20–24, they are likely to have arrived in England and Wales already married. Furthermore, in all years with substantial sample sizes, the proportion was higher among immigrant business owners compared to immigrant workers, suggesting that it is associated with the likelihood of *starting* a business. Arriving with a family could have promoted entrepreneurship in two ways. First, the necessity of supporting a family may have made wage labour less attractive, especially if immigrants were restricted in kinds of wage labour they could obtain, as suggested above. Second, families provided important sources of capital and labour which were less readily available to unmarried individuals (Young, 1995: 406–9; Crossick and Haupt, 1995: 90–107). Even if immigrants did not arrive already married, they tended to marry people from the same community; half of all immigrant entrepreneurs in 1891 were married to people with the same birthplace as themselves, with similar proportions in the other later census years where the data are most reliable. Such high rates of endogamy suggest that the immigrant communities were more closely integrated than native communities and this had advantages in terms of networks and the ability to find employees or raise capital (Levie, 2007; Fairlie and Robb, 2008). Consequently, the higher propensity of immigrants to start businesses was in part a factor of their life cycle; that is, they migrated and therefore entered the population under study at the moment they were most likely to start a business. This suggests that demographic and life-cycle factors were as important as the cultural factors more often cited when immigrant entrepreneurship is studied (Foreman-Peck and Zhou, 2013).

10.5   Internal migration

In addition to international immigration, there was considerable movement within the UK. For example, in 1891 the economically active population of England and Wales included 215,717 people born in Scotland and 281,440 born in Ireland. Furthermore, 38.5 percent of the total economically active population born in England or Wales, 4,621,426, were living in a county different from the one in which they were born. This high degree of mobility was in large part because of the uneven pace of economic development, with patterns of movement recognised as closely associated with the developing economic geography of the country (Pooley and Turnbull, 1998: 149; Goose, 2014: 159–69; Hatton, 2014: 105–7).

Table 10.12 shows the entrepreneurship rates for Irish, Scottish, and English and Welsh internal migrants. It shows that while Scottish and internal migrants from England or Wales had similar rates of business ownership to individuals who did not migrate, the Irish were significantly less entrepreneurial, something reinforced by the results of the model shown in Table 10.7.

Ireland

Why were Irish migrants less entrepreneurial than other internal migrants? Partly it reflects the more transitory nature of much Irish migration to England

Table 10.12 Entrepreneurship rates, internal migrants, 1851–1911

Year	Irish	Scottish	England and Wales Internal	Non-migrants
1851	10.1	15.0	16.0	15.5
1861	8.5	13.4	14.8	14.6
1881	9.9	13.8	13.9	13.9
1891	10.3	12.9	13.9	13.8
1901	9.0	12.6	13.6	13.0
1911	8.8	12.1	12.6	11.1

Source: BBCE database.

and Wales. Many Irish migrants were only temporary residents, and an individual was unlikely to set up a business if they were only going to be in the country for a matter of months.[11] However, it also reflects the place of Irish migrants within British society. Contemporaries reflected on the relative lack of Irish businesses; just before our period Reverend Edward Peach commented that the Irish in Birmingham 'never look for any trade or business; they merely seek to get their living, as their fathers have done, by labour'.[12] John Denvir[13] in his survey of the Irish in Britain found that the situation was a little improved by the end of the century but noted that the entrepreneurial spirit of the Irish had few outlets:

> Irish intellect and Irish courage have, in thousands of cases, brought out people to their proper place in the social scale, but it only too often happens that adverse circumstances drive the great bulk of them to the hardest, the most precarious, and the worst paid employments in the English labour market. The Irish of Liverpool frequently show a remarkable aptitude for dealing, which goes to show that, under the fostering care of a native government, ours would develop into a great commercial people.
>
> (Denvir, 1894: 437)

The Irish population in England and Wales had always been more complex than much commentary focused on the very poorest migrants suggested. Furthermore, as Denvir noted, by the end of the nineteenth century the Irish middle class had grown considerably (Denvir, 1894: 398–9, 416, 440; Belchem, 2006: 129–51; MacRaid, 2011: 57–9). However, business proprietors still remained a comparatively small section of the Irish population, especially when compared to other groups such as the Jewish community in London. Both were predominantly poor communities with small middle classes; however, the Jewish community reacted to this precariousness, as we have seen, by starting businesses, while the Irish in England and Wales frequently remained in a range of unskilled and semi-skilled occupations. Partly this reflected the fact that Irish men and women found it easier to enter the wage labour market. Irish individuals were not restricted to precarious occupations in a limited number of sectors like Jewish immigrants. Thus, the Irish in London could find employment in a wider range of occupations than immigrants from the Russian Empire.[14] For example, of 125 I–CeM occupation categories that had 50 or more Irish people in them in 1901, only 61 categories had 50 or more Russian immigrants. The Irish managed to access a number of key London occupations that remained closed to Jewish immigrants, such as clerical work, dock labouring and the building trades. These occupations were not well paid, but the ability of Irish migrants to access them does suggest that the kind of barriers to wage labour which prompted immigrants of most other nationalities to start businesses were not as severe for the Irish population.

Additionally, Irish workers were less likely to work for Irish business proprietors. For example, in 1901 Russian workers made up 21 percent of the workers employed in tailoring in London while 30 percent of all tailoring business proprietors were immigrants from the Russian Empire. There are no such industries in which the Irish dominated both the workforce and the employer population. If there is a path dependency element to immigrant entrepreneurship, if immigrants starting businesses were more likely to start them in occupations which fellow immigrants had previously succeeded in, then the Irish were at a disadvantage. Furthermore, much Irish employment was in occupations in which there was little possibility for social mobility within the occupation: labouring and domestic service (which offered few employer openings) or coal mining and dock work (which generally required large capital assets). The capital, skills and contacts required to set up your own business could be developed while working for an East End tailor, but not when working on a London dock or in a coal mine in North-East England. This is seen at an aggregate level in Table 10.13 where the occupational structure of the Irish, Scottish, and English and Welsh population in 1901 is shown, along with the entrepreneurship rates for each sector. Many of the sectors characterised by high proportions of business proprietors had relatively few Irish-born individuals, although the Irish in those sectors were broadly as entrepreneurial as people born in England and Wales (with the exception of farming and estate work). However, the most important sectors for Irish employment (manufacturing, transport, domestic service and labouring) were characterised by little or no Irish business ownership. Those sectors provided sufficiently regular employment and income to ensure that Irish workers had no need to start businesses. This suggests that the lack of entrepreneurship shown by Irish migrants in this period was caused by their socio-economic position rather than any predisposition against business proprietorship, much as Denvir argued in the 1890s.

Scotland

Migrants from Scotland had slightly lower levels of entrepreneurial activity compared to people born in England and Wales. Scottish migration to England is surprisingly understudied and, consequently, explaining their actions is difficult

(McCarthy, 2002: 511). However, the occupational data in I-CeM allow some conclusions to be made. Table 10.13 shows that Scottish migrants were over-represented in manufacturing, but that Scottish people involved in manufacturing were less likely to be business proprietors than the English and Welsh. This heavy concentration in a sector characterised by low levels of entrepreneurship is partly explained by the large size of many of the employers. This is responsible for most of the small difference in overall entrepreneurship ratios between the Scottish migrants and the English- and Welsh-born population. This fits with the nascent history of Scottish migration to England which argues that much

Table 10.13 Occupational structure of Irish and Scottish migrants, 1901

Sector	England and Wales			Ireland			Scotland		
	Total	% of Total	Ent Ratio	Total	% of Total	Ent Ratio	Total	% of Total	Ent Ratio
Farming and estate work	1,142,242	8.8	23.3	12,739.45	4.9	7.2	10,311.03	4.0	27.8
Mining and quarrying	712,671.3	5.5	1.2	12,534.24	4.8	0.8	7,632.187	3.0	2.4
Construction	1,016,192	7.9	11.6	19,235.38	7.4	4.1	17,855.95	6.9	9.9
Manufacturing	2,887,127	22.3	5.1	49,890.35	19.1	3.0	77,205.83	29.9	3.9
Maker–dealing	1,054,656	8.2	30.9	15,227.16	5.8	26.2	15,660.11	6.1	31.6
Retailing	496,937.5	3.8	35.5	9,461.936	3.6	46.7	11,865.21	4.6	40.9
Transport	991,735.7	7.7	4.2	30,170.38	11.5	1.5	16,954.68	6.6	3.5
Professional and business services	512,182.3	4.0	10.5	7,216.485	2.8	12.7	14,708.63	5.7	13.3
Personal services	707,150.4	5.5	23.1	20,087.79	7.7	21.8	17,250.96	6.7	26.8
Agricultural processing and dealing	104,332.6	0.8	19.4	1,539.755	0.6	12.0	1,747.18	0.7	22.2
Food sales	575,396.9	4.5	40.3	5,856.233	2.2	49.7	8,544.339	3.3	40.6
Refreshment	294,957.3	2.3	43.4	6,202.747	2.4	37.8	5,516.506	2.1	43.1
Finance and commerce	159,807.8	1.2	16.3	2,525.515	1.0	25.6	5,880.467	2.3	25.2
Public administration, military and clergy	372,901	2.9	n/a	21,829	8.3	n/a	14,672	5.7	n/a
Domestic service	1,473,275	11.4	n/a	27,145	10.4	n/a	26,260	10.2	n/a
Undefined general labourers	419,447	3.2	n/a	19,836	7.6	n/a	5,812	2.3	n/a

Source: BBCE database.

of it was driven by skilled workers who could access higher wages in England than in Scotland (Devine, 2011: 104–5; Burnett et al., 2012: 79, 84). However, the industrial nature of Scottish migration should not be overstated. The 14 percent employed in professional, business and personal services, and finance or the 5 percent employed in retail were smaller but still important aspects of the Scottish migrant community; these exhibited higher rates of business proprietorship than the English- and Welsh-born population. Again, as with immigrants and the Irish cases discussed above, the level of entrepreneurship demonstrated by the group in question was a function of their socio-economic position, rather than inherent cultural characteristics of migrant populations. This could take the form of class differences, as in the contrasting entrepreneurial activity of Irish and Scottish migrants, or occupational differences, as in the different behaviours of Irish migrants and Jewish immigrants. As a result the Scottish entrepreneurship rates had dual characteristics: some high, as in the professional and business services areas, others lower, notably manufacturing.

England and Wales internal migration

There was considerable internal migration in nineteenth-century England and Wales. Table 10.14 shows the numbers in each census living in counties different from those of their birth. This is an imperfect measure of migration as moves from Cumbria to Devon appear as identical to moves of a few miles across a county border, such as someone moving four miles from Hinckley in Leicestershire to Nuneaton in Warwickshire; or in London people changed county by moving very short distances; for example, moving from Southwark to Whitechapel appears as a migrant. It also gives no idea of movement within counties. This is problematic as most movement in nineteenth-century England and Wales was short-distance migration, apart from movement to London and to some industrial areas for short periods (such as to South Wales in the second half of the nineteenth century) (Pooley and Turnbull, 1998: 3, 12–13; Friedlander

Table 10.14 Internal migration of English- and Welsh-born population, 1851–1911

Census Year	Total Population		Business Proprietors	
	% Non-Migrant	% Migrant	% Non-Migrant	% Migrant
1851	70.1	29.9	65.0	35.0
1861	68.7	31.3	64.1	35.9
1881	69.7	30.3	64.5	35.5
1891	67.2	32.8	58.2	41.8
1901	67.4	32.6	57.6	42.4
1911	66.6	33.4	56.1	43.9

Source: BBCE database.

Note: Visitors have been removed from the population.

and Roshier, 1966: 252–5, 262–3; Day, 2015). However, it is a useful indicator of migration, even if it underestimates total internal migration.

Table 10.14 shows a slow rise in migration across this period, something mirrored by the proportion of business proprietors who were living in a county different to that in which they were born. Although modern studies often find that businesses are more likely to be run by individuals born in that location, and that such local-run businesses are more successful than those run by migrants (Michelacci and Silva, 2007; Dahl and Sorenson, 2012; Figueiredo et al., 2002), the situation in nineteenth-century England and Wales was somewhat different. The proportion of businesses run by internal migrants is lower than that run by non-migrants; however, the entrepreneurship ratios given in Table 10.12 suggest that an internal migrant, consistently across all years, was slightly more likely to have been a business proprietor than someone living in their county of their birth. Consequently, Table 10.14 reflects the general distribution of internal migrants. However, the patterns varied strongly for different locations. For example, in 1901 the percentage of internal migrant businesses ranged from 60 percent in Essex to 10 percent in Cornwall.[15]

Table 10.14 shows that migrants were more likely to be business proprietors than migrants in the general population on average, for all years. There was also a strong correlation between the share of the county's population that were internal migrants and the share of the businesses in that county run by internal migrants, as Figure 10.1 shows. However, the variation between places in this figure shows that on average internal migration levels were almost the same in all counties. The two exceptions in 1901 were Carmarthenshire and

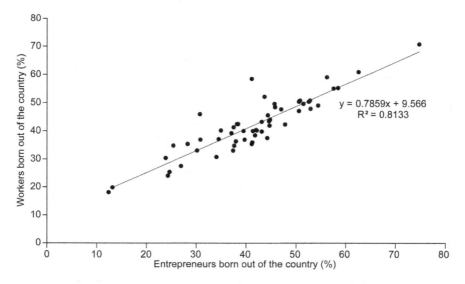

Figure 10.1 County internal migrant populations and business proprietors, 1901

Source: BBCE database.

Radnorshire where the proportion of the workforce born outside the county was not reflected in the proportion of internal-migrant business proprietors. In both counties internal migrants were excluded from the main source of entrepreneurial activity: farming. In Radnorshire, 61.5 percent of Radnorshire-born entrepreneurs were in farming, compared to 39.7 percent of those business proprietors born outside of the county; for Carmarthenshire the figures were 46.8 percent and 19.6 percent for non-migrants and migrants respectively. Consequently, fewer migrants were entrepreneurs and more worked as waged labour in manufacturing and transport, sectors with lower entrepreneurship rates.

The local bias in entrepreneurship in modern economies is expected from theory: entrepreneurs usually have greater start-up and transfer costs than workers. In modern analyses it has also been attributed to local business proprietors' greater local knowledge which allows them to more easily identify market opportunities, raise capital and secure labour (Michelacci and Silva, 2007: 627–30; Dahl and Sorenson, 2012: 1059–61; Figueiredo et al., 2002: 356). However, the historical situation seems different with internal migrants looking as entrepreneurial as non-migrants, except in Carmarthenshire and Radnorshire. This holds even when we break migrants down into recent arrivals and long-term residents. Thus, in 1901 the age-standardized entrepreneurship rate of internal migrants with a child younger than age 3 born in the county in which they are living was 12.4 compared to 13.0 for non-migrants; for long-term migrants (those with children born in the county of residence aged between 10 and 15) the entrepreneurship rate was 13.4 (with rates standardized so that the recent migrants and long-term resident migrants had the same age structure as the non-migrant population).

The difference between the historical and the contemporary situation relates, in part, to the changing role of financial institutions in driving business creation. Most small and medium-sized firms of the nineteenth and early twentieth centuries still required little capital, and much of their financing was provided through familial contacts which need not be local, rather than formal financial institutions (Çrouzet, 1982; Davidoff, 2012: 57–65). Even if local firms had possessed an advantage in terms of access to finance in the first part of this period, this disappeared towards the end of the century. By the early twentieth century local and regional banks had almost completely disappeared and most were joint stock national banks with local branches throughout the country (Cottrell, 1980, 2004). The managers of these branches usually had less discretion over the size of loans and amount of security required; consequently, the provision of finance became more regular and there was less room for local knowledge and reputation to affect the ability of an individual to obtain industrial finance (Carnevali, 2005: 16–17; Cottrell, 1980: 194–8; Capie and Collins, 1996: 36–7).

The situation in the labour market was more complex. There were some occupations dominated by migrant labour and migrant employers. For example, the professions were characterised by highly mobile workforces and employers; in 1911: 67 percent of English and Welsh entrepreneurs and 60 percent of workers in journalism were internal migrants; and for schoolteachers 61 percent

Table 10.15 Entrepreneurship rates of internal migrants by sector, 1901

Occupation Category	Internal Migrant	Non-Migrant
Farming and estate work	22.8	23.5
Mining and quarrying	1.3	1.1
Construction	11.5	11.7
Manufacturing	6.4	4.5
Maker-dealing	34.4	29.2
Retailing	36.2	35.1
Transport	3.6	4.5
Professional and business services	12.7	8.9
Personal services	23.3	22.8
Agricultural processing and dealing	20.0	19.1
Food sales	41.2	39.8
Refreshment	45.2	41.9
Finance and commerce	19.5	14.0

Source: BBCE database.

of employers and own-account proprietors, and 48 percent of workers were internal migrants in 1911. Other occupations had a high proportion of internal migrant business proprietors but the migrant share of the workforce was low; for example, 46 percent of business proprietors making umbrellas in 1911 were internal migrants, but only 21 percent of the workforce were living in counties different from those of their birth. Yet other industries had low proportions of both internal migrant workers and business proprietors, such as japanning where, in 1911, 16 percent of entrepreneurs and 23 percent of workers were internal migrants. Table 10.15 shows the entrepreneurship rates of internal migrants and non-migrants. In most sectors the rates were similar. However, internal migrants were more likely than non-migrants to start businesses in maker-dealing, professional and business services, refreshment and finance and commerce. In no sectors were non-migrants especially more entrepreneurial than internal migrants. These sector-specific rates and the overall entrepreneurship rate for internal migrants suggest that locals had no advantage in terms of securing a workforce, otherwise their entrepreneurship rates would have been significantly lower (as found in modern Italy; Michelacci and Silva, 2007: 630).

10.6   Conclusion

This chapter has discussed the patterns of business proprietorship among four different sets of migrants. In each case their business activities reflected their socio-economic context. Scottish and English and Welsh migrants generally exhibited similar rates of entrepreneurship compared to the non-migrant population in large part because their position in the labour market in England

and Wales was very similar to that of non-migrant English- and Welsh-born individuals. All three groups had similar options available to them; they could enter the waged labour market with relative ease, and their tendency to operate businesses was more reflective of their life-cycle position, most notably their marital status, than any cultural tendency. International immigrants and Irish migrants occupied a more disadvantaged socio-economic position than the other migrant groups; however, their entrepreneurial activity was markedly different. Again, this difference related to their position in relation to the labour market. International immigrants tended to struggle to access the waged labour market and when they did it was often in low-paid low-status occupations. Yet some of these occupations offered substantial opportunities for entrepreneurship, most notably tailoring, leading to precarious employment but also abundant entrepreneurship. It is notable that many of the nationalities with long-standing communities in England and Wales had entrepreneurship rates similar to those of the non-migrant population, for example, the Dutch and the Nordic and Scandinavian nations which constituted the 'Northern Europe' category discussed above. In contrast, the Irish population, while similarly precariously situated in the nineteenth-century social order, exhibited low levels of business proprietorship. In their case, the Irish tended to have similarly low-waged and low-status occupations, but in industries in which there was little opportunity for small-scale entry-level entrepreneurship, notably mining and transport, or which were inherently worker-only, as for domestic service and labouring. The nineteenth-century labour market saw relatively little horizontal mobility between trades, and so the Irish population had far fewer opportunities for starting and running businesses (Williamson, 1990: 148).

Notes

1 TNA, Manuscript Census Enumerators Book (CEB), 1881 Census of England and Wales, *TNA*, RG11/5096/95/52.
2 H.W.B., 'The "Alien" Coster', *Pall Mall Gazette*, 24 Mar. 1902, 1–2; *Royal Commission on Alien Immigration. Minutes of Evidence taken before the Royal Commission on Alien Immigration, Vol. II, PP*, IX (1903), 259–65, 719–21.
3 *Census of England and Wales, 1891, Vol. IV, General Report, with summary tables and appendices, PP*, CVI (1893–4), 6–5.
4 TNA, Manuscript CEB, 1891 Census of England and Wales, RG12/4229/51/17; Manuscript CEB, 1901 Census of England and Wales, RG13/330/153/33.
5 TNA, Duplicate Certificates of Naturalisation, HO334/25/9440, Nathan Shonman, 19 Jan. 1897.
6 Germany, Russian Empire, France, British Empire, Italy, United States, South America, Northern Europe, Southern Europe, Central Europe and the Balkans, Central America and the Caribbean, Africa, the Middle East, and Asia and the Pacific.
7 *Census of England and Wales, 1911, Vol. IX, Birthplaces of persons enumerated in administrative counties, county boroughs, &c., and ages and occupations of foreigners, PP*, LXXVIII (1913), xv.
8 *Royal Commission on Alien Immigration, Vol. II*, 693–4.
9 The 10 most common occupations in London in other census years varied somewhat, but not significantly.
10 In 1891, 29.5 percent of all bakery businesses in London were owned by immigrants and 25.2 percent of tailoring enterprises.

11 *Report and Tables Relating to Migratory Agricultural Labourers in Ireland, 1900, PP*, CI (1900), 12–13, 21.
12 *Royal Commission on the Condition of the Poorer Classes in Ireland, Appendix G. Report on the State of the Irish Poor in Great Britain, PP*, XXXIV (1836), 475.
13 Denvir and brother Bernard were notable Liverpool-Irish entrepreneurs, running a publishing business which produced, among other things, a trade directory listing Irish-owned businesses; see Belchem, 2007: 48–9.
14 The census does not identify people by religion; however, the majority of migrants from the Russian Empire can be assumed to have been Jewish, see Godley, 2001: 29–30.
15 Surrey has a higher percentage of internal migrant business proprietors at 73 percent; however, this is misleading as the London problem noted above inflates the population of internal migrants.

11 Portfolio businesses

11.1 Introduction

Portfolio businesses are those that have different business activities with different earning streams under the same proprietor(s). These may be distinct from each other, such as someone running a textile factory and a farm, or closely related, such as a dairy farmer who is also a milk seller. It is important for studies of entrepreneurship to understand how business proprietors assembled portfolios, since this gives insight into adaptation to different sector and market opportunities, as well as how this interacted with the personal and household strategies of the proprietors themselves and any other partners or families involved. Entrepreneurs' choices to start a second or further enterprise was strongly influenced by their personal, economic and geographical context. As discussed in Chapter 6, portfolios could relate to family life cycle or to responses to changed opportunities or to changes in the application of resources. They could be used to hedge against risk, to respond to opportunities for diversification, to facilitate transitions between different stages of the business or the family life cycle or to respond to changing economic conditions. However, such possibilities were not available to all entrepreneurs in all sectors. Starting a second business required time, capital and labour in addition to that already used in an entrepreneur's first business. The choice to start an additional concern was therefore limited by the extent to which an individual's original business offered opportunities to diversify or constrained their ability to access the required additional resources. This was affected by sector, gender, location and other factors. It was also affected in many cases by family circumstances.

As recognised in literature on modern businesses, for many small as well as some large enterprises, the firm is not the only unit of analysis: a firm can also be analysed as the composite of all the different business activities of the business proprietor and their spouse, associates and kin (see e.g. Rosa and Scott, 1999; Carter and Ram, 2003; Alsos et al., 2003; Rønning and Kovereid, 2006). If listed under one individual in their census response, such composites form a portfolio of activities as defined here. Despite their potential significance, portfolio businesses have been given little attention in historical literature, and where referred to have been included under the catch-all term 'by-employment' (Keibek and

Shaw-Taylor, 2013) or 'dual occupations' (Bellamy, 1978). But these terms only give a partial picture since they emphasise worker occupations. Similarly, more modern research on portfolio businesses often combines employers and employees under terms such as 'double jobholding', 'moonlighters', 'weekend workers', 'variable-day workers', 'rotating employment', 'irregular employment' and 'part-time workers' (see e.g. Alden, 1977). Research on farmers, because it has often been the most frequent sector to develop portfolios, has more directly addressed employer business diversification (see Harrison, 1975; OECD, 1978; and Fuller, 1983 for some early contributions). But even in farming, portfolios are often included in 'pluriactivity' (adopted from the French *pluriactivité*) (Carter, 2001), whether entrepreneurial or waged, and hence akin to by-employment (Evans and Ilbery, 1993; Niemelä and Häkkinen, 2014).

This chapter focuses on the employer and own-account multiple business activities in order to draw some conclusions about business strategy in the past. It first assesses what we know about nineteenth-century portfolio businesses from previous research. It then presents the methodology for extraction of portfolio businesses from the BBCE database. The main body of the chapter then presents estimates of the population of portfolio businesses, their sector and inter-sector composition, and their relationship to business sector, gender and family structure.

11.2   Existing literature on nineteenth-century portfolio businesses

There has been little previous research on nineteenth-century portfolio businesses, and nothing which allows a large-scale assessment of their relative importance within the business population. Crossick (1984: 62–3; Crossick and Haupt, 1995: 38–42) has argued that much of this neglect arises because of the difficulties of classifying the emerging 'petty bourgeoisie': they were neither waged labour nor great capitalists, causing particular neglect and misclassification of small-scale farmers (Reed, 1986: 89–91). For the 1851 census there was a published table of the portfolios of 'farmers and occupiers of land who returned themselves as engaged in other pursuits besides farming'.[1] This is the first and only estimate of the phenomenon in the nineteenth-century censuses. Re-analysing this table to align with the definitions used later in the chapter gives an estimate of 6.95 percent of farmers with multiple activities, though this included portfolios as workers as well as business proprietors. The four most frequent categories in rank order, accounting for 42 percent of portfolios of farmers, were beer seller, miller, innkeeper, and butcher; the next six occupations were carpenter, grocer, woollen cloth manufacturer, shoemaker, carrier and maltster (accounting for a further 23 percent). This provides a useful benchmark, but to make progress requires use of the original CEBs.

There have been pilot studies using the CEBs. The most valuable, by Woollard (2004), took a sample of three counties (Cornwall, Derbyshire and Westmorland) and four occupational categories (grocers, dentists, wheelwrights and auctioneers) in 1851 and 1881. He found that, in 1851, 9.5 percent of grocers had multiple occupations, 8 percent of dentists, 4 percent of wheelwrights and 7 percent of auctioneers. By 1881, these numbers had risen to 13 percent for grocers, 26 percent for dentists, 22 percent for wheelwrights, and 13 percent for auctioneers (re-calculated from Woollard, 2004: Tables 1–6). Woollard did not distinguish between workers and entrepreneurs, and included all household occupants and institutions, but his figures are useful indicators, and his method guides our approach. Similar ranges were also found by Sunderland (2007: Tables 9.5–9.7) using trade directory listings as a source for Bolton (Lancs.). For the period 1829–61 he quotes 15.2 percent of business owners had multiple occupations across related sectors, and 4 percent across unrelated sectors. This had remained similar since the 1780s. Engineering and metals, retail and consumer services and other manufactures were the most diversified into related sectors (each over 20 percent of businesses); the least were textiles (9.6 percent), bleachers (6 percent) and professionals (1 percent). The most frequent unrelated sector combinations were retailing with manufacturing, which echoes the Report of the Census Committee (1890) about the difficulties of separating manufacturers and dealers.[2]

For farmers in the 1870s–90s, Bellerby (1956), using information in the Royal Commissions of 1879–82, and 1895–97,[3] noted that 'part time farming' was extremely common, with supplementary occupations including fishing, retailing, road haulage and carrying, wholesale distribution, factory work and agricultural work on other farms. The 1895–97 Commission argued that this was a useful support to living standards of agricultural labourers. However, Crossick and Haupt (1995: 57) comment that most farming as a secondary activity was carried out by artisans and small business proprietors rather than labourers. Davies' (1909) survey found that over one-third of farmers had another occupation in the early 1900s in Corsley, Wiltshire. Similarly, in a review of the discrepancy between the great number of farmers and the small number of farm holdings in the 1851 and 1871 censuses, Reed (1986: 86–8) summarises case studies and contemporary accounts confirming the widespread development of ancillary occupations to farming.

Other case studies indicate differences in local opportunities. A pilot study for this book by Radicic et al. (2017) for 1881 using I-CeM data confirms that location was a key factor influencing portfolios in farming. It also confirms Winstanley's (1996) case study using contrasted industrial and non-industrial Lancashire districts for 1881, demonstrates that farmers close to urban settlements developed a wider range of opportunities, often gaining their principal income from selling their produce to the growing workforce in industrial textile districts: especially poultry, eggs and milk. They were not wholesalers to an advanced system of distribution, but primarily 'producer-retailers . . . able to secure profits absorbed elsewhere by wholesalers and retailers' (Ibid., 173). Other opportunities available from close urban centres allowed secondary farm occupations in beer retailing, innkeeping or carting. These additional occupations generally decreased with farm size: from 36 percent for farms of 1–5 acres to

6 percent for those of over 50 acres in non-industrial districts, but in industrial districts 70 percent for farms of 1–5 acres, decreasing to 21 percent for those over 50 acres (Ibid.: Table 7). Much of this diversification was possible through family to support marketing and retailing thus increasing (Ibid.: Table 9).

Studies by Hallas (1990; 1999: 54–5) suggest that portfolios were more prevalent in northern and more marginal agricultural areas, especially in mining areas. Nenadic et al. (1992) and Nenadic (1993) using directories and census entries identified multiple enterprises in Edinburgh in dealing, artisan, catering and carrying trades. She suggested that these were predominantly responses to changing market conditions, in part related to family development. At a smaller scale, using biographical material, Davidoff and Hall (1997: 200–19, 240–65; Davidoff, 2012) demonstrate that family and kinship in family businesses encouraged portfolio business development to meet the needs of offspring for business opportunities, with women often playing a pivotal role. In the studies by Anderson (1971), Malcolmson (1981: 23, 39) and Pahl (1984: 46–52), such examples covered a wide range of the population in the nineteenth and early mid-twentieth centuries, indicating widespread portfolio businesses for certain types of activity, and a high level of dual occupations more generally.

Samuel (1975, 1977) classified the disparate portfolio experiences he recorded into three broad types: (i) survival strategies where workers 'do a bit on the side' (Hill, 1982); (ii) farmers who had developed some diversified retailing or agricultural processing; and (iii) development of businesses in new directions, often as a means to share activities across different household members. An additional category can be added, perhaps the most lucrative multiple businesses: (iv) those which became the subject of individual business histories, major biographies and entries in the *Dictionary of Business Biography* and the *Dictionary of National Biography*. By using landed wealth, or the proceeds from large-scale manufacturing or commerce, major railway and canal undertakings, and successful financial services and speculation, diversification often occurred into new fields including building and land development, entrepreneurial projects overseas, as well as more mundane investment of wealth into farms and estates either as a passive investment or as part of a residential lifestyle decision (see e.g. Jeremy, 1984; Payne, 1988; Miles, 1999; Rubinstein, 2006; Nicholas, 2000, 2000). This also frequently included directors with portfolios of companies.

It is clear from the nature of these different portfolios that few in category (i) are relevant since most were by-employed workers. Benson (1983) refers to these as 'penny capitalists' among the working classes who had minor self-employments; usually spare time, often occasional or seasonal. Pahl (1984: 46) termed such by-employment 'occupational easement', where earnings were otherwise often low or insufficient. On the other hand, categories (ii) and (iii) are important and should be relatively fully recorded in the census, albeit with the usual proviso regarding the recording of female economic activity. Category (iv) is likely to be patchily returned. However, multiple activities of large proprietors will be captured in employer census returns where it is non-corporate; and we restrict analysis in this chapter to such activity.

The data from I–CeM can be compared with more modern estimates. Harrison (1975) provides one of the earliest and widest studies, finding in 1969 that over 30 percent of business partners on farms had other occupations, 55 percent of which were full time, indicating that farming was a secondary business. Indeed, 80 percent of farmer portfolios provided equal or greater earnings than farming (see also Gasson, 1967). Carter's (2001) study of Cambridgeshire farmers found that younger farmers were more likely to be portfolio owners; nonportfolio farmers tended to operate smaller farms (less than 100 hectares), while portfolio farmers operated larger farms (see also Grande et al., 2011). However, in a larger-scale study Gasson (1967) found multiple activities highest for farms under 10 hectares (25 acres) and decreased with farm size over 50 hectares (124 acres). There was enormous diversity of these portfolios 'from peer to roadman, from professor to domestic cleaner' (Gasson, 1983: 46). OECD (1978) and EC (1981) recognised this pattern as long-standing across advanced economies.

11.3 Data and extraction method

This chapter focuses on the non-corporate portfolios evident from the census; corporate director portfolios are assessed in other publications. However, it is important to note that portfolios were more common for directors than for other entrepreneurs: almost 40 percent were involved in more than one company in 1881, and 33 percent in 1911. About half had two directorships, with another 20 percent involved in three companies. Directorships in more than five companies was rare, but became slightly more common over time: while only 8 percent of the portfolio directors had more than five directorships in 1881, this increased to 12 percent in 1911. One director held 40 directorships, these were almost all in mines in South Africa.

In the 1851–1901 censuses respondents were asked, if they had more than one occupation, to state them in order of their significance. For example, the 1891 CEB instructions stated, 'A person following several distinct occupations must state each of them in the order of their importance'. Similar instructions were given in other census years; however, in 1911 this instruction was changed to 'state that by which living is mainly earned' and not list other activities, which may create a discontinuity with earlier censuses. However, 1911 is very different in our database in having the original household responses rather than CEBs. As a result, we find that, despite the instruction, it includes many portfolios, and can be analysed essentially in the same way as the earlier censuses. This differs from censuses after 1911 where only published tables are available, so that if individual responses included portfolios we cannot retrieve them.

The GRO when tabulating the occupational information adopted a somewhat different approach to portfolio importance to that suggested by the household instructions. The 1881 census report stated that when coding multiple occupations 'a mechanical handicraft or construction occupations should invariably be preferred to a mere shop-keeping occupation'; 'that, if one of the diverse occupations seemed of more importance than the others, it should be selected' and that if neither of these criteria applied they would assume people gave the occupation they primarily earned a living from first. There were further considerations regarding certain occupations, thus clergymen with additional occupations, such as teaching, were usually tabulated as their second occupation because 'the total number of clergy could be ascertained by other means'; similarly, MPs who gave an additional occupation were coded to that rather than as MPs. These criteria were followed in the other census years.[4] It is also clear that published tables gave precedence to farming in most cases over other occupations (Higgs, 2015). The coding instruction to clerks was dropped in 1911 because the information on additional occupations was not used in tabulations.[5] This indicates that a mix of income, 'rank' and social status influenced GRO tabulations, while concern with 'mechanical' or 'construction occupations' over retail reflected the long-standing preoccupation with the effects of industrial work on health (Higgs, 1991). However, respondents had no knowledge of Census Office instructions to clerks. Hence, we can assume that the instruction to householders to state occupations in order of importance was followed.

For the 1851–81 censuses the number of extracted employers and masters was small enough to check all by hand to identify any portfolios that failed to use one of these terms; for example, 'baker farmer employing ten men'. Unfortunately, the numbers involved in the 1891–1911 census meant this was impossible and the string searches had to suffice. This developed from the method used by Woollard (2004). Having extracted the entrepreneurs in each year, their occupational strings were searched for any that included 'and', '&', 'also' and '+'. These strings were then divided into their component parts using the position of the word or symbol to indicate multiple activities; for example, 'grocer and baker' was divided into two parts: 'grocer' and 'baker'. The individual parts were then given occupation codes. At this stage three types of false positives were removed. First, those we define as semantically or functionally indistinguishable. For example, 'carpenter and joiner' or 'boot and shoe maker' were extracted as potential portfolio occupations but we treat them as functionally the same and not genuine portfolios. Second, individuals with a non-economic second occupation, such as 'Farmer and Justice of the Peace', were removed from business portfolios. This means that we classify the very numerous second occupations of clergy differently from GRO publications: they were clerics, not business proprietors, whereas in many cases GRO would table them according to their second business. Third, additional occupations were excluded if non-entrepreneurial, such as 'grocer and postmaster' (where the latter is assumed an employee status in this book). The distinction between entrepreneur and non-entrepreneur categories is the same as used throughout this book, as defined in Chapter 3 (Tables 3.3 and 3.4), WP 3 and the download accompanying WP 5.

The genuine multiple business strings were then coded to their portfolio components; thus, 'grocer and baker' has two occupational codes, 'farmer, miller and innkeeper' has three, and so on. A final correction was made by hand to re-order portfolios so that the presumed primary business was listed first; this as far as possible matches the instruction in the census, as noted above. This primarily aimed at correcting I-CeM miscoding that had picked up only part of a string which was a secondary activity. But it also corrected obvious ordering errors. These were chiefly portfolio businesses that were coded to farming irrespective of the size of their other business or the order given in the returns; for example, 'flax spinner and farmer of 350 acres employing 400 workpeople' was coded in I-CeM as a farmer even though spinning was clearly the major business.

Since the coding of portfolios was only undertaken on identified entrepreneurs, the analysis in this chapter is carried out on a more limited selection of data than used in other chapters. Because of concern to reflect *actual* census responses, for 1851–81 only the extracted Groups 1–6 as defined in Chapter 4 are analysed, not the reconstructed employers and own-account proprietors. This means that tabulations make no attempt to identify portfolios among non-respondents, except for farmers where all could be defined as employers or own-account proprietors using extraction groups (Montebruno et al., 2019a). For 1891–1911 the *unweighted* data on employers and own-account proprietors are used because the weighting process did not take multiple occupations into account. Thus, the groups analysed differ in definition and scale between 1851–81 and 1891–1911 and (except for farmers) between this chapter and Chapters 7–10.

11.4 Portfolio businesses: numbers and trends

Table 11.1 gives the total number of identified portfolio businesses in each census year and as a percentage of the appropriate population of entrepreneurs. While the change in census practice and our extraction strategy makes comparison across the whole period difficult, it is clear that the proportion of entrepreneurs with portfolio business activities was fairly constant within each period. The overall proportions fell somewhat between 1851 and 1881, but this fall was mainly driven by a decline in the number of own-account proprietors running portfolio businesses and is likely to be an effect of the imperfect extraction of own-account proprietors in the earlier censuses. Between 1891 and 1911 the portfolio proportion for employers and own-account proprietors both increased. The increase for employers happened first, before own-account; however, in both cases the change was small.

The drop in portfolio entrepreneurs in the first period was caused mainly by a significant decrease in the number of own-account portfolio farmers, from 4,795 in 1861 to 2,341 in 1881. This was the opposite of the overall change in own-account farm numbers which increased over this period. Although we should not go too far in interpreting trends, given data uncertainties, it is likely that the agricultural depression forced the more precarious farmers to either leave agriculture or to move to wage labour rather than diversifying their business. It suggests that whilst the agricultural depression after 1873 stimulated a switch from employers to using only their own labour as own account (and perhaps undeclared use of their spouse and families), they were less able to operate additional activities. Thus, contrary to literature that suggests entrepreneurs

Table 11.1 Portfolio entrepreneurs, 1851–1911; number and percentage of all extracted entrepreneurs

The extreme for 1861 is driven by a big drop in number of own-account farmers and also partly a drop in extracted own account, which fell from 83,075 in 1851 to 70,153 in 1861 before rising to 101,895 in 1881. This is likely to result from variations in census recording and transcription thoroughness.

	Employer	Own Account	Total	% All Employers	% Own Account	% Total
1851	20,760 (17,492)	7,798	28,558	9.4 (8.7)	9.4	9.8
1861	21,859 (17,156)	9,313	31,172	9.0 (9.7)	13.3	10.0
1871	17,685 (12,988)	5,531	23,216	10.0 (9.2)	6.2	8.7
1881	22,418 (18,918)	6,551	28,969	9.4 (10.3)	6.4	8.5
1891	60,193	60,074	120,267	11.1	6.2	8.0
1901	69,638	72,456	142,094	12.6	6.4	8.4
1911	82,681	73,979	156,660	12.1	7.4	9.3

Source: BBCE database.

Note: Figures for employers with reported employee numbers in brackets for 1851–81; provided here as a stricter comparative sample.

diversify under economic stress, in farming at this time under severe price pressures many instead had to focus more effort on their main farm activity.

The slight increase in the proportion of own-account portfolios between 1901 and 1911 was driven less by expansion of portfolios and more by the decrease in the overall number of own-account businesses in that period. This suggests that own-account portfolio businesses were better able to cope with the pressures that forced many other own-account proprietors out of business in the first decade of the twentieth century (as indicated in Chapter 4), in contrast to farmers in the 1870s and 1880s.

The trends in rates of portfolio activities are shown in Figure 11.1. Although complex, they follow a different pattern to the trends in rates of entrepreneurship discussed in Chapter 4. The bases used for the two rate calculations differ in size because of the different data comparators; for this reason, the own-account rates for 1851–81 in Table 11.1 are not used in Figure 11.1. The figure shows that whereas the total rate of entrepreneurship follows a generally downward trend over the period (mainly as a result of increasing worker numbers), within this the proportion of portfolios showed at first a slight decline and then an increase. Similarly, for employers the rate of entrepreneurship generally declined, but the proportion with portfolios generally increased.

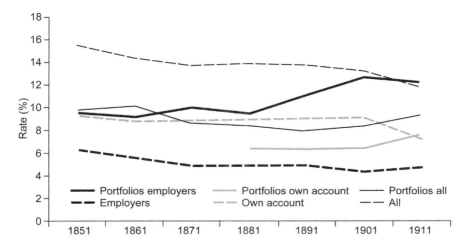

Figure 11.1 Rates of portfolio entrepreneurship (Table 11.1) compared to total rates of entrepreneurship (Table 4.1), 1851–1911

Source: BBCE database.

For own account, the proportion of portfolios and the rate of entrepreneurship are similar to each other 1891–1901, but show a marked divergence for 1911 when own-account entrepreneurship declined, but the portfolio proportion continued the increasing trend begun in 1891. The end of the 'age entrepreneurship' noted earlier thus seems to have been accompanied by pressures to diversify or extend businesses to maintain viability, and this was a similar trend for employers and own account alike. Although the different way of recording portfolios in 1911 (from householders' responses rather than the CEBs) may influence this trend (perhaps exaggerating own-account portfolios in 1911), the fact that the upward trend in portfolio rates began in 1891 indicates that the trend was probably real.

It is also important to see how the experiences of farm and non-farm businesses differed. Apart from the drop in the number of own-account portfolio farmers, the balance between farm and non-farm portfolio employers was fairly stable over 1851–81. However, over 1891–1911 the two groups diverged: farmer portfolios declined and non-farm portfolios increased, as Table 11.2 shows. The exception was 1871 because of missing data, as discussed in Chapter 3, rather than real change. Some of the decrease seen in Table 11.2 was caused by the general decline in farming: in 1891, 23.5 percent of all employers and 6.3 percent of all own-account proprietors were farmers; by 1911 these numbers had fallen slightly to 20.3 percent and 6.2 percent (in 1901 the own account was 5.9 percent). However, between 1891 and 1911 the proportion of farmers among the portfolio employers and own-account proprietors fell more sharply.

Table 11.2 Farm and non-farm portfolio entrepreneurs, 1851–1911; percentages in brackets

	Farm Employer	Non-Farm Employer	Farm Own Account	Non-Farm Own Account
1851	3,288 (15.8)	17,472 (84.2)	2,704 (34.7)	5,094 (65.3)
	2,353 (13.5)	*15,139 (86.5)*		
1861	3,361 (15.4)	18,498 (84.6)	4,795 (51.5)	4,518 (48.5)
	2,253 (13.1)	*14,903 (86.9)*		
1871	4,295 (24.3)	13,390 (75.7)	0 (0.0)	5,531 (100.0)
	1,800 (13.9)	*11,188 (86.1)*		
1881	3,372 (15.0)	19,046 (85.0)	2,341 (35.7)	4,210 (64.3)
	2,453 (13.0)	*16,465 (87.0)*		
1891	7,088 (11.8)	53,105 (88.2)	3,233 (5.4)	56,841 (94.6)
1901	5,796 (8.3)	63,842 (91.7)	3,817 (5.3)	68,639 (94.7)
1911	4,631 (5.6)	78,080 (94.4)	2,700 (3.6)	71,279 (96.4)

Source: BBCE database.

Notes: Farm and non-farm based on first occupation stated; 1871 not fully comparable. Figures for employers with stated workforce numbers in *italics* for 1851–81; provided as a stricter comparative sample.

This fall in importance of farm portfolios was a more extreme version of the general decrease in the importance of farming entrepreneurs, and suggests that for farms running adjunct businesses was becoming less feasible or less attractive in the early twentieth century.

The decrease in portfolio own-account agriculture was considerable: in 1861, 11 percent of own-account farmers ran multiple businesses, by 1881 it was just 4 percent. The proportion of employer farmers with portfolio occupations remained stable between 1851 and 1881, at about 2–3 percent. Therefore, it seems that diversification helped a small number of employers maintain their status in the face of the pressures which drove more marginal own-account farmers out of business. Diversification as a business strategy in farming could help entrepreneurs cope with difficult conditions but it was not a universal panacea; it could help more substantial businesses, namely those employing workers, but for more precarious entrepreneurs it seemingly offered little assistance.

For non-farming the trends were similar for employers. In 1851–81, 16–18 percent of extracted employers were portfolio entrepreneurs; in 1891, this was 12.8 percent; in 1901, 14.9 percent; and in 1911, 14.4 percent. Thus, as with farmers, non-farm portfolio firms were a stable proportion of extracted employers, again suggesting that for a minority of firms with workers, diversification was a useful business strategy or that diversifying required employees. For non-farm own-account proprietors 1851–81, the proportion of portfolios varied between 10 percent and 13 percent, and for 1891–1911 the proportion was 6–7 percent. The fact that there was not the same decline in the incidence of portfolios as seen in farming, suggests that portfolio entrepreneurship remained an attractive option for non-farming own-account proprietors, albeit less attractive than for employers.

The trends also varied by gender, shown in Table 11.3. The proportion of female employers with multiple occupations remained fairly stable across the whole period, before rising in 1901 and 1911, a similar pattern to male employers. The poor recording of own-account proprietors in the earlier censuses requiring reconstruction means that these figures are harder to interpret. However, for 1891–1911 the proportion of female and male own-account proprietors running portfolio operations was stable over 1891 to 1901, before rising slightly in 1911. While the trends were similar for men and women, male entrepreneurs were always more likely to run more than one business than female entrepreneurs. Taking just the most complete data, 1891–1911, we see that 8–13 percent of male employers had portfolio businesses, compared to 5–7 percent of female employers. Those who have examined this issue using case studies have tentatively suggested that female business proprietors were more likely to have multiple businesses (Nenadic, 2007: 277, 281), but the evidence has been scanty and largely based on urban case studies, and hence excludes most farmers. When farmers and non-farmers are analysed separately, in Table 11.4, the picture is more complex. Once again, the divide between the early and later censuses make long-run comparison difficult, especially in terms of own-account proprietors; however, the drop between 1871 and 1881 in the proportion of female non-farm entrepreneurs running multiple businesses suggests that earlier in the period this was a more viable activity for female entrepreneurs. It also reflects the changing possibilities for female entrepreneurship. Between 1871 and 1881 the number of own-account music teachers increased substantially; the emergence of this and other occupations which provided more opportunities for self-employed sole-proprietor income for women, without needing to be combined with other activities, meant that female portfolio activities were less important to the overall structure of female own-account entrepreneurship.

Table 11.3 Percentage of entrepreneurs with portfolio businesses by gender, 1851–1911

	Employers		Own Account		All Entrepreneurs	
	Female	Male	Female	Male	Female	Male
1851	5.3	8.3	6.2	9.7	5.6	8.6
1861	5.3	9.3	8.1	13.8	6.1	10.3
1871	6.8	10.3	3.8	6.5	5.6	9.0
1881	5.3	9.7	1.8	7.4	3.4	9.1
1891	5.4	11.9	2.6	8.4	3.0	10.0
1901	7.1	13.2	2.9	8.5	3.3	10.5
1911	6.5	12.9	3.6	9.2	4.2	10.9

Source: BBCE database.

Table 11.4 Percentage of non-farm entrepreneurs with portfolio businesses by gender, 1851–1911

	Employers		Own Account		All Entrepreneurs	
	Female	Male	Female	Male	Female	Male
1851	18.3	17.3	18.2	13.1	18.3	16.1
1861	16.8	18.9	11.6	15.8	15.2	18.2
1871	19.4	21.3	19.1	16.8	19.3	19.8
1881	13.1	16.6	2.2	13.1	5.8	15.8
1891	5.7	14.1	2.6	8.7	3.0	10.8
1901	8.3	15.7	2.9	8.7	3.4	11.3
1911	7.3	15.4	3.7	9.6	4.3	12.2

Source: BBCE database.

Table 11.5 Urban and rural portfolio entrepreneurs, 1851–1911 (percent in each category)

	1851	1861	1871	1881	1891	1901	1911
Non-Farmer							
Urban	29.0	31.2	34.9	38.2	61.3	66.4	71.7
Transition	31.6	30.4	31.8	26.8	18.1	15.3	14.8
Rural	39.4	38.4	33.4	35.0	20.7	18.3	13.5
Farmer							
Urban	13.4	15.9	14.1	18.4	19.5	21.3	25.5
Transition	37.1	34.4	35.6	29.7	24.9	23.2	25.2
Rural	49.4	49.7	50.3	51.9	55.5	55.5	49.3

Source: BBCE database.

Note: Urban and urban-transition categories combined to give a single urban category.

Using the urban classification (defined in Chapter 3) we can examine the geographical distribution of these portfolio business proprietors, shown in Table 11.5, broken down by whether their first occupation was in farming. Even with the break between 1881 and 1891 the pattern is clear. Portfolio farmers were generally found in rural and transition areas, which is unsurprising as these two categories include most farmland in England and Wales. However, the increased proportion present in urban locations by the 1900s indicates both the spread of urban areas and the importance of such areas to portfolio activity; running an additional business was more attractive to a farmer with an appropriate market nearby, as found in case studies by Winstanley (1983) and in 1881 by Radicic et al. (2017).

The non-farmer figures are harder to interpret. The steady decline in transition and rural categories and the growth of urban portfolios partly reflects the expansion of urban locations. The urban population grew faster than that in other locations and thus the share of portfolio entrepreneurs in urban places inevitably expanded compared to rural and transitional locations. However, it was also linked to economic necessity; if a second business was to be successful, it required a market, and this was more likely to be found in the major population centres than rural areas. The transition areas were mixes of smaller towns and rural areas, and the decline in the proportion of portfolio businesses in these areas was accompanied by a shift in the character of those businesses. In 1851, 37 percent of the portfolio entrepreneurs' second businesses in these areas were in agriculture, but by 1911 this had fallen to just 10 percent. Therefore, the shift away from farming and from rural areas was not solely driven by population distribution; it also reflected the declining feasibility of agriculture as a secondary activity; the butcher in a small town who in 1851 diversified by maintaining a smallholding instead ran a grocer's shop in 1911. The growth in urban population and the increasingly integrated national market for food and other goods meant that portfolio entrepreneurs were increasingly found in urban locations, whether in the large towns included in the urban category in Table 11.5 or in the smaller towns in the transition category.

The overall pattern of portfolio entrepreneurs as a percentage of all entrepreneurs in 1911 is shown in Figure 11.2 for England and Wales. Portfolios were on average 9.3 percent of all proprietors. The areas where the proportion significantly exceeded this average were concentrated on urban fringes, but mainly in Lancashire and the West Riding, Derbyshire, Nottinghamshire and Staffordshire: this type of portfolio business was interrelated with heavy industrial areas. Elsewhere portfolios were mainly in rural and mixed small town areas, usually on the main rail lines. These appear large on the map because the RSD sizes are larger than urban and fringe areas. They mainly occurred in Wiltshire-Berkshire, around the South East, and in Lincolnshire and East Anglia. They were notably absent in rural Wales and other upland locations distant from rail access in the Pennines, Lake District, North York Moors and the South West. The mix of urban opportunity and rural necessity thus shows clearly: portfolio proprietors were more likely to be found in urban locations, a tendency which only strengthened as farmers became less likely to start second businesses, and as farming became a less attractive option for others looking to diversify their business activities.

11.5 Portfolio businesses: sectors and occupations

Table 11.2 has already given the breakdown of farm and non-farm portfolios according to the first occupations given by census respondents. From that we have seen that farming became progressively less common as first occupation in a portfolio. Table 11.6 shows the proportion by their first occupation, organised into the 13 sectors used in earlier chapters. In this table a portfolio is counted in the same way as previously, between distinct occupations, but these are now summarised for aggregate sectors so that some portfolios are within their aggregate sector and some between. For instance, a butcher and baker had a portfolio

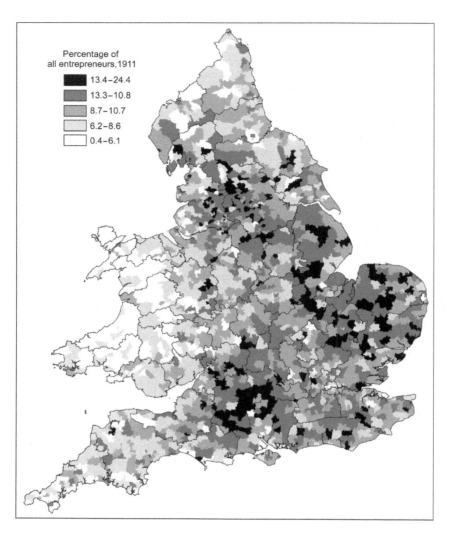

Figure 11.2 Portfolio proprietors as a percentage of all proprietors in 1911, by RSD
Source: BBCE database.

business within food sales, while a butcher and farmer had a portfolio between food sales and farming. A similar decline to that in farming occurred in agricultural processing and dealing. Construction, manufacturing, maker-dealers and food sales remained the most common first sectors for portfolios throughout this period, with manufacturing slightly increasing in importance, while maker-dealers and food sales increased more substantially. Retail portfolios grew in importance over the period to become one of the most common first sectors, but

Table 11.6 Portfolio entrepreneurs' first occupations, 1885–1911 (each column sums to 100 percent)

	1851	1861	1871	1881	1891	1901	1911
Farming and estate work	22.6	27.9	20.4	21.9	10.4	9.6	7.6
Mining and quarrying	1.8	1.9	3.2	2.5	1.0	1.1	1.0
Construction	14.2	13.5	14.5	15.5	15.3	14.9	13.9
Manufacturing	11.7	11.2	12.5	12.7	13.8	13.8	14.2
Maker-dealer	9.9	8.9	9.0	8.4	13.1	10.5	12.3
Retail	5.2	4.6	5.5	5.4	8.9	10.4	11.6
Transport	1.2	0.9	2.3	1.4	1.9	2.2	2.0
Professional and business services	1.4	1.7	1.6	2.2	3.7	3.9	4.1
Personal Services	0.5	0.5	0.7	0.4	3.0	3.0	3.3
Agricultural produce processing and dealing	8.5	7.3	7.7	7.7	3.7	3.2	2.3
Food sales	10.4	10.7	11.5	12.7	19.4	22.1	23.6
Refreshment	11.5	9.9	9.7	8.5	4.6	4.1	3.0
Finance and commerce	1.0	1.0	1.2	0.8	1.2	1.1	1.1

Source: BBCE database.

refreshment declined sharply. While we analyse company director portfolios in detail elsewhere, it is important to note their contrast with other entrepreneurs: mining and transport consistently had the highest ratios of directorship portfolios in a different sector, while the lowest ratios were found for maker-dealing, retail and refreshments.

Tables 11.7 and 11.8 expand this by showing the relationship between first and second occupations in 1851 and 1911. It gives the number of each combination as a percentage of the total number of portfolio entrepreneurs in each year (i.e. all entries in the tables sum to 100 percent). In 1911, most entrepreneurs starting a second portfolio business did so in the same sector as their initial enterprise (those down the diagonal, top left to bottom right). In four of the five most frequent portfolio sectors, the most common second business was in the same sector as the first: construction, manufacturing, retail and food sales. However, in 1851 it was different, with agriculture as the most common second sector. It was particularly common as a second sector for food sales and refreshment, two sectors in which there was utility for entrepreneurs having a smallholding to support and improve their primary business: a butcher could keep livestock, innkeepers could use farmland to grow crops and livestock for use in their business whether serving food or brewing beer. However, the degree of change should not be overstated; in 1851 in construction and manufacturing the same sector was the most common source of secondary businesses, in maker-dealing it was retailing, a closely related sector; all were the same in 1911.

Table 11.9 shows the percentage of portfolio entrepreneurs whose second business was, variously, in the same sector as their first, in farming, and in

Table 11.7 Portfolio entrepreneur first and second occupations, 1851

	Farming and estate work	Mining and quarrying	Construction	Manufacturing	Maker-dealer	Retail	Transport	Professional and business services	Personal Services	Agricultural produce processing and dealing	Food sales	Refreshment	Finance and commerce
Farming and estate work	2.7	1.3	1.6	3.1	1.4	1.2	1.0	0.3	0.0	3.3	3.0	3.5	0.1
Mining and quarrying	1.5	0.1	0.0	0.1	0.0	0.0	0.0	0.0	0.0	0.0	0.0	0.0	0.0
Construction	2.8	0.1	7.4	2.2	0.3	0.2	0.0	0.1	0.0	0.1	0.3	0.6	0.0
Manufacturing	3.2	0.1	0.6	4.4	0.9	1.4	0.1	0.2	0.0	0.2	0.2	0.3	0.1
Maker-dealer	3.1	0.0	0.2	0.9	1.1	3.3	0.0	0.0	0.1	0.1	0.7	0.4	0.0
Retail	1.1	0.0	0.1	1.2	1.2	0.5	0.1	0.0	0.0	0.1	0.7	0.1	0.0
Transport	0.6	0.0	0.0	0.1	0.1	0.1	0.0	0.0	0.0	0.0	0.0	0.1	0.0
Professional and business services	0.8	0.0	0.2	0.2	0.0	0.0	0.0	0.1	0.0	0.0	0.0	0.0	0.1
Personal services	0.2	0.0	0.0	0.2	0.0	0.0	0.0	0.0	0.0	0.0	0.0	0.0	0.0
Agricultural produce processing and dealing	5.5	0.0	0.0	0.2	0.0	0.2	0.0	0.0	0.0	1.1	0.9	0.3	0.1
Food sales	5.6	0.0	0.1	0.2	0.4	1.2	0.1	0.0	0.0	0.7	1.8	0.3	0.0
Refreshment	9.3	0.0	0.5	0.4	0.5	0.1	0.1	0.0	0.0	0.2	0.3	0.0	0.0
Finance and commerce	0.4	0.0	0.0	0.1	0.1	0.0	0.3	0.0	0.0	0.1	0.0	0.0	0.0

Source: BBCE database.

Table 11.8 Portfolio entrepreneur first and second occupations, 1911

	Farming and estate work	Mining and quarrying	Construction	Manufacturing	Maker-dealer	Retail	Transport	Professional and business services	Personal services	Agricultural produce processing and dealing	Food sales	Refreshment	Finance and commerce
Farming and estate work	1.8	0.1	0.4	0.3	0.3	0.7	0.6	0.2	0.0	0.4	1.8	0.7	0.2
Mining and quarrying	0.1	0.0	0.2	0.1	0.0	0.3	0.0	0.0	0.0	0.1	0.0	0.0	0.1
Construction	0.4	0.1	9.2	2.2	0.9	0.4	0.1	0.1	0.1	0.0	0.1	0.2	0.1
Manufacturing	0.2	0.1	1.3	5.7	0.9	4.2	0.2	0.4	0.3	0.2	0.3	0.1	0.5
Maker-dealer	0.4	0.0	0.1	4.8	1.6	3.8	0.1	0.1	0.3	0.1	0.8	0.2	0.2
Retail	0.4	0.1	0.2	2.0	2.8	3.7	0.4	0.2	0.1	0.2	1.1	0.1	0.3
Transport	0.3	0.0	0.4	0.4	0.1	0.3	0.2	0.0	0.0	0.0	0.1	0.1	0.1
Professional and business services	0.2	0.0	0.1	0.3	0.1	0.3	0.0	2.5	0.2	0.0	0.1	0.0	0.2
Personal services	0.1	0.0	0.1	0.8	0.9	0.4	0.0	0.2	0.8	0.0	0.1	0.0	0.0
Agricultural produce processing and dealing	0.5	0.0	0.0	0.2	0.1	0.3	0.0	0.0	0.0	0.7	0.3	0.1	0.1
Food sales	1.6	0.0	0.2	0.3	1.0	3.8	0.2	0.1	0.0	0.6	13.4	2.2	0.2
Refreshment	0.9	0.0	0.1	0.1	0.1	0.3	0.1	0.1	0.0	0.1	0.8	0.4	0.0
Finance and commerce	0.0	0.0	0.0	0.3	0.1	0.2	0.0	0.2	0.0	0.0	0.0	0.0	0.2

Source: BBCE database.

Table 11.9 Portfolio entrepreneurs, percentages with second occupations in the same sector, for farming and other sectors, 1851 and 1911

	1851			1911		
	% Same	% Farm	% Other	% Same	% Farm	% Other
Farming and estate work	12.1	–	87.9	23.2	–	76.8
Mining and quarrying	4.4	81.6	14.0	3.4	5.7	91.0
Construction	52.3	19.6	28.1	66.5	2.8	30.7
Manufacturing	37.4	27.3	35.2	39.8	1.6	58.6
Maker-dealer	11.0	31.0	57.9	12.9	3.3	83.8
Retail	9.7	21.5	68.9	31.7	3.1	65.1
Transport	1.5	50.3	48.2	9.1	14.4	76.5
Professional and business services	10.6	57.3	32.2	62.1	4.0	33.9
Personal services	4.0	33.1	62.9	22.8	1.7	75.5
Agricultural produce processing and dealing	12.8	65.5	21.6	28.2	21.3	50.5
Food sales	17.4	53.3	29.3	56.7	6.7	36.6
Refreshment	0.2	80.9	18.9	13.3	28.5	58.1
Finance and commerce	1.4	39.8	58.8	16.0	3.0	81.0

Source: BBCE database.

other sectors. In both years farming had a high percentage of entrepreneurs with second businesses in other sectors, while the other main portfolio sectors (construction, manufacturing, maker-dealers, retail, food sales and refreshment, the other sectors have far fewer portfolios) tended to have second businesses in the same sector or similar ones. Thus, in 1851, 33 percent of maker-dealers with second businesses had them in retail and 9 percent in manufacturing; in retail 23 percent had a second business in manufacturing and 24 percent in maker-dealing. In 1911, 31 percent of portfolio maker-dealers had second businesses in retail and 39 percent in manufacturing, while 24 percent of portfolio retailers ran a second concern in maker-dealing and 17 percent in manufacturing. There was an important change over time as well; the proportion of portfolios where the second sector was in farming declined substantially. In food sales and refreshments the decline of agricultural second businesses was accompanied by an increase in entrepreneurs whose second enterprises were in the same or similar sectors, which were natural areas for diversification. In other words, outside of agriculture it was rare for entrepreneurs to have businesses in widely different sectors, and this tendency became rarer over time as agriculture contracted. This was particularly noticeable in mining, but the portfolio numbers in this and some other sectors were small so the changes may be exaggerated.

Sectors hide interesting aspects of portfolio combinations between more detailed occupations, as shown in Table 11.10 for the 10 most common

Table 11.10 Most common portfolio businesses, 1851–1911 (male and female)

1851	1861	1871	1881	1891	1901	1911
Innkeeper–farmer	Innkeeper–farmer	Innkeeper–farmer	Innkeeper–farmer	Grocer–draper	Baker–confectioner	Baker–confectioner
Miller–farmer	Farmer–innkeeper	Miller–farmer	Miller–farmer	Carpenter–builder	Carpenter–builder	Grocer–provision dealer
Butcher–farmer	Miller–farmer	Butcher–farmer	Butcher–farmer	Baker–confectioner	Builder–contractor	Builder–contractor
Plumber–painter	Butcher–farmer	Farmer–innkeeper	Farmer–innkeeper	Tailor–draper	Grocer–draper	Carpenter–builder
Farmer–innkeeper	Plumber–painter	Tailor–draper	Plumber–painter	Baker–grocer	Grocer–provision dealer	Architect–surveyor
Tailor–draper	Tailor–draper	Plumber–painter	Carpenter–builder	Innkeeper–farmer	Plumber–painter	Plumber–painter
Farmer–miller	Farmer–miller	Carpenter–builder	Tailor–draper	Plumber–painter	Architect–surveyor	Builder–painter
Carpenter–farmer	Farmer–grocer	Grocer–farmer	Carpenter–farmer	Grocer–provision dealer	Baker–grocer	Grocer–draper
Farmer–butcher	Grocer–farmer	Farmer–miller	Grocer–farmer	Builder–contractor	Grocer–shopkeeper	Baker–grocer
Blacksmith–farmer	Farmer–butcher	Carpenter–farmer	Farmer–miller	Farmer–innkeeper	Innkeeper–farmer	Carpenter–wheelwright
Grocer–farmer	Carpenter–builder	Farmer–grocer	Grocer–draper	Watchmaker–jeweller	Tailor–draper	Grocer–confectioner
Carpenter–builder	Carpenter–farmer	Grocer–draper	Farmer–butcher	Grocer–baker	Carpenter–wheelwright	Grocer–baker
Painter–glazier	Grocer–draper	Farmer–butcher	Farmer–carter	Architect–surveyor	Watchmaker–jeweller	Watchmaker–jeweller
Grocer–draper	Farmer–commercial traveller	Plumber–Painter	Baker–grocer	Carpenter–wheelwright	Grocer–Baker	Innkeeper–farmer
Farmer–grocer	Blacksmith–farmer	Lead mining–farmer	Auctioneer–farmer	Butcher–farmer	Farmer–innkeeper	Grocer–beer seller

Source: BBCE database.

occupation pairs for each census year. Many of the same pairs re-appear year on year, simply changing order. They reflect two main kinds of portfolio business. Some were portfolios because of the nature of their sector. Thus, building entrepreneurs with portfolio businesses had more than one branch to their construction firm because of the high level of sub-contracting in that industry. The building industry was characterised by a multitude of specialized small firms; portfolio firms either embraced two branches of construction (such as plumbers and painters) or a single specialism and the more general term 'builder' (such as carpenter and builder). In the first case, diversification aided survival through increasing the kinds of sub-contracting work which they could carry out. The other type is harder to generalise about as the term 'builder' was ambiguous; however, it presumably meant that such firms both carried out jobs as part of larger projects and carried out their own projects, either bidding for contracts or building speculatively, most obviously seen in the 'builder and contractor' firms which appear with regularity from the 1890s onwards. This also reflects a more general shift to general builders and contractors as major firms in the sector (Pollins, 1969; Cooney, 1980: 157). It reflects a flexibility that would have allowed such firms to adapt to the kind of contracts on offer and the nature of the economic climate, key given the volatility of the building cycle in Victorian and Edwardian England and Wales (Powell, 1980: 78–88). A similar process occurred for the one type of professional portfolio which appears in this table: architect and surveyor. Both professions expanded significantly in the nineteenth century driven by the building boom arising from continued urbanization and infrastructure development. A firm that could offer the services of both an architect and surveyor had a better chance of obtaining work, especially given the still unregulated entry into these professions (Powell, 1980: 76–7; Brodie et al., 2001: II, xiv).

A second group of portfolio firms were those diversifying into similar or directly connected trades. Some of these were obvious expansions into closely related trades, such as baking and confectionary, or grocery and provision dealing. In such cases diversification both helped spread risk and responded to increased demand for a wider variety of goods; for example, grocery and provision dealers emerged in response to the greater supply of, and demand for, imported provisions such as tea, bacon, sugar and pre-processed goods (Jeffreys, 1954: 126–31; Winstanley, 1983: 123), and also reflected de-regulation after abolition of tea and coffee excise licenses in 1870 allowed other retailers to expand into this field.[6] Diversification was also a strategy adopted by some grocers to deal with the increasingly precarious market when faced with growing competition from co-operatives and local branches of multiple retailers (Shaw, 1982; Shaw and Tipper, 1997; Winstanley, 1983: 120–2). The third group were less directly connected, such as grocery and drapery. Many such businesses were portfolios because they provided a range of services to areas where specialist retailers could not have survived. The case of grocery and drapery is indicative; in 1901, 51 percent of businesses combining grocery with drapery were in rural areas, with a further 25 percent in rural–urban transition locations. Diversification into similar or related trades was therefore driven by different market opportunities and economies of scale in different locations. The choice made by these entrepreneurs was constrained by the particularities of the local market; in urban areas diversification helped such retailers cope with pressure from mass retailers, in rural areas diversification offered a solution where demand for a variety of goods existed but was insufficient to support separate enterprises.

Farming portfolios were similar in nature to this second type. Farmers operating a second business entered into a number of occupations: innkeeper, miller, butcher, grocer and carter were the most common. Some of these had obvious connections to agriculture, notably milling and butchery, where the farmer could expand by moving into processing their own agricultural produce. Carting was somewhat different and has been previously recognised as a common offshoot that all farmers engaged in given that they often transported goods to markets (Turnbull, 1979; Everitt, 1976: 179; Barker and Gerhold, 1995: 15–20). Finally, the other farm portfolios involved retailing to urban inhabitants or providing accommodation to travellers, both of which relied on proximity to urban centres and good transport links. As a result, portfolio farming was slightly more likely to occur near urban locations than non-portfolio farming; in 1851, 64 percent of non-portfolio farmers lived in rural areas, 27 percent in transition areas and just 8 percent in urban locations, whereas for portfolio farmers 49 percent were in rural, 37 percent in transition and 13 percent in urban areas. As Winstanley argues, such farmers were well-placed to respond to growing demand for food and drink and accommodation created by urbanization (Winstanley, 1996). Farm portfolio businesses also tended to be smaller; in 1851, the average acreage of farmer employers who had a second business was 102 acres, compared to 156 acres for non-portfolio farmer employers; in 1861, the figures were 125 and 166; in 1871, 139 and 179; and in 1881, 122 and 185. This suggests that they had greater need to diversify because they had less scope to increase their scale as farmers. Therefore, it was farmers with small or medium farms and those nearer urban areas which tended to start second businesses, consistent with modern studies (Gasson, 1983).

Table 11.11 shows the 10 most common occupation pairings for female portfolio entrepreneurs. Many of these were the same as the pairings in the total population. However, few female portfolio entrepreneurs were involved in construction; and dressmaking and millinery were far more important portfolios for women than for the total population of proprietors. This is unsurprising as female entrepreneurs were relatively rare in construction, and clothes manufacturing was a very common activity for female business proprietors (as Chapter 8). However, the fact that there was so much overlap between female portfolio entrepreneurs and the population of business proprietors as a whole suggests that the portfolio choice was driven more by the structure of particular trades rather than the character of the individual entrepreneurs. In many

Table 11.11 Most common female portfolio businesses, 1851–1911

1851	1861	1871	1881	1891	1901	1911
Innkeeper–farmer	Innkeeper–farmer	Innkeeper–farmer	Innkeeper–farmer	Milliner–dressmaker	Baker–confectioner	Baker–confectioner
Milliner–dressmaker	Farmer–innkeeper	Farmer–innkeeper	Miller–farmer	Grocer–draper	Grocer–draper	Grocer–confectioner
Farmer–innkeeper	Miller–farmer	Miller–farmer	Grocer–farmer	Dressmaker–milliner	Grocer–shopkeeper	Grocer–provision dealer
Miller–farmer	Farmer–grocer	Grocer–farmer	Farmer–innkeeper	Grocer–provision dealer	Grocer–provision dealer	Confectioner–tobacconist
Plumber–glazier	Grocer–farmer	Milliner–dressmaker	Farmer–miller	Baker–confectioner	Grocer–confectioner	Grocer–draper
Farmer–miller	Farmer–miller	Farmer–miller	Farmer–Grocer	Milliner–draper	Milliner–draper	Grocer–shopkeeper
Grocer–farmer	Butcher–farmer	Tailor–draper	Plumber–painter	Grocer–beer seller	Grocer–beer seller	Milliner–draper
Butcher–farmer	Milliner–dressmaker	Grocer–draper	Butcher–farmer	Grocer–baker	Glass worker–pottery dealer	Fishmonger–coffeehouse keeper
Farmer–grocer	Plumber–glazier	Farmer–grocer	Grocer–draper	Baker–grocer	Draper–milliner	Draper–milliner
Maltster–farmer	Farmer–shopkeeper	Butcher–farmer	Baker–confectioner	Innkeeper–farmer	Grocer–baker	Tobacconist–confectioner
Shopkeeper–farmer	Grocer–draper	Grocer–baker	Baker–grocer	Glass worker–pottery dealer	Baker–grocer	Newsagent–tobacconist
Farmer–dressmaker	Farmer–butcher	Farmer–butcher	Shopkeeper–farmer	Grocer–confectioner	Confectioner–tobacconist	Grocer–beer seller
Farmer–weaver	Farmer–maltster	Plumber–glazier	Beer seller–farmer	Draper–milliner	Draper–dressmaker	Grocer–baker
Grocer–draper	Tailor–draper	Shopkeeper–farmer	Printer–stationer	Draper–grocer	Draper–grocer	Confectioner–baker
Beer seller–farmer	Farmer–laundry	Plumber–painter	Farmer–shopkeeper	Draper–dressmaker	Innkeeper–farmer	Baker–grocer

Source: BBCE database.

trades, no matter how successful they were, portfolio firms were rare: heavy manufacturing and the professions being notable in this regard. Nor, it would seem, did entrepreneurs in such sectors turn to diversification in order to cope with competition and uncertainty. In contrast, business proprietors in grocery, dressmaking, baking and other such trades often diversified, sometimes to deal with uncertainty and competition, sometimes because local circumstances were propitious, sometimes because their success allowed them to expand; however, the data from the censuses suggest that such moves were mainly dependent on the nature of trade or industry in which the entrepreneur was active, rather than any other factor.

11.6 Firm size and resources

As noted at the outset of this chapter, firms could adapt to different sector and market opportunities in different ways, of which portfolios was just one. This adaptation interrelated with the resources of the firm. Human capital resources could be hired as waged employees or could be provided by spouses and family. The latter in turn interacted with the personal and household strategies of the proprietors, their partners and their families. We can investigate these interrelations in two ways: analysis of portfolios by the number of employees and analysis by possible family involvement.

Figures 11.3 shows firm size by number of employees for portfolio businesses compared to non-portfolio businesses. In farming, portfolio firms were slightly more likely to have larger workforces than non-portfolio farms; however, the numbers involved were small, for example, in 1851 there were just 137 portfolio farmers employing between 20 and 49 people. For non-farmers, portfolios were slightly more common for larger businesses than for smaller; however, the difference was small. Portfolio employers were more likely to run medium-size businesses and less likely to run very small businesses, although the majority of both portfolio and non-portfolio employers ran small businesses: 70–78 percent of portfolio and 70–80 percent of non-portfolio employers employed fewer than 10 people. Such small differences suggest that most of these businesses were not successful firms seeking to expand through diversification, but rather that, in both farming and non-farming sectors, they reflected personal or local opportunities. The trends were also the same over time.

Chapter 7 showed that employers who employed co-resident family and non-family members tended to be more marginal than those who did not. Table 11.12 shows that the proportion of farming portfolio employers who employed co-resident household members in their primary or secondary business was generally lower than the proportion of non-portfolio employers.[7] Again, it is hard to interpret trends because of the break between the early and late censuses, with the farm data more complete in 1851–81, and due to the small number of portfolio farmers. The table shows that, given the association of co-resident employees with more precarious entrepreneurship, portfolio farmers were slightly less marginal than non-portfolio farmers (except in 1851). For

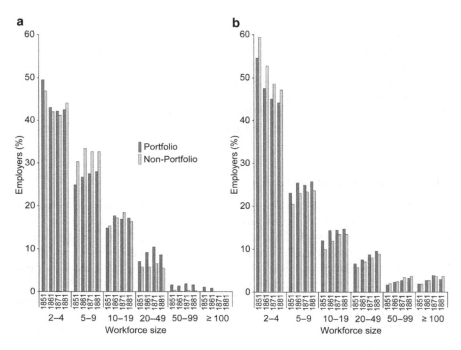

Figure 11.3 Firm size distribution of portfolio and non-portfolio employers, 1851–81: (a) farm; (b) non-farm

Source: BBCE database.

non-farmers the picture was different, with portfolio employers more likely to employ co-resident household members than non-farmers who did not run a second business. This suggests that portfolio non-farmers were likely to be more marginal than non-portfolio employers in the same trades. It also reflects the fact that many portfolio employers were in trades where live-in staff were common: maker–dealers and retail, for example, as Tables 11.7 and 11.8 and Chapter 7 have shown. However, the numbers are small, even in 1911 there were only 14,045 portfolio employers with co-resident workers.

Figure 11.3 and Table 11.12 can also be compared with the modern GHS. Alden (1977: 18–23; Alden and Saha, 1980) showed that second jobbing generally had a reverse 'J' distribution across earnings levels (which we can approximate by firm size): low-income people had a high level of double jobbing, with the rate declining as income increased until upper-middle-income levels where second jobs rates increased, though this might also be referred to as a form of 'U-shape'. The former would be referred to as 'survival' strategies, and the latter 'opportunity' strategies, in line with GEM (2009; 2018). The historical data thus

Table 11.12 Family and household firms as a percentage of portfolio and non-portfolio employers, 1851–1911

Year	Farm Household Firms		Non-Farm Household Firms	
	% of Portfolios	% of Non-Portfolios	% of Portfolios	% of Non-Portfolios
1851	52.7	52.3	39.1	23.9
1861	38.4	40.3	30.2	18.6
1881	40.0	44.4	27.4	15.8
1891	40.3	49.0	22.9	13.3
1901	49.0	58.6	24.3	16.8
1911	46.0	60.3	15.3	10.7

Source: BBCE database.

evidence that there was some continuity of the portfolio structures over the long term: at the bottom of the size and earnings scale as survival, and for large firm sizes a diversification to follow opportunities.

11.7 Conclusion

Portfolio entrepreneurs were a significant component of the entrepreneurial population in Victorian and Edwardian England and Wales. They accounted for 9–12 percent of all employers, 6–13 percent of own-account proprietors and 8–10 percent of all entrepreneurs, figures similar to previous research for 1851 and 1881 (Woollard, 2004) and to modern non-farm comparisons (Alden, 1977), but lower than for the eighteenth century (Keibek and Shaw-Taylor, 2013). Farming was an important sector for portfolio activity, both as a sector to diversify out of (forward diversification), and one to enter into when for a second business (backward diversification). However, even in 1851 portfolio activity was not as common in farming as it had been in the eighteenth century, and agriculture as a source of portfolio entrepreneurship declined over the period 1851–1911, suggesting that in both farming and other sectors it was becoming less common. However, the decline in portfolio activity by farmers is out of line with modern estimates, which suggest high levels of multiple occupations among farmers in modern England (Harrison, 1975; Gasson, 1983; Evans and Ilbery, 1993).

Most portfolio entrepreneurs' second businesses were in the same broad sector as their original enterprise or in an allied sector. The main exception was agriculture, but even in those cases there was often significant overlap; butchers keeping land to graze livestock or farmers opening a mill to grind their own grain. This was a change from the eighteenth century where manufacturers were more likely to expand into agriculture. In the second half of the nineteenth century manufacturers were more likely to run second businesses in another manufacturing trade or in retail. This reflects the decline in the appeal of agriculture as an economic activity and growing demand for manufactured goods of all kinds.

The decline in portfolio farming and the fact that few outside farming entered it suggests that the second half of the nineteenth century was a particular moment in English and Welsh farming when agriculture either provided sufficient income for most farmers or that they did not have the time and resources to engage in other business activities. Similarly, given high capital and labour costs, and the falling returns in farming (particularly high farming), especially after the agricultural depression, it is unsurprising that manufacturers and retailers did not look to farming as a viable secondary concern.

Portfolio entrepreneurship was primarily an urban activity, a tendency which strengthened over time. Urban locations provided markets for many of the goods portfolio entrepreneurs produced and sold, especially for those farmers who moved into food processing or accommodation. However, portfolio activity was not absent from rural areas. In such locations communities could only support so many businesses and thus portfolios were a useful strategy to maximise outcomes in a market with limited opportunities: if a village could not support two businesses independently, then one entrepreneur running both could provide the services at lower costs.

Contrary to previous suggestions based on case studies, portfolio entrepreneurship was more common amongst men than women. This was driven by the gendered nature of many of the sectors in which portfolio businesses were particularly common. Thus, construction, which provided many of the most common portfolio businesses, was dominated by male employers and own-account proprietors. Here, therefore, as in many aspects of portfolio entrepreneurship, the structure of the particular sectors and markets shaped who did and who did not start a portfolio business, rather than the simple argument that diversification was a solution to precarious positions within the economy or indeed that portfolio businesses were necessarily successful entrepreneurs simply expanding their activities.

Notes

1 *Census of Great Britain, 1851, Population Tables, II, Ages, civil conditions, occupations and birthplace of the people with the numbers and ages of the blind, the deaf-and-dumb, and the inmates of workhouses, prisons, lunatic asylums, and hospitals, Vol. I, Parliamentary Papers,* LXXXVIII (1852–53), cclxxxv.

2 Report of the Committee Appointed by the Treasury to Inquire into Certain Questions Connected with the Taking of The Census, *Parliamentary Papers,* LVIII (1890).

3 *Parliamentary Papers:* Royal Commission on Depressed Condition of Agricultural Interests (1879–82) 3 vols.; Royal Commission on Agricultural Depression (1895–7).

4 *Census of England and Wales, 1881, Vol. IV, General Report, Parliamentary Papers,* LXXX (1883), 28; see also, *Census of Great Britain, 1851, Population Tables, II, Vol. I,* lxxxii; *Census of England and Wales, 1861, General Report, Parliamentary Papers,* LIII (1863), 30; *Census of England and*

Wales, 1891, Vol. IV, General Report with summary tables and appendices, Parliamentary Papers, CVI (1893–4), 37; TNA, RG27/16, Instructions to clerks, 1901, v.

5 TNA, RG19/48B; Committee on the Census of 1911: proceedings of meetings, 19 April 1910.

6 Kelly, *Directory of Grocery, Oil and Colour Trades*, 1877, p. v, Kelly, London.

7 The definition of household firm here has been expanded from that used in Chapter 7 to include workers who were in the same occode as either of the employers' first or second occodes.

12 Conclusion

Re-positioning the entrepreneur in history and the present day

12.1 Introduction

This book has aimed to provide the first large-scale, long-term and detailed assessment of the history of entrepreneurship in Britain from 1851 to 1911 in detail using individual-level data on the 160 million people in the censuses, and in lesser detail up to the present. It rests upon an entirely novel database of all identifiable business proprietors in each of the seven censuses between 1851 and 1911, combined with more recent census and other data, and a separate linked database of directors of public companies. The database provides a surrogate 'British Business Census of Entrepreneurs' (BBCE) now available at the UK Data Archive. This book provides an entry point to that database with supplementary material provided in working papers listed in the references. These data on entrepreneurship, and the analysis of them, are the first on this scale in historical scholarship and the first to link whole-population estimates from 1851 to the present.

12.2 Re-positioning entrepreneurship studies

This book has adopted a broad definition of an entrepreneur. This contrasts with much modern and historical research on entrepreneurs that has focused on innovators; indeed many commentators restrict the definition of entrepreneurship to those who innovate. Our broad approach defines entrepreneurs as all proprietors who were responsible for the key decisions in their business at a given point of time. This means that we adopt a definition based on all self-employed. This has six key advantages outlined in Chapters 1 and 2: it is generally simple to define, it is inclusive of all categories of business by size and legal/taxation basis, it can be applied to corporate and non-corporate structures, it is available from both the historical and modern records on a consistent basis, it accords with economic definitions of entrepreneurs as the recipients of entrepreneurial income rather than wages and it fits with measured data in historical national income accounts for England and Wales which can also be compared on a uniform basis internationally. These advantages allow the key contribution of this book: to isolate the distinctions between business proprietors and waged workers. This allows an important new avenue of research to be opened for making long-term comparisons of business, sector and industry development. This should provide a useful stepping stone for future work on entrepreneurship, whether historical or modern.

Of course if the censuses contained information on issues such as innovation these would have been important to include. But the fundamental advantage of a broad definition is that it permits whole population analysis. Subsequent research can focus on any sub-categories within this which can be identified, such as innovators, permitting for the first time these specific categories to be compared against the whole population or selected parts of it. This overcomes the key drawbacks of most previous research on historical entrepreneurship summarised in Chapter 1: that they are mainly restricted to small samples and case studies, biased towards the large and usually towards the most successful, that contain various other selection biases with often unknown effects. Selection of samples can now be developed on a proper statistical basis and the whole distribution examined.

This approach also has the advantage of integrating modern understanding more fully with entrepreneurship as it was understood by contemporaries. This will of course always be imperfect, as individuals like Cantillon, Say, Mill or Marshall did not have the benefit of modern interpretations. But it is clear from the review of those who sought to understand entrepreneurship in the past, in Chapter 2, that entrepreneurship was seen as encompassing all business proprietors from the smallest own-account operation to the great manufacturers and merchants with major overseas trade. The broad approach, rooted in this historical discourse, thus applies relevant criteria to modern understanding of historical assessments of risk, success and failure: that even necessity entrepreneurs have to bear risk, evaluate market opportunities and adapt in order to survive. This approach also highlights the extent to which success is dependent on context as well as entrepreneurs' individual characteristics: a business proprietor may be working hard and constantly implementing small-scale innovations to achieve profit or survival, but their potential for profit and relative success is limited by the context in which their business operates. Using the whole population allows the outcomes from their business decisions (their continued existence and the size of their business) to be understood against the broadest range of research questions: their personal position in household and other networks; the business sector in which they operate; and their location with its history of related and other businesses affecting the local competitive conditions, externalities and the overall environment for entrepreneurship.

12.3   Historical and modern entrepreneurship

There have been many previous efforts to assess entrepreneurship in England and Wales in the Victorian and Edwardian periods. These have generally focused on its supposed 'decline'. However, previous research has tended to rely on case studies, small samples, aggregates of general economic activity or broad generalisations. The wholly original analysis presented in this book has confirmed many of the existing scholarship's arguments, but it also shows two key aspects to be wayward and opened up new areas of investigation.

First, and contrary to many previous discussions of entrepreneurship in this period, the long-run time series in Chapter 4 demonstrate that this period saw entrepreneurship increase, not decline. Second, we show female entrepreneurship to be frequent, not rare. Moreover, although the overall rate of entrepreneurship declined as a proportion of the economically active, this was against a background of rapidly rising population. But even then the rate of entrepreneurship equalled or exceeded that achieved in England and Wales up to 2017; and not until the 1990s has the level of entrepreneurial activity even approached that found in the late nineteenth century (Figures 4.8 and 4.9). Indeed, whilst there are limitations to the 1851–1911 data, these are generally downward biases, whilst the modern data have limitations that generally have upward biases (Figures 4.10 and 4.11): indicating that modern rates of entrepreneurship are only beginning to match the Victorian period.

This suggests significant alterations to the historiography of the Victorian and Edwardian economy: it is hard to sustain arguments that there was a decline in entrepreneurial spirit in a period which saw the highest rate of business proprietorship ever recorded. This underpins our recognition of the 1851–1911 period as the 'age of entrepreneurship'. There were fundamentals about this period encouraging business proprietors in a way that has not yet been repeated. Moreover this was not just about sole proprietor own-account businesses prepared to survive on low incomes at the margins, though many of these indeed existed. The number of employers of others and their rate of entrepreneurship also equalled those of today.

The key drivers of growing business numbers among those identified in Chapter 1 appear to be rapid general population growth that stimulated demand, a period of open trade that offered a wide range of opportunities, urbanisation that broadened the market potential for many of the smallest as well as large firms and a final breakdown in traditional systems limiting market entry into many sectors to skilled craftsmen. But countervailing limitations to small business growth were beginning to emerge: the increasing dominance of larger firms that could develop products and services at lower prices, reaping the benefits of economies of scale (especially in manufacturing), perhaps aided by a growing switch toward managerial and hierarchical control; increasing development of national and regional brands and branch networks (especially in retail, wholesale and services) that could extend into all localities and recruit many would-be entrepreneurs into managerial positions; and the increasing ability of corporations to reap these benefits compared to non-corporate proprietors.

As a result of these shifts, the analysis in Chapters 4 and 5 shows that the nature of entrepreneurial activity was changing over the main period of analysis. We have been able to enlarge significantly the range of information that can be drawn on to demonstrate that many business sectors were concentrating into larger sizes and that corporate activity was becoming increasingly important.

One effect was that non-corporate proprietors, whilst continuing to grow in numbers, had to adjust to a more slowly growing pool of profits as companies absorbed a larger share of the most profitable activities, with these effects accelerating from the 1890s. Hence incomes were shared more thinly, and this seems to have been a key driver that reduced the numbers of own-account proprietors and the smallest firms (those with fewer than 10 employees) from the 1870s, but especially after 1901 (Figures 5.10 and 5.11). The census data for 1901 generally represent a high point for own-account activity which began to slow in rate of increase, or decline, under pressure from employer-led businesses, who were themselves increasingly concentrating and growing, while also experiencing pressure from corporate businesses. Small businesses would remain important throughout the twentieth and twenty-first centuries, but would never again be as significant as they were between 1851 and 1901; they were pushed out by competition from larger firms and the larger capital needs of mechanisation and other developments.

This changed the makeup of choices; with expanding waged work available, people increasingly turned to it rather than own-account entrepreneurship, and entrepreneurs increasingly focused on larger-scale businesses that needed lots of workers. Furthermore, as Chapters 6 and 9 show, the national market was ever more integrated with accessibility increasingly influencing decisions. Rural areas were, consequently, becoming less entrepreneurial than they had once been, especially in the maker-dealer sectors. Small communities were more able to purchase goods produced elsewhere, and thus local small-scale manufacturing and maker-dealing in items such as clothes, shoes and other consumer goods declined. Furthermore, one of the key sectors, agriculture, often ignored in studies of entrepreneurship, was in long-term decline in terms of employment throughout this period, albeit business numbers remained remarkably stable and even slowly increased (Figures 4.4–4.6). This meant that entrepreneurship did not decline in agriculture, but shifted its form towards own account and small employers. Hence in contrast to analyses based on occupational change and proportions of the workforce, there was no shift in entrepreneurship out of agriculture, but a relative growth of worker opportunities in larger firms in other industries. All these changes meant that in 1911 and later periods the English and Welsh population was more divided between employers and workers than it had been since 1851 (and perhaps earlier periods). Entrepreneurial activity was being reshaped by changing contexts beyond the control of most, and choices made were tipping towards favouring waged work.

The analysis has also demonstrated that female entrepreneurship was dramatically more common than previously suggested (Chapter 8). Moreover the evidence of the major role played by married women in operating businesses shows that previous comment on different types of female business activity must be radically reassessed. The census remains an imperfect record of female economic activity, but even given its drawbacks the census reveals female business proprietorship in general, and married women's activity in particular, to be on a level far beyond that previously recognised. Women most commonly ran own-account businesses, most frequently when married or widowed, but also when single, in a limited array of sectors: clothes making, food sales, retailing, accommodation and refreshments. In those sectors, they were of great significance as a substantial part or majority of all entrepreneurs.

However, for both men and women the chance of being an entrepreneur was closely related to various demographic factors, discussed in Chapters 6 and 7, of which marital status, position within the household and age were key influences. Our analysis reinforces arguments about the centrality of the family to the Victorian economy. This often had the consequence of hiding the economic activity of women, who supported family entrepreneurship in ways that are hard to recover from the census. However, the analysis of co-entrepreneurs in Chapter 8 and the family firm in Chapter 7 reveals their importance in the specific businesses that can be identified as based on the household as a unit.

Throughout this volume it has been clear that the men and women of Victorian and Edwardian England and Wales made the choice of whether or not to start a business under circumstances not of their own making. Their decision was shaped, limited and enabled by a set of interlocking contexts: the family, their location and the sector. Each of these has been shown to interact with the choice of entrepreneurship in ways which render any easy equation of business proprietorship with economic success, risk-taking or innovation difficult to reduce to simple measures of the incidence of entrepreneurship, something Chapter 9 shows in its discussion of the changing geography of entrepreneurship and the difficulty of measuring rates at a local level. This reveals some of the difficulties of the measures built into modern rate calculations, such as those used to make international comparisons in GEM (2018).

A key aspect of the difficulties of rate measures is the locational unit used. But also important is how an entrepreneur is to be distinguished from others in their supporting environment on whom they depend. Married male heads were the most common entrepreneurs in the Victorian period, but they were supported by spouses, family members and resident servants and assistants. Women often ran own-account businesses whilst their husbands were engaged in waged labour. Migrants, as Chapter 10 shows, were often more entrepreneurial than individuals born in England and Wales, but this was shaped by their inability to access waged labour markets and their form of entrepreneurship was determined by the sectors they could access, such as the Jewish tailors in the East End. In each of these cases, and many more illustrated in this book, individual entrepreneurs were part of a business unit or a wider social unit. This underpins the importance of the modern literature that focuses on broader definitions of entrepreneurship within family and other enterprises.

12.4   Future research

This volume presents one of the most detailed uses of big data in historical scholarship based on construction of one of the largest databases ever assembled on entrepreneurs, which has a reasonable claim to offer a surrogate 'British Business

Census'. It demonstrates, along with recent work by others on demography, the potential for using large-scale individual level data in historical and other research (Schürer et al., 2018). The most obvious benefit of the database is that it contains the whole population and thus avoids the issues of sampling and selection bias which have troubled previous studies of entrepreneurship and business history. The database offers considerable potential for further development and analysis. Some of this is being undertaken by the authors, such as analysis on partnerships, firm size, farm size and more detailed work on the impact of transportation. But in addition to the authors' further research the potential of the database should also be an attraction to other researchers. The key dimensions for further analysis fall into three groups.

First, there is considerable scope to investigate many of the more fine-grained developments of the 1851–1911 period. We have focused primarily in this book on drawing out the aggregate trends and the key influences on entrepreneurial choice. Whilst we have analysed data at the 797 occode level, we have mainly had to focus on aggregate sectors, using the EA13 and EA44 definitions. The database provides great scope to develop national whole-population studies for individual business categories (at the level of individual occodes, e.g. jewellers, blacksmiths) and other sectoral aggregations that move away from our sector definitions to fit other specific research questions. Similar fine-grained questions can be developed on different types of individuals within families and households, taking further the work by Davidoff on cousins and aunts, or investigating boarders and lodgers, or any other relationship category. The unoccupied and unemployed are also an interesting and valuable category to assess more fully than possible here, offering potential to address research questions about labour force participation and stocks and flows within the labour market. At the geographical level more details studies can be developed for specific cities, towns, villages or other spatial units of interest. Wider groupings of different types of spatial unit can be investigated moving on from our factor analyses. Migration can be analysed at finer level of parishes or towns rather than our more aggregate areas. Local and regional aggregates can also be assessed within economic growth models; we have posed various questions in Chapter 2 about endogenous growth which used as a background for some interpretations, but can be more fully addressed using linkage with other data – of which the most valuable would be wage rates. The 1851–1911 analysis can be extended to later censuses: modern census data already available digitally at the individual level, and the censuses of 1921 and 1931 once they have been encoded.

Second, we hope we have opened the way for using the BBCE as a data source that can be built on by others to create a more general resource for business historians. The database so far constructed has all identifiable census respondents that ran businesses of all sizes. While Scotland's data unfortunately was not ready for analysis in this book, it has since been added to the BBCE database. Although the database has to be anonymised because of restrictions from the licence holder for I-CeM (FindMyPast), the names and addresses of census respondents can be accessed through a special licence via the UKDA. This opens the way to add to the database. We believe the data are near-complete for non-corporates, though are bound to have some omissions. Other contributors can add to these data by supplying business connections which have not been so far identified. This can be done at various levels:

- Individual firms not included in the database but found to exist by other users can be linked to the database by infilling details of that business, or infilling lost and truncated information on existing entries;
- Specific search strategies at local, sector or other levels to fill out 'all' firms; e.g. by using record linkage to trade directories;
- Additional data can be added about these firms, including information such as capital levels, sales or profit information if known from other sources;
- Developing infills based on specific research questions, such as those relating to innovation, through record linkage of innovators known from other sources to their census records and attempting matched samples against comparable sub-sets of individuals, opening the way for a better founded sample for innovation and other specific categories;
- Considerably developing the linkage to the corporate sector, by extending the record linkage we have been able to achieve of about 36 percent of *Directory of Directors* listings matched to the census to those unmatched from the *Directory*; and also searching for other known directors among census respondents using other sources, especially linked to the stock exchange data.

Such studies will have the benefit to put individual dimensions of analysis in their place: for example, for the first time putting 'Schumpeterian innovation' in its proper context compared to the mass of other entrepreneurs. We believe there is enormous scope for integrated studies of business history along these lines although, beyond focused research studies, there will be challenges to how more general database enhancement is organised, achieves consistency, and is integrated with the UKDA BBCE data deposit. The inputs could be derived from many sources, ranging from academic researchers to family historians and crowd-sourcing.

Third, as well as extending record linkage to other sources, there is considerable scope for intercensal record linkage. This would allow tracking of firms over time, or tracking of individual's movements between firms or other occupations. We have begun this process for the employer categories over 1851–91, focusing on the Group 1 respondents who gave workforce sizes in 1851–81, and developed record linkage for about 30 percent of this group. This will be reported in future publications and a future data deposit. But this only begins to scratch the surface of the larger scale of record linkage now possible from the BBCE database, especially as this can be linked with the wider I-CeM database to attempt to record-link the whole population which would allow family reconstruction, migration tracking and panel comparisons of workers and the unoccupied with entrepreneurs. This would allow dynamic analyses of choice equivalent to the cross-sections to which we have been restricted here, as well as investigating a wider range of research questions. Once such panel samples have been constructed much greater potential for econometric analysis is also opened up, allowing stronger causal inferences to be drawn. This would offer considerable potential for spatial econometric analysis, and the ability to compare spatial and individual-level record linkage and casual modelling.

These groups of future research directions do not exhaust the possibilities. What we hope the BBCE database deposit will achieve, and this book has helped to open up, is the start of a journey towards a wider understanding of business development over time based on whole-population analysis for research communities in many disciplines.

References

Acheson, G.C., Campbell, G., Turner, J. and Vanteeva, N. (2015) Corporate ownership and control in Victorian Britain, *Economic History Review*, 68, 911–36.

Acland, A.H.D. and 45 others (1888) Memorandum on the improvement of census returns, especially as regards occupations and industry, in *Report of the Committee Appointed by the Treasury to Inquire Into Certain Questions Connected with the Taking of the Census, Parliamentary Papers*, 58(1890), 118–20.

Acs, Z.J. and Audretsch, D.B. (1990) *Innovation and Small Firms*, Cambridge, MA: MIT Press.

Acs, Z.J. and Armington, C. (2009) *Entrepreneurship, Geography, and American Economic Growth*, Cambridge: Cambridge University Press.

Acs, Z.J., Braunerhjelm, A., Audretsch, D.B. and Carlsson, B. (2009) The knowledge spillover theory of entrepreneurship, *Small Business Economics*, 32(1), 15–30.

Aghion, P. and Howitt, P. (1992) A model of growth through creative destruction, *Econometrica*, 60(2), 323–51.

Alchian, A.A. and Demsetz, H. (1972) Production, information costs, and economic organisation, *American Economic Review*, 62(5), 777–95.

Alden, J.D. (1977) The extent and nature of double jobbing in Great Britain, *Industrial Relations Journal*, 8, 14–24.

Alden, J.D. and Saha, S.K. (1980) A regional analysis of double jobholding in the UK, 1969–1975, *Regional Studies*, 14(5), 367–79.

Alderman, G. (1973) *The Railway Interest*, Leicester: Leicester University Press.

Aldrich, H.E. and Cliff, J.E. (2003) The pervasive effects of family on entrepreneurship: Toward a family embeddedness perspective, *Journal of Business Venturing*, 18(5), 573–96.

Aldrich, H.E. and Waldinger, R. (1990) Ethnicity and entrepreneurship, *Annual Review of Sociology*, 16, 111–35.

Allanson, P. (1992) Farm size structure in England and Wales, 1939–89, *Journal of Agricultural Economics*, 43(2), 137–48.

Alsos, G.A., Ljunggren, E. and Pettersen, L.T. (2003) Farm-based entrepreneurs: What triggers the start-up of new business activities? *Journal of Small Business and Enterprise Development*, 10(4), 435–43.

Anderson, M. (1971) *Family Structure in Nineteenth Century Lancashire*, Cambridge: Cambridge University Press.

Anderson, M. (1972) The study of family structure, in E.A. Wrigley, ed., *Nineteenth-Century Society: Essays in the Use of Quantitative Methods for the Study of Social Data*, Cambridge: Cambridge University Press, 47–81.

Anderson, M. (1984) The social position of spinsters in Mid-Victorian Britain, *Journal of Family History*, 9(4), 377–93.

Anderson, M. (1988) Households, families and individuals: Some preliminary results from the national sample from the 1851 Census of Great Britain, *Continuity and Change*, 3(3), 421–38.

Anderson, M. (1990) The social implications of demographic change, in F.M.L. Thompson, ed., *The Cambridge Social History of Britain, 1750–1950: Volume 2: People and Their Environment*, Cambridge: Cambridge University Press, 1–70.

Anderson, M. (1999) What can the Mid-Victorian censuses tell us about variations in married women's employment?, *Local Population Studies*, 62, 9–30.

Anderson, M., Collins, B. and Scott, C. (1979) *National Sample from the 1851 Census of Great Britain*. [data collection], UK Data Service, http://doi.org/10.5255/UKDA-SN-1316-1.

Andersson, L. and Hammarstedt, M. (2010) Intergenerational transmissions in immigrant self-employment: Evidence from three generations, *Small Business Economics*, 34, 261–76.

Ang, J.S., Cole, R.E. and Lin, J.W. (2000) Agency costs and ownership structure, *Journal of Finance*, 55(5), 81–106.

Armstrong, W.A. (1972) The use of information about occupations, in E.A. Wrigley, ed., *Nineteenth-Century Society: Essays in the Use of Quantitative Methods for the Study of Social Data*, Cambridge: Cambridge University Press, 191–210.

Ashton, T.S. (1961) *The Industrial Revolution in the Eighteenth Century: An Outline of the Beginnings of the Modern Factory System in England*, London: Johnathan Cape.

Ashworth, W. (1962) *A Short History of the International Economy since 1850*, London: Longman.

Aston, J. (2016) *Female Entrepreneurship in Nineteenth-Century England, Engagement in the Urban Economy*, Basingstoke: Palgrave Macmillan.

Atack, J. and Bateman, F. (1999) U.S. historical statistics: Nineteenth century U.S. industrial development through the eyes of the census of manufactures, *Historical Methods*, 32, 177–88.

Atack, J., Bateman, F., Haines, M. and Margo, R.A. (2011) Railroads and the rise of the factory: Evidence for the United States, 1850–1870, in P.W. Rhode, J.L. Rosenbloom, and D.F. Weiman, eds., *Economic Evolution and Revolution in Historical Time*, Stanford, CA: Stanford University Press, 162–79.

Baines, D. (1995) *Emigration from Europe, 1815–1930*, Cambridge: Cambridge University Press.

Baines, D. and Johnson, P. (1999) Did they jump or were they pushed? The exit of older men from the London labor market, 1929–1931, *The Journal of Economic History*, 59(4), 949–71.

Baines, D. and Woods, R. (2004) Population and regional development, in R. Floud and P. Johnson, eds., *The Cambridge Economic History of Modern Britain: Volume II: Economic Maturity, 1860–1939*, Cambridge: Cambridge University Press, 25–55.

Baker, A.P. (2004) Leslie, Andrew (1818–1894), in *Oxford Dictionary of National Biography*, Oxford: Oxford University Press.

Baker, T. and Welter, F. eds. (2015) *The Routledge Companion to Entrepreneurship*, London: Routledge.

Bannock, G. (1989) *Small Business Statistics: A Feasibility Study Prepared for the Department of Employment*, London: Graham Bannock & Partners.

Barker, H. (2006) *The Business of Women: Female Enterprise and Urban Development in Northern England, 1760–1830*, Oxford: Oxford University Press.

Barker, H. (2017) *Family and Business during the Industrial Revolution*, Oxford: Oxford University Press.

Barker, T. and Gerhold, D. (1995) *The Rise and Rise of Road Transport, 1700–1990*, Cambridge: Cambridge University Press.

Barnes, G.A. and Guinnane, T.W. (2012) Social class and the fertility transition: A critical comment on the statistical results reported in Simon Szreter's fertility, class and gender in Britain, 1860–1940, *Economic History Review*, 65(4), 1267–79.

Barreto, H. (1989) *The Entrepreneur in Microeconomic Theory: Disappearance and Explanation*, London: Routledge.

Barro, R.J. and Sala-i-Martin, X. (1995) *Economic Growth*, Cambridge, MA: MIT Press.

Baumol, W.J. (1990) Entrepreneurship: Productive, unproductive, and destructive, *Journal of Political Economy*, 98(5), 893–921.

Baumol, W.J. (2010) *The Microtheory of Innovative Entrepreneurship*, Princeton, NJ: Princeton University Press.

Becattini, G., Bellandi, M. and de Propis, L. eds. (2009) *A Handbook of Industrial Districts*, London: Edward Elgar.

Belchem, J. (2006) *Merseypride: Essays in Liverpool Exceptionalism*, second edition, Liverpool: Liverpool University Press.

Belchem, J. (2007) *Irish, Catholic and Scouse: The History of the Liverpool-Irish, 1800–1939*, Liverpool: Liverpool University Press.

Bellamy, J.E. (1953) A note on occupational statistics in British censuses, *Population Studies*, 6(3), 306–8.

Bellamy, J.E. (1978) Occupational statistics in the nineteenth century censuses, in R. Lawton, ed., *The Census and Social Structure: An Interpretative Guide to Nineteenth Century Censuses for England and Wales*, London: Frank Cass, 165–78.

Bellerby, J.R. (1956) *Agricultural and Industrial Relative Income*, London: Macmillan.

Bendix, R. (1974) *Work and Authority Industry*, Berkeley, CA: University of California Press.

Bennett, R.J. (2011) *Local Business Voice: The History of Chambers of Commerce in Britain, Ireland and Revolutionary America, 1760–2011*, Oxford: Oxford University Press.

Bennett, R.J. (2016) Interpreting business partnerships in late-Victorian Britain, *Economic History Review*, 69(4), 1199–227.

Bennett, R.J. and Newton, G. (2015) Employers in the 1881 population census of England and Wales, *Local Populations Studies*, 29–49.

Bennett, R.J., Smith, H. and Montebruno, P. (2019a) The population of non-corporate business proprietors in England and Wales 1891–1911, *Business History*, http://doi.org/10.1080/00076791.2018.1534959

Bennett, R.J., Montebruno, P., van Lieshout, C. and Smith, H. (2019b) Firm size and railway development in England and Wales 1851–81, forthcoming.

Benson, J. (1983) *Penny Capitalists: A Study of Nineteenth-Century Working-Class Entrepreneurs*, Dublin: Gill and Macmillan.

Berg, M. (1993) Small producer capitalism in eighteenth-century England, *Business History*, 35(1), 17–39.

Berg, R. van den (2012) 'Something wonderful and incomprehensible in their œconomy': The English versions of Richard Cantillon's essay on the nature of trade in general, *European Journal of Economic Thought*, 19(6), 868–907.

Bianchi, S.M. and Milkie, M.A. (2010) Work and family research in the first decade of the 21st century, *Journal of Marriage and Family*, 72(3), 705–25.

BIS (2014) *Business population estimates for the UK and regions*, Department of Business Innovation and Skills, London.

Blanchflower, D. (2000) Self-employment in OECD countries, *Labour Economics*, 7(5), 471–505.

Blanchflower, D. and Shadforth, C. (2007) *Entrepreneurship in the UK*, Speech, Bank of England. www.bankofengland.co.uk/publictaions/Pages/speeches/default.aspx

Booth, C. (1886) Occupations of the people of the United Kingdom 1801–1881, *Journal of the Royal Statistical Society*, 49(2), 314–435.

Booth, C. (1902–3) *Life and Labour of the People in London*, second series, 17 volumes, London: Macmillan.

Boschma, R.A. (2009) *Evolutionary Economic Geography and Its Implications for Regional Innovation Policy*, Paris: OECD.

Bowley, A.L. (1919) *The Division of the Product of Industry: An Analysis of National Income before the War*, Oxford: Oxford University Press.

Bowley, A.L. (1937) *Wages and Incomes in the United Kingdom since 1860*, Cambridge: Cambridge University Press.

Bowley, A.L. and Stamp, J. (1927) *The National Income 1924: A Comparative Study of the Income of the United Kingdom in 1911 and 1924*, Oxford: Clarendon Press.

Boyer, G.R. and Hatton, T.J. (1997) Migration and labour market integration in late nineteenth-century England and Wales, *Economic History Review*, 50(4), 697–734.

Boyer, G.R. and Hatton, T.J. (2002) New estimates of British unemployment, 1870–1913, *Journal of Economic History*, 63(2), 643–75.

Brewer, A. (1992) *Richard Cantillon: Pioneer of Economic Theory*, London: Routledge.

Briggs, A. (1990) *Victorian Cities*, London: Penguin.

Broadberry, S. (1997) *The Productivity Race: British Manufacturing in International Perspective, 1850–1990*, Cambridge: Cambridge University Press.

Broadberry, S. (2006) *Market Services and the Productivity Race, 1860–2000: British Performance in International Perspective*, Cambridge: Cambridge University Press.

Broadberry, S. (2014) The rise of the service sector, in R. Floud, J. Humphries, and P. Johnson, eds., *The Cambridge Economic History of Modern Britain, Volume 2, 1870 to the Present*, Cambridge: Cambridge University Press, 330–61.

Broadberry, S., Federico, G. and Klein, A. (2010) Sectoral developments, 1870–1914, in S. Broadberry and K. O'Rourke, eds., *The Cambridge Economic History of Modern Europe Volume 2, 1870 to the Present*, Cambridge: Cambridge University Press, 59–83.

Brodie, A., Felstead, A., Franklin, J., Pinfield, L. and Oldfield, J. (2001) *Directory of British Architects*, 2 volumes, London: Continuum.

Brodie, M. (2004) *The Politics of the Poor: The East End of London, 1885–1914*, Oxford: Oxford University Press.

Brown, B.J.H. (1943) *The Tariff Reform Movement in Great Britain, 1881–1895*, New York: Columbia University Press.

Buckley, P.J. (1989) *The Multination Enterprise: Theory and Applications*, Basingstoke: Palgrave Macmillan.

Burnett, J.A., Hughes, K., MacRaild, D. and Smith, M. (2012) Scottish Migrants in the Northern 'Irish Sea Industrial Zone', 1841–1911: Preliminary Patterns and Perspectives, *Northern History*, 49(1), 73–95.

Burnette, J. (2008) *Gender, Work and Wages in Industrial Revolution Britain*, Cambridge: Cambridge University Press.

Bythall, D. (1978) *The Sweated Trades: Outwork in Nineteenth-Century Britain*, London: Batsford.

Cain, P.J. and Hopkins, A.G. (1986) Gentlemanly capitalism and British overseas expansion, I: The all-colonial system, 1688–1850, *Economic History Review*, 39(4), 501–25.

Cain, P.J. and Hopkins, A.G. (1987) Gentlemanly capitalism and British overseas expansion, II: New Imperialism, 1850–1945, *Economic History Review*, 40(1), 1–26.

Cain, P.J. and Hopkins, A.G. (2002) *British Imperialism 1688–2000*, second edition, London: Longmans.

Campagnolo, G. and Vivel, C. (2012) Before Schumpeter: Forerunners of the theory of the entrepreneur in 1900s German political economy: Werner Sombart, Friedrich von Wieser, *European Journal of Economic Thought*, 19(6), 908–43.

Campbell, G. and Turner, J.D. (2011) Substitutes for legal protection: Corporate governance and dividends in Victorian Britain, *Economic History Review*, 64(2), 571–97.

Cantillon, R. (1734/1755) *Essai sur la Nature du Commerce en général translated as the Analysis of Trade: Commerce . . . Banks, and Foreign Exchanges*, London: Gyles.

Capie, F. and Collins, M. (1996) Industrial lending by English commercial banks, 1860s–1914: Why did banks refuse loans?, *Business History*, 38(1), 26–44.

Caree, M.A., Stel, A. van, Thurik, A.R. and Wennekers, S. (2007) *The Relations between Economic Development and Business Ownership Revisited*, Discussion Paper TI 2007–022.3. Tinbergen Institute, Amsterdam/Rotterdam.

Carnevali, F. (2003) 'Malefactors and Honourable Men': The making of commercial honesty in nineteenth-century industrial Birmingham, in J.F. Wilson and A. Popp, eds., *Industrial Clusters and Regional Business Networks in England, 1750–1970*, Aldershot: Ashgate, 192–207.

Carnevali, F. (2005) *Europe's Advantage: Banks and Small Firms in Britain, France, Germany and Italy since 1918*, Oxford: Oxford University Press.

Carter, S. (2001) Multiple business ownership in the farm sector: Differentiating monoactive, diversified and portfolio enterprises, *International Journal of Entrepreneurial Behavior & Research*, 7(2), 43–59.

Carter, S. and Ram, M. (2003) Reassessing portfolio entrepreneurship, *Small Business Economics*, 21(4), 371–80.

Casson, M. (1982) *The Entrepreneur: An Economic Theory*, Oxford: Robertson.

Casson, M. (1999) The economics of the family firm, *Scandinavian Economic History Review*, 27(1), 10–23.

Casson, M. (2003) *The Entrepreneur: An Economic Theory*, second edition, Cheltenham: Edward Elgar.

Casson, M. ed. (2010) *Entrepreneurship: Theory, Networks, History*, Cheltenham: Edward Elgar.

Casson, M. and Godley, A. (2010) Entrepreneurship in Britain, 1830–1900, in D.S. Landes, J. Mokyr, and W.J. Baumol, eds., *The Invention of Enterprise: Entrepreneurship from Ancient Mesopotamia to Modern Times*. Princeton, NJ: Princeton University Press, 211–42.

Chandler, A.D. (1962) *Strategy and Structure: Chapters in the History of the Industrial Enterprise*, Cambridge, MA: MIT Press.

Chandler, A.D. (1977) *The Visible Hand: The Managerial Revolution in American Business*, Cambridge, MA: Harvard University Press.

Chandler, A.D. (1990) *Scale and Scope: The Dynamics of Industrial Capitalism*, London: Belknap Press.

Chapman, A.L. and Knight, R. (1953) *Wages and Salaries in the United Kingdom, 1920-1938*, Cambridge: Cambridge University Press.

Chapman, S.D. (1967) *The Early Factory Masters: The Transition to the Factory System in the Midlands Textile Industry*, Newton Abbot: David & Charles.

Chapman, S.D. (1984) *The Rise of Merchant Banking*, London: Allen & Unwin.

Chapman, S.D. (1972) *The Cotton Industry in the Industrial Revolution*, London: Macmillan.

Chapman, S.D. (1992) *Merchant Enterprise in Britain: From the Industrial Revolution to World War I*, Cambridge: Cambridge University Press.

Checkland, S.G. (1964) *The Rise of Industrial Society in England 1815–1885*, London: Longmans.

Cheffins, B.R. (2008) *Corporate Ownership and Control: British Business Transformed*, Oxford: Oxford University Press.

Church, R.A. (1968) The effect of the American export invasion on the British Boot and Shoe Industry, 1885–1914, *The Journal of Economic History*, 28(2), 223–54.

Church, R.A. (1993) The Family Firm in Industrial Capitalism: International Perspectives on Hypotheses and History, *Business History*, 35(4), 17–43.

Clapham, J.H. (1926) *An Economic History of Modern Britain, Vol. 1: The Early Railway Age, 1820–1850*, Cambridge: Cambridge University Press.

Clapham, J.H. (1932) *An Economic History of Modern Britain, Vol. 2: Free Trade and Steel 1850–1886*, Cambridge: Cambridge University Press.

Clapham, J.H. (1938) *An Economic History of Modern Britain, Vol. 3: Machines and National Rivalries (1887–1914) with an Epilogue (1914–1929)*, Cambridge: Cambridge University Press.

Clark, C. (1957) *The Conditions of Economic Progress*, third edition, London: Macmillan.

Clark, G. (2010) The macroeconomic aggregates for England, 1209–2008, in A.J. Field, G.G. Clark, and W.A. Sundersrom, eds., *Research in Economic History*, Volume 27. London: Emerald, 51–119.

Clark, P. (2000) *British Clubs and Societies 1580–1800*, Oxford: Clarendon Press.

Colli, A. (2003) *The History of the Family Business, 1850–2000*, Cambridge: Cambridge University Press.

Colli, A. (2013) Risk, uncertainty, and family ownership, in P. Fernández Pérez and A. Colli, eds., *The Endurance of Family Businesses: A Global Overview*, Cambridge: Cambridge University Press, 85–108.

Colli, A., Fernández Pérez, P. and Rose, M. (2003) National determinants of family firm development? Family firms in Britain, Spain, and Italy in the nineteenth and twentieth centuries, *Enterprise and Society*, 4(4), 28–64.

Colli, A. and Rose, M. (2008) Family business, in G. Jones and J. Zeitlin, eds., *The Oxford Handbook of Business History*, Oxford: Oxford University Press, 194–218.

Collins, E.J.T. (2000) Rural and agricultural change, in E.J.T. Collins, ed., *The Agrarian History of England and Wales, Vol. VII, 1850–1914: Part One*, Cambridge: Cambridge University Press, 72–190.

Collins, M. and Baker, M. (2003) *Commercial Banks and Industrial Finance in England and Wales, 1860–1913*, second edition, Oxford: Oxford University Press.

Congregado, E., Golpe, A.A. and Parker, S. (2009) The dynamics of entrepreneurship: Hysteresis, business cycles and government policy, *IZA Discussion Paper No. 4093*, Bonn.

Conrad, F.G., Couper, M.P. and Sakshaug, J.W. (2016) Classifying open-ended reports: Factors affecting the reliability of occupation codes, *Journal of Official Statistics*, 32(1), 75–92.

Cooney, E.W. (1980) The building industry, in R. Church, ed., *The Dynamics of Victorian Business: Problems and Perspectives to the 1870s*, London: Allen & Unwin, 142–60.

Copelman, D.M. (1996) *London's Women Teachers: Gender, Class and Feminism, 1870–1930*, London: Routledge.

Cottrell, P.L. (1980) *Industrial Finance 1830–1914: The Finance and Organisation of English Manufacturing Industry*, London: Methuen.

Cottrell, P.L. (2004) Domestic finance, 1860–1914, in R. Floud and P. Johnson, eds., *The Cambridge Economic History of Britain, Vol II, Economic Maturity 1860–1939*, Cambridge: Cambridge University Press, 253–79.

Crafts, N.F.R. (1985) *British Industrial Growth during the Industrial Revolution*, Oxford: Oxford University Press.

Crafts, N.R.F. (1997) Economic history and endogenous growth, in D.M. Kreps and K.F. Wallis, eds., *Advances in Economics and Econometrics: Theory and Applications, Volume 2*, Cambridge: Cambridge University Press, 43–78.

Crafts, N.F.R. (2005) Market potential in British regions 1871–1931, *Regional Studies*, 39(9), 1159–66.

Crafts, N.F.R. and Mulatu, A. (2005) What explains the location of industry in Britain, 1871–1931?, *Journal of Economic Geography*, 5(4), 499–518.

Craig, B. (2016) *Women and Business since 1500, Invisible Presences in Europe and North America?*, London: Palgrave.

Crossick, G. (1977) The emergence of the lower middle class in Britain, a discussion, in G. Crossick, ed., *The Lower Middle Class in Britain, 1870–1914*, London: Croom Helm, 11–60.

Crossick, G. (1978) *An Artisan Elite in Victorian Society: Kentish London 1840–1880*, London: Croom Helm.

Crossick, G. (1984) The Petite Bourgeoisie in nineteenth-century Britain: The urban and liberal case, in G. Crossick and H.-G. Haupt, eds., *Shopkeepers and Master Artisans in Nineteenth-Century Europe*, London: Methuen, 62–94.

Crossick, G. (2000) Meanings of property and the world of the petit bourgeoisie, in J. Stobart and A. Owens, eds., *Urban Fortunes: Property and Inheritance in the Town, 1700–1900*, Aldershot: Ashgate, 50–78.

Crossick, G. and Haupt, H.-G. (1995) *The Petite Bourgeoisie in Europe 1780–1914: Enterprise, Family and Independence*, London: Routledge.

Çrouzet, F. (1982) *The Victorian Economy*, trans. A. Foster, London: Methuen.

Çrouzet, F. (1985) *The First Industrialists*, Cambridge: Cambridge University Press.

Curthoys, M. (2004) *Governments, Labour, and the Law in Mid-Victorian Britain: The Trade Union Legislation of the 1870s*, Oxford: Oxford University Press.

Dahl, M.S. and Sorenson, O. (2012) Home Sweet Home: Entrepreneurs location choices and the performance of their ventures, *Management Science*, 58(6), 1059–71.

Daunton, M. (1983) *House and Homes in the Victorian City: Working-Class Housing, 1850–1914*, London: Edward Arnold.

Daunton, M. (1985) *Royal Mail: The Post Office since 1840*, London: Athlone.

Daunton, M. (1991) 'Gentlemanly capitalism' and British industry 1820–1914, *Past & Present*, 122, 119–58.

Daunton, M. (2007) *Wealth and Welfare: An Economic and Social History of Britain 1851–1951*, Oxford: Oxford University Press.

Davidoff, L. (1995) The separation of home and work? Landladies and lodgers in nineteenth and twentieth century England, in L. Davidoff, ed., *Worlds between: Historical Perspectives on Gender & Class*, London: Routledge, 151–80.

Davidoff, L. (2012) *Thicker Than Water: Siblings and Their Relationships 1780–1920*, Oxford: Oxford University Press.

Davidoff, L. and Hall, C. (1997) *Family Fortunes: Men and Women of the English Middle Class 1780–1850*, revised edition, London: Routledge.

Davies, M.F. (1909) *Life in an English Village: An Economic and Historical Survey of the Parish of Corsley in Wiltshire*, London: T. F. Unwin.

Day, C. (1927) *The Distribution of Industrial Occupations in England, 1841–61*, New Haven, CT: Yale University Press.

Day, J. (2015) *Leaving home and migrating in nineteenth-century England and Wales: Evidence from the 1881 census enumerators books (CEBs)*, Ph.D. thesis, Cambridge University.

DBEIS (2017) *Business Population Estimates 2017*, London: Department for Business, Energy & Industrial Strategy.

De Vries, J. (1984) *European Urbanisation 1500–1800*, London: Methuen.

Denvir, J. (1894) *The Irish in Britain from the Earliest Times to the Fall and Death of Parnell*, second edition, London: Kegan Paul, Trench and Trübner & Co.

Devine, T.M. (2011) *To the Ends of the Earth: Scotland's Global Diaspora, 1750–2010*, London: Allen Lane.

Digby, A. (1994) *Making a Medical Living: Doctors and Patients in the English Market for Medicine, 1720–1911*, Cambridge: Cambridge University Press.

DE (1991) *Small Firms in Britain*, Department of Employment, London.

DTI (2009) *SME Statistics*, Department of Trade and Industry, London.

Duranton, G. and Puga, D. (2004) Micro-foundations of urban agglomeration economies, in J.V. Henderson and J.-F. Thisse, eds., *Handbook of Regional and Urban Economics, Vol. 4: Cities and Geography*, Amsterdam: North-Holland, 2063–117.

EC (1981) *Factors Influencing Ownership, Tenancy, Mobility and the Use of Farmland in the United Kingdom*, Information on Agriculture No. 74, Brussels: European Commission.

Edelstein, M. (1982) *Overseas Investment in the Age of High Imperialism*, London: Methuen.

Ekelund, R.B. and Hébert, R.F. (1983) *A History of Economic Theory and Method*, second edition, New York: McGraw Hill.

Erickson, A.L. (1993) *Women and Property in Early Modern England*, London: Routledge.

Erickson, A.L. (2008) Married women's occupations in eighteenth-century London, *Continuity and Change*, 23(2), 267–307.

EU (2001) 2001 *Innovation scoreboard*, Commission Staff Working, Paper SEC (2001) 1414, Brussels.

Evans, N.J. and Ilbery, B.W. (1993) The pluriactivity, part-time farming, and farm diversification debate, *Environment and Planning A: Economy and Space*, 25(7), 945–59.

Everitt, A. (1976) Country carriers in the nineteenth century, *Journal of Transport History*, 3, 179–202.

Evert, R.E., Martin, J.A., McLeod, M.S. and Payne, T. (2016) Empirics in family business research: Progress, challenges, and the path ahead, *Family Business Review*, 29(1), 17–43.

Fang, H.-T. (1930) *The Triumph of the Factory System*, Philadelphia, PA: Porcupine Press.

Fairlie, R.W. and Robb, A.M. (2007) Families, human capital, and small business: Evidence from the characteristics of business owners survey, *Industrial and Labor Relations Review*, 60(2), 225–45.

Fairlie, R.W. and Robb, A.M. (2008) *Race and Entrepreneurial Success: Black-, Asian-, and White-Owned Businesses in the United States*, Cambridge, MA: MIT Press.

Feinstein, C.H. (1972) *National Income, Expenditure and Output of the United Kingdom 1855–1965*, Cambridge: Cambridge University Press.

Feldman, D. (1994) *Englishmen and Jews: Social Relations and Political Culture, 1840–1914*, New Haven, CT: Yale University Press.

Feldman, D. (2000) Migration, in M. Daunton, ed., *Cambridge Urban History: Volume III, 1840–1950*, Cambridge: Cambridge University Press, 185–206.

Fernández Pérez, P. and Colli, A. (2013) Introduction, in P. Fernández Pérez and A. Colli, eds., *The Endurance of Family Businesses: A Global Overview*, Cambridge: Cambridge University Press, 1–10.

Field, J. (2018) Economic change in a London Suburb: Southwark, c. 1601–1881, *The London Journal*, 43(3), 243–66.

Figueiredo, O., Guimarães, P. and Woodward, D. (2002) Home-field advantage: Location decisions of Portuguese entrepreneurs, *Journal of Urban Economics*, 52(2), 341–61.

Finn, M. (1996) Women, consumption and coverture in England, c. 1760–1860, *Historical Journal*, 39(3), 703–22.

Fitton, R.S. and Wadsworth, A.P. (1958) *The Strutts and the Arkwrights, 1758–1830: A Study of the Early Factory System*, Manchester: Manchester University Press.

Fitzgerald, M.A. and Muske, G. (2002) Copreneurs: An exploration and comparison to other family businesses, *Family Business Review*, 15(1), 1–16.

Fitzpatrick, D. (2010) Emigration, 1871–1921, in W.E. Vaughan, ed., *A New History of Ireland, Volume VI: Ireland Under the Union II: 1870–1921*, Oxford: Oxford University Press, 606–52.

Fogel, R.W. (1964) *Railroads and American Economic Growth: Essays in Econometric History*, Baltimore, MD: Johns Hopkins University Press.

Foreman-Peck, J. and Hannah, L. (2012) Extreme divorce: The managerial revolution in UK companies before 1914, *Economic History Review*, 65(4), 1217–38.

Foreman-Peck, J. and Zhou, P. (2013) The strength and persistence of entrepreneurial cultures, *Journal of Evolutionary Economics*, 23(1), 163–87.

Francois, P. and Lloyd-Ellis, H. (2003) 'Animal spirits' through creative destruction, *American Economic Review*, 93(3), 530–50.

Fraser, D. (2009) *The Evolution of the British Welfare State: A History of Social Policy since the Industrial Revolution*, fourth edition, Basingstoke: Palgrave Macmillan.

Friedlander, D. and Roshier, R.J. (1966) A study of internal migration in England and Wales: Part I, *Population Studies*, 19(3), 239–79.

Frost, D. (1995) Racism, work and unemployment: West African seamen in Liverpool, 1880s-1960s, in D. Frost, ed., *Ethnic Labour and British Imperial Trade: A History of Ethnic Seafarers in the UK*, London: Frank Cass, 22–33.

Fuller, A.M. (1983) Part-time farming and the family farm, *Sociologica Ruralis*, 23(1), 5–10.

Gamber, W. (1997) *The Female Economy: The Millinery and Dressmaking Trades, 1860–1930*, Chicago, IL: University of Illinois Press.

Garrett, E., Reid, A., Schürer, K. and Szreter, S. (2001) *Changing Family Size in England and Wales: Place, Class and Demography, 1891–1911*, Cambridge: Cambridge University Press.

Gasson, R. (1967) Some characteristics of part-time farming in Britain, *Journal of Agricultural Economics*, 18(1), 111–20.

Gasson, R. (1983) *Gainful Occupations of Farm Families*, Ashford: Wye College, School of Rural Economics.

Gatrell, V.A.C. (1977) Labour, power and the size of firms in Lancashire cotton in the second quarter of the nineteenth century, *Economic History Review*, 30(1), 95–139.

Geary, F. and Stark, T. (2015) Regional GDP in the UK, 1861–1911: New estimates, *Economic History Review*, 68(1), 123–44.

GEM (2009) *2007 Report on Women and Entrepreneurship*, Babson, MA: Global Entrepreneurship Monitor.

GEM (2018) *Global Entrepreneurship Monitor: Global Report, 2017–18*, London: London Business School, Global Entrepreneurship Research Association.

Geroski, P. (1995) What Do We Know about Entry? *International Journal of Industrial Organization*, 13(4), 421–40.

Gilbert, D. and Southall, H. (2000) The urban labour market, in M. Daunton, ed., *The Cambridge Urban History of Britain: Volume III, 1840–1950*, Cambridge: Cambridge University Press, 593–628.

Gilbert, E.M. (1975) *Brighton, Old Oceans Bauble: The Growth of the English Sea-Side*, Hassocks: Flare Books.

Glaeser, E.L., Keer, S.P. and Kerr, W.R. (2015) Entrepreneurship and urban growth: An empirical assessment with historical mines, *Review of Economics and Statistics*, 97(2), 498–520.

Gleadle, K. (2001) *British Women in the Nineteenth Century*, Basingstoke: Palgrave Macmillan.

Godley, A. (1996) Immigrant entrepreneurs and the emergence of London's east end as an industrial district, *The London Journal*, 21(1), 38–45.

Godley, A. (2001) *Jewish Immigrant Entrepreneurship in New York and London, 1880–1914: Enterprise and Culture*, Basingstoke: Palgrave Macmillan.

Goldberg, L.R. and Velicer, W.F. (2006) Principles of exploratory factor analysis, in S. Strack, ed., *Differentiating Normal and Abnormal Personality*, second edition, New York: Springer Publishing Co.

Goose, N. (2004) Farm service in Southern England in the mid-nineteenth century, *Local Population Studies*, 72, 77–82.

Goose, N. (2006) Farm service, seasonal unemployment and casual labour in mid nineteenth-century England, *Agricultural History Review*, 54, 274–303.

Goose, N. (2007) The straw plait and Hat trades in nineteenth-century Hertfordshire, in N. Goose, ed., *Women's Work in Industrial England: Regional and Local Perspectives*, Hatfield: Local Population Studies Supplement, 97–137.

Goose, N. (2014) Regions, 1700–1870, in R. Floud, J. Humphries and P. Johnson, eds., *The Cambridge Economics History of Modern Britain: Volume I, 1700–1870*, Cambridge: Cambridge University Press, 149–77.

Gospel, H. (1992) *Markets, Firms and the Management of Labour in Modern Britain*, Cambridge: Cambridge University Press.

Gospel, H. (2008) The management of labor and human resources, in G. Jones and J. Zeitlin, eds., *The Oxford Handbook of Business History*, Oxford: Oxford University Press, 421–64.

Gough, J.W. (1969) *The Rise of the Entrepreneur*, London: Batsford.

Grande, J., Madsen, E.L. and Borch, O.J. (2011) The relationship between resources, entrepreneurial orientation and performance in farm-based venture, *Entrepreneurship & Regional Development*, 23(3–4), 89–111.

Gray, R. (1996) *The Factory Question and Industrial England, 1830–1860*, Cambridge: Cambridge University Press.

Green, D.R., Owens, A., Maltby, J. and Rutterford, J. (2009) Lives in the balance? Gender, age and assets in late-nineteenth-century England and Wales, *Continuity and Change*, 24(2), 307–35.

Grigg, D.B. 1989. *English Agriculture*, Oxford: Basil Blackwell.

Guide to Trade (1843) *The Dress-Maker, and the Milliner*, London: Charles Knight.

Gunn, S. (2000) *The Public Culture of the Victorian Middle Class: Ritual and Authority in the English Industrial City, 1840–1914*, Manchester: Manchester University Press.

Hallas, C. (1990) Craft occupations in the late nineteenth century: Some local considerations, *Local Populations Studies*, 44, 18–29.

Hallas, C. (1999) *Rural Responses to Industrialization: The North Yorkshire Pennines 1790-1914*, Bern: Peter Lang.

Hamlin, C. (1988) Muddling in Bumbledom: On the enormity of large sanitary improvements in four British towns, 1855–1885, *Victorian Studies*, 31(1), 55–83.

Hannah, L. (1983) *The Rise of the Corporate Economy*, second edition, London: Methuen.

Hannah, L. (1986) *Inventing Retirement: The Development of Occupational Pensions in Britain*, Cambridge: Cambridge University Press.

Hannah, L. (2007) The 'Divorce' of ownership from control from 1900 onwards: Re-calibrating imagined global trends, *Business History*, 49(4), 404–38.

Hannah, L. (2014) Corporations in the US and Europe 1790–1860, *Business History*, 56(6), 865–99.

Hannah, L. and Kay, J.A. (1977) *Concentration in Modern Industry: Theory, Measurement and the UK Experience*, London: Macmillan.

Hansmann, H. and Kraakman, R. (2000) The essential role of organizational law, *Yale Law Review*, 110(3), 387–440.

Harper, M. and Constantine, S. (2010) *Migration and Empire*, Oxford: Oxford University Press.

Harris, R. (2000) *Industrializing English Law: Entrepreneurship and Business Organization, 1720–1844*, Cambridge: Cambridge University Press.

Harrison, A. (1975) *Farmers and Farm Business in England*, Department of Agriculture, Economics and Management, Studies No. 62, University of Reading.

Hart, P.E. (1960) Business Concentration in the United Kingdom, *Journal of the Royal Statistical Society Series A (General)*, 123(1), 50–8.

Hatton, T.J. (2014) Population, migration and labour supply: Great Britain, 1871–2011, in R. Floud, J. Humphries and P. Johnson, eds., *The Cambridge Economic History of Modern Britain: Volume II, 1870 to the Present*, Cambridge: Cambridge University Press, 95–121.

Hatton, T.J. and Bailey, R.E. (2001) Women's work in census and survey, 1911–1931, *Economic History Review*, 54(1), 87–107.

Hawke, G.R. (1970) *Railways and Economic Growth in England and Wales, 1840–1870*, Oxford: Clarendon Press.

Hébert, R.F. and Link, A.N. (2009) *The History of Entrepreneurship*, London: Routledge.

Hennock, E.P. (1973) *Fit and Proper Persons: Ideal and Reality in Nineteenth-Century Urban Government*, London: Edward Arnold.

Higgs, E. (1983) Domestic servants and households in Victorian England, *Social History*, 8(2), 201–10.

Higgs, E. (1987) Women, occupations and work in the nineteenth century censuses, *History Workshop Journal*, 23, 59–80.

Higgs, E. (1988) The struggle for the occupational census, 1841–1911, in R.M. McLeod, ed., *Government and Expertise: Specialists, Administrators and Processionals, 1860–1914*, Cambridge: Cambridge University Press, 73–86.

Higgs, E. (1991) Disease, Febrile poisons, and statistics: The census as a medical survey, 1841–1911, *Social History of Medicine*, 4(3), 465–78.

Higgs, E. (1995) Occupational censuses and the agricultural workforce in Victorian England and Wales, *Economic History Review*, 48(4), 700–16.

Higgs, E. (2004) *Life, Death and Statistics: Civil Registration, Censuses and the Work of the General Register Office, 1836–1952*, Hatfield: Local Population Studies Supplement.

Higgs, E. (2005) *Making Sense of the Census Revisited: Census Records for England and Wales 1801–1901*, London: Institute of Historical Research and National Archives.

Higgs, E., Jones, C., Schürer, K. and Wilkinson, A. (2015) *Integrated Census Microdata (I-CeM) Guide*, second edition, Colchester: University of Essex History Department.

Higgs, E. and Wilkinson, A. (2016) Women, occupations and work in the Victorian Censuses revisited, *History Workshop Journal*, 81, 17–38.

Higgs, H. ed. (1931) *Essai sur la Nature du Commerce en General, by Richard Cantillon*, London: Macmillan, for the Royal Economic Society.

Hill, B. (1982) Concepts and measurement of the incomes, wealth and economic well-being of farmers, *Journal of Agricultural Economics*, 33(3), 311–24.

Hirst, P. and Zeitlin, J. (1991) Flexible specialization vs. Post-Fordism: Theory evidence and policy implications, *Economy and Society*, 20(1), 1–55.

Holmes, D. (2009) Development of the boot and shoe industry in Leicester during the nineteenth century, *Transactions of the Leicestershire Archaeological and Historical Society*, 83, 175–218.

Honeyman, K. (1983) *Origins of Enterprise: Business Leadership in the Industrial Revolution*, New York: St. Martins Press.

Honeyman, K. (2007) Doing business with gender: Service industries and British business history, *Business History Review*, 81(3), 471–4.

Honeyman, K. (2009) Invisible entrepreneurs? Women and business in twentieth-century Britain, in R. Coopey and P. Lyth, eds., *Business in Britain in the Twentieth Century: Decline and Renaissance?*, Oxford: Oxford University Press.

Honeyman, K. and Goodman, J. (1991) Women's work, gender conflict, and labour markets in Europe, 1500–1900, *Economic History Review*, 44(4), 608–28.

Hoppit, J. (2011) Bounties, the economy and the state in Britain, 1689–1800, in P. Gauci, ed., *Regulating the British Economy, 1660–1850*, Ashgate, Farnham, 139–60.

Hoppit, J. (2018) Petitions, economic legislation and interest groups in Britain, 1660–1800, *Parliamentary History*, https://doi.org/10.1111/1750-0206.12329

Horrell, S. and Humphries, J. (1995) Women's labour force participation and the transition to the male-breadwinner family, 1790–1865, *Economic History Review*, 48(1), 89–117.

Hoselitz, B.F. (1951) The early history of entrepreneurial theory, *Explorations in Entrepreneurial History*, 3(4), 193–220.

Hoselitz, B.F. (1960) *Theories of Economic Growth*, Glencoe IL: Free Press of Glencoe.

Howe, A. (1997) *Free Trade and Liberal England 1846–1946*, Oxford: Clarendon Press.

Howkins, A. and Verdon, N. (2008) Adaptable and sustainable? Male farm service and the agricultural labour force in midland and southern England, c. 1850–1925, *Economic History Review*, 61(2), 467–95.

Howorth, C., Rose, M., Hamilton, E. and Westhead, P. (2010) Family firm diversity and development: An introduction, *International Small Business Journal*, 28(5), 437–51.

Hudson, P. ed. (1989) *Regions and Industries: A Perspective on the Industrial Revolution in Britain*, Cambridge: Cambridge University Press.

Humphries, J. (2010) *Childhood and Child Labour in the British Industrial Revolution*, Cambridge: Cambridge University Press.

Humphries, J. and Sarasúa, C. (2012) Off the record: Reconstructing women's labor force participation in the European past, *Feminist Economics*, 18(4), 39–67.

Hunt, E.H. (1973) *Regional Wage Variations in Britain, 1850–1914*, Oxford: Oxford University Press.

Hunt, E.H. (1986) Wages, in J. Langton and R.J. Morris, eds., *Atlas of Industrializing Britain, 1780–1914*, London: Methuen, 60–8.

ICSER (1951) *Guides to Official Source, No. 2. Census Reports of Great Britain, 1801–1931*, London: Interdepartmental Committee on Social and Economic Research, HMSO.

Ingram, P. (2000) *British provincial dressmakers in the nineteenth century*, Ph.D. thesis, De Montfort University.

Isard, W. (1956) *Location and Space Economy: A General Theory Relating to Industrial Location, Market Areas, Land Use, Trade, and Urban Structure*, New York: MIT Press and John Wiley.

Jackson, G. (1988a) The ports, in M.J. Freeman, and D.H. Aldcroft, eds., *Transport in Victorian Britain*, Manchester: Manchester University Press, 218–52.

Jacobs, J. (1969) *The Economy of Cities*, New York: Random House.

Jacobs, J. (1984) *Cities and the Wealth of Nations*, New York: Random House.

James, H. (2013) Family values or crony capitalism?, in P. Fernández Pérez and A. Colli, eds., *The Endurance of Family Businesses: A Global Overview*, Cambridge: Cambridge University Press, 57–84.

Jason, L. (2013) The surprising social mobility of Victorian Britain, *European Review of Economic History*, 17(1), 1–23.

Jefferys, J.B. (1938) *Business organisation in Great Britain 1856–1914*, Ph.D. thesis, University of London; reprinted Arno Press, New York, 1977.

Jefferys, J.B. (1954) *Retail Trading in Britain, 1850–1950: A Study of Trends in Retailing with Special Reference to the Development of Co-Operative, Multiple Shop and Department Store Methods of Trading*, Cambridge: Cambridge University Press.

Jenks, L.H. (1944) Railroads as an economic force in American development, *Journal of Economic History*, 4(1), 1–20.

Jensen, M.C. and Meckling, W.H. (1976) Theory of the firm: Managerial behaviour, agency costs and ownership structure, *Journal of Financial Economics*, 3(4), 305–60.

Jeremy, D.J. (1984) Anatomy of the British Business Elite, 1860–1980, *Business History*, 26(1), 2–23.

Jeremy, D.J. (1998) *A Business History of Britain, 1900–1990s*, Oxford: Oxford University Press.

Jeremy, D.J. and Shaw, C. eds. (1984–6) *Dictionary of Business Biography: A Biographical Dictionary of Business Leaders Active in Britain in the Period 1860–1980*, 5 volumes, London: Butterworths.

Jevons, W.S. (1881) Richard Cantillon and the nationality of political economy, *Contemporary Review*, January, (reprinted in Jevons *Principles of Economics*, 1905; re-edited with noted by Higgs, 1931, 333–60).

Johnson, E.A.J. (1937) *Predecessors of Adam Smith: The Growth of British Economic Thought*, London: P. S. King.

Johnson, Paul (1994) The employment and retirement of older men in England and Wales, 1881–1891, *Economic History Review*, 47(1), 106–28.

Jones, G. and Rose, M.B. (1993) Family capitalism, *Business History*, 35(4), 1–16.

Jovanovic, B. and Rousseau, P.L. (2007) The small entrepreneur, in E. Sheshinski, R.J. Strom, and W.J. Baumol, eds., *Entrepreneurship, Innovation, and the Growth Mechanism of the Free-Enterprise Economies*, Princeton, NJ: Princeton University Press, 140–57.

Joyce, P. (1980) *Work, Society and Politics: The Culture of the Factory in Later Victorian England*, Brighton: Harvester.

Kay, A.C. (2009) *The Foundations of Female Entrepreneurship: Enterprise, Home and Household in London, c. 1800–1870*, London: Routledge.

Keeble, D.E. and Tyler, P. (1995) Enterprising behaviour and the urban-rural shift, *Urban Studies*, 32(6), 975–97.

Keeble, D.E. and Walker, S. (1994) New firms, small firms and dead firms: Spatial patterns and determinants in the United Kingdom, *Regional Studies*, 28(3), 411–27.

Keibek, S.A.J. and Shaw-Taylor, L. (2013) Early modern rural by-employments: A re-examination of the probate inventory evidence, *Agricultural History Review*, 61(2), 244–81.

Kennedy, W.P. (1991) Portfolio behaviour and economic development in late nineteenth century Great Britain and German: Hypotheses and conjectures, in J. Mokyr, ed., *The Vital One: Essays in Honor of Jonathan R.T. Hughes*, Greenwich, CT: Research in Economic History Supplement 6, Research Annual, JAI Press, 93–130.

Keynes, J.M. (2015) The general theory of employment, interest and money, in R. Skidelsky, ed., *The Essential Keynes*, London: Penguin.

Kinross, F. (1991) *Coffee and Ices: The Story of Carlo Gatti in London*, England: Kinross.

Kirzner, I.M. (1973) *Competition and Entrepreneurship*, Chicago, IL: Chicago University Press.

Kirzner, I.M. (1979) *Perception, Opportunity and Profit: Studies in the Theory of Entrepreneurship*, Chicago, IL: Chicago University Press.

Kirzner, I.M. (1985) *Discovery and the Capitalist Process*, Chicago, IL: University of Chicago Press.

Kirzner, I.M. (1997) Entrepreneurial discovery and the competitive market process: An Austrian approach, *Journal of Economic Literature*, 35(1), 60–85.

Kish, L. (1967) *Survey Sampling*, second edition, New York: Wiley & Sons.

Kitching, J. and Rouse, J. (2017) Opportunity or dead end? Rethinking the study of entrepreneurial action without a concept of opportunity, *International Small Business Journal*, 35(5), 558–77.

Knight, F.H. (1921) *Risk, Uncertainty and Profit*, Boston, MA: Houghton Mifflin; reissued with additional Prefatory Essay, London School of Economics, 1933.

Koning, N. (1994) *The Failure of Agrarian Capitalism: Agrarian Politics in the United Kingdom, Germany, the Netherlands and the USA 1846–1919*, London: Routledge.

Koster, S. and Venhorst, V.A. (2014) Moving shop: Residential and business relocation by the highly educated self-employed, *Spatial Economic Analysis*, 94(4), 436–64.

Krugman, P. (1991) *Geography and Trade*, Cambridge, MA: MIT Press.

Kussmaul, A. (1981) *Servants in Husbandry in Early Modern England*, Cambridge: Cambridge University Press.

Kuznets, S. (1926) *Cyclical Fluctuations: Retail and Whole-Sale Trade, United States, 1919–1925*, New York: Adelphi.

Kuznets, S. (1940) Schumpeter's business cycles, *American Economic Review*, 30(2), 257–71.

Kuznets, S. (1966) *Modern Economic Growth: Rate: Structure and Spread*, New Haven, CT: Yale University Press.

Kuznets, S. (1974) *Population, Capital, and Growth: Selected Essays*, London: Heinemann.

Kuznets, S., Epstein, L. and Jenks, E. (1941) *National Income and Its Composition, 1919–1938, vol. 1.*, New York: National Bureau of Economic Research.

La Porta, R., Lopez-de-Silanes, F. and Schleifer, A. (1999) Corporate ownership around the world, *Journal of Finance*, 54(2), 471–517.

La Porta, R., Lopez-de-Silanes, F. and Schleifer, A. (2008) The economic consequences of legal origins, *Journal of Economic Literature*, 42(2), 285–332.

La Porta, R., Lopez-de-Silanes, F., Schleifer, A. and Vishny, R.W. (1998) Law and finance, *Journal of Political Economy*, 106(6), 1113–55.

Lamoreaux, N.R. and Rosenthal, J.-L. (2005) Contractual tradeoffs and SMEs' choice of organizational form: A view from U.S. and French history, 1830–2000, *American Law and Economics Review*, 7, 28–61.

Landes, D.S. (1969) *The Unbound Prometheus: Technological Change and Industrial Development in West Europe from 1750 to the Present*, Cambridge: Cambridge University Press.

Langton, J. (1984) The Industrial Revolution and the Regional Geography of England, *Transactions of the Institute of British Geographers*, 9(2), 145–67.

Langton, J. (2000) Urban growth and economic change: From the late seventeenth century to 1841, in P. Clark, ed., *The Cambridge Urban History of Britain, Vol. II 1540–1840*, Cambridge: Cambridge University Press, 453–90.

Laslett, P. (1972) Introduction: The history of the family, in P. Laslett and R. Wall, eds., *Household and Family in Past Times*, Cambridge: Cambridge University Press, 1–90.

Law, C.M. (1967) The growth of urban population in England and Wales, 1801–1911, *Transactions of the Institute of British Geographers*, 41, 125–43.

Lawton, R. and Pooley, C.G. (1992) *Britain 1740–1950: An Historical Geography*, London: Edward Arnold.

Lazonick, W. (1990) *Competitive Advantage on the Shopfloor*, Cambridge, MA: Harvard University Press.

Lazonick, W. (1991) *Business Organization and the Myth of the Market Economy*, Cambridge: Cambridge University Press.

Lee, C.H. (1981) Regional growth and structural change in Victorian Britain, *Economic History Review*, 34(3), 438–52.

Lee, C.H (1984) The service sector, regional specialization, and economic growth in the Victorian economy, *Journal of Historical Geography*, 10(2), 139–55.

Levi, L. (1870) On joint stock companies, *Journal of the Statistical Society of London*, 33(1), 1–41.

Levie, J. (2007) Immigration, in-migration, ethnicity and entrepreneurship in the United Kingdom, *Small Business Economics*, 28(2–3), 143–69.

Lévesque, M. and Minniti, M. (2006) The effect of aging on entrepreneurial behavior, *Journal of Business Venturing*, 21, 177–94.

Lewis, S.I. (2009) *Unexceptional Women: Female Proprietors in Mid-Nineteenth-Century Albany, New York, 1830–1885*, Columbus, OH: Ohio State University Press.

Littler, C.R. (1982) *The Development of the Labour Process in Capitalist Societies: A Comparative Study of the Transformation of Work Organization in Britain, Japan and the USA*, Aldershot: Gower.

Lösch, A. (1937) Population cycles as a cause of business cycles, *Quarterly Journal of Economics*, 51(4), 649–62.

Lösch, A. (1943/1952) *The Economics of Location*, translated from 1943 second edition by W.H. Woglom and W.F. Stolper, New York: John Wiley.

Lyberg, L. and Kasprzykm, D. (1997) Post-survey processing and operations, in L. Lyberg, P.P. Biemer, M. Collins, E. de Leeuw, C. Dippo, N. Scwharz and D. Trewin, eds., *Survey Measurement and Process Quality*, New York: Wiley, 353–70.

MacRaid, D. (2011) *The Irish Diaspora in Britain, 1750–1939*, Basingstoke: Palgrave Macmillan.

Malcolmson, R.W. (1981) *Life and Labour in England 1700–1780*, London: Hutchinson.

Malcolmson, P.E. (1986) *English Laundresses: A Social History, 1850–1930*, Urbana and Chicago, IL: University of Illinois Press.

Marlow, S., Henry, C. and Carter, S. (2009) Exploring the impact of gender upon women's business ownership, *International Small Business Journal*, 29(6), 717–35.

Marshall, A. (1919) *Industry and Trade: A Study of Industrial Technique and Business Organization; and Their Influence on the Conditions of Various Classes and Nations*, London: Macmillan.

Marshall, A. (1961) *Principles of Economics*, ninth edition with annotation of 1920 edition, London: Macmillan.

Marshall, A. and Marshall, M.P. (1879) *The Economics of Industry*, London: Macmillan.

Martin, J., Bushnell, D., Campanelli, P. and Thomas, R. (1994) A comparison of interviewer and office coding of occupations, Survey Methods Centre Newsletter, *Social and Community Planning Research*, 15(2), 18–25.

Martin, R. (1988) The political economy of Britain's North-South divide, *Transactions of the Institute of British Geographers*, 13(4), 389–414.

Mason, C. (1994) Spatial variations in enterprise: The geography of new firm formation, in R. Burrows, ed., *Deciphering the Enterprise Culture: Entrepreneurship, Petty Capitalism and the Restructuring of Britain*, London: Routledge, 74–106.

Mayer, C., Siegel, D.S. and Wright, M. (2018) Entrepreneurship: An assessment, *Oxford Review of Economic Policy*, 24(4), 517–39.

McCarthy, A. (2002) The Scottish diaspora since 1815, in T.M. Devine and J. Wormald, eds., *The Oxford Handbook of Modern Scottish History*, Oxford: Oxford University Press, 510–32.

McGeevor, S. (2014) How well did the nineteenth century census record women's regular employment in England and Wales? A case study of Hertfordshire in 1851, *The History of the Family*, 19(4), 489–512.

McKay, J. (2007) Married women and work in nineteenth-century Lancashire: The evidence of the 1851 and 1861 census report, 164–181, in N. Goose, ed., *Women's Work in Industrial England: Regional and Local Perspectives*, Hatfield: Local Populations Studies Supplement, 164–81.

McKibbin, R. (2013) Political sociology in the guise of economics: J.M. Keynes and the Rentier, *English Historical Review*, 128(530), 78–106.

Meager, N. and Bates, P. (2004) Self-employment in the United Kingdom in the 1980s and 1990s, in R.A. and W. Müller, eds., *The Re-Emergence of Self-Employment: A Comparative Study of Self-Employment Dynamics and Social Inequality*, Princeton, NJ: Princeton University Press, 135–69.

Michelacci, C. and Silva, O. (2007) Why so many local entrepreneurs?, *Review of Economics and Statistics*, 89(4), 615–33.

Miles, A. (1999) *Social Mobility in Britain, 1837–1914*, Basingstoke: Palgrave Macmillan.

Mill, J.S. (1867) *Principles of Political Economy with Some of Their Applications to Social Philosophy*, London: Longmans Green.

Mills, D.R. (1999) Trouble with farms at the Census Office: An evaluation of farm statistics from the censuses of 1851–1881 in England and Wales, *Agricultural History Review*, 47(1), 58–77.

Mises, L. von (1949) *Human Action: A Treatise on Economics*, New Haven, CT: Yale University Press.

Mitchell, B.R. (1964) The coming of the railway and United Kingdom economic growth, *Journal of Economic History*, 24(3), 315–36.

Mitchell, B.R. (1988) *British Historical Statistics, 1750–1970*, Cambridge: Cambridge University Press.

Mitchell, B.R. and Deane, P. (1962) *Abstract of British Historical Statistics*, Cambridge: Cambridge University Press.

Mokyr, J. (1990) *The Lever of Riches: Technological Creativity and Economic Progress*, Oxford: Oxford University Press.

Mokyr, J. (2009) *The Enlightened Economy: An Economic History of Britain, 1700–1850*. New Haven, CT: Yale University Press.

Mokyr, J. (2010) Entrepreneurship and the industrial revolution in Britain, in D.S. Landes, J. Mokyr and W.J. Baumol, eds., *The Invention of Enterprise: Entrepreneurship from Ancient Mesopotamia to Modern Times*, Princeton, NJ: Princeton University Press, 183–210.

Mohr, J. and Spekman, R. (2006) Characteristics of partnership success: Partnership attributes, communication behavior, and conflict resolution techniques, *Strategic Management Journal*, 15(2), 135–52.

Montebruno, P., Bennett, R.J., van Lieshout, C. and Smith, H. (2019a) Shifts in agrarian entrepreneurship in mid-Victorian England and Wales, *Agricultural History Review*, 67(1).

Montebruno, P., Bennett, R.J., van Lieshout, C. and Smith, H. (2019b) A tale of two tails: Do power law and lognormal models fit firm-size distributions in the mid-Victorian era? *Physica A: Statistical Mechanics and its Applications*, 523(1), 858–75.

Moore-Colyer, R.J. (2000) Wales, in E.J.T. Collins, ed., *The Agrarian History of England and Wales: Volume VII, 1850–1914, Part 1*, Cambridge: Cambridge University Press, 427–52.

Morris, R.J. (1990) *Class, Sect and Party: The Making of the British Middle Class: Leeds, 1820–50*, Manchester: Manchester University Press.

Morris, R.J. (2005) *Men, Women and Property in England, 1780–1870: A Social and Economic History of Family Strategies amongst the Leeds Middle Classes*, Cambridge: Cambridge University Press.

Morton, J.C. ed. (1855) *A Cyclopedia of Agriculture, Practical and Scientific*, Glasgow: Blackie and Son.

Moser, C.A. and Scott, Wolf (1961) *British Towns: A Statistical Study of Their Social and Economic Differences*, London: Oliver and Boyd.

Mukhtar, S.M. (1998) Business characteristics of male and female small and medium enterprises in the UK: Implications for gender-based entrepreneurialism and business competence development, *British Journal of Management*, 9(1), 41–51.

Murphy, A. (1986) *Richard Cantillon: Entrepreneur and Economist*, Oxford: Clarendon Press.

Muske, G., Fitzgerald, M.A., Haynes, G., Black, M., Chin, L., MacClure, R. and Mashburn, A. (2009) The intermingling of family and business financial resources: Understanding the copreneurial couple, *Journal of Financial Counselling and Planning*, 20(2), 27–47.

Nenadic, S. (1993) The small family firm in Victorian Britain, *Business History*, 35(4), 86–114.

Nenadic, S. (1998) The social shaping of business behaviour in the nineteenth-century women's garment trades, *Journal of Social History*, 31(3), 625–45.

Nenadic, S. (2007) Gender and the rhetoric of business success: The impact of women entrepreneurs and the 'new woman', in Later Nineteenth-Century Edinburgh, in N. Goose, ed., *Women's Work in Industrial England: Regional and Local Perspectives*, Hatfield: Local Population Studies Supplement, 269–88.

Nenadic, S., Morris, R. J., Smyth, J. and Rainger, C. (1992) Record linkage and the small family firm: Edinburgh 1861–1891, *Bulletin of the John Rylands Library*, 74(3), 169–88.

Nicholas, T. (1999a) Wealth making in nineteenth and early twentieth century Britain: Industry v. commerce and finance, *Business History*, 41(1), 16–36.

Nicholas, T. (1999b) Clogs to Clogs in three generations? Explaining entrepreneurial performance in Britain since 1850, *Journal of Economic History*, 59(3), 688–713.

Nicholas, T. (2000) Wealth Making in the nineteenth-and early twentieth century: The Rubinstein hypothesis revisited, *Business History*, 42(2), 155–68.

Niedomysl, T., Källström, J., Sierdjan, K. and Östh, J. (2018) Interregional migration of business owners: Who moves and how does moving affect firm performance? *Regional Studies*, 53(4), 503–16. https://doi.org/10.1080/00343404.2018.1462486

Niemelä, T. and Häkkinen, R. (2014) The role of puriactivity for continuity and survival in family farm firms. *Journal of Entrepreneurship Management and Innovation*, 10(4), 7–43.

North, D.C. (1990) *Institutions, Institutional Change and Economic Performance*, Cambridge, Cambridge: Cambridge University Press.

North, D.C. (2005) *Understanding the Process of Economic Change*, Princeton, NJ: Princeton University Press.

Nye, J.V.C. (1991) Lucky fools and cautious businessmen: On entrepreneurship and the measurement of entrepreneurial failure, in J. Mokyr, ed., *The Vital One: Essays in Honor of Jonathan R.T. Hughes*, Greenwich, CT: Research in Economic History Supplement 6, Research Annual, JAI Press, 131–52.

OECD (1978) *Part-Time Farming in OECD Countries*, Paris: OECD.

Ó Grada, C. (1995) *Ireland: A New Economic History, 1780–1939*, Oxford: Oxford University Press.

OPCS (1977) *Guide to Census Reports: Great Britain, 1801–1966*, London: Office of Population Censuses and Surveys HMSO.

Osborne, J.W. and Costello, A.B. (2005) Best practices in exploratory factor analysis: Four recommendations for getting the most from your analysis, *Practical Assessment, Research & Evaluation*, 10(7), 1–9.

Owen, R. (1857) *The Life of Robert Owen, Written by Himself, Volume 1*, London: E. Wilson.

Owens, A. (2002) Inheritance and the life-cycle of family firms in the early industrial revolution, *Business History*, 44(1), 21–46.

Pahl, R.E. (1984) *Divisions of Labour*, Oxford: Basil Blackwell.

Panayi, P. (1995) *German Immigrants in Britain during the Nineteenth Century*, Oxford: Berg.

Panayi, P. (2010) *An Immigration History of Britain: Multicultural Racism since 1800*, Harlow: Longman.

Parker, S.C. (2004) *The Economics of Self-Employment and Entrepreneurship*, Cambridge: Cambridge University Press.

Parker, S.C. ed. (2011) *Entrepreneurship in Recession*, Cheltenham: Edward Elgar.

Parker, S.C. (2018) Entrepreneurship in economic theory, *Oxford Review of Economic Policy*, 34(4), 540–64.

Parris, H. (1965) *Government and the Railways in Nineteenth Century Britain*, London: Routledge.

Payne, P.L. (1967) The emergence of the large-scale company in Britain, 1870–1914, *Economic History Review*, 20(3), 519–42.

Payne, P.L. (1984) Family business in Britain: An historical and analytical survey, in A. Okochi and S. Yasuoka, eds., *Family Business in the Era of Industrial Growth: Its Ownership and Management*, Tokyo: University of Tokyo Press, 171–206.

Payne, P.L. (1988) *British Entrepreneurship in the Nineteenth Century*, second edition, London: Macmillan.

Peneder, M. (2001) *Entrepreneurial Competition and Industrial Location: Investigating the Structural Patterns and Intangible Sources of Competitive Performance*, Cheltenham: Edward Elgar.

Peneder, M. and Resch, A. (2015) Schumpeter and venture finance: Radical theorist, broke investor, and enigmatic teacher, *Industrial and Corporate Change*, 24(6), 1315–52.

Penrose, E. (1959) *The Theory of the Growth of the Firm*, Oxford: Oxford University Press.

Perkyns, A. (1996) Age checkability and accuracy in the census of six Kentish parishes, 1851–1881, in D. Mills and K. Schürer, eds., *Local Communities in the Victorian Census Enumerators Books*, Oxford: Leopards Head Press, 115–34.

Phillips, N. (2006) *Women in Business 1700–1850*, Woodbridge: Boydell Press.

Piketty, T. (2014) *Capital in the Twenty-First Century*, Cambridge, MA: Belknap Press.

Piori, M.J. and Sabel, C.F. (1984) *The Second Industrial Divide: Possibilities for Prosperity*, New York: Basic Books.

Pollard, S. (1968) *The Genesis of Modern Management*, Harmondsworth: Penguin.

Pollard, S. (1984) *The Neglect of Industry: A Critique of British Economic Policy since 1870*, Rotterdam: Erasmus Universiteit, 1984.

Pollins, H. (1969) Railway contractors and the finance of railway development in Britain, in M.C. Reed, ed., *Railways in the Victorian Economy: Studies in Finance and Economic Growth*, Newton Abbot: David & Charles, 212–28.

Pooley, C.G. (1977) The residential segregation of migrant communities in mid-Victorian Liverpool, *Transactions of the Institute of British Geographers*, 2(3), 364–82.

Pooley, C.G. and Turnbull, J. (1997) Leaving home: The experience of migration from the parental home in Britain since c. 1770, *Journal of Family History*, 22(4), 390–424.

Pooley, C.G. and Turnbull, J. (1998) *Migration and Mobility in Britain since the Eighteenth Century*, London: UCL Press.

Popp, A. (2013) *Entrepreneurial Families: Business, Marriage and Life in the Early Nineteenth Century*, London: Pickering and Chatto.

Popp, A. and Wilson, J.F. (2007) Life cycles, contingency, and agency: Growth, development and change in English industrial districts and clusters, *Environment and Planning A: Economy and Space*, 39(12), 2975–92.

Porter, B. (1979) *The Refugee Question in Mid-Victorian Politics*, Cambridge: Cambridge University Press.

Porter, T.M. (1986) *The Rise of Statistical Thinking 1820–1900*, Princeton, NJ: Princeton University Press.

Postlethwayt, M. (1749) *A Dissertation on the Plan, Use, and Importance, of the Universal Dictionary of Trade and Commerce*, London: Knapton.

Powell, C. (1980) *The British Building Industry since 1800: An Economic History*, London: E. & F.N. Spon.

Prais, S.J. (1964) A new look at the growth of industrial concentration, *Oxford Economic Papers*, 26(2), 273–88.

Prais, S.J. (1981) *The Evolution of Giant Firms in Britain: A Study of the Growth of Concentration in Manufacturing Industry in Britain 1909–70*, Cambridge: Cambridge University Press.

Prest, J. (1990) *Liberty and Locality: Parliament, Permissive Legislation, and Ratepayers Democracies in the Nineteenth Century*, Oxford: Oxford University Press.

Prothero, R. (1912) *English Farming, Past and Present*. London and New York: Longmans, Green.

Radicic, D., Bennett, R.J. and Newton, G. (2017) Portfolio entrepreneurship in farming: Empirical evidence from the 1881 Census for England and Wales, *Journal of Rural Studies*, 55, 289–302.

Redlich, F. (1949) On the origin in of the concepts of 'entrepreneur' and 'creative entrepreneur', *Explorations in Entrepreneurial History*, 1(2), 1–7.

Reed, M. (1986) Nineteenth-century rural England: A case for 'peasant studies'?, *Journal of Peasant Studies*, 14(1), 78–99.

Reeder, D. and Rodger, R. (2000) Industrialisation and the city economy, in M. Daunton, ed., *The Cambridge Urban History of Britain:Volume III, 1840–1950*, Cambridge: Cambridge University Press, 553–92.

Richards, E. (1974) Women in the British economy since about 1700: An interpretation, *History*, 59(19), 337–57.

Roberts, E. (1988) *Women's Work 1840–1940*, Cambridge: Cambridge University Press.

Robinson, R. (1986) The evolution of railway fish traffic policies, 1840–66, *Journal of Transport History*, 7(1), 32–44.

Robson, B. (1973) *Urban Growth: An Approach*, London: Methuen.

Romer, P.M. (1986) Increasing returns and long-run growth, *Journal of Political Economy*, 94(5), 1002–37.

Romer, P.M. (1990) Endogenous technological change, *Journal of Political Economy*, 98(5), 71–102.

Rønning, L. and Kovereid, L., 2006. Income diversification in Norwegian farm households: Reassessing pluriactivity. *International Small Business Journal*, 24(4), 405–20.

Rosa, P. and Hamilton, D. (1994) Gender and ownership in UK small firms, *Entrepreneurship Theory and Practice*, 18(3), 11–27.

Rosa, P. and Scott, M. (1999) The prevalence of multiple owners and directors in the SME sector: Implications for our understanding of start-up and growth, *Entrepreneurship and Regional Development*, 11(1), 21–37.

Rose, M.B. (1993) Beyond Buddenbrooks: The family firm and the management of succession in nineteenth-century Britain, in Jonathan Brown and Mary B. Rose, eds., *Entrepreneurship, Networks and Modern Business*, Manchester: Manchester University Press, 127–43.

Royle, V. (1833) *The Factory System Defended, in Reply to some parts of the Speech by G. Condy, Esq.*, Manchester: T. Sowler.

Rubinstein, W.D. (1977) Wealth, Elites, and the Class Structure of Modern Britain, *Past and Present*, 76, 99–126.

Rubinstein, W.D. (1993) *Capitalism, Culture and Economic Decline in Britain, 1750–1990*, London: Routledge.

Rubinstein, W.D. (2006) *Men of Property: The Very Wealthy in Britain since the Industrial Revolution*, second edition, London: Social Affairs Unit.

Rutterford, J., Green, D.R., Maltby, J. and Owens, A. (2011) Who comprised the nation of shareholders? Gender and investment in Great Britain, c. 1870–1935, *Economic History Review*, 64(1), 157–87.

Samuel, R. (1975) *Village Life and Labour*, London: Routledge and Kegan Paul.

Samuel, R. (1977) *Miners, Quarrymen and Saltworkers*, London: Routledge and Kegan Paul.

Sanderson, M. (1995) *Education, Economic Change and Society in England 1780–1870*, Cambridge: Cambridge University Press.

Savary de Bruslons, J. (1723) *Dictionnaire Universel de Commerce*, 2 volumes, Paris: Jacques Etienne.

Say, J.B. (1827) *A Treatise on Political Economy: Or the Production, Distribution, and Consumption of Wealth*, translated from the fourth edition of the French by C.R. Prinsep, London: Longman, Hurst, Rees, Orme & Brown.

Schloss, D.F. (1899) *Methods of Industrial Remuneration*, London: Williams and Norgate.

Schumpeter, J.A. (1927) The explanation of the business cycle, *Economica*, 21(1), 286–311.

Schumpeter, J.A. (1934) *The Theory of Economic Development*, Cambridge, MA: Harvard University Press.

Schumpeter, J.A. (1939) *Business Cycles: A Theoretical, Historical and Statistical Analysis of the Capitalist Process*, New York: McGraw Hill.

Schumpeter, J.A. (1942) *Capitalism, Socialism and Democracy*, New York: Harper & Brothers.

Schürer, K. (1991) The 1891 census and local population studies, *Local Population Studies*, 47, 16–29.

Schürer, K., Garrett, E., Jaadla, H. and Reid, A. (2018) Household and family structure in England and Wales (1851–1911): Continuities and change, *Continuity and Change*, 33(3), 365–411.

Schürer, K., Higgs, E., Reid, A.M. and Garrett, E.M. (2016) *Integrated Census Microdata 1851–1911, version V.2 (I-CeM.2)*, [data collection], UK Data Service, SN: 7481, http://dx.doi.org/10.5255/UKDA-SN-7481-1; enhanced.

Schürer, K. and Woollard, M. (2000) *1881 Census for England and Wales, the Channel Islands and the Isle of Man (Enhanced Version)* [data collection]. Federation of Family History Societies, Genealogical Society of Utah, [original data producers]. UK Data Service, SN: 4177, http://doi.org/10.5255/UKDA-SN-4177-1.

Schürer, K. and Woollard, M. (2002) *National Sample from the 1881 Census of Great Britain 5% Random Sample: Working Documentation Version 1.1*, Colchester: Historical Censuses and Social Surveys Research Group, University of Essex.

Scott, A.J. and Storper, M. (1987) High technology industry and regional development: A theoretical critique and reconstruction, *International Social Science Journal*, 112, 215–32.

Scott, P. (2007) *Triumph of the South: A Regional Economic History of Early Twentieth-Century Britain*, Aldershot: Ashgate.

Seccombe, W. (1993) *Weathering the Storm: Working-Class Families from the Industrial Revolution to the Fertility Decline*, New York: Verso.

Seed, J. (2006) Limehouse Blues: Looking for Chinatown in the London Docks, 1900–40, *History Workshop Journal*, 62, 58–85.

Segerstrom, P.S., Anant, T.C.A. and Dinopoulos, E. (1990) A Schumpeterian model of the product life cycle, *American Economic Review*, 80(5), 1077–91.

Shane, S. and Venkataraman, S. (2000) The promise of entrepreneurship as a field of research, *Academy of Management Review*, 25(1), 217–26.

Shannon, H.A. (1932) The limited companies of 1866–1883, *Economic History Review*, 4(1), 290–316.

Shaw, G. (1982) *British Directories as Sources in Historical Geography*, Norwich: Geo Abstracts.

Shaw, G. (2004) Marks, Michael (1859–1907), in *Oxford Dictionary of National Biography*, Oxford: Oxford University Press.

Shaw, G. and Tipper, A. (1997) *British Directories: A Bibliography and Guide to Directories Published in England and Wales (1850–1950) and Scotland (1773–1950)*, second edition, London: Mansell.

Shaw-Taylor, L. (2005) Family farms and capitalist farms in mid nineteenth-century England, *The Agricultural History Review*, 53(2), 158–191.

Shaw-Taylor, L. (2007) Diverse experiences: The geography of adult female employment in England and the 1851 census, in N. Goose, ed., *Women's Work in Industrial England: Regional and Local Perspectives*, Hatfield: Local Populations Studies Supplement, 29–50.

Shaw-Taylor, L. (2012) The rise of agrarian capitalism and the decline of family farming in England, *Economic History Review*, 65(1), 26–60.

Shaw-Taylor, L. and Wrigley, E.A. (2014) Occupational structure and population geography, in R. Floud, J. Humphries, and P. Johnson, eds., *The Cambridge Economic History of Modern Britain: Volume I, 1700–1870*, Cambridge: Cambridge University Press, 53–88.

Sherrington, C.E.R. (1934) *A Hundred Years of Inland Transport, 1830–1933*, London: Duckworth.

Simmons, J. *The Railway in Town and Country 1830–1914*. Newton Abbot: David and Charles, 1986.

Smiles, S. (1859) *Self-Help: With Illustrations of Character and Conduct*, London: John Murray.

Smith, A. (1904) *An Inquiry Into the Nature and Causes of the Wealth of Nations*, ed. Edwin Cannan, London: Methuen.

Smith, H. (2015) William Hutton and the Myths of Birmingham, *Midland History*, 40(1), 53–73.

Smith, H., Bennett, R.J. and Radicic, D. (2018) Towns in Victorian England and Wales: A new classification, *Urban History*, 45(4), 568–94.

Smith, H., Bennett, R.J. and van Lieshout, C. (2019) Entrepreneurship in Birmingham and Manchester, 1851–1911, forthcoming.

Smith, R. (1961) An Oldham limited liability company 1875–1896, *Business History*, 4(1), 34–53.

Sorenson, O. (2017) Regional ecologies of entrepreneurship, *Journal of Economic Geography*, 17(5), 959–74.

Sparks, E. (2006) *Capital Intentions: Female Proprietors in San Francisco, 1850–1920*, Chapel Hill: University of North Carolina Press.

Spengler, J.J. (1954) Richard Cantillon: First of the moderns. I and II, *Journal of Political Economy*, 62(4), 281–95; 62(5), 406–24.

Spring, D. (1971) English Landowners and nineteenth century industrialism, in J.T. Ward and R.G. Wilson, eds., *Land and Industry: The Landed Estate and the Industrial Revolution*, Newton Abbot: David & Charles, 16–62.

Stamp, J. (1916) *British Income and Property: The Application of Official Statistics to Economic Problems*, London: King.

Stedman Jones, G. (2013) *Outcast London: A Study in the Relationship between Classes in Victorian Society*, third edition, London: Verso.

Storey, D.J. (1994) *Understanding the Small Business Sector*, London: Routledge.

Stuetzer, M., Obschonka, M., Audretsch, D.B., Wyrwich, M., Rentfrow, P.J., Coombes, M., Shaw-Taylor, L. and Satchell, M. (2016) Industry structure, entrepreneurship, and culture: An empirical analysis using historical coalfields, *European Economic Review*, 86, 52–72.

Sunderland, D. (2007) *Social Capital, Trust and the Industrial Revolution, 1780–1880*, London: Routledge.

Swift, R. and Campbell, S. (2017) The Irish in Britain, in E.F. Biagini and M.E. Daly, eds., *The Cambridge Social History of Modern Ireland*, Cambridge: Cambridge University Press, 515–33.

Szreter, S. (1996) *Fertility, Class and Gender in Britain, 1860–1940*, Cambridge: Cambridge University Press.

Tabili, L. (2011) *Global Migrants, Local Culture: Natives and Newcomers in Provincial England, 1841–1939*, Basingstoke: Palgrave Macmillan.

Tatomir, S. (2015) Self-Employment: What can we learn from recent developments? *Bank of England Quarterly Bulletin*, Q1, 56–66.

Taylor, F.W. (1911) *The Principles of Scientific Management*, New York: Harper & Brothers.

Taylor, M. (1997) *The Changing Picture of Self-Employment in Britain*, Discussion paper 97/2, ESRC Research Centre on Macro-Social Change, University of Essex.

Teitelbaum, M.S. (1984) *The British Fertility Decline: Demographic Transition in the Crucible of the Industrial Revolution*, Princeton, NJ: Princeton University Press.

Thane, P. (2011) The Experience of Retirement in Britain, Past and Present, *Österreichische Zeitschrift für Geschictswissenschaften*, 22(3), 13–32.

Thomson, D. (1996) Age reporting by the elderly and the nineteenth-century census, in D. Mills and K. Schürer, eds., *Local Communities in the Victorian Census Enumerators Books*, Oxford: Leopards Head Press, 86–99.

Thünen, J.H. von (1826/1966) *Isolated State*, translation from 1826 edition by C.M. Wartenberg, Oxford: Pergamon.

Todd, G. (1932) Some aspects of joint stock companies 1844–1900, *Economic History Review*, 4(1), 46–71.

Turnbull, G.L. (1979) *Traffic and Transport: An Economic History of Pickfords*, London: George Allen & Unwin.

Turner, J.D. (2009) Wider share ownership?: Investors in English and Welsh bank shares, *Economic History Review*, 62(1), 167–92.

Turnock, D. (1998) *A Historical Geography of Railways in Great Britain and Ireland*. Aldershot: Ashgate.

Ure, A. (1835) *The Philosophy of Manufactures, or an Exposition of the Scientific, Moral, and Commercial Economy of the Factory System of Great Britain*, London: Charles Knight.

Vickery, A. (1993) Golden age to separate spheres? A review of the categories and chronology of English women's history, *The Historical Journal*, 36(2), 383–414.

Wall, R. (2002) Elderly widows and widowers and their coresidents in late 19th and early 20th-century England and Wales, *History of the Family*, 7(1), 139–55.

Wallis, P. (2014) Labour markets and training, in R. Floud, J. Humphries, and P. Johnson, eds., *The Cambridge Economic History of Modern Britain: Volume 1, 1700–1870*, Cambridge: Cambridge University Press, 178–210.

Ward, J.T. ed. (1970) *The Factory System: Volume 1: Birth and Growth*, Newton Abbot: David & Charles.

Wardley, P. (1999) The emergence of big business: The largest corporate employers of labour in the United Kingdom, Germany and the United States c. 1907, *Business History*, 41(4), 88–116.

Wardley, P. (2001) On the ranking of firms: A response to Jeremy and Farnie, *Business History*, 43(3), 119–34.

Warren, K. (1986) Chemicals, in J. Langton and R.J. Morris, eds., *Atlas of Industrializing Britain, 1780–1914*, London: Methuen, 114–18.

Webb, S and Webb, B. (1920) *The History of Trade Unionism*, second edition, London: Longmans.

Weber, A. (1909/1929) *The Location of Industries*, translation of 1909 edition by C.J. Friedrich, Chicago IL: University of Chicago Press.

Webster, W. (2011) The Empire comes home: Commonwealth migration to Britain, in A. Thompson, ed., *Britain's Experience of Empire in the Twentieth Century*, Oxford: Oxford University Press, 122–60.

Welton, T.A. (1911) *England's Recent Progress*, London: Chapman and Hall.

Wennekers, S., Stel, A. van, Carree, M. and Thurik, R. (2010) *The Relationship between Entrepreneurship and Economic Development: Is It U-Shaped?* EIM Research Reports, Zoetermeer.

Westhead, P. and Howorth, C. (2007) 'Types' of private family firms: An exploratory conceptual and empirical analysis, *Entrepreneurship & Regional Development*, 19(5), 405–31.

Whaples, R. (2013) Economic history and entrepreneurship, in R. Whaples and R.E. Parker, eds., *Routledge Handbook of Modern Economic History*, London: Routledge, 71–81.

Whyte, I.D. (2000) *Migration and Society in Britain, 1550–1830*, Basingstoke: Palgrave Macmillan.

Wiener, M.J. (1981) *English Culture and the Decline of the Industrial Spirit, 1850–1914*, Cambridge: Cambridge University Press.

Williams, P.L. (1978) *The Emergence of the Theory of the Firm: From Adam Smith to Alfred Marshall*, London: Macmillan.

Williamson, J.G. (1990) *Coping with City Growth during the Industrial Revolution*, Cambridge: Cambridge University Press.

Williamson, O.E. (1985) *The economic institutions of capitalism: Firms, markets, relational contracting*, New York: Free Press.

Wilson, J.F. and Popp, A. eds. (2003) *Industrial Clusters and Regional Business Networks in England, 1750–1970*, Ashgate, Aldershot.

Wilson, J.F. and Singleton, J. (2003) The Manchester industrial district, 1750–1939: Clustering, networking and performance, in J.F. Wilson and A. Popp, eds., *Industrial Clusters and Regional Business Networks in England, 1750–1970*, Ashgate, Aldershot, 44–67.

Wise, M.J. (1949) On the evolution of the jewellery and gun quarters in Birmingham, *Transactions and Papers (Institute of British Geographers)*, 15, 59–72.

Winstanley, M. (1983) *The Shopkeepers World, 1830–1914*, Manchester: Manchester University Press.

Winstanley, M. (1996) Industrialization and the small farm: Family and household economy in nineteenth-century Lancashire, *Past and Present*, 152, 157–95.

Woods, R. (2000) *The Demography of Victorian England and Wales*, Cambridge: Cambridge University Press.

Woodward, D. (1995) *Men at Work: Labourers and Building Craftsmen in the Towns of Northern England, 1450–1750*, Cambridge: Cambridge University Press.

Woollard, M. (1997a) Creating a machine-readable version of the 1881 census enumerators books, in C. Harvey and J. Press, eds., *Databases in Historical Research: Theory, Methods and Applications*, Basingstoke: Palgrave Macmillan, 98–101.

Woollard, M. (1997b) 'Shooting the Nets': A note on the reliability of the 1881 census enumerators books, *Local Population Studies*, 59, 54–7.

Woollard, M. (1999) *The Classification of Occupations in the 1881 Census of England and Wales*, Colchester: Department of History, University of Essex.

Woollard, M. (2002) The employment and retirement of older men, 1851–1881: Further evidence from the census, *Continuity and Change*, 17(3), 437–63.

Woollard, M. (2004) The classification of multiple occupational titles in the 1881 census of England and Wales, *Local Population Studies*, 72, 34–49.

Worswick, G.D.N. and Tipping, D.G. (1967) *Profits in the British Economy 1909–1938*, Oxford: Blackwell.

Wright, C.D. (1882) The factory system as an element of civilisation, *Journal of Social Science*, 16(1), 101–26.

Wright, C.D. (1883) Report on the factory system of the United States, in *Report on the Manufactures of the United States at the Tenth Census (June 1, 1880)*, Washington, DC: Government Printing Office, 527–606.

Wrigley, E.A. (1975) Baptism coverage in early nineteenth-century England: The Colyton area, *Population Studies*, 29(2), 299–316.

Wrigley, E.A. (2006) The transition to an advanced organic economy: Half a millennium of English agriculture, *Economic History Review*, 59(5), 435–80.

Wrigley, E.A. (2011) *The Early English Censuses*. Oxford: Oxford University Press.

You, X. (2014) *Women's Employment in England and Wales, 1851–1911*, Ph.D. thesis, Cambridge University.

Young, C. (1995) Financing the micro-scale enterprise: Rural craft producers in Scotland, 1840–1914, *Business History Review*, 69(3), 398–421.

Zona, F. (2015) Board ownership and processes in family firms, *Small Business Economics*, 44(1), 105–22.

Zucchi, J.E. (1999) *The Little Slaves of the Harp: Italian Child Street Musicians in Nineteenth-Century Paris, London and New York*, Liverpool: Liverpool University Press.

Working Papers

A detailed guide to the data used in this book is contained in Working Papers with additional data downloads. These also provide the definitions and main guide to the UKDA database deposit of the 'British Business Census of Entrepreneurs'. The list of papers is being added to. These can be downloaded from the website for ESRC project ES/M010953: *'Drivers of Entrepreneurship and Small Business'* at: www.campop.geog.cam.ac.uk/research/projects/driversofentrepreneurship/

WP 1: Bennett, R.J., Smith, H.J., van Lieshout, C. and Newton, G. (2017) *Drivers of entrepreneurship and small businesses: Project overview and database design*. https://doi.org/10.17863/CAM.9508

WP 2: Bennett, R.J., Smith, H.J. and van Lieshout, C. (2017) *Employers and the self-employed in the censuses 1851–1911: The census as a source for identifying entrepreneurs, business numbers and size distribution*. https://doi.org/10.17863/CAM.9640

WP 3: van Lieshout, C., Bennett, R.J., Smith, H.J. and Newton, G. (2017) *Identifying businesses and entrepreneurs in the Censuses 1851–1881*. https://doi.org/10.17863/CAM.9639

WP 4: Smith, H.J., Bennett, R.J. and van Lieshout, C. (2017) *Extracting entrepreneurs from the Censuses, 1891–1911*. https://doi.org/10.17863/CAM.9638

WP 5: Bennett, R.J., Smith, H.J., van Lieshout, C. and Newton, G. (2017) *Business sectors, occupations and aggregations of census data 1851–1911*. https://doi.org/10.17863/CAM.9874 Data download of classification file: https://doi.org/10.17863/CAM.9874

WP 6: Smith, H.J. and Bennett, R.J. (2017) *Urban-rural classification using census data, 1851–1911*. https://doi.org/10.17863/CAM.15763

WP 7: Smith, H., Bennett, R.J. and Radicic, D. (2017) *Classification of towns in 1891 using factor analysis*. https://doi.org/10.17863/CAM.15767

WP 8: Bennett, R.J., Smith, H. and Radicic, D. (2017) *Classification of occupations for economically active: Factor analysis of Registration Sub-Districts (RSDs) in 1891*. https://doi.org/10.17863/CAM.15764

WP 9: Bennett, R.J., Montebruno, P., Smith, H. and van Lieshout, C. (2019) *Reconstructing entrepreneurship and business numbers for censuses 1851–81*. https://doi.org/10.17863/CAM.37738

WP 10: Bennett, R.J., Smith, H. and Radicic, D. (2018) *Classification of environments of entrepreneurship: Factor analysis of Registration Sub-Districts (RSDs) in 1891*. https://doi.org/10.17863/CAM.26386

WP 11: Montebruno, P. (2018) *Adjustment weights 1891–1911: Weights to adjust entrepreneur numbers for non-response and misallocation bias in Censuses 1891–1911*. https://doi.org/10.17863/CAM.26378 Adjustment weights: https://doi.org/10.17863/CAM.26376

WP 12: van Lieshout, C., Day, J., Montebruno, P. and Bennett, R.J. (2018) *Extraction of data on Entrepreneurs from the 1871 census to supplement I-CeM.* https://doi.org/10.17863/CAM.27488

WP 13: van Lieshout, C. and Bennett, R.J. (2019) *Extracted data on employers and farmers compared with published tables in the xensus general reports, 1851–1881.* https://doi.org/10.17863/CAM.37165

WP 14: van Lieshout, C., Bennett, R.J. and Montebruno, P. (2019) *Company directors: Directory and census record linkage.* https://doi.org/10.17863/CAM.37166

WP 15: Bennett, R.J., Montebruno, P., Smith, H. and van Lieshout, C. (2019) *Entrepreneurial discrete choice: Modelling decisions between self-employment, employer and worker status.* https://doi.org/10.17863/CAM.37312

WP 16: Satchell, M., Bennett, R.J., Bogart, D. and Shaw-Taylor, L. (2019) *Constructing Parish-level and RSD-level data on transport infrastructure in England and Wales 1851–1911.* https://doi.org/10.17863/CAM.37313

Index

technology 22, 47, 49
telegraph 15
telephones 15
textile manufacture 13, 26, 39, 55, 79, 195, 213, 219, 221, 225, 236, 241, 249–50, 259, 279
thatchers 78
Thünen, J.H. von 49–52, 55
ties *see* kin; networks; relationships
timber dealers 79, 122, 233–5
Tinsley, E. 214
tobacconists 75, 78, 79, 110, 242, 244, 300
toolmaking 78, 235–6, 238, 244
Torquay 246–8
towns 14–17, 50, 74, 118, 149, 189, 211–12, 219–37, 246–51, 260–2, 291, 311
toy-making 236, 254
transaction costs 31–2, 140, 162
transcriptions, errors ix, 23, 57–9, 64, 286
transition economy 35
transportation 3–5, 14–15, 17, 23–4, 31, 40, 50–1, 78–9, 95–6, 99
transport industries 3, 4, 14–15, 17–18, 23–4, 31, 34, 40, 50–1, 78–9, 93–6, 99, 108, 126, 128, 133, 143–8, 150–3, 167, 173–6, 184–5, 188, 200, 202, 213–14, 218–19, 233–6, 240–9, 252–4, 261, 271–7, 293–6, 299, 311
truck system 22
truncations of I-CeM records 7, 23, 64; *see also* transcription
trundlers 8, 10
trust (personal) 18, 140; *see also* informal
trusts (legal bodies) 111
Turner, J.D. 75, 198

UK *see* Britain
UK Data Archive vii–xi, 23, 311–12
uncles 177
unemployed 7, 100, 130, 194, 266, 311
unoccupied in census 61, 88–9, 226, 311–12
urban businesses 15, 17–18, 53, 73–6, 96, 117–22, 142, 145–60, 183, 193, 197, 221–51, 254, 262, 281, 289–91, 299, 304
urban definitions xii, 74–5, 142, 221
urban location/growth/occupations 15, 17–18, 31, 53, 73, 76, 118–19, 122, 145–6, 148–51, 158–60, 183, 193, 197, 221–5, 227, 237, 239–46, 248–50, 254, 281, 289–91, 299, 304; *see also* town names
urban migration 96, 262

urban transport 14, 50, 57, 122
Ure, A. 44
US Census of Manufacturers 52, 112
'U' shaped evolution of entrepreneurship 85, 102–8, 192
utilities 19, 76–8, 93, 122, 128, 133–4, 155–7

vagrants 88
VAT (value added tax) 103–4
venture capital 26, 47–8, 57

wages, waged employment 4, 6–7, 11, 16, 21–2, 27–30, 32–5, 39–41, 46–7, 51, 68, 73, 93, 96, 103, 108, 114, 133, 141–4, 153, 158–60, 162–4, 168, 171, 174, 176, 178, 185, 189, 192, 208, 210–11, 220, 226–7, 247–51, 254, 259, 265, 268–71, 275–7, 280, 285, 301, 306, 309–11; *see also* worker
Wakefield 254
Wales 35, 74, 118, 120, 182, 188–9, 212, 223–7, 234, 257, 273, 291
Walsall 220
Wardley, P. 7, 128, 134
Warrington 234
Warwickshire 223, 273
washing *see* laundry
watchmakers 34, 79, 124, 241, 243, 297
water industry 18, 38, 79, 320; *see also* utilities
waterproof goods industry 79
waterways 14, 31, 148–52; *see also* transportation
weavers 79, 300; *see also* textiles
Weber A. 49–52, 55
Wednesbury 246
weights for estimation 62, 88–9, 102, 109, 144, 285, 232
Wennekers. S. 85
Westhead, P. 145, 180
Westmorland 280
Whaples, R. 8, 26
Whitaker's *Red Book of Commerce* 76
Whitby 226, 246–8
whitesmiths 78, 123
widow 70, 141–57, 147, 178, 182, 190, 193, 206, 209, 211–14; *see also* widower
widower 142–56, 178, 190; *see also* widow
Widnes 220
wife 69, 112, 140, 186, 212; census definition 'wife of …' 69–70, 196, 212; *see also* husband; marriage